Companion to Heidegger's
Contributions to Philosophy

Studies in Continental Thought

Companion to Heidegger's
Contributions to Philosophy

Edited by
**Charles E. Scott,
Susan M. Schoenbohm,
Daniela Vallega-Neu,**
and
Alejandro Vallega

Indiana University Press
Bloomington & Indianapolis

This book is a publication of

Indiana University Press
601 North Morton Street
Bloomington, IN 47404-3797 USA

http://iupress.indiana.edu

Telephone orders 800-842-6796
Fax orders 812-855-7931
Orders by e-mail iuporder@indiana.edu

Manufactured in the United States of America

Library of Congress Cataloging-in-Publication Data

Companion to Heidegger's Contributions to philosophy /
edited by Charles E. Scott . . . [et al.].
p.   cm. — (Studies in Continental thought)
Includes bibliographical references and index.
ISBN 0-253-33946-4 (alk. paper)—ISBN 0-253-21465-3 (pbk. : alk. paper)
1. Heidegger, Martin, 1889-1976. Beiträge zur Philosophie.
I. Scott, Charles E. II. Series.
B3279.H48 B4516   2001
193—dc21   00-053952

1 2 3 4 5   06 05 04 03 02 01

Contents

Introduction: Approaching Heidegger's *Contributions
to Philosophy* and Its Companion
Charles E. Scott   1

Part 1. Approaches

1. Reading Heidegger's *Contributions to Philosophy:* An Orientation
Susan M. Schoenbohm   15

2. Strategies for a Possible Reading
Dennis J. Schmidt   32

3. "Beyng-Historical Thinking" in Heidegger's *Contributions to Philosophy*
Alejandro Vallega   48

4. Poietic Saying
Daniela Vallega-Neu   66

5. The Event of Enthinking the Event
Richard Polt   81

6. *Contributions to Philosophy* and Enowning-Historical Thinking
Friedrich-Wilhelm von Herrmann   105

Part 2. Readings

7. The Time of *Contributions to Philosophy*
William McNeill   129

8. Turnings in Essential Swaying and the Leap
Kenneth Maly   150

9. Da-sein and the Leap of Being
Walter A. Brogan   171

10. Grounders of the Abyss
John Sallis   181

11. Forgetfulness of God: Concerning the Center
of Heidegger's *Contributions to Philosophy*
Günter Figal   198

12. The Last God
David Crownfield   213

13. On "Be-ing": The Last Part of *Contributions to Philosophy*
(From Enowning)
Parvis Emad   229

Contributors   247
Index   251

Introduction: Approaching Heidegger's
Contributions to Philosophy and Its Companion

Charles E. Scott

An unusual way of thinking comes to expression in Heidegger's *Contributions To Philosophy (From Enowning)*.[1] He "made" this "book" by combining reflections on an extraordinary number of topics that include thoughts on thinking and the grounds for thinking, observations about Platonism, nature and earth, critical studies of history and language, reconsiderations of key ideas and descriptions in *Being and Time*, and, above all, explorations in a performative thinking of the truth of "being." I have marked the words "made," "book," and "be-ing" because I believe that Heidegger did not experience himself as making a book when he wrote the words and sentences and fragments of sentences that are intended to bring to thought and to language an interrupted and highly elusive word for the enactment—the "enownment"—of the living occurrences of beings. *Contributions* does indeed have in its dynamic form a well-planned approach on the order of a fugue (which many of the essays in this volume address). All of the aphorisms, short discussions, paragraphs, repetitions, re-considerations, departures and returns to major themes, and considerations of Western histories and futures are gathered together by a title, section headings, and numbered sub-section headings—it looks like a book. And I suppose it should be called one. But it pushes the limits of "a book" in the way that a group of meditations in a diary that are held together by a long trip pushes the meaning of "book." Heidegger is in the midst of an *Erfahrung*—an experience of traveling along, a "progress" in older usage—as he writes; but instead of being centered in his own private world of feeling and observation as many travelers are, he finds that he is drawn out by a troubling, persistent, indeterminate thought that is not his to own. 'It' has no clear way leading to it. This thinking is thus more like exploring than like a trip defined by a destination, and it does not present itself as naming any specific thing. It is like a new thought a-borning, one bred in years of strict, philosophical learning and discipline, one that does not come ready made or clearly produced, and one that challenges not only other thoughts of being but challenges as well the way thinking (and books) usually takes place. The new thought that is finding its birth is the thought of be-ing. It is thought that does not find its destination in a group of beliefs, a system of reasons, or a summarizable body of contents. This new thought composes a way of thinking with our philosophical heritage—our reflective commonwealth—a way that is less a position than it is a manner of disciplined alertness with the occurrence of being. Such occurrence appears to be the same for everything that is alive and present, and 'its' sameness appears not to be any thing. 'It' appears as beings come to pass, and Heidegger wishes to think alertly in the eventuation of this happening.

I believe that a person would be mistaken to expect in *Contributions* either a clearly marked philosophical path or a helter-skelter of notes. Heidegger is certainly exploring and experimenting in the book's language and thought. You could use his logging-path metaphor and say that he goes up (or down) one path after another and finds them all going in the same region and in what appears to be a similar direction but also finds each way leading to clearings that dwindle into over-grown, dense, and dark forest. Or you might think of Nietzsche's play on *Versuch* (which can mean attempt or temptation) and say that Heidegger's attempts in thinking compose a temptation that is not completely within his control, that his very exploration shows in its life a strange and perhaps dangerous draw, promising neither vortex nor golden city, to something missing, uncertain but important, even crucial, but not a specific being. Do we join in?

Heidegger's thought obviously clears out a region of words and considerations—I have at times the impression that he is whacking away at underbrush—but it is not so much a well defined path that he clears as an area for thought—I also find him coming back toward me while I am trying to determine where he is going. In my image he is not so much lost as he is preoccupied, as though caught in between leading and following in a region without clear signs or maps. It is not as though he were proceeding to a summit or even to the end of a track. I believe that most readers of *Contributions* will say that it consists in thought in a strange and demanding region, a region that provides a different environment—a different living space—for thought's eventuation. Finding ourselves in this often shadowy area, we do not perceive one defining method or a neat piece of analysis—not even a nicely outlined group of lectures. We find an extremely intense, utterly determined process of thinking that is moved—and I repeat this for emphasis—by 'something' that Heidegger finds he cannot make or control, 'something' that is not a thing in any sense, 'something' that is neither human nor god, that ungrounds grounds while enabling them. Heidegger's effort is to think the living core of Western sensibility and thought, to find traces there of 'something' that is mostly missing in our culture and missing to our culture's great detriment. His intention in *Contributions* is to see if he might be able to travel with those traces and questions and explore them in his reflections. If he can pull that off, if he can find the discipline that allows him to come to an *Erfahrung*—*a traveling*—with be-ing in his thought, he will have made, on his terms, an immeasurable contribution to philosophy.

A clearing, I have said, not quite a way, certainly a far cry from an open country path through hill and dale, that invites a Sunday afternoon's stroll. Heidegger's thought in this book might be compared with the kind of expectation that a coach might have for a young team: with hard work a few disciplined people can learn to play this game. Except what Heidegger offers is not quite a game. He offers, perhaps, a field for training, a site of conditioning, an occasion for learning new moves, for becoming accustomed to a special rigor of approach and a new intensity of discipline. But victory is not a goal here. Something else is, and so much 'else' is it that I believe you will find the general attraction and value of 'goal' diminishing as you work your way through his "book."

Part of the experimental rigor comes with the words that Heidegger uses and the English words that the translators of *Beiträge* choose. If you are reasonably literate in the history of philosophy and of reasonably sound mind, you might be at least puzzled and more than a little put off at first by such experimental words as "enowning," "fore-grasping," "ab-ground," "essential swaying," "projecting-open," "charming-moving-unto," "enseeing," "enthinking," "enopening," "enquivering," and "encleaving." What kind of en-clearing is this?! It is, as I have said, one that requires exploration into relatively uncharted areas of thought, experimentation with language before a strange withdrawal of meaning in traditional intelligence and in ordinary cultural life. Heidegger's thinking is before 'something' irritating and even offensive to the ways we usually think and figure things out. For Heidegger is attempting to bring to thought a dimension of our tradition that has been terribly misshaped by many metaphysical, religious, and ethical ways of thinking; and if his thought has merit, these traditional forms of intelligence must be turned out from within, turned out toward a different intelligence and sensibility. That is part of the discipline of learning to travel with *Contributions'* thought—finding ways whereby one might break out of the limits of traditional intelligence, but break out of them by intense enough engagements *in* them to find traces of what they are overlooking or covering over. Heidegger finds that there is no way around the canons of Western culture. The clearing comes through them and by their means. He has no tolerance for easy mysticism and "special" gifts of knowledge that claim sight without the rigorous discipline of learning to read and think in the Western canon. And within this discipline there also comes from the pen of this seemingly conservative man a continuous effort to find the words and turns of thought that will allow his thought to follow an else-than, an other to the motivations, sensibilities, and ways of life ensconced in Western cultures' best ideas and images. If you find some of the words in *Contributions* unhelpful or wrong-headed, look for options. Follow your intuitions with as much self-awareness as you can maintain. Take a walk with Heidegger down a path and through a clearing and see if you can hear what he senses, hear the faint echo of 'something' missing in the satisfactions of our productive culture, hear with his words in their attempts, and find better ones if they are available to you.

Reading *Contributions* is a joint enterprise, an engagement with Heidegger's thought, at best an unsentimental effort at hearing well and addressing carefully what you hear. And addressing also what you overhear, what cannot be said directly and counts all the more for its generative, originary, and suggestive power.

I speak personally when I say that the best experiences with *Contributions* happen when readers feel no requirement to agree or disagree but feel a drawing allowance to encounter Heidegger in the processes of this thought with as much thoughtful intensity as they can stand. I believe that it is the quality of the engagement that most counts, not agreements. The issue is whether people can think with Heidegger well enough to experience the movements and forces of his mentation and in that process find their own voices as they undergo the question of being.

The stakes are high for Heidegger as he makes his "contributions" to philosophy. They address issues of cultural survival that range *from* unconscious boredom and an accompanying frenzy of production, consumption, and search for distracting novelty and projects, from easy, thoughtless identification of people and things *to* moments of crystal, physical insight when the entire world shimmers with fragile, passing sufficiency of meaning and beauty, when each being stands forth in the uniqueness of its own event, a moment in which an enowning enactment of each being brings together a strange unity that offers everything and is without the sustained presence of any thing. Heidegger was persuaded from his early years in college that superficiality is a malaise that brings with it a deadening of human life; and by the time he wrote *Contributions*, he had come to believe that institutional systematization of peoples' lives, whether secular or religious, destroyed the freshness and freedom that originality and alertness with the life of events require. He believed firmly that frivolity is not innocent in corruptions of human sensitivity, and he knew as well as he knew anything that in the *events* of consumptive production and unthinking lives there are also echoes of a vastly more profound and vitalizing dimension of being that one can find waiting, as it were, to be said and thought for the enormous benefit of Western communal life. Throughout *Contributions* we can find Heidegger's despair over the banality of ordinary perception and intuition and his commitment to the possibility of a much less destructive, much more deeply engaged encounter with all beings that disclose themselves and constitute the world in their intricate interweavings. We find echoes and hints and possibilities for a less belligerent and self-protective living, for bringing people into an alert touch with the genuinely originative fragility of being here. We find echoes, hints and possibilities for engendering dispositions toward conserving 'what' is most precious in life and 'what' is least to be objectified and used. These are hints and possibilities for 'what' has never been quite reached by Western endeavor and evaluation—they are found in their elusive and withdrawing visage and murmur and call out continuously to and in Heidegger's thought. His stern experimentations in *Contributions* revolve fugally with a strange combination of assertion and reticence around this intimating center of uncertain promise and give this book its singular, sometimes maddening, always demanding quality of judgment and affirmation.

Heidegger's education in theology and philosophy had prepared him to think that spiritual growth can reach a substantial, fundamental, and true reality. In the context of *Contributions*, we may see a residue of that training in mainstream Christian spirituality and metaphysics. In *Being and Time* his thought had constituted a process of taking apart that tradition from the inside and turning it toward a way of thinking that finds its origins in the temporal disclosiveness of beings instead of in a transcendent reality. Although he continued to interpret everyday living as usually superficial and ignorant of what is most profound and important for human life, he no longer perceived that superficiality and ignorance in relation to a fundamental and true being. Rather, the question of being in *Being and Time* and, in *Contributions*, the enowning event of be-ing, were the guides for the thinker who could find a measure of freedom from easy assumptions and ill-considered meanings. Our tradition, he found, has largely blinded us to an alertness that it also covertly bears: alertness to the coming and passing of gods and to the occurrence of truth, truth not as correspondence of objects with representations but as the mortal, uncovering presentation of beings. This turn requires from him a renewal of our traditional language, a renewal that turns to a range of sensitivities that it both bears and obscures, *almost* a different language, a language of "da-sein" and "unconcealing," a language that shows the turning passage of metaphysical thought with its emphasis on timeless, universal reality. He sought a way of thought that would call people out of their unalert and insensitive lives with beings and would recover alertness to the temporal eventuation, not the spiritualization, of living things in their coming to pass. For Heidegger's mature thought there is no dimension *in* which there are beings. There is, rather, the dimensionality *of* their happening, their being here as disclosive occurrences.

So *Contributions* is a renewing and revolutionary engagement with the happening of beings. It is not about a ground of being or a region that is beyond, below, or behind being. It is not about *a* particular, primary being or group of beings. *Contributions* is an attempt by Heidegger to think—we might say, to allow a thinking of—the temporal enactment

of beings without turning such enactment into yet another being: as he
addresses the question of *a* defining ground he finds, in the force of the
thought of be-ing, that such a ground is ungrounded.

Heidegger wrote the reflections and meditations that compose *Contributions* in response to interpretations of *Being and Time* that failed to
understand that the book addressed the question of the meaning of be-
ing, the question that requires a thinker to confront mortal temporality
without a grounding being. He wrote in response to interpretations of
his account of dasein that said it was a novel account of subjectivity, and
to other interpretations of "my-ownness" and "authenticity" as solipsis-
tic in the lineage of Descartes. He wrote these contributions in author's
distress when he saw that his own language was used against that language's defining purposes. Heidegger also saw that his thought in *Being
and Time* at times suggested the very metaphysical conceptuality that he
wanted to avoid because of such concepts and imagery as horizon, ontological conditions for the possibility of specific existing structures, and
being's transcendence of beings. How might he bring to bear in his
thought and language the question of the meaning of being, the priority
of disclosure for the meaning of truth, the priority of temporal eventuation for the meaning of disclosures—come to think in the priority of
eventuation (or enownment) of the truth of be-ing—and bring disclosiveness to bear so that his thought composes a decisive departure from
philosophical language that is dominated by the value of special beings
and of substantial presence? How might his thought compose a leap
into a way of thinking that holds itself open to the eventful disclosure of
beings and that protects such eventful disclosure from such colonializ-
ing beings as subjectivity, reason, God, and representative thought?
How might he re-think the meaning of the question of being so that be-
ing's eventfulness suggests only the happening of beings?

Heidegger attempts in *Contributions* to give an occasion—to provide
an historical happening—in which the meaning of being appears differently from its previous figurations in Western thought. This is an occasion for a different thinking, a different saying of being, so different, in
fact, that another sense of being needs a departure that is figured in the
word itself. He uses an earlier spelling of the word *Sein, Seyn,* which the
translators of *Beiträge* render as 'be-ing' (and which some of the authors
in this book translate as 'beyng') in their efforts to attend to a breakage in
traditional meanings for being. *Seyn* names an unthought dimension in
our history's preoccupations with life and its meaning. *Seyn* suggests
origination—the happening of what is—that is elusive and difficult to
attend to, not an enduring ground of being that is "there" and not
noticed. Be-ing appears like a dimensionality in the disclosures of living
events that has not come to thought. Heidegger describes hints and resonances of be-ing, a draw like that of a ship's wake—a draw of with-

drawal, not completely unlike an indeterminate sense of loss or a vague unease before something's missing. He wishes to find ways to cultivate thought in the hints and resonances, in recognition of terrible insufficiency in our Western culture, so that the thinking and language of his meditations are not so much about be-ing as they are an *Erfahrung* of be-ing, a traveling with be-ing in its virtual withdrawal from ordinary thought, evaluation, and recognition. Heidegger wished to give rise to an event of thinking that made a decisive difference in Western culture, an event of origination and departure, an historical happening in which the strange dimension of the withdrawal of be-ing from our cultural lives composes a fleeting guide in disclosures of beings for thoughtful consideration. Heidegger intended to occasion an event in which be-ing's faint disclosure of withdrawal in events of beings guides philosophical thought, occasions a happening of be-ing, no matter how tentative, in an unmistakably historical moment of thinking.

Many of the writers in this volume discuss in a variety of contexts these themes and words that I have noted. In these discussions you will find subtle and not so subtle differences of emphasis and translations of important words—a small democracy of voices; and these differences bear testimony to the original quality of Heidegger's thought in *Contributions* as well as to the elusiveness of be-ing. There is no one authoritative interpretation; and insofar as translations are interpretations, there is no one authoritative rendering into English of Heidegger's language. One of this book's purposes is to present interpretive work on *Contributions* by people who know the book well and who engage it with different interests, angles of perception, and manners of thought.

Indeed, Heidegger's own thought is one of translation. The eventuation of beings and the many ways in which it has come to expression in the Western tradition do not give him a definitive pattern or guide to follow. He must carry over to thought and language—trans-late—a dimension of disclosive occurrence that lacks an established and determined norm. Just as words often carry in their lively meanings and histories multiple and even contradictory suggestions and connotations, the eventuation of being in the world is without a single, objective and re-presentable determination. When people establish forms of completion for interpreting living beings (i.e., "authoritatively" translate them), the lives of those beings never quite fit the completion. They spill over and beyond the established limits in their living incompletenesses, in their unforeseeable possibilities, in *their* happenings and fugitive, restless moments. Heidegger's thought is attuned to the otherness, the difference, of beings' occurrences, to the uncapturable quality in their lives as he attempts to carry over their eventuation into the specificities of written and meditative expression. Hence the rigor of his thought as he finds inappropriate systems of reflection that command determined limits for the temporal indeterminacy of disclosing beings. To carry over, to translate in determined ways such indeterminacy requires a discipline of careful, reserved and attentive listening that he finds largely missing in the frequent aggressiveness of Western thought. His is not a discipline that aims to satisfy interests in controlling establishments of final definitions or to answer with determined directness and objectivity the questions that we ordinarily expect philosophy to resolve.

So there is a coordination of uncertainty—a joining in uncertainty—that these essays spell out in their interpretive and translational differences and that marks Heidegger's attempt to think with appropriateness to be-ing as he engages the eventfulness of beings. I believe that the essayists and Heidegger jointly know that translation leaves out something of the translated life, leaves openings for new encounter, and in this openness projects the frustrations and vitality of incompleteness and possibility. Such thought composes engagements and encounters with events that are not prone to definitional or systematic sufficiency. That observation suggests that readers might well find the *differences* among these writers as worthy of considerations as the specificity of their claims.

When people work in *Contributions* or in *Beiträge,* they have the opportunity to encounter Heidegger in his singularity. They will find in his aphorisms and paragraphs his intense worry and anger over the triumph of objectification and usage in "machination," his offense before a culture abandoned by the question of being and any sense of the truth of be-ing. I believe that I can trace in his chapters sorrow and mourning in the impact on him of *Being and Time*'s reception as well as in that of a world that appears to him to be abandoning its own life. I find an unresolved struggle to stay with a way of thinking that he expects to be incommunicable at the same time that he experiences a passion to communicate by means of this thought. There is a considerable amount of loneliness in his words as well as defiance and determination. Were he painting, I believe that he would often use colors of intense darkness, apocalyptic flashes of light, splotches of terrible reds and blues, as well as beautiful, fading pastels. *Contributions* presents a passionate man who is struggling—is driven—at every level of his person to bring to thought 'something' that has not been thought and that eludes his own extraordinary powers of conception. At times he seems to me to be writing in a whisper. At other times he fairly shouts. He is past argument, and he is not into a project of making disciples. He certainly does not write from the serene transcendence of a wise man who wishes to show people the way they should be. Rather than instruct, he agonizes. He pushes words to their extremity, agonizing them, recomposing and rehearsing them, often twisting them toward new expression. He rethinks his own landmark book, *Being and Time*, with little compassion for its "mistakes," pushing himself in the process to a new level of style and mentation. In all of this he wants to make a contribution to philosophy that never repeats its conceptual movements without placing them in vigorous transitions, often in movements of thought that are harsh toward any complacency or satisfaction that they might offer.

I make these observations about the personal singularity of Heidegger's thought in order to emphasize what I take to be a fact: no matter that the thought of be-ing, or indeed thought in general, may not belong exclusively or even primarily to an individual's efforts, such mentation is never without its singular, individualistic dimensions. That is part of the meaning of "enownment": Heidegger is speaking from and to the enactment of beings, enactment that is not a being and that is never without beings. When his thought shows ("says") its own enactment, it will show at once Heidegger the individual and the specificity of the time in which he thought as he did.

I find one of the most telling aspects of *Contributions* its success as it leaves behind the dualism of transcendence/immanence. It provides a reorientation of thinking without invocation of 'transcendence' or 'immanence' as it enters the sway of the event of be-ing. The event of be-ing is *at once* eventuation of beings. I thus expect Heidegger's thought in *Contributions* to be appreciated fully only when people hold firmly in mind that its agonized language is struggling to engage the lives of beings more thoroughly than we can engage them under the sway of another, transcendent, and defining being. *Er-eignis*, en-ownment, and eventuation of beings, I emphasize again, never refer to a being or a group of beings; and that is because beings are so singular in their events, so specific, that one can be taken to define sufficiently the others only at the palpable cost of loss of vitality in cultural life. Were be-ing a transcendent being in relation to beings, Heidegger would not think the nonreducible specificity of beings that enowning eventuates; for beings are enowned, and in their enownment they are each themselves quite singular, given to be themselves (enowned) only as they are in their mortal coming to pass. And were be-ing an immanent 'it' there would be no withdrawing non-presence in the presentation of beings. He must find other options for thinking.

In order to reach such a place of experimentation and affirmation regarding be-ing, however, Heidegger found necessary singular attention to the *question* of being and *its* turn in Western thought — a rigor that is congenial to beings in its steadfast inattention to them, but a rigor that comes close at times, in my opinion, to assigning an Olympian role to "the essential sway" of the truth of be-ing. A complex and steadfast conviction governs *Contributions*: *only* by overturning the prevailing and lived meanings for being in Western experience, by following the hints

and resonances of be-ing's truth and in this following breaking away
from the domination of thought by the presence of privileged beings, by
recognizing the devastating need and danger that now quietly savage
the very appearances of beings, and by attending to the decisive turn offered by be-ing's truth toward opportunities for basically different kinds
of experiences of the world—*only* by such overturning, following,
breaking away, recognizing, and attending do we have a possibility for
ways of life that are in tune with the enactment of beings and hence in
tune with beings in their singular disclosures. Corollary with this conviction is another that I have noted: beings do not depend in their disclosive lives on something that transcends them and supports them.
Their being—their enactment—composes their essence. The essence of
beings is not an identity of any kind but is their own, strangely be-
stowed coming to pass, the "essential sway" of be-ing. And finally, a
third, now familiar conviction: only by attending single-mindedly to be-
ing in its questionable, i.e., mortal and temporal fragility of enactment,
can people come to manners of alertness and ways of living that will be
salutary for the lives of living beings. So in *Contributions* Heidegger will
not pay much attention to specific beings, including "humanity," because *the* issue is the occurrence of the being of beings. Olympian or not,
we must reach some participatory sense of the *enactment* of beings before we can appropriately engage them; and without that sense we
would be capable only of furthering the travail of a suicidal machinational world that sucks out the marvelous lives of beings in a frenzy of
useful assignation and objective recognition. Such frenzy, such "using
up" and objectification of beings, constitutes an embodiment—a living
understanding—of being as a subjective and sustaining presence that
transcends and gives meaning to finite existences. Heidegger is looking
toward a fundamental shift in the course of worldly events, and that shift
requires a fundamental alteration in the way being and its meaning is
understood before we can turn appropriately to beings in their
specificity—because the way their specificity shows up is dependent on
the meaning of being that composes the ways they show themselves in
the world.

In this companion, you will find first, in chapters 2 through 6, a
series of essays that address in an introductory manner *Contributions* as
a whole. In each you will find emphases and orientations that are different from the others and that provide a particular entry into Heidegger's book. Chapters 7 through 13 are essays on major sections and
themes in *Contributions*. In them the authors frequently circle back to
the first step of learning to read *Contributions* and connect their central
themes to other sections in the book. This process reflects the fugal
movement of *Contributions* and the need that it embodies for returns to

beginnings and for reconsiderations of questions and issues that have come to view and now carry new implications and bearings for thought.

All of the authors have experienced the frustration of writing discussions that cannot cover fully their topics as well as that of being driven at times to commenting on a way of thinking that requires people to leap into a dimension of mentation that commentary leaves untouched. I believe that all of the authors would tell you that they feel unfinished in the specific engagements with *Contributions* that comprise their chapters and that this sense of incompleteness is an aspect not only of their present writing but also of the thinking that the book inspires in its disconcerting way.

Our intention is to carry out the mandate of a companion, to accompany readers of *Contributions* as they work in Heidegger's volume; to point out what is singular in it and the ways various words and thoughts interconnect and suggest each other; to show now and then how one might take a next step or avoid a distracting turn. These essays also give readers occasions to engage the interpretations, discoveries, and insights of people who have concentrated for years on Heidegger's book, thought long and hard with it, and can speak of it with experience.

The editors asked each essayist to refer to the pages of the Emad/ Maly translation, especially when he or she chose translations of key words that differ from the published edition. By this strategy we hope that readers might enter into the always unfinished process of translating and have the advantage of considering different ways of reading the German text. All of the contributors worked in the German text during the ten years before the publication of the translation and had preferred and well-considered renderings for many of its words and phrases. We believe that when new readers consider these preferences in relation to the published version, they will benefit their understanding of Heidegger's thought, increase their appreciation for the issues that any translator of *Beiträge* must face, and perhaps relive the inevitability that thinking itself is a process of translating.

If you have not worked in *Beiträge* prior to reading this companion, we recommend that you read the discussions in the first seven chapters prior to those on the specific parts of Heidegger's book. More informed readers might wish to read the essay that addresses directly the part of *Contributions* on which they are working.

Notes

1. Citations from volumes of Heidegger's Gesamtausgabe appear in the body of the text as GA followed by a volume and page number. For the English as well the German titles of volumes of the Gesamtausgabe, see *Heidegger Studies* 15 (1999): 185–92.

Beiträge zur Philosophie (Vom Ereignis) was written between 1936 and 1938 and first published in 1989 as volume 65 of the Gesamtausgabe (Frankfurt am Main: Vittorio Klostermann). References to *Beiträge* in the essays in this book cite GA 65 followed by a page number. The English translation by Parvis Emad and Kenneth Maly, *Contributions to Philosophy (From Enowning)* (Bloomington: Indiana University Press, 1999), is cited as CP followed by a page reference.

Part 1. Approaches

1. Reading Heidegger's *Contributions to Philosophy:*
An Orientation

Susan M. Schoenbohm

How are we to orient ourselves in our approach to this text? This essay aims to provide a few helpful pointers to readers, especially those who come to it for the first time. English and German readers alike may be put off at first by the text's strange form, structure, and vocabulary. An expectation of immediate or easy access to the matter to be thought here is only to be met with disappointment. In this essay, we shall see that the text's strangeness is to be thought as appropriate to the main issue or matter (*Sache*) that Heidegger attempts to work out in it. By engaging this strangeness, by allowing it to determine one's own thinking as much as possible, the reader will find this strangeness effective in carrying out the text's strategies. The commonly held belief that the success of a piece of writing can be measured by the degree to which an author makes something readily intelligible to already familiar ways of understanding is inappropriate here. We need to be venturesome, to allow our familiar ways of understanding, which are at best limited, to be challenged, perhaps then to become opened to interestingly different ways of thinking.

Heidegger's initial statement of the task that he is undertaking which will guide us here is: "to attempt . . . as in a preparatory exercise [*Vorübung*] a thoughtful saying of philosophy . . . in an age of transition [*Übergang*] from metaphysics into be-ing-historical thinking"[1] and "to think according to a more originary basic position [*Grundstellung*] within the question of the truth of be-ing."[2] This essay seeks to help the reader to begin to gain some sense for the meaning of this transition and this saying.

The text requires a philosophical orientation. But at the outset we need to be clear as to what the word "philosophy" means for Heidegger, since it means for him something different than it might mean in other contexts or to other people. Heidegger explicitly characterizes what he means by "philosophy" in this text as "questioning into being [das Fragen nach dem Sein]."[3] We will expect then a questioning into being to happen in working through this text.

With respect to this philosophical questioning into being, we recall that this is also the primary focus of Heidegger's first major work, *Being and Time*. In that work, Heidegger develops the importance of retrieving the question of the meaning of being from out of the obscurity produced by a metaphysical tradition of thought. The retrieval is enacted by a renewed raising of the question of the meaning of being. In *Being and Time*, Heidegger shows that for traditional metaphysics, the word

"being" is no longer in question. It is tacitly assumed to mean something like "being-ness," that is, something like a most common, general,
or universal concept, or a highest, allegedly permanent, ever-lasting or
timeless being that supposedly unifies or grounds beings. And yet the
meaning of this being, for example, the relation of this being to the
worldly beings that it is supposed to ground, remains insufficiently
clear. Thus, for Heidegger such metaphysical interpretations of being
are not only themselves still questionable and uncertain, they obscure
the way that the meaning of being itself continues to be most question-
worthy. In *Being and Time,* Heidegger orients his rethinking of the question of the meaning of being by giving priority to the temporality and
disclosive phenomenality of beings, that is, to temporality as the occurrence of being in distinction to a representation of beingness. In this
way, *Being and Time* begins Heidegger's reorientation of philosophy to
the task of engaging in the as yet insufficiently answered question of
the meaning of being by locating itself where it is, namely, within temporal, historical, always questionable being-in-the-world. Philosophy
thus also entails a rethinking of traditional metaphysics in its own questionable, temporal/historical character, a character that has also been
obscured by the metaphysical positing of timeless meaning. Thus,
working carefully through *Being and Time* is very useful, perhaps indispensable, to readers of *Contributions.* Through reading *Being and Time,*
we come to understand that the meaning of being, however it comes to
be understood or interpreted, is temporal.[4] Meanings are temporally/
historically disclosed;[5] the temporal disclosure of beings, their aletheic
coming-into and withdrawing from appearing, their coming to pass
(*Wesen*) does not have the character of permanence. Being's temporality means that there is no meaning of being—nor any being—that is
permanent, ever-lasting, or unchanging. The meaning of being thus
must be thought in a way different from metaphysics.

Contributions takes up the main thematics of *Being and Time,* that is,
the question of being, temporality, historicality, and truth in an even
more radical way. The philosophical orientation of thinking called for
when thinking through *Contributions* is also one that no longer assumes
that the meaning of the being of beings is nontemporal, permanent
presence, or that this meaning is to be located in the positing of a highest, best, most all-inclusive, most general, or most common being.
Heidegger's thinking in *Contributions* is oriented, as in *Being and Time,* by
the temporal character of being and thus by the untenability of assuming that there "is" behind or above or beneath beings any atemporal, su-
prahistorical being as their ultimate ground. As we read *Contributions,*
our thinking will be drawn into the draft of the question of the meaning
of being—which also is a question of *our* being—in the experience of the
insufficiency and untenability of metaphysically oriented interpreta-

tions of being. Thinking in *Contributions* will *not* think that be-ing[6] means a being of any kind. It will rather turn attention toward the question-worthy, temporal, disclosive character of be-ing, toward its "truth" character, its *Wahrheit,* that is, the question-worthiness of the very *occurring* of beings. Here it is important to note that the *question* of be-ing, which includes but is not reducible to the question of the occurring of beings, implicates as well a question of the character of thinking. Just as there is no timeless being grounding beings, there is also no eternal soul or transcendent subject of thinking doing it. Rather, thinking is a temporal and disclosive enactment "of" be-ing. This will be further clarified below.

Unlike other ways of thinking that may call themselves philosophical, then, philosophy, as Heidegger understands it in *Contributions,* endeavors to think of the most question-worthy disclosiveness of being as it inquires into its meaning. Attending carefully to the question-ableness and uncertainty of be-ing, to the strangeness of there being anything at all, coupled with the undeniable facticity of being-in-the-world characterizes philosophy for Heidegger both in *Being and Time* and in *Contributions.*

Keeping the above pointers in mind, in the remainder of this essay we will attempt further to orient our thinking and our efforts to gain a sense of what Heidegger is up to in *Contributions* by what we can glean from the first major part of the text, entitled "Preview" (*Vorblick*). The title *Contributions to Philosophy (From Enowning),* we read, "corresponds to the issue or matter [*Sache*]"[7] of thinking to be enacted in the text. Again, Heidegger articulates this matter as one of attempting "to think out of the more original basic position [*Grundstellung*], within the question concerning the truth [*Wahrheit*] of be-ing."[8] Such an attempt, he says, occurs "in the age of the transition [*des Übergangs*] from metaphysics into be-ing-historical thinking [*seynsgeschichtliche Denken*]."[9] We can now already understand these sentences to indicate a dynamic of thinking,[10] one that in its occurrence is attuned to temporal disclosiveness that we can expect to be enacted in the text. Perhaps we can also anticipate to some extent the difference that such a way of thinking opens up for *our* thinking as we attempt to think through its matter.

In the "Preview," Heidegger also points in an abbreviated way to the fugal character of the text's structure[11] and lists certain basic organizing words that will provide much of the text's texture. As we progress through the "Preview" and into the other major parts of *Contributions,* we will need to think of what each of these words means as all corresponding or belonging, each in a different, singular way, to the text's "matter." Each of these words says—or means—the very coming-to-meaning of the question of the truth of be-ing. The words articulate be-ing's questionableness, its disclosive coming-to-pass.

Heidegger goes on to say that this transitional thinking/saying "gathers be-ing into an initial sonority [or sounding out, *Anklang*][12] of be-ing's own coming-to-pass [*Wesen*][13] which itself sounds out from this coming to pass."[14] Heidegger is attempting to allow the question-worthy coming-to-pass of be-ing itself to come to a provisional articulation in words in this writing. The saying that arises as one thinks in this manner is an exploratory attempt to allow be-ing's enactment to be articulate in words. This attempt is in turn to be thought as belonging and responding to be-ing's own originary sounding out, that is, the saying is to be thought to belong and respond (*gehören*) to be-ing's own enactment. What will be said in the preparatory exercise that is enacted in this text, again,

> is a *question*, which is neither a purposive doing of an individual nor any narrow calculation of a group, but rather before everything, is the further beckoning of a hint that comes from that most-worthy-of-questioning, and remains attributed to it.[15]

Subjectivity, whether of an individual or a group, does not ground this saying. The "question" enacted here then needs to be distinguished from any action of a subject and also from any particular way in which any person or people (including Heidegger) actually attempts to pose or follow it out. For Heidegger, far from an act of a subject, "question" is an essential (*wesentlich*) aspect of the enactment of "that most worthy of questioning," namely be-ing itself.[16] The dimension of be-ing that is its *question*, then, remains distinct, although not separate from, whatever determinations of be-ing, whatever meanings, arise through it. This dimension of question, we will see, is linked with be-ing's "not-character," that is, with be-ing's not-being *a* being, with be-ing's difference from any determinate being. In be-ing as eventuation (en-owning, *Er-eignis*) the occurrence of this question-dimension of be-ing occurs, we might say provisionally, as the withdrawal-dimension of be-ing from beings, as be-ing's withdrawal from beings, as abyss (*Ab-grund*). This will be elaborated further below.

The "thinking/saying" that is enacted in this text, then, "does not describe or explain, does not proclaim or teach. This saying does not stand over against what is said" (GA 65, 4; CP, 4). It is not attributable to any subject or transcendent being but "attributed to" be-ing. At best, it arises from and returns to the very questionable occurrence that calls it forth, which Heidegger calls the en-owning eventuation (*Er-eignis*) of be-ing in and as truth (*Wahrheit*).[17] As we move through the text, we will be attempting to attend not only to the saying but to that occurring movement that the saying enacts and attempts to articulate.

The preparatory, provisional, and above all transitional character of Heidegger's attempt here is enacting a transit out of metaphysical ways of thinking to an other, quite different manner of thinking. The transitory character in turn means that this thinking is not expecting completion. But in its transit, there eventuates a lighting up of "the until now altogether concealed region of the coming passing [*Wesung*] of be-ing."[18] As we think, we too are engaged in this transitional traversal of thinking. Our "engagement" means that the movement of transition determines *our da-sein*,[19] here and now. The very determinations of this new and different region (our da-sein) that we are traversing are coming into awareness, even as the traversing occurs, and we will see that there is a profound accord between "enowning character" and our worldly existence.

Bearing in mind the transitional character of the thinking in which we are engaged, then, we might attend further to the way in which the transition also implicates a change in human being (*Wesenswandel des Menschen*).[20] As the meaning of be-ing transists, so also does the meaning of "human being." More specifically, Heidegger says, the transition into be-ing-historical thinking involves a change *from* taking the basic meaning of human being to be something metaphysical, something along the lines of "rational animal," *to* orienting our thinking according to da-sein in its temporal, disclosive character.

At least since Aristotle, we humans have thought of ourselves metaphysically, as beings among other beings that are distinguished from them by a lasting essence, that is, our ability to reason and speak. The consequences of this interpretation include virtually all of the ways that we have thought and behaved with respect to others in the world. The transition from metaphysical thinking to be-ing-historical thinking enfolds a change in this thinking of humans—that is, in our being—*from* thinking and experiencing ourselves in terms of some permanent essence *toward* a thinking of "self" as having whatever character or meaning it has only in virtue of be-ing-t/here in the world. *We* are now implicated in the *question* of the very determination of this, our da-sein. We can then no longer assume any metaphyiscal interpretation of any aspect of the t/here, including our "practices," "institutions," and "knowledge." We can no longer assume either that "we" are as or what we have thought ourselves to be or that things are as we have thought: we can no longer assume that whatever we have thought "world" to mean is its meaning. "We" are called into an abyssal possibility, of thinking no longer and otherwise than according to previous interpretations bequeathed to us by metaphysical *Historie*, that have arisen out of what Heidegger names "the history of the first beginning."[21] Again, in this transition, neither da-sein nor be-ing itself are to be thought metaphysically. Rather, both are to be thought in their temporal, revealing/concealing, appearing/withdrawing character. They are also to be thought rather than in general terms or as instances of a species, as singular and unprecedented. The question of the meaning of be-ing involves "us" in the question of the meaning of our being in the withdrawal of metaphysical possibilities for determining that meaning.

As Heidegger draws out this change in human being, he also says that the meaning of care (*Sorge*) — the basic ontological character of dasein in *Being and Time* — changes. In *Contributions*, care is also thought as a basic character of da-sein, but more radically. Care means the standing-in (*Inständigkeit*) amidst beings that, in question, also stands out from them.²² Care means both standing determinately in the midst of determinate beings and yet not being enmeshed with them (i.e., standing out from them), allowing them their determinations as enowned by be-ing. In this way, care cares not just for beings in their (questionable) determinations but for be-ing in its twofold, emerging, and abysally withdrawing, truth character. Care then, is characterized in *Contributions* as primarily for the sake of be-ing, for the manner in which be-ing occurs in its granting, sheltering, withdrawing truth-character as this occurs.

The transitional thinking that is happening here occurs both as a dynamic standing among beings that together manifest whatever t/here 'is,' and, in question, as a standing out in the abyssal "ground" that, other than any being, "is" no-thing. This abyssal ground "is" be-ing's "not-character," that dimension of be-ing that enables and characterizes the very possibility of thinking questioningly and not metaphysically of beings. Questioning-thinking, en-owned by be-ing, eventuates as the question-worthy be-ing of the t/here in its temporal, not metaphysical, determinations (*Bestimmungen*). It is oriented by, is called and belongs listeningly to (*gehört*) the en-owning of be-ing's coming-passing, appearing-withdrawing, *Wahrheit*. "We" (as da-sein) are both in and of the enactment of the enjoining en-owning of be-ing, which enactment occurs as singularly determinate, and thus enacts provisionally the unique and unprecedented history, that is, the determination, of be-ing in its "other" beginning.

An abyssal sense of being-without-ground is unavoidable in this transitional thinking. Along with everything and every known interpretation of things, the very "self" of "ourselves" is in question and without metaphysical foundation in this transition.²³ The transition, then, is a radical shift or draw (*Ruck*) out of metaphysical thinking and interpretation of being in the world (da-sein) into the unprecedented, be-ing historical thinking. In this other thinking, the question of be-ing has priority and one thinks in as well as about the way in which be-ing occurs *as dasein*, occurs, that is, as a singular, unique appearing-withdrawing-from-appearing, coming-passing occurrence. This is thinking that is 'of' *Er-eignis*, of en-owning, that has nothing further grounding it. The task then is to remain engaged in the *question* of the manner in which 'we ourselves,' that is, 'our' da-sein is to be thought henceforth, as this thinking without metaphysical ground occurs in the "no-thing," the abyss (*Ab-grund*) of be-ing.

And yet, all the while, da-sein and thinking do occur. Things are still happening, in spite of their appearing without metaphysical grounds. This is indeed strange: even in their utter questionability, even though there is no available accounting either for 'human' being or for the being of things, things persist nevertheless. In the abyssal experience of the untenability, the being-without-permanent-ground, of virtually all previous interpretations of being, t/here nevertheless still 'is' or appears a t/here, even though this 'is' does not have whatever sense we may have thought it to have. This 'is'—the question-worthy being of the t/here—'is' nevertheless. Yet in what way may this be thought? Asking this question further intensifies the experience of the way of thinking that Heidegger is attempting to work out here. It deepens thinking's engagement with that matter (*Sache*) that calls for thinking in the context of Heidegger's *Contributions*, that calls thinking into an entirely unprecedented, unique, singular (*einzig*) disclosure. This matter includes the question of the very occurring of the disclosing that happens in and as this da-sein. This matter, the question of the determination of the very be-ing of the t/here, 'is' now strangely beyond whatever familiarity people might have had regarding it, and it elicits and draws—or more accurately, is in the need (*Not*) of—the very enactment of original thinking. Human being *needs* an other, non-metaphysical determination, for the matter in question 'is' closer than hands and feet, even here and now coming to pass. It is a matter of *our* being.

> In and *as* da-sein, be-ing enowns the truth [*Wahrheit*] which it manifests as [refusal] [*Verweigerung*], as that domain of hinting and withdrawal—of stillness. . . . For that man can do nothing—least of all when he has been given the task of preparing for the grounding of da-sein—so much so that this task once again inceptually determines what is ownmost to humans. (GA 65, 20; CP, 15 [translation modified])

The compelling and compelled character of this thinking that Heidegger enacts in his writing and that enjoins "our" thinking as we read is now unmistakable. "We" are now compelled, as was Heidegger, not only by the question of the very be-ing which we "are" but the question of that be-ing in which "we" come to pass. In following the lead of this question, there eventuates a falling away of familiar-seeming ways of thinking and familiar-sounding terminology, and an opening of what Heidegger calls a great stillness (*Stille*) in which thinking is also disinclined to revert to previous ways of thinking. Attention to the stillness that opens in the falling away of metaphysical determinations now attunes thinking, returning it to that abyssal and yet somehow grounding aspect of be-ing's question, in which unprecedented determinations of da-sein are awaited, emerge, and pass away.

Heidegger also indicates that in the first experiences of thinking's being so drawn back into question out of familiarity with beings, a "tonality"

(*Stimmung*) of "startled dismay" (*Erschrecken*)²⁴ approaching out-and-out terror, qualifies it.

> Startled dismay: This can be most appropriately contrasted with the grounding-attunement [*Grundstimmung*] of the first beginning, with *wonder* [*Erstaunen*]. . . . [It] means faring back [*Zurückfahren*] out of the familiarity of easy comportments into the open of the press of the self-concealing [*Sichverbergenden*], in which openness the hitherto familiar indicates itself as the estranging and fettering.²⁵

This attunement arises out of the experience of being drawn out of any familiarity with beings and becoming attuned to the strangeness of things even, and perhaps especially, in their apparent familiarity, when no metaphysical ground is t/here to account either for their being at all or for their coming-to-pass as they do. Heidegger sets this moodal attunement of *Erschrecken* in contrast with the basic attunement of thinking in the first beginning, namely, wonder (*Erstaunen*). While we might suppose that in wonder, which was the basic attunement of ancient Greek thinkers, there may well have been more of a sense of the overwhelming presence of a vast superfluity of arising and readily apparent beings than of the questionability of their being at all, the attunement of *Erschrecken* that arises in the experience of the utter questionability of beings without ground is accompanied by a sense of dire need (*Not*), namely, a need to seek a way of thinking of the mean-ing of be-ing in its most strange and question-worthy character. *Erschrecken* is the tonality that at least at first accompanies a thinking that thinks and experiences, without protection, the absence of ground, the withdrawal in da-sein of whatever may have once been meant by being. Through *Erschrecken*, we might say, thinking is attuned more to the withdrawal of beings than to their wondrous arising. Not turning away from this experience, allowing it to determine thinking, not seek-ing (even if vainly) to return to familiar ways of thinking of beings deepens, then, into a reticence (*Verhaltenheit*) in the thinking-experience of da-sein. Reticence, Heidegger says, is the "creative 'hanging-in' [*Aus-halten*] in the abyss."²⁶ In reticence, the self-concealing and withdrawal of be-ing from beings, its abyssal question-dimension, opens up, taking thinking with it, as it were, in its draft. "Hanging in" with the stillness and utter strangeness that such an experience inaugurates, one becomes singularly disinclined to speak or think in any familiar, that is, meta-physical, manner. This falling silent (*Verschweigung*) enables a listening/belonging (*Zugehören*) to be-ing in its abyssal character of withdrawal. Silently, one awaits in this question a determination of da-sein different from any previous one, that is, as "grounded" in the abysmal dimension of the *question* of be-ing. Falling silent and attuning to the great stillness, according to Heidegger, characterizes the meditative awareness (*Besinn-*

ung) of thinking in the transition from the first to the other beginning of history. "Hanging-in" simultaneously opens one to the strange, unprotected, utterly mortal fragility of unprotected beings in their ungrounded coming to pass. In reticence, "beings themselves, and [one's] relation to them, want to be guarded."[27] The "guarding" here, which might suggest the *Scheu*, the "awe" that, according to the text, also characterizes attunement to them, means allowing them to occur as they do, that is, as utterly singular and irredeemable.

Further, reticence is also a kind of "gathering of human being to itself" [Verhaltenheit vermag allein Menschenwesen und Menschenversammlung auf es selbst . . . zu sammeln (GA 65, 34; CP, 24–25)]. It thus constitutes a preparedness (*Bereitschaft*) for experiencing the withdrawing refusal (*Verweigerung*) of be-ing as a kind of gifting (*Schenkung*). This gifting involves the coming to pass of beings in their singular, unprecedented character. That is, the preparedness for experiencing the apparent withdrawal of be-ing from beings enables an experience of this withdrawal as belonging to and as needful (*Notwendig*) in be-ing's enowning character. In turn, this preparedness increasingly draws thinking farther away from any tendency to try to return to familiarity. It allows be-ing *its* own, most strange and question-worthy way of determining da-sein, of determining beings anew, as enowned in be-ing's own eventuation.

A way of thinking and experiencing thus emerges that no longer wants the traditional familiarity of beings and is no longer involved in a fruitless attempt to be blindly enmeshed with them. In question, thinking draws away from beings' dominance and into a difference from beings that enables them to occur in their singularity as enowned by be-ing and thus as disclosive of be-ing's 'own' singularity. In this movement away from enmeshment and into 'something' else, thinking is oriented to seek *be-ing*, a seeking that Heidegger says is "the goal" [Das Suchen selbst ist das Ziel] (GA 65, 18; CP, 17). It is a seeking that is attuned not primarily by beings but to be-ing's abysally remote distance from beings, to its utter questionability. This seeking, oriented by the abyssal character of be-ing, yields a da-sein unlike any previous determination of da-sein.

The name Heidegger gives for be-ing's originary, most question-worthy opening-out-into and abyssal drawing away from determinations is *Entrückung*.[28] He calls the dimensionality of be-ing's opening and drawing away from, through which be-ing's differentiation from determinate things occurs and in which determinate things are differentiated and 'placed' together and apart from one another, time/space. The opening of time/space, as the dimensionality of determinations of be-ing, is itself different (but not separated) from the beings that come to pass 'in' that dimensionality. Within the opening of time/space, things come to

pass. Thinking follows, or is drawn out by and into, the opening and
coming to pass of things. This being-drawn out into can also turn
into a fascinated enmeshment or enchantment with things, which Heidegger names *Bezauberung*.[29] In a fascinated preoccupation with things,
the very opening (*Lichtung*) of things, as well as the dimension of the
abyssal withdrawal of be-ing (be-ing's difference from beings), remains
unthought, concealed and forgotten. In the enchantment process, thinking is *necessarily* drawn out *away* from the question, and this being
drawn out is an aspect of the disclosive event itself. Things seem so
familiar and without question that their abyssal "ground" is forgotten.
Thus, in any thinking that focuses primarily on the beings that are disclosed in and as da-sein, a withdrawing and concealing of the abyssal
dimension of be-ing occurs. Whatever is thought to happen in and as
the t/here — as da-sein — draws thinking simultaneously away from be-
ing's abyssal nothing-ness, which Heidegger also characterizes as "preg-
nant fullness [*Reife*]."[30] In thinking primarily of beings, thinking draws/
is drawn away from encountering 'itself,' away from its own question,
away from asking: how does the be-ing of the t/here itself come to
pass? Thinking tends thus to revert to ways of thinking of da-sein that are
oriented primarily by *what* occurs. Such thinking, according to Heidegger, has given rise to the manifold metaphysical ways of thought that
characterize what he calls the first beginning of history. Metaphysical
thought continues to interpret things in familiar ways that are oriented
primarily by beings. This tendency, the allure of metaphysics, attests to
the power of the first beginning of history, in which things first
emerged as persisting things. The draw of thinking into *what* happens
tends to cover over again and again the abyssal question of the very
occurrence of be-ing, the disclosive eventfulness which comes to pass
and which, as it were, both withdraws and is 'itself' sheltered in the singular disclosing of da-sein.[31] We need then to be mindful, especially in
our reading of *Contributions*, of the way in which our thinking has a tendency to revert back to traditions from which it takes its departure. This
is not just a matter of tending to posit once again some permanent
ground of beings as the source of their meaning. Rather, it involves an
aspect of the truth of be-ing itself, namely, the potentially fascinating
power of the disclosure of beings. The event of be-ing in its difference
from the disclosure of things, although profoundly obscured, occurs
through the very disclosures of the traditions of the first beginning of
history; and the thinker undergoes a draw toward the traditional
thought as well as away from it. This helps explain why Heidegger is
clear that thinking that is oriented by be-ing must be thought in relation to traditional thought.[32] Our philosophical tradition provides the
'site' where both the anticipation and the transition from the first to the
other beginning of history can happen.

Although thinking may tend to be fascinated by beings, the move-ment of the thinking in *Contributions* attests to the way in which be-ing itself not only enables thinking to become familiar with things that are disclosed. Be-ing also eventuates as a withdrawal of familiarity, for ex-ample, through death.[33] Be-ing thus eventuates (as) a kind of double-movement, a drawing of thinking *both* into *and* back out of familiarity. This double movement is doubly abyssal: in being-drawn toward and into engagement with disclosed beings, thinking tends to lose attention to the abyssal character of their disclosure. This loss is itself abyssal, since it is a loss of an awareness of beings' belonging to be-ing's event-fulness. However, as thinking experiences itself as being drawn back out of everyday familiarity into the question of being that, for example, an experience of death can elicit, thinking draws/is drawn back into the ungrounding ground, the not-character of be-ing, the abyssal question in which da-sein originally emerges. Be-ing itself thus draws thinking back into the very occurring of being-in-question that familiarity covers over. Transitional thinking of be-ing occurs then as what might be called an oscillation of draws toward and away from the potentially fascinating power of beings, toward and away from its own abyssal occurrence.

Whether or not in any moment of da-sein thinking is or is not drawn back and displaced (*verrückt*) from apparent familiarity with beings into the ungrounding, abyssal dimension of the question of be-ing's singu-lar, disclosive eventfulness requires a decision (*Entscheidung*) that deter-mines the way da-sein occurs.[34] And although this decision happens in and as a determination of da-sein, it is not a decision that is attributable to the action of any agent. Although a thinker may experience this de-cision as it occurs, subjective choice is not at issue. Rather, a decision concerning da-sein's primary draw and basic determinations eventuates as an occurrence of be-ing. The issue remains open: both the site that da-sein 'is' and its specific, determinate character are eventuated (*er-eignet*) in be-ing. Thinking thus always has the possibility of temporally being drawn away from its abyssal questionability into engagement pri-marily with beings; it can continue indefinitely to attend primarily to the ways that beings (including human beings) occur "in site" in their physical interrelationships. Thinking may largely continue to interpret things in the manifold metaphysical ways that give priority to what is there rather than to the question of their occurrence, to continuing presence rather than to ungrounding ground of da-sein. This remains an open possibility because da-sein happens always with beings, in their passing presence, and with the draw of their fascination. And yet, inso-far as the enactment of thinking is also always, in however hidden a manner, also enactment of be-ing in question, the determination of thinking as a thinking of da-sein has its abyssal "ground" that is not any 'what,' not any being, but 'is' the coming-passing of be-ing 'itself.'

We have seen that no being can provide any lasting or enduring ground for the occurring of beings. Relatively lasting beings and determinations of thinking strangely emerge and so find whatever temporal ground they seem to have in *question*. However, *this* question, we recall, can be no determinate question. Rather, this question is a dimension of be-ing that occurs as the eventuation in be-ing of the withdrawal, the passing away of any certain or familiar determinations. Question belongs both to beings' determinations and to the occurring of be-ing in its truth. Be-ing's truth character comes to pass as the coming-to-pass of da-sein, as arising determinations withdraw simultaneously from determination passing "back" into question. Be-ing occurs through the eventuation of things as they occur. The abyssal ground and the inevitability of question that always, however hidden, accompanies da-sein's determinations, is disclosed through the always question-worthy enactment of beings, through their coming-to-pass, which articulates the coming-passing (*Wesung*) of be-ing's truth.

This way of thinking, although frequently hidden in familiar ways of thinking of beings, emerges through a careful attention not only to the emergence of beings but also to their withdrawing. Both emerging and withdrawing simultaneously characterize the be-ing of beings. Said another way, with primary reference to be-ing rather than to beings, thinking in the draft of the emerging and withdrawing of beings, in the attentiveness to the singularity of the way in which beings occur in and as *this* da-sein, attests to be-ing's own en-owning character.

This makes clearer what Heidegger means when he says that be-ing shelters 'itself' in beings: Be-ing is *at once* disclosed through (sheltered in) beings and withdraws from them back into indeterminacy. This withdrawal of be-ing exposes the sheltering as itself passing, as an occurrence of the ungrounding of its own manifest determinations. This ungrounding-sheltering occurs in and as our da-sein. Without da-sein, without manifest, passing determinations of be-ing in beings, there would only be no thing. That beings are thus means that be-ing 'is' en-owning (as) da-sein, and da-sein 'is' be-ing's abyssal grounding of the coming to pass of beings' determinations.

What becomes increasingly clear through reading *Contributions* is that, although the truth of be-ing is sheltered in beings, be-ing cannot be thought from (out of) beings, whether individually or altogether. Be-ing must be thought out of 'itself.'[35] The transition of thinking that is enacted in *Contributions* enables us to understand why, in the earlier part of the text, Heidegger states provisionally that "beings are. Be-ing comes-to-pass [*west*],"[36] and then, toward the end of the text, says rather,

> the full, coming-passing of be-ing in the truth of en-owning allows us to realize that be-ing and only be-ing "is" and that a being [or beings] is/are

not. . . . Be-ing is—that is to say that be-ing alone comes-to-pass (west) [as] the coming to pass of itself (en-owning).[37]

We can no longer think, therefore, that beings "are"; we think rather of the coming-passing (*Wesung*) of be-ing "itself" as we think through the coming-to-pass of determinations of da-sein, here and now.

Heidegger's attempt in *Contributions* at a thoughtful saying of philosophy in the other beginning of history, and our attempts to join with him in this thinking, are attempts to think in and through the opening of metaphysical thought to its being-yet-without that ground that it had assumed is t/here. As we continue to think through the way of thinking enacted in this text, we are called continually to return not only to the questionability, and the need, to re-think traditional ways of positing being as enduring presence, we also are called continually to return to the ungrounding, questionable character of our being t/here and to engage decisively in the open issue of its determination. It is to the experience of the untenability of metaphysical ways of thinking that Heidegger's thought would call us 'back,' and so, call us toward a different, unprecedented and singular, other beginning of history.

Notes

1. GA 65, 3, translation mine; cf. CP, 3. For bibliographical information on the texts referred to here, see the introduction to this volume, note 1. I have found the Emad/Maly translation of *Beiträge* to be valuable and have consulted it in all cases. I have, however, frequently chosen a different rendering of particular passages, which I will indicate as mine. Where the differences are more than slight, I will attempt to explain why I chose the renderings I did.

2. GA 65, 4, translation mine; cf. CP, 4.

3. See his explicit statement to this effect in §259. In this section, Heidegger goes on to outline the two ways in which this characterization can be interpreted. He states that, whereas "initally and throughout the long history between Anaximander and Nietzsche, inquiring into being is only the question concerning the being of beings [*das Sein des Seienden*]," what is at stake in the question of being is the developing of a way of thinking that no longer takes its cues primarily from beings but rather from be-ing (*das Seyn*) itself. As the translators point out (see CP, xxii) the differences in the spelling of "being" (*Sein* and *Seyn*) indicate differences in the manner in which being is thought: in the context of metaphysics and in the context of what Heidegger calls "be-ing-historical-thinking [*seynsgeschichtliches Denken*]," respectively. The difference involves the transitional (das *Übergängliche*) way of thinking that Heidegger works out in *Contributions*. In the last major part of the text, entitled "Be-ing," which includes §259, Heidegger also explicitly states his understanding of the difference of what he calls philosophy from *Historie* and *historische* ways of thinking. In §258, for example, Heidegger says, "At present and in the future the essential grasping of the concept of philosophy is historical [*geschichtliche*] grasping (not

historical [as a discipline] [*historische*])" (translation mine). In what follows, we shall see more clearly the importance of the difference between these two ways of thinking of "philosophy" as corresponding to the differences in the two manners in which being can be thought.

4. In this regard, see Heidegger's discussion of temporality as the ontological meaning of care in *Being and Time*, §§65ff. He further elaborates this meaning in terms of the temporality of the "everydayness" of dasein in the sections that follow §65.

5. For an introduction to Heidegger's discussion of truth as *aletheia*, see *Being and Time*, §44, and the essay "Vom Wesen der Wahrheit" ("On the Essence of Truth"). A first version of the latter was delivered as a lecture in 1930 and published in 1943. It may be found in a later version in English in *Basic Writings*, ed. David Farrell Krell (New York: Harper & Row, 1977).

6. Again, spelling be-ing in this way indicates that "being" is no longer thought metaphysically or in terms of permanent presence.

7. GA 65, 3, translation mine; cf. CP, 3.

8. Ibid., translation mine.

9. Ibid., translation mine. We have already seen that what Heidegger means by "be-ing-historical thinking" will occur otherwise than metaphysical thinking, insofar as the former no longer is oriented primarily by a thinking of being in terms of a most common, transcendent, timeless, or highest being. As we shall see below, be-ing historical thinking means the eventuation of a thinking whose orientation is primarily to be-ing itself rather than primarily to beings.

10. In concord with the translators' remarks to this effect, most of the essays in this volume (see, e.g., Vallega, Vallega-Neu, Brogan, Emad, Maly, von Herrmann) stress the importance of the "passage-character" of this thinking, indicated by Heidegger's italicizing the ending in the word Gedanken-*gang*, which appears immediately following the sentences cited above. This passage-character is the character of enactment or performance of thinking that is occurring in the text. And as we read, the movement of our thinking too joins in this enactment.

11. See CP, 5, 7; see also the discussion of the importance of this structure in essays in this volume, for example, Brogan, Emad, and von Herrmann.

12. Emad and Maly's translation of this passage is: "This saying gathers being's essential sway unto a first sounding, while it itself [this saying] sounds only out of this essential sway" (GA 65, 4; CP, 4). Unfortunately, they do not discuss their choice of translation of this key word in their foreword. Whereas they translate the word elsewhere as "echo," I prefer their translation of *Anklang* in this passage as "sounding (out)." I think it is better than "echo" since what is at stake is a sounding-out or bell-like ringing out, albeit tentative, that is, an initial, preparatory "sonance" that may gain a hearing of a different way of thinking of be-ing. One hears in "echo" or even "re-sonance" some sort of reference to something that has already sounded previously.

13. As the translators of *Contributions* helpfully point out in their foreword, *Wesen* as well as *Wesung*, both of which Heidegger will frequently use in the context of attempting to think of be-ing otherwise than with primary reference to beings, are among the Heideggerian terms most difficult to translate. Not only do they not have any readily corresponding words in English, but the ways in which *Wesen* has been translated in traditional philosophy easily mislead a

reader into thinking of something like "essence" or "essential nature." In the context of thinking of be-ing, in contrast, these words mean something like the way(s) in which be-ing occurs as always "coming to pass" or "coming-passing." Thus, my translation of *Wesen* as "coming-to-pass" and *Wesung* as "coming-passing." In the latter case, this translation also retains a sense of *Verwesung*, which one may overhear in *Wesung*. Unlike *Wesung*, a term that Heidegger appears to coin, *Verwesung* is a fairly common German word and means, as Vallega also points out in his essay, something like "decomposition" or "decay." *Wesung*, then, means something like the simultaneous arising-and-falling or appearing-withdrawing of be-ing.

14. GA 65, 4, translation mine.

15. Ibid., translation mine.

16. Thus, Heidegger will say a bit later that "everything is posed . . . upon . . . questioning" (translation mine); the original reads, "Alles ist auf . . . das Fragen . . . gestellt" (GA 65, 10). The translation of this passage in *Contributions* reads: "Everything is geared toward . . . questioning" (CP, 7). But this translation misses the manner in which, in some sense, every thing that comes to pass comes to pass in question, the manner in which "question" itself, quite different from any metaphysical ground, might be thought to serve as "that in which" or "that upon which" everything is posed or comes to be.

17. Recall here that *Wahrheit* names for Heidegger a dynamic, aletheic movement of the appearing and withdrawing from appearing.

18. GA 65, 3, translation mine; cf. CP, 3. See note 10 above.

19. As Emad and Maly note in their foreword, "the difficulty of translating Heidegger's word Da has been recognized all along by Heidegger's translators" (CP, xxxiv). The word dasein is used in common as well as philosophical German to indicate the manifest existence or existential character of a being of beings within definite worldly situations. As Vallega-Neu writes in this volume (see chapter 4, note 24), the word indicates not simply presence but the way in which situated things occur. Dasein frequently appears in hyphenated form in *Contributions* (da-sein), to indicate that the way its meaning is to be thought is different from the way in which it is thought in other contexts, including from the way in which it is thought in *Being and Time*. In *Contributions*, he says, for example, that "the t/here [Da] is the occurring, en-owned and insisting [*inständliche*] site for the moment of the turning [*Wendungsaugenblicksstätte*] for the clearing of beings in enownment" (GA 65, 273, translation mine; cf. CP, 192). See Vallega-Neu's note on this translation of *inständliche*, which I prefer to Emad/Maly's "inabiding." The beginning sections of the fifth major part of *Contributions* entitled "Gründung" elaborate the way in which da-sein should be understood within the context of *Contributions*. For Heidegger, it becomes increasingly important to think of "our" being as da-sein rather than in any traditional metaphysical terms. I will discuss this further below.

20. GA 65, 3: "[The matter to be thought] amounts to an essential transformation of the human from 'rational animal' (*animal rationale*) to Da-sein." Heidegger further addresses this transformation of the way in which "human being" comes to be thought later in the "Preview," for example, §19.

21. GA 65, 169–70, particularly §87; CP, 119–20. See also note 3 above.

22. "Sorge [ist] . . . die das Da ausstehende Inständigkeit" ("Care [is] . . . the

standing-in that stands out from the t/here") (GA 65, 35, translation mine; cf. CP, 25).

23. The withdrawal and experience of the untenability of metaphysical meaning introduces the possibility of nihilism. Heidegger gives an analysis of nihilism in *Contributions* (see, e.g., §72).

Although this topic is too broad to discuss in detail in this essay, we might at least broach it by saying that the experience of there not being any metaphysical meaning or any stable or permanent ground grounding phenomena is extremely dis-orienting. We will discuss this further below. This dis-orientation can elicit a variety of responses. One is to believe, as Nietzsche's work draws out, that nothing is worth anything anymore, that there are no values, that there "is" only nothing. Another possible response is to try to ignore the questionability of holding metaphysical beliefs and to try to repeat metaphysical thinking ad infinitum. In *Contributions,* Heidegger points out the destructive consequences of both of these responses. His attempt in *Contributions* is to work out a way of thinking that follows neither of these courses but rather, staying with the experience of da-sein in the passage of metaphysical ways of thinking, allows something different, a different way of being and thinking to emerge.

24. Although the Emad/Maly translation of the word *Erschrecken* as "startled dismay" may be accurate, I believe that the word carries an even stronger meaning. What's important here is not just an intellectual but also a moodal attunement to the experience of no longer being able to rely on previous interpretations of one's being in order to make sense of it, the experience of being without any ground. This experience shakes one up. The mood that accompanies it is one of being shaken down to the very roots of whatever hold on anything that one may have thought oneself to have. I doubt there is one word that could carry this sense. To "understand" it, it must be experienced by undergoing the transition of thinking that Heidegger is speaking of throughout *Contributions.*

25. GA 65, 15, translation mine; cf. CP, 11.

26. GA 65, 36, translation mine; cf. CP, 24. Emad/Maly translate this passage as follows: "the creative sustaining in ab-ground." The question I would raise here is, what does this "sustaining" sustain? How is the sustaining to be understood? Certainly thinking sustains no-thing. Rather, thinking awaits—unprecedented determination(s) of being-t/here as gifted, as *er-eignet.*

27. Ibid., translation mine.

28. Important passages that develop the meaning of the terms *Entrückung* and its corollary, *Berückung,* which Emad/Maly translate respectively as "removal-unto" and "charming-moving-unto," include, for example, GA 65, 34, 70, 237, 260, 268, 272, 316; CP, 24, 48, 168, 184, 189, 192, 222. Heidegger employs these terms to designate the aletheic, double movement of thinking in terms of *Zeit/Raum,* time-space, whereby both da-sein and be-ing occur as temporal and spatial, that is, as temporal-spatial disclosure.

29. See, for example, GA 65, 124; CP, 86.

30. See, for example, GA 65, 268; CP, 189.

31. Heidegger refers in several places to the way in which be-ing shelters itself/is sheltered in beings. The terms that he uses for this sheltering are *Bergen, Bergung, Sichverbergen,* and *Verbergung.* See, for example, GA 65, 70–71, 96, 330; CP, 49, 66, 231.

32. See, for example, his statement in §81: "The encounter of the necessity of the other beginning out of the originary positioning of the first" (translation mine). Many of the sections in the third major part of *Contributions* entitled "Zuspiel" ("Playing-Forth") have to do with this differentiating/interrelating of the first and the other beginning.

33. See in this regard the discussion of death in *Contributions*, §§160–63.

34. For a more explicit discussion of decision (*Entscheidung*), see, for example, *Contributions*, §§43–49.

35. GA 65, 7, translation mine; cf. CP, 5.

36. GA 65, 30, translation mine; cf. CP, 22.

37. GA 65, 472–73, translation mine; cf. CP, 332–33.

2. Strategies for a Possible Reading

Dennis J. Schmidt

About a decade ago a book landed on our desks that married all the complicated features of a whale and a riddle: large and apparently offering no easy way for a hapless reader to see directly into its concerns (to look it in the eye as it were, for that, in some sense, is what one does with a book), it sometimes read like a hieroglyph for which the code was lost. The text was hermetically sealed: imagine a 510-page poem by Paul Celan. Oedipus confronting the riddle of the Sphinx had an easier time. And yet the stakes seemed almost as high as the city that Oedipus would save: long before its publication, rumor of *Beiträge zur Philosophie (Vom Ereignis)* had circulated, fueled by three powerful fires. First, Heidegger's own comments about the importance of this book (the secretiveness which surrounded the withheld publication of the book only whet the appetite further). Second, the eventual circulation of an unauthorized and, in my case at least, incomplete manuscript of the book, which gave some indication of what large claims were to be offered up in this work (further amplified by remarks which threw down a gauntlet and egged the reader on: "No one understands what 'I' am thinking here").[1] Third, the anticipation surrounding this text was increased further still by Otto Pöggeler's oft-cited remark that *Beiträge zur Philosophie,* or *Contributions to Philosophy,* is Heidegger's "true magnum opus."[2] The anticipation of the publication of this book could not have been greater. I take the relative quiet which has been maintained about it over the past decade to be one indicator of just how stunned we have been by the reality of this work. Now we must confess just how unprepared we were (and perhaps remain) to come to terms with the claims and achievements of this large and, despite every anticipation, unexpected work.[3]

Recently, this same book resurfaced, much like Moby Dick, but this time wearing the mask of a translation. Now it is in English—or at least something resembling the English language.[4] And now it seems that we cannot escape the fact that it is time to come to some terms with the claims of this work. But my suspicion is that it will be quite some while before we can begin to be comfortable with just what it is that this book would ask of its readers. We have grown accustomed to having Heidegger surprise and challenge us with the nuanced style of his thought and its rigorous, at times almost acrobatic, language; but nothing which we have been able to read up to this point has posed such profound challenges and surprises—to this reader at least—as his *Contributions.* While I confess that, unlike Pöggeler, I do not regard this as Heidegger's real masterwork (at least from the point of view of my present understanding of this work), I do believe that this book merits the serious attention and effort that it demands of one who would take it to heart. This is so for two reasons. First, in *Contributions* we find Heidegger talking only with Heidegger—this is a profoundly intimate work, and so provides a glimpse into the workings of an original mind struggling to find a way to a radically new point of view and struggling with the need that it set for itself of establishing a new philosophical lexicon. Exceedingly self-reflexive, *Contributions* is indispensable for one who would take Heidegger seriously since in it Heidegger's concerns are folded back upon themselves and compressed by the effort to generate a new philosophical vocabulary which does not let those concerns be translated out of their proper idiom. As a consequence, it is something like a hitherto missing link in the evolution of Heidegger's thought, since here we see the crucible in which so many of the early themes and so much of the language undergo a sort of alchemy which opens up a still different—or at least differently configured—idiom and set of concerns. One must also say that, in some sense, this is the *ultimate* work we have from Heidegger: it is hard to imagine a work which would be more embedded in a realm which Heidegger himself has sought to define and chart. But the second, and to my mind more important, reason this hard nut of a book merits the serious effort it requires is that in *Contributions* we find the avenues down which we can begin to understand what might emerge from Heidegger's thought as a politics. Not unjustly did Reiner Schürmann suggest that we could read these "Contributions to Philosophy" "as a monstrous 'Contribution to Politics.'"[5]

The purpose of this essay, which must, for many reasons, remain modest (especially in contrast to the grand ambitions of the text about which I will speak), is twofold: first, I would like to propose some strategies for reading *Contributions;* and second, I would like to explain why it is that here, in this idiosyncratic work, we might just find something of the contours of a possible Heideggerian politics. I readily concede that the sweep of this work far surpasses the reach of my remarks. So I make no pretense of offering anything more than a simple set of strategies for reading this seemingly impenetrable text and of proposing what I see to be one productive, and largely unexamined, thematic axis along which a more systematic interpretation of this text might be undertaken.

Honesty governs every good strategy of reading, and I must be honest and say that what is most prominent about this book is that it is *exceedingly difficult.* One might justly suggest that this is a downright uninviting work: it makes little to no effort to engage a reader, it spins out a vocabulary very insulated from anything outside itself, it indulges in grammatical and syntactical abuses that would never pass the scrutiny of a copy editor, and it sometimes masks its own topic.[6] How then can one begin to speak of this book without some acknowledgment of the difficulties which it generates for one who would read it? Addressing the specific character of its difficulty is the best way to work through it in order to open the book to the forms of reflection which it would engage. There seem to be three aspects of *Contributions* which constitute obstacles for one who would read the text: first, its language; second, its context; third, its intentions. Some comments on these key, yet enigmatic elements of any possible reading of *Contributions* might be the best way to enter the text.

Referring to Hölderlin's translations of Sophocles into German, Benjamin famously remarked that here one confronted "the monstrous and original danger of all translation: that the gates of a language which has been expanded slam shut and that the translator is enclosed in silence."[7] It is a sentence which, for many reasons, aptly applies to Heidegger's *Contributions*, especially since language, translatability, danger, monstrosity, and silence constitute some of its most evident themes. Indeed, this sense that language threatens to shut down in *Contributions* is one of its very first concerns. The first sentence of the text announces Heidegger's own disillusion with the "public" title of his text, suggesting that nothing that could be said publicly would do justice to its heart (the subtitle, which is secluded in parentheses, is, however, "essential"). And the second sentence of the text tells us why this is the case: "Philosophy cannot make an appearance in public in any other way [than "flat and customary and non-speaking" (GA 65, 3; cf. CP, 3)], since all essential titles have been rendered impossible in the abuse of all fundamental words and the destruction of the genuine relation to the word" (GA 65, 3; cf. CP, 3).[8] From the outset this failure of inherited language becomes a guiding theme for what follows. At the other end of the text, Heidegger concludes *Contributions* with reflections on language, this time a reflection upon its greatest possibility: "When the gods summon the earth and in the summons echo a world, and thus the summons resonates as Da-Sein of human being, then there is language as historical, as the word grounding history. . . . Language is grounded in silence. Silence is the most hidden holder of measure. It *holds* the measure insofar as it first sets up the measure" (GA 65, 510; cf. CP, 358–59).

One does well to bear in mind that the entire text of *Contributions* is sandwiched between remarks on language. Opened and closed by an explicit discussion of language—opened by reference to its poverty in the present, closed with an allusion to the measure-setting possibility of silence—*Contributions* is governed *at every turn* by Heidegger's struggle against a language already co-opted by (and for) the purposes of metaphysics, and by the struggle to open a new dimension of language which would properly be spoken of and from "the event" which has always escaped the reflections of metaphysics. While the question of language is explicitly thematized at various points in *Contributions*, the most important form in which Heidegger's concern with language is played out is *performatively*. Language operates here in a manner that asks the reader to attend to its "how" as well as (perhaps even first of all) its "what." In light of this, one would do well to approach this text with many of the interpretive demands one places upon oneself when reading a poem: its movement, which is frequently borne by language rather than conceptual argument, is very much a part of what one needs to follow. Whether or not Heidegger has succeeded in this great experiment with the language of thinking remains to be seen (I suspect that our decision in this matter will have to be a split decision: in some points he has indeed opened creative possibilities for a language which would evade, and undermine, the presumptions of metaphysics, while in other regards his effort seems to have failed).[9]

To follow this thread of language—both thematically and operatively—it is helpful to recall that it is the *exhaustion* of language in the present age, its "destruction" even, which haunts what can be said of language at all.[10] But how did this happen? How did we "use up" language? What is capable of "destroying" even "essential words"?

The answer is, in one sense, easy to announce: metaphysics. More precisely, it is the capacity of metaphysics, as a way of thinking and speaking, to cover over by ossifying the original event of the truth [or: truing] of beyng, which "is and remains *my* question and my *sole* question, for it qualifies as the most singular question" (GA 65, 10; cf. CP, 8).[11] But there is clearly nothing simple, no easy resolution in this remark. Heidegger is at least clear about the task he has set himself as a necessary accomplishment; and he concedes that it is at best preliminary with respect to the full needs which he will outline, needs which he argues far outstrip what he believes can be accomplished in this transitional age: "The truth of beyng does not let itself be said with the customary language which today is ever more widely used abused and destroyed by talking. Can the truth of beyng be said at all immediately if all language is still the language of beings? Or can a new language be invented for beyng? No. . . . Only one thing matters: to say the most nobly formed language in its simplicity and its essential power, to say the language of beings as the language of beyng" (GA 65, 78; cf. CP, 54). In other words, what must be accomplished is a renewal, as a transformation in which it is heard anew, of the language which we already speak. This we achieve insofar as the essential power of words is recuperated.

Of course, that is what Heidegger understands himself to be doing in this text, and that is the reason he has stretched language in this text so very far. It is also the reason that he insists on having us hear some commonplace words in a quite unusual register (e.g., "Ereignis," "Dasein," "Wesen," "Abgrund," "Gründung"—the list could easily be extended), and that is the reason he resorts to neologisms and archaic spellings (e.g., "Seyn"). All of this is part of an extended effort to demand that the reader think about what it is that the language of this text is saying. It is also part of the effort to articulate a way of speaking and thinking which does not submit itself in advance to the logic and presumptions of the language of the idea. The difficulty we have in reading *Contributions* is the difficulty of following along in a language which does not abide by the logic of our own expectations. It might also, in part at least, be a consequence of Heidegger's own difficulty in coming by the proper relation to language.

But Heidegger readily admits that in the matter of this renewal of the power of elemental words it is the poetic relation to language which will lead the way. He becomes even more specific, not merely referring us on this matter to poets generally; it is *Hölderlin* above all who opens up the possibilities of language in a manner that Heidegger finds full of promise: "The historical determination of philosophy peaks in the knowledge of the necessity of making Hölderlin's word be heard" (GA 65, 422; cf. CP, 297). And so, "Hölderlin is the poet of those of the future who comes from farthest away and thus the most futural poet. Hölderlin is the most futural of those to come because he comes from farthest away, and in this distance *traverses* and transforms what is greatest" (GA 65, 401; cf. CP, 281). In the end, Hölderlin, perhaps more than any other figure, is the one with whom Heidegger is dialoguing in *Contributions*. Much is to be learned about the language that Heidegger suggests is proper to the event of the truth of beyng from Hölderlin. Above all, one learns that it is a language that does not calcify time; that it is a language wedded to the disposition of reticence; and that it is a language that names the holy. It is, in the end, the language of tragedy which is possible in these times.

But to fully develop this topic of language and the role that Hölderlin plays in how this topic unfolds in *Contributions* is beyond the scope of this essay. It does, however, point to the second issue, which I consider a necessary concern for one who would breach the extraordinary difficulty of *Contributions*, namely, the context in which this work is to be read.

There are three sorts of contexts which help frame any reading of *Contributions:* first, the *historical* moment in which it was written; second, the *philosophical* itinerary which was guiding Heidegger at this stage in his work; and third, the *dialogue partners* Heidegger had in this project of forging a new and revolutionary conception of the task of thinking. The remarks that follow begin with the final and most easily defined of these three ways in which this text reaches beyond its own internal limits.

Proper names are, as is often the case with Heidegger's texts, remarkably few and far between for one so concerned with the force of history in thinking. For the most part, the list of those named in *Contributions* is a list of the usual suspects for Heidegger. Plato, Aristotle, Pindar, Descartes, Kant, and Hegel all make some form of appearance in these reflections. But there are four figures who, even if not always explicitly mentioned, seem to be the true dialogue partners in Heidegger's project: Hölderlin, Nietzsche, Schelling, and Jünger—each in his own way (in the case of Jünger this means only tacitly)—come to help Heidegger define his own efforts. The time of the composition of *Contributions* is the time of Heidegger's deep involvement in teaching and reading each of these three writers (the designation "writer" rather than "philosopher" is all-important since each of these figures thinks and writes outside the orbit of what typically qualifies as philosophizing; each is deeply committed to articulating a manner of thinking as a *linguistic* experience that refuses to be reduced to a conceptual argument).

At the risk of being reductive, it is worth noting that there is a theme which Heidegger seems to connect most powerfully with each of these figures. So it is that Heidegger turns most of all to Hölderlin in order to reflect upon the character of *language,* which is requisite for thinking; he turns to Nietzsche to clarify the task of overcoming *metaphysics;* he turns to Schelling for much of his *philosophical vocabulary* and for an understanding of the role that *freedom* plays in these issues; and he turns to Jünger to gain some insights into the nature of *modern technicity* and the logic of *machination.* While the role of Nietzsche, Schelling, and Hölderlin in Heidegger's thought has, in some measure, been acknowledged, the role of Jünger in the formation of his thought has yet to be fully understood and will perhaps prove to be of the most assistance for one who would read this text. Indeed I would argue that if one is to understand how to engage *Contributions* and to understand how it is not simply a self-enclosed text, an understanding of the significant extent to which it is a dialogue with Jünger's reflections in *Der Arbeiter* is requisite.[12] While Heidegger's notion of "machination," which is so central to the arguments of *Contributions,* does not derive from Jünger's work, it is clearly the case that the specific shape and many of the particulars of Heidegger's diagnosis of the character of machination in Western culture are deeply influenced by Jünger.

But the context of this work is not only shaped by a dialogue with others; it is equally shaped by Heidegger's dialogue with himself. *Contributions* is a curiously self-reflexive work, one that is deeply engaged in Heidegger's efforts to come to terms with both the achievements and the limitations of his own contributions to philosophy up to this point. This project of self-assessment, which is so basic to the development of *Contributions,* manifests itself in the frequent references to

Heidegger's other works (no other author is footnoted in the book as often as Heidegger himself). From his first works, Heidegger has self-consciously positioned himself as an outsider and a *revolutionary* with respect to the Western tradition, which has been guided by the assumptions of metaphysics—assumptions about time (as eternity), nature (as substance), truth (as correctness), and language (as conceptual); and one of Heidegger's central concerns in *Contributions* is to come to some understanding of the direction in which he must move if this revolution in thinking is to be advanced. One sees this peculiar form of textual self-consciousness working through the language of the text where notions developed elsewhere both draw upon and transform the senses they previously had. This is perhaps most evidently the case with the use of the word "Da-sein" in *Contributions,* which Heidegger now writes in hyphenated form to accentuate the idea that it names being that is "there" in the world.[13] Whereas in *Being and Time*, Dasein is a theme for an existential analytic, here in *Contributions* it becomes that which human being must *become*. Da-sein now becomes something of a task, "because human being has become too feeble for Da-sein" (GA 65, 8; cf. CP, 6). Heidegger has now come to understand that the revolution he is calling for requires "a complete transformation of human being into Da-sein" (GA 65, 475; cf. CP, 334), even though the starting point for this transformation is itself problematic since "no existing and customary conception of human being can serve as the starting point" (GA 65, 439; cf. CP, 439). The path by which one arrives at the understanding of human being as Da-sein is thus a thorny one since even the starting point which we assume in reflections upon the being that we are is problematic: "The most stubborn resistance to originary thinking is found in the unexpressed self-conception which contemporary human being has of itself" (BP, 42/61). My point is not to trace the evolution of the notion of Dasein from *Being and Time* through *Contributions* (though attention to such a development would be interesting), but to indicate just one of the important ways in which one can see how it is that the work of *Contributions* both self-consciously continues and revises Heidegger's own earlier contributions. A question haunts this text and even contributes to the sense of urgency that one finds in its tone: to what extent has Heidegger indeed contributed to the revolution in thinking that he has long been calling for and promising? Heidegger is in dialogue with himself more than any figure; and while that might be said to be the case with all of us, in some sense that self-conversation is especially powerful here.

There are perhaps many reasons that this is the case, but there is, I believe, one very important reason for the unusual intensity of Heidegger's self-involvement in this text. From its outset, Heidegger's philosophical agenda—which it was the plan of *Being and Time* to thematize[14]—was self-avowedly revolutionary; and the nature of this revolution as Heidegger conceives it is wide: it is a revolution in the fundamental assumptions guiding, grounding, and animating Western culture.[15] Only two years prior to beginning *Contributions,* Heidegger sought to enlist his own project of a philosophical revolution with the greatest possible travesty of what that revolution might mean. His brief and disastrous involvement with the National Socialists during the period of his rectorship would define him—even if at times by virtue of a deliberate avoidance—for a long time to come; and *Contributions,* as much if not more than any other work, needs to be read in the light of this definition.

This brings me to the third context for a possible reading of *Contributions,* namely the way in which it must be seen as in a dialogue with its own historical moment. Of course, that means that it needs to be read against an era that might well come to be the definitive expression of Western culture, namely the time of the Shoah. Though it is not always easy to see the manner in which *Contributions* addresses its times, I believe that it is crucial that we learn how to read this work as very much an engagement with the cultural situation of the period in which it was composed.[16] I would even argue that *Contributions* might well prove to be among Heidegger's most direct—if still oblique and obscure—efforts to confront the historical present. There are several ways in which one can see this happening; nonetheless, I will refer only to the four themes where I see this being most in evidence: the theme of distress (and its lack), the theme of machination, the theme of race, and the theme of lastness. Of course, each of these themes needs to be read as contributing to the revolutionary character of the historical present in which *Contributions* is composed.

One of the first and most enduring claims of this book is that this is a time of a peculiar crisis which Heidegger refers to with the word "distress" [*Not*]. More precisely, this is the time of "the highest distress: *the distress of the absence of distress*" (GA 65, 108; cf. CP, 75). Heidegger will repeat this claim at several points in the text, often with only slight variation, and so it almost takes on the status of the chorus in the text. This form of the "abandonment of/by beyng" (GA 65, 109; cf. CP, 77), a notion which clearly resonates with the opening remarks of *Being and Time,* which refer to the "forgetfulness of being," is the most pernicious form of the historical possibilities opened for us because it is a form in which the oblivion we suffer is squared: our distress is that we have not yet experienced the distress which is proper to our times.[17] What is important beyond the details of Heidegger's diagnosis of these times is that this theme of a historical *crisis* is one of the conducting wires of *Con-*

tributions; and this crisis, which defines the present age, needs to be understood as the unfolding of the logic of a long history.[18]

Of course, that history is the history of metaphysics. But here in *Contributions* the present character of that history gets a new specification, namely "machination." Now the project of the overcoming of metaphysics gets a distinctive task, one that separates it—at least in some measure—from Nietzsche's project of overcoming metaphysics.[19] Demonstrating that the roots of machination are found in the simple human capacity for making—and so linking this to the analyses of *techne* and *poiesis*[20]—Heidegger rapidly moves to argue that in the modern age these capacities have come to be governed by the logics of calculability, speed, and enormity. Machination is the form which the abandonment of beyng now takes, as the effort to secure a constant presence—ultimately as the effort to stave off death, which is "the utmost and most extreme testimony of beyng" (GA 65, 284; cf. CP, 200)—machination marks the final possible obliteration of the event that Heidegger is arguing belongs at the sources of thinking which is alive. It is the most extreme form of the denial of the incalculable which is the elemental character of the event.

One of the manners in which the logic of machination unfolds itself is in a further transformation of the self-understanding of human being.[21] Under the logic of machination what is being prepared for is "the *transition to a technicized animal*" (GA 65, 98; cf. CP, 68); in other words, the deepening of the cultural form which metaphysics takes, the saturation of the forms of life by the logic of machination, entails a deepening of the obliteration of Da-sein as that which human being must become. This alteration of our self-understanding is the obliteration of the relation of Da-sein and the event; it is, one might say, the erasure of history from our self-understanding. This brings me to the third feature of Heidegger's engagement with his historical present, namely, his concern with *race.*

One is struck by the remarkable frequency of Heidegger's remarks about race and blood in *Contributions.* Together with concomitant discussions of biologism and of "the people," it becomes abundantly clear that Heidegger is engaging the National Socialist ideology on a point that he would later indicate was a basic difference between his political views and those espoused by the Nazi party.[22] The critique of Nazi racial policy is clear and unmistakable: it is but "a hitherto unknown dressing for the old trimmings of school philosophy [i.e., metaphysics]" (GA 65, 19; cf. CP, 14). But the grounds of this critique are not what one might expect. Heidegger's clear criticisms of the notion of race and blood, and of the forms in which those notions are mobilized in his times, is not based upon what one might traditionally conceive of as *moral* grounds; rather, the problem with these notions is that they mark a further obliteration of the recognition of *history* in human self-understanding. So Heidegger writes that "it is no accident that 'modernity' brings historicity [the technologized conception of history and its task] to genuine domination. This domination today (in the beginning of the decisive period of modernity) already extends itself so far that . . . history [in the proper sense] is pushed into what is history-less. . . . Blood and race become the bearers of history. *Pre*history now gives historicity the character of legitimacy" (GA 65, 493; cf. CP, 347). This is the final obliteration of the life of time and history in human being. Locating our self-understanding in "biological" notions, notions which of themselves give no testimony to history, is the last form in which metaphysics expresses itself.

This brings me at last to the final form of Heidegger's dialogue with the historical present, namely his concern with "last things." The two briefest parts of *Contributions*, "The Futural Ones" (VI) and "The Last God" (VII), make clear that the historical present is the time of exhaustion, of "decline" (GA 65, 397; cf. CP, 278), and of last things. The part entitled "The Last God," which is the final part of the six "facets"[23] seems to be almost a privileged part of the text (and it is a part that one might even choose to read first after the "Preview") since in it the issue of the extremity of history is finally named.

Heidegger had been moving toward the sense that our historical present represents a time of utmost extremity for several years by this point. One finds this expressed pointedly in a letter to Elisabeth Blochmann, written on April 10, 1932: "But here—in the these years that which the Greeks designated '*acme*' presses itself into our Dasein. The edge of the knife, upon which all decides itself and has been decided and where the distinctiveness of the individual wants to become something essential in the whole."[24] Here, in *Contributions*, the true starting point for Heidegger's contributions is announced in the first short part of this "facet" of the text entitled "The Last God": "The last is that which not only requires the longest pre-decessorship, but itself *is*, not the cessation, but rather the deepest beginning, which reaches furthest and catches up with itself with great difficulty. Therefore, the last withdraws itself from all calculation and must for this reason be able to bear the burden of the loudest and most frequent misinterpretation (GA 65, 405; cf. CP, 285). An understanding of lastness, of the specific character of this historical present, is thus the starting point which Heidegger is trying to attain in *Contributions*. If this work accomplishes the task which it has set for itself, then the full import of this, its final part will be evident. For that to happen, we must become clear about why it is that Heidegger chooses to speak of the last "god" of all possible forms of lastness.[25]

While it is in some sense undeniable that here one finds the development of, if not a theology, something like a "theological difference,"[26] it is most important to understand the ways in which the discussion of the last god is not, in the first instance at least, a theological discussion. Heidegger says this clearly: "The last god has its singular singularity and thus stands outside of that calculative determination which is meant by titles such as "mono-theism," "pan-theism," and "a-theism" (GA 65, 411; cf. CP, 289). It is rather a commentary upon history, above all upon the form of history in the present age; and it is a linchpin in how such a time opens the prospects of community: "A people is *only* people when it receives its history as distributed in the discovery of its god. ... This god will set up this simple but extreme opposition [between earth and world] over its people as the paths upon which this people wanders beyond itself, in order to find once again its essence and to exhaust the moment of its history" (GA 65, 398–99; cf. CP, 279–80). And it is the task of those who belong to the future, to the poets above all—here Hölderlin stands as exemplary—to summon this moment into being.

Saying this, drawing this final and decisive discussion of the future and of the last god away from prophecy and theology (where the titles they bear might lead one), and so embedding the concerns of *Contributions* ever more deeply in the question of history, one begins to see how it is that one might argue that in *Contributions* we find a contribution to politics.[27] It goes without saying that this is a very different conception of politics than one typically expects from a theory of political life and its possibilities: here there is no utopian vision, no normative basis of critique, no set of standards of good and evil. Here even the very notion of "theory" in the matter of political life is problematized—no normativity could ever be thinkable—and from the outset the discourse here proposes itself as beyond the calculus of good and evil. Even more: Heidegger went to great lengths to disparage the words "politics" and "ethics," suggesting that they were simply the public forms of metaphysics and ultimately only calculuses of values and prejudices. He never made the question of political life easy for those who would take to heart the possibilities of his contributions to philosophizing.

Nonetheless, this is perhaps the work by Heidegger which will let us open the way to the question of how we are to think about our shared life in time in the wake of what we have learned about ourselves and the nature of time from Heidegger. This is the work in which the project of the destruction of metaphysics is linked most clearly to the region of concerns that usually go under the heading of cultural life—machination and technology, language and a people, race and history—and this is the work in which Heidegger struggles mightily to come to terms with the failure of his revolutionary conception of the possibilities of philosophizing to lead the way in the crisis of the historical present. In order to read *Contributions* as the contribution to a possible politics, it is necessary that we begin to pose questions about what we can legitimately expect from any politics in the contemporary world. Is a discourse on justice even *thinkable* in the present age? Can one still speak of the good? Or is it the case, as I believe Heidegger argues in *Contributions,* that these very notions, which have long guided political reflections in the West, have themselves become suspect? Might it just be the case that we need new words which might name what it is we seek, and ask, from one another as we share our lives in time?

In *Contributions* we find only hints of what Heidegger calls "originary thinking," the forms of thinking which have set themselves free from the calcifications and presumptions of metaphysics. No positive theory or doctrine of political life is proffered. But there is a sharp and far-reaching critique leveled against the forms of contemporary life and thinking, especially as those forms have emerged out of Western metaphysics. It is an unusual critique, one that does not arrogate to itself any standards of justice, good or evil, since, whatever else it is, this critique is a call to move the language of reflection upon how we come together in history beyond such notions. We find here a powerful criticism of the logic of repression, of the extinction of history, which operates in the tradition of metaphysics.[28] It also, rather clearly, contains an undeniable criticism of the forms of thinking governing Germany at the time this book was composed. Simply because we do not find this criticism being formulated on clearly *moral* grounds, on the grounds that here is evil being done, does not mean we should overlook the criticism being developed here. This is especially the case when we recall that a key feature of Heidegger's argument about such matters is that he, like Nietzsche, wants us to consider seriously the failure of any "ethics" or "politics" which operates according to the oppositional logics of "good" and "evil": the good has shown itself too easy, too ready, to the self-righteous enemy of its own intentions (or worse: it has shown itself to be but a mask for evil itself). What is necessary then for us to learn if we are to learn to read *Contributions* is simply this: that we ask ourselves what is required if we are indeed to take seriously the claim that the presumptions of metaphysics have exhausted themselves and that consequently we can no longer carry forward with a theory of politics as we have been accustomed to do. To what must thinking turn if it is to index itself to the prospect of freedom without grounding itself in the calculus of good and evil?

It seems to me that one of Heidegger's most significant contributions in the difficult and enigmatic text is precisely to begin to explore this possibility and to begin to pose questions about the fundaments which animate the shape of life in history in the present age.

Notes

1. GA 65, 8; cf. CP, 6. For bibliographical information on the texts referred to here, see the introduction to this volume, note 1. All the translations here are my own. It will be clear that in some cases I have chosen to vary the translation of key words such as "Ereignis," which I translate as "event" rather than as "enowning," and "Wesen," which I translate as "essence" rather than "essential sway." Other significant differences from the Emad/Maly translation are indicated in the following notes.

2. Otto Pöggeler, "Heidegger und die hermeneutische Theologie," in *Verifikationen: Festschrift für Gerhard Eberling,* ed. Eberhard Jüngel (Tübingen: J. C. B. Mohr Verlag, 1982), p. 481.

3. There have been efforts to come to terms with *Contributions.* To mention only a few of the earlier efforts: Joan Stambaugh, *The Finitude of Being* (Albany: State University of New York Press, 1992); David Farrell Krell, *Daimon Life* (Bloomington: Indiana University Press, 1992); Friedrich-Wilhelm von Herrmann, *Wege ins Ereignis: Zu Heideggers "Beiträgen zur Philosophie"* (Frankfurt am Main: Vittorio Klostermann, 1994); Daniela Neu, *Die Notwendigkeit der Gründung im Zeitalter der Dekonstruktion* (Berlin: Duncker & Humblot, 1997); Reiner Schürmann, "Riveted to a Monstrous Site," in *The Heidegger Case: On Philosophy and Politics,* ed. Tom Rockmore and Joseph Margolis (Philadelphia: Temple University Press, 1992); and my own "On the Memory of Last Things," *Research in Phenomenology* 23 (1993).

4. This is not entirely a jab at the translation. *Contributions* self-consciously stretches the meanings of German words and syntax. Reiner Schürmann put it well when he said that "the language is more ponderous than in any of his other writings; at times one may think one is reading a piece of Heideggerian plagiarism: so encumbered it is with ellipses and assertoric monoliths. . . . An atrophy of grammar . . . a cacotrophy of logic . . . a hypertrophia of rhetoric. Litotes, hyperbole, sentence fragments, questions left open, nouns reduced to their verbal origins" ("Riveted to a Monstrous Site," p. 314). Naturally, any translation will require a creative relation to language and will need to stretch, perhaps even torture, the target language. I will refrain from commenting upon the new translation of the work. Suffice it to say that the translators have my admiration for having undertaken an impossible task and so given us the assignment of coming to terms with Heidegger's claims in English.

5. Ibid., p. 313.

6. In this regard, Rüdiger Safranski recounts a joke that Carl Friedrich von Weizsäcker once told Heidegger: "A man is sitting in a bar mumbling to himself, 'Yes, my wife!' — 'What is going on with her?' — 'She talks and talks and talks and talks . . .' — 'What does she talk about then?' — 'That she doesn't say!'" Heidegger responded to this story by saying, "That is the way it is." Safranski interprets Heidegger's reply as in some manner a commentary on himself and his own sense that no one really knew what he was saying. See Rüdiger Safranski, *Ein Meister aus Deutschland: Heidegger und seine Zeit* (Munich: Hanser Verlag, 1994), p. 361.

7. Walter Benjamin, "Die Aufgabe des Übersetzers," in *Gesammelte Schriften,* vol. 4, no. 1 (Frankfurt am Main: Suhrkamp Verlag, 1980), p. 21.

8. This remark about the impossibility of philosophy making an appearance

in public, written just two years after the debacle of Heidegger's own appearance in the public realm (the legacy of which is still very much alive), cannot be read without a sense that Heidegger is still burned by the trauma of his own failure. So much of *Contributions* is driven by this trauma. To think through Heidegger's own relation to his historical present, a genuinely philosophical issue, one would do well to take up once again Plato's Seventh Letter and his own efforts to give an account of his political failure. Just as the *Laws* needs to be read in the light of Plato's efforts to grapple with the relation of philosophizing to its times, so too does Heidegger's *Contributions* need to be read as such an effort.

9. Because of the weight borne by the language of this text, the stakes of the translation are raised even higher than usual. What is needed is a translation which operates in English in the same manner that Heidegger's language worked upon German.

10. Again the parallel between Plato's Seventh Letter and Heidegger's concern with the possibilities of writing a text needs attention here. One cannot avoid being reminded of Plato's claim that "no serious man will ever think of writing about serious realities for the general public" (344c). Like Heidegger, Plato is haunted by the question of the possibility of a proper philosophic style and idiom. Ironically, it is precisely the neologisms which Plato introduces into philosophizing (in order to escape what he takes to be the poverty of the possibilities of language in his historical present) which form the targets of many of Heidegger's criticisms.

11. I prefer to translate Heidegger's use of the word "Seyn" by this archaic English word.

12. One exception to this lacuna is Michael E. Zimmerman, *Heidegger's Confrontation with Modernity: Technology, Politics, and Art* (Bloomington: Indiana University Press, 1990).

13. It should be noted that although Heidegger continued to permit future German editions of *Sein und Zeit* to be published with "Dasein" written as one word (although from the initial publication there were sections of the text in which it was written as hyphenated), he did request that future translations of that book into English write the word as hyphenated. The difference here between the impact of the word in English, where it strikes one as a technical term, and German, where it is a quite common word, should be taken into consideration when trying to make sense of this request.

14. And here, as always, it is important to remember that *Being and Time* is a self-aborting text; we have only two of the announced six parts of the plan which it lays down for itself in the introduction. The "failure" of that project as it had projected itself guides much of Heidegger's work in the decade following the publication of *Being and Time*. *Contributions* is the work in which Heidegger becomes self-conscious about the need for a different approach to the same plan announced in *Being and Time*.

15. This is the place to say that while all of Heidegger's work has a rather strong non-Western dimension, this resistance to Western assumption is perhaps most pronounced in *Contributions*.

16. I say this fully aware that Heidegger had an allergy to the use of the word "culture." The reasons he rejected its use are subtle, if nonetheless important;

but I do not believe that they should preempt the use of that notion altogether by those of us trying to understand Heidegger.

17. In this one is reminded of Socrates' argument, put most directly in the *Apology*, that while he might suffer from his own ignorance, at least he was wiser than those who were ignorant of their own ignorance.

18. On this, see Hans Sluga, *Heidegger's Crisis* (Cambridge, Mass.: Harvard University Press, 1993); see also my "Heidegger and 'the' Greeks: History, Catastrophe and Community," in *Heidegger toward the Turn: Essays on the Work of the 1930's,* ed. James Risser (Albany: State University of New York Press, 1999).

19. One might suggest that in the notion of machination, Heidegger's involvement with Nietzsche marries his involvement with Jünger. Heidegger does not shed Nietzsche's efforts to identify the truth of metaphysics in terms of nihilism and Christianity—both of which come to be symptoms of a culture in decay; Heidegger links these with machination, suggesting that "machination contains the *Christian-biblical* interpretation of beings" (GA 65, 132; cf. CP, 92)—but he does suggest that the deeper roots of this decay are evidenced most clearly in the form that machination takes in modern technicity, which is the greater, more urgent threat we face. It is an insight that will, of course, be developed frequently in the later years, most notably perhaps in *Die Frage nach der Technik.*

20. And in so doing we find an important link to Heidegger's analysis of these notions in his "Ursprung des Kunstwerkes."

21. A full discussion of this notion of "machination" would be well advised to take a careful look at a text which was composed right on the heels of the composition of *Contributions.* I am referring to those texts published in volume 69 of the Gesamtausgabe under the title "Koinon: Aus der Geschichte des Seyns" (1939/40).

22. See, for instance, "Das Rektorat 1933/34: Tatsache und Gedanken," in volume 16 of the Gesamtausgabe (Frankfurt am Main: Vittorio Klostermann, 2000), p. 381.

23. This is how I prefer to translate the word "Fügung" with which Heidegger describes the six parts which he deems the text proper (see, e.g., GA 65, 9; CP, 7; the first part, entitled "Preview," and the final, one entitled "Beyng," are outside the framework of the text proper as Heidegger presents it). While "facet" is not a legitimate translation of the word "Fügung," I believe that it conveys the character of the relation of the parts of the text to one another better than the word "jointure," which the translators have chosen for the English text.

24. *Martin Heidegger—Elisabeth Blochmann: Briefwechsel 1918-1969,* ed. Joachim Storck (Marbach am Neckar: Deutsche Schillergesellschaft, 1989), p. 49.

25. The phrase "the last god" was also used by Schelling in his *Philosophie der Kunst,* where he writes: "It is as if Christ, as the sacrifice of the infinite having become finite in human form, constituted the conclusion of the *old* time; he is merely there in order to mark the limit—the last god." See F. W. J. Schelling, *Philosophie der Kunst* (Darmstadt: Wissenschaftliche Buchgesellschaft, 1966), p. 76.

26. See Heidegger's "Zeit und Sein" for a clarification of this notion; see also von Herrmann, *Wege ins Ereignis,* p. 39.

27. The claim that Heidegger is, in some clear measure, engaging the question of political life is one that has been made well by Philippe Lacoue-Labarthe

in his *La fiction du politique* (Breteuil-sur-Iton: Christian Bourgois Editeur, 1987). See also Miguel de Beistegui, *Heidegger and the Political* (London: Routledge, 1998). That this is a concern of Heidegger's at this time is also recognized by von Herrmann; see chapter 2 of his *Wege ins Ereignis.*

28. On this, see John McCumber, *Metaphysics and Oppression: Heidegger's Challenge to Western Philosophy* (Bloomington: Indiana University Press, 1999).

3. "Beyng-Historical Thinking" in Heidegger's *Contributions to Philosophy*

Alejandro Vallega

In the introductory section of *Contributions to Philosophy (From Enowning)*, Heidegger says that this title does not define nor does it attempt to speak about "some-thing." The thinking of *Contributions*, he states, may only occur as "an *attempt*" (*ein Versuch*) to think the question of the truth of beyng out of its originary ground in a time of transition (*Übergang*). Heidegger says, "in the age of the crossing from metaphysics into be-ing-historical thinking, one can venture only an *attempt* to think according to a more originary basic stance within the question of the truth of beyng."[1] This thinking in the transition Heidegger calls a beyng-historical thinking (*seynsgeschichtliches Denken*). In this essay I try to understand the motion of thought behind this "attempt," i.e., how beyng-historical thinking may be understood not just as a thinking in "transition" from one epoch to another but in itself as transitional (*Übergänglich*), as a thinking of passage.

This essay is divided into four parts. In the first I direct my attention to the question of the matter (*die Sache*) given to be thought at the end of metaphysics, and how this task is taken up in *Contributions*.[2] In the second, in order to come closer to the term beyng-historical thinking in *Contributions*, I point out Heidegger's distinction between "historiography" (*Historie*), and "history" or "historical occurrence" (*Geschichte*).[3] This differentiation is then developed in its more essential aspect in the third part, where I discuss its temporal foundation by discussing its "passing" and inceptual character. In considering the temporal character of the thinking of beyng in *Contributions*, it becomes clear that the "essential-swaying of beyng" (*Wesung des Seyns*)[4] occurs as a passage (a coming to be in passing away), and a leap (*Sprung*): a leap that in its occurrence not only enacts the unsettling of any conception of beyng in terms of the logic of presences and ever-lasting, unchangeable essences or origins, but occurs itself as its own unsettling overcoming passage. In the final part I indicate that *Contributions*, with its fugal structure, enacts (*vollzieht*) this leap of the passage of beyng.

Almost at the Closure

What if there were nothing behind the appearing[5] that we call world? How would one think this nothingness? Certainly not in terms of the metaphysical structures that would always suggest "something else" eternal and unchanging underneath or above the surface of the appearing. But this would also mean that this "nothing" would not be what is not presence, what is set against presence at hand, since this presence would no longer be dictated by the traditional configurations that could give "meaning," or "essence," to the appearing as the "whatness" of what appears. It would then be a question of a certain "nothingness" — neither empty, as it might be understood in contrast to things present at hand, nor senseless, as understood in contrast to the logic or reason of metaphysics and transcendental philosophies. In other words, and other words would be needed precisely in the light of the question of this nothingness, the question would be one of thinking a way of being utterly other: other to objective presence and fact, other to the conceptual configurations of presence, and other to the sufficient reason that sustains the logic of presence.

When we look at the beginning of *Contributions* we can see that Heidegger's thinking begins at the closure of metaphysics, i.e., at the limit of Nietzsche's thought of nihilism. In the first pages of *Contributions* Heidegger refers to the task announced by the title of the book as an "attempt" (*Versuch*) to think the question of the truth of beyng out of its originary grounding.[6] This attempt occurs "in the time of the transition (*Zeitalter des Übergang*s) from metaphysics to beyng-historical thinking."[7] The thinking of *Contributions* occurs as such in a certain "transition" (*Übergang*).

In his lecture on Nietzsche's thinking of nihilism, winter semester 1937/38, the time of the composition of *Contributions*, Heidegger directly broaches the subject of the "transition" from metaphysics to the beyng-historical thinking of *Contributions*. In this lecture Heidegger writes, "This end of the first beginning (*erster Anfang*) of Western philosophy is Nietzsche; from here and only from here must his work be developed, if it is to be what each end must be — a transition (*Übergang*)."[8]

Nietzsche's Nihilism, the very discovery that "God is dead," that behind the appearing there is nothing, is not only the end of metaphysics, but this end remains to be thought in its very occurrence (*Ereignis*) as the "transition" from metaphysics, the first beginning, to beyng-historical thinking.

The seeming overlapping of Nietzsche's nihilism and Heidegger's own thinking does not mark a direct continuity between the two. Heidegger's thought only touches on Nietzsche at the limit of Nietzsche's thinking of nihilism. Later, in "European Nihilism," a series of lectures written in 1940 as part of Heidegger's ongoing meditation on Nietzsche, Heidegger writes,

> The end of metaphysics discloses itself as the collapse of the reign of the transcendent and the "ideal" that sprang from it. But the end of metaphysics does not mean the cessation of history (*Geschichte*). It is the beginning (*Beginn*) of a serious struggle with that "occurrence" (*Ereignis*): "God is dead . . ."[9]

The end of metaphysics does not mean an end, a cessation of the occurrence, *Ereignis*, or history, *Geschichte*, of being. From nihilism we
might learn that metaphysics is not to be repeated; but, at the same time,
the end of metaphysics cannot be abandoned as if meaningless. To the
end of metaphysics, to the death of God, belongs a historical occurrence
that does not stop, nor end, and that remains to be thought as it gives itself to be thought. Thinking would now remain, stay with, what is given
to be thought in the occurrence of the end of metaphysics: in the very
occurrence of the death of God, what is given to be thought is this death
in itself, this nothingness. As Heidegger concludes, Nietzsche's thought
marks the beginning of "a serious struggle with that occurrence [*Ereignis*]: the death of God." It is this struggle to think in the death or absence
of God and metaphysical meanings that is indicated in the supplemen-
tary title to *Contributions*, where Heidegger has already situated the
thinking of the book as occurring out of and in this struggle, as a thinking *vom Ereignis*.[10]

But Nietzsche's thought itself only intimates what is given to be
thought. In "The Will to Power as Art," Heidegger expressly states that
Nietzsche takes the "leading question" (*Leitfrage*) of philosophy, the
question of the being of beings, as "the" question, and neglects to ask
the "ground-question" (*Grundfrage*), the question of being as such (*Was
ist das Sein selbst?*).[11] According to Heidegger, with the doctrine of the
will to power Nietzsche's thought withdraws from his own insight concerning nihilism and ultimately remains metaphysical, thus failing to
ask the essential question of the truth of being as such.

Bringing Nietzsche's realization that there is nothing behind the appearing of the appearances to the ground question of philosophy (*Grundfrage*) would not be a matter of seeking another kind of account to be
given about beings. Rather, the very question asked would change.[12] In
bringing nothing as such into question, one would have to think this appearing in its occurrence, as such: the question would then be that of the
appearing in its appearing as such. Beyng-historical thinking as the
thinking of the transition would think the very occurrence of the death
of God; it would think what gives itself to be thought in this passage; it
would not only think in the light of the very awareness that behind the
appearances there is nothing; but it would think in this passage, and out
of this nothingness.

High in the lower Alps lies a small cemetery. There a young man is
being buried, one who was so consumed by life as to pass away at an
early age. The funeral is simple—a few friends, but mostly strangers to
the young man, like myself. After a few words have been spoken by a
priest and others have recalled the young man at the request of his
mother, the urn filled with his ashes is brought to its resting place. As

the cemetery worker tries to set the urn in its place in a marble wall, silence falls upon all those present. Someone begins a prayer destined to return to silence. Silence.

Silence, and then, after some time, voices begin to echo. Not unified voices in prayer, or recollections of the dead, but conversations that spring from utter silence, echoes out of silence; conversations as diverse as the foliage and flowers that almost overrun the cemetery and the marble wall. Conversations that are fleeting and yet light as clouds and sky. Conversations amongst strangers, like myself . . . where do these elemental words come from? How is it that out of silence might come such disclosure of living configurations?

In *Die Geschichte des Seyns* [The history of beyng],[13] a work that belongs to *Contributions* as well as expands it, one that was composed immediately after it in 1938/39, Heidegger makes the following brief remark about beyng-historical thinking:

The first leap (*Sprung*) of thinking thinks:
Beyng is nothing (*Das Seyn ist das Nichts*).
Nothing nothings (*Das Nichts nichtet*).[14]

In these lines we hear the radical difference between Heidegger's thought and Nietzsche's, at least as understood by Heidegger.[15] For Heidegger, Nietzsche's question of being is still the question of the beingness of beings, being as the presence of beings out of their need to be, a need gathered conceptually by Nietzsche under the five rubrics that form one metaphysical interpretation of being.[16] For Heidegger the question of beyng is outside the logic and necessity of presence: beyng is not any thing. The abrupt leap from Nietzsche to Heidegger is marked by the "y" of "beyng" (*Seyn*).[17] Heidegger's return to the archaic spelling of being (*Sein*) marks this leap. This leap opens the question of beyng anew: beyng is not to be thought now in terms of presence but as nothing. Heidegger says, "Das Nichts nichtet." We can get a glimpse of the question that has opened even as we translate this brief passage into English: "nothing nothings." It is not "no-thing" but a certain occurrence (*Ereignis*) that is given to be thought. We might repeat the last word of the last phrase, "nothings," in another way that places it at the center of *Contributions:* the expression "nothings" recalls us to our need to think beyng's essential swaying (*die Wesung des Seyns selbst.*)

In this first section I have situated the thinking in *Contributions* at the closure (not the end) of the history of metaphysics. This is a significant move because it lets us see certain fundamental aspects of beyng-historical thinking. From what we have discussed it is clear that beyng-historical thinking does not occur as the continuation or outcome of historiographical developments. Rather, it takes place as a re-turning of the death of God and the closure of the metaphysical interpretation of the world as constituted by a dualism of changing beings and unchanging being. This indicates a second characteristic. Beyng-historical thinking has a beginning in the interruption of the metaphysical interpretation of living configurating events, in the gap between Nietzsche's Will to Power and Heidegger's thinking-saying, and in the leap we are called to make if we are to think the matter that is given to be thought by nihilism and yet remains without articulation in Nietzsche.

Furthermore, this problematization of nihilism brings with it two questions that are already indicated by the very expression *seynsgeschicht-lich*. If in *Contributions* Heidegger thinks out of the closure of metaphysics, his thinking must occur otherwise than in terms of the ontological difference between beings and being. This is the case for the metaphysical interpretation of this relation, the difference between changing and unchanging essences, as well as for transcendental articulations of beyng, including Heidegger's own in *Being and Time*. There he speaks of an ontological difference between entities at hand and being. Indeed, the very term *seynsgeschichtlich* indicates a single motion of thought, a single matter to be thought in this motion, a single temporal occurrence beyond this ontological dualism.

This also means that the dense living occurrences that have been interpreted as the objective facts of historiography or as the expression of a logical motion underlying it, are now to be rethought and understood for themselves, in their own occurrence, i.e., beyond their interpretation as either objective or logical. The question is, how are we to grasp the term beyng-historical thinking?

Historical-Beyng, not Historiography

At the beginning of *Contributions*, Heidegger speaks of the work in the book as an attempt at a "beyng-historical thinking" (*seynsgeschichtliches Denken*).[18] The term is translated by Emad/Maly as "be-ing-historical thinking." I prefer to translate it into English as "beyng-historical thinking."[19] The word that is translated as "historical" in both cases is not its German cognate *historisches*, but *geschichtliches*. Heidegger's choice is significant. *Geschichtliches* refers not to the measurable and factual time of objective presence and its historiography (*Historie*).[20] Rather, the word attempts to sound out the very occurrence (*Ereignis*) of appearing as such, the essential swaying of beyng as such (*die Wesung des Seyns selbst*).

The words *geschichtlich* and *Geschichte* find their verbal form in *geschehen*, which means "to occur." The three terms are rooted in the word *giskiht*, from Old High German.[21] *Giskiht*, as echoed in *geschehen*, bespeaks the momentary and contingent character of any event, incident, or episode.[22] *Giskiht* also sounds out not only particular events[23] but the occurrence of their gathering into a meaningful whole.[24] From this etymology we may see that *Geschichte* and *geschichtlich* echo the occurring of beings not in their determinate analyzable objectivity, not as things already determined, not as unchanging essences, but in their essential temporality. Heidegger's choice of words echoes an opening, momentary and unpredictable, a passage that is unanalyzable as well as unpredictable, although given for the gathering of beings in their configurations.

This differentiation between *Geschichte* and *Historie* does not begin with Heidegger. We may trace it back to the roots of hermeneutics. The differentiation is first made by the German theologian M. Kähler and is then systematically sustained in the hermeneutics of scripture from Dilthey to Bultmann.[25] In Heidegger's own work we find the differentiation already made in the hermeneutics of *Being and Time*, where he differentiates specifically between the historicity (*Geschichtlichkeit*) of the opening of being as given with dasein, and the historiography that is possible in the light of this disclosing occurrence.

> Temporality reveals itself as the *historicity* (*Geschichtlichkeit*) of dasein. The statement that dasein is historical is confirmed as an existential and ontological fundamental proposition. It is far removed from merely ontically ascertaining the fact that Dasein occurs in a "world history" (*Weltgeschichte*). The historicity of dasein, however, is the ground of a possible historiographical understanding (*historisches Verstehen*) that in its turn harbors the possibility of getting a special grasp of the development of historiography as a science (*Historie als Wissenschaft*).[26]

This articulation of the difference between *Historie* and *Geschichte* remains limited by the transcendental direction of the dasein analytic toward an essential temporal ground/horizon in *Being and Time*, and it is therefore to be rethought in *Contributions*. However, the distinction between historiography (*Historie*) and the occurrence (*Geschichte*) of beings in the opening of beyng may be followed through to *Contributions* and traced back from *Contributions* to the thinking of temporality that Heidegger is already coming to in *Being and Time*.[27]

The differentiation between factual history (*Historie*) and historical occurrence as such (*Geschichte*) is indicated by Heidegger's language in *Contributions*. Heidegger speaks in *Contributions* of beyng-historical thinking as a "transition" (*Übergang*), and he also calls this thinking a thinking "underway" (*Gedanken-gang*).[28] In the second case Heidegger emphasizes the passage of thinking underlining and separating *-gang* from *Gedanken*. The two terms directly refer the thinking of *Contributions* to Heidegger's understanding of the way beyng is given to be thought in

Greek experience. The opening of beyng occurs for the Greeks and is thus indicated with the word *phusis*. This word Heidegger takes to indicate the very *Wesung des Seyns*, the passing in coming to be of beyng, translated as the "essential swaying of being."[29] Heidegger translates *phusis* as *Aufgehen*, or *Aufgang*: a word that recalls the springing forth, taking place, coming out that echoes in *phusis*.[30] Thus, *Übergang* and *Gedanken-gang* recall the *Auf-gang*, the passage in the very occurrence of the coming to be in passing away of beyng.

The Passing of Beyng-Historical Thinking

In the beginning part (*Vorblick*) of *Contributions*, Heidegger speaks of beyng-historical thinking as a "transition" (*Übergang*) from metaphysics to "the other beginning of thinking" (*der andere Anfang des Denkens*),[31] i.e., from the interpretation of being in terms of beings that occurs with Greek thought at the beginning of our metaphysical tradition, to the other beginning. This thinking motion is for Heidegger not a bridge but a thinking that itself occurs as a passage. Heidegger calls his thinking a thinking underway (*Gedanken-gang*).[32] The terms "first," "other," and "transition," do not refer to two points, an origin and its other, which are to be bridged by a certain crossing over from one location to another in history.[33] Heidegger says in *Contributions* that the other beginning is "the only other out of relation to the one and only first beginning [*aus dem Bezug* zu *dem einzig einen und ersten Anfang*]".[34] What is to be thought is a single occurrence, a single passage, the only one and first beginning of thinking. Beyng-historical thinking would occur then as an attempt at beginning, an attempt at an "inceptual thinking," an attempt at an *anfängliches Denken*.[35] Therefore, in order to understand beyng-historical thinking, we would have to enter the play of this attempting beginning, we would have to stand in the in-between that is the place or passage of the occurrence of this thinking.

Heidegger asks in *Contributions*, "What is the beginning [Anfang]?" He replies,

> It is the essential swaying of being itself [*die Wesung des Seins selbst*]. But this beginning first becomes enactable as the other beginning in its encounter [*Auseinandersetzung*] with the first. Beginning—understood inceptually [*anfänglich begriffen*]—is beyng itself.[36]

In this passage we find two aspects of "beginning" (*Anfang*). Heidegger first says that beginning is the essential swaying of beyng itself. But then he goes on to make the following observations: beginning in the sense of beyng itself can only occur in the encounter (*Auseinandersetz-*

ung) of the first and other beginning. The first and the other beginning do not define points in history, as if we were to accomplish a move from point A to point B.[37] It is in the encounter of first and other beginning, in their playing off each other, that they enact the opening of beyng. Furthermore, what Heidegger is saying is that the one and only beginning is beyng itself as it occurs in the play-encounter of first and other beginning. The "beginning" *(Anfang),* as the "one and only beginning" being enacted, cannot be understood as an "origin" that is unchanging, because beyng can only occur in and as enactment *(Vollzug).* In other words, there is not an unchanging origin or beginning to which thinking might return.[38] To deepen the play-encounter of the beginnings by reducing them to a representation of a certain "original event" would be to lose precisely the thought that takes place in *Contributions.* The encounter of the first and other beginning can be understood out of the originary temporality of the opening of beyng itself.

Geschichtliches Denken, the thinking of the history of beyng as such, occurs otherwise than in the traditional sense of history, metaphysics, or transcendental philosophy. Put in another way, beyng-historical thinking does not occur in the terms of the logic that has held and given meaning to the tradition since the Greeks. As I have pointed out above, according to Heidegger it is the setting up of a certain logic of affirmation and presence that reduces the question of being as such to the question of the beingness of beings at the beginning of Greek philosophy.[39] With this logic comes the intrinsic association of the question of being with that of production. According to Heidegger it is this association of being as such with *poiesis* and *techne* that erases the question of the passage of beyng. This production-oriented logic that is then assumed and attributed, dictated to being, is also used in the interpretation of temporality. In this way time is divided into present, past, and future, sections of temporality that as such make time march according to the logic of presence, make it quantifiable, fixable, and producible.[40]

If we now go back to the passage on "beginning" from *Contributions,* according to Heidegger, the other beginning occurs in play with "the only one and first beginning." This means that the other beginning occurs always and only along with a first beginning. The "other" beginning can only make any sense in the play with the first beginning. What occurs here is a strange turn, a re-turn of the first beginning. I say re-turn because in the motion of going over to the other beginning, and since the other beginning can only occur in the light of the first, there must always be a certain recalling of the first beginning, a certain turning again of the first beginning that unsettles and overcomes the very concept of a first unchanging origin.

The play-encounter of first and other beginning occurs only in the enactment of an originary event that has no metaphysical origin. In the

re-turning motion of beyng-historical thinking, nothing is left to oblivion, nothing remains undisturbed. In the last section of *Die Geschichte des
Seyns*, Heidegger writes a list of enactments, of moments of configuration of the history of beyng. Near the end, referring to Hölderlin's poetry, Heidegger writes a single name, "Mnemosyne."[41] This name brings
to mind memory and temporality, but it does so by appealing to the
overturning or transformative power inherent in memorial events.
Mnemosyne is the name of the river that runs outside the logic of beings and their history: the name marks the motion of a river that runs
backwards. We might consider this recalling of the river in trying to understand the motion of thought behind the "going-over." To say that a
river runs backwards is not to say that a river runs its course to an "end"
and then returns to an ever present "beginning'" or "origin."[42] There is
no geometrical possibility for Mnemosyne. To flow backwards is to con-
tradict any linear or objective temporal logic. A river flowing backwards
defeats any teleology or projected horizon, since in its motion it goes
back only in going forward, and at the same time, it goes forward only
by claiming its past, its origin. Furthermore, its going backwards is a going on that in moving toward the past decenters every occurrence in
that past, so that the going on is at once an appropriation and decenter-
ing of all origins.[43]

In figuring this re-turning or overcoming motion of beyng-historical
thinking, we are now speaking of the motion by which what remains
the unthinkable "empty," or "no-thing," in the tradition of metaphysics, is brought forth as the matter to be thought if beyng as such is to be
thought. With each re-turning, the first beginning is brought forth not
in the repetition of an unchanging origin but in the opening possibility
of the event of alterity that is inherent to its occurrence. One might
think back to the "death of God" and how for Heidegger this is not the
end of history, the closure of the question of essence, but a moment of
passage given to be understood, withstood, and undergone in its full
density and concreteness as the matter to be thought is given in that
death, i.e., in its density thinking has no closure in the overcoming
motion of the essential swaying of being. This is what Heidegger is
pointing out when he says in *Geschichte des Seyns*, "*Das Nichts nichtet.*"[44]

Because nothing does not have a place in the logic of beings, this
otherness, arisen in the overcoming motion of the history of beyng,
cannot be reinscribed into the first metaphysical beginning. Since the
first beginning has itself been recalled in the light of its otherness, and
this otherness cannot be thought in terms of it, the first beginning
would itself be thinkable otherwise than in the traditional way. But this
would be because what gives itself to be thought is no longer the being
of beings but the passage of beyng in its truth (*die Wahrheit des Seyns*).[45]

This unsettling or overcoming motion is characteristic of beyng-historical thinking. In thinking in this re-turn we come to a passage that, in enacting its taking place, has always already gone outside, beyond its originary occurrence; or to put it inversely, the passage of beyng always must remain unsurpassable, since its beginning has always already been overcome by its very occurrence. In the openness of temporality as such, ordering belongs not to logic and production but to temporality in its one single opening in which past, present, and future are at play at once.

We find this characteristic re-turning of beyng-historical thinking indicated in the first part of *Contributions,* where Heidegger says that "The thinking of the future is a thinking underway (*Gedanken-gang*)."[46] In the light of the overcoming character of beyng-historical thinking, we can now say that the thinking to come[47] is not some other account of being. Rather, it is a thinking "to come" because it must inhabit its place in the future by undergoing its own passing, by being a thinking that in its overcoming passing must always remain underway. But that Heidegger would indicate that beyng-historical thinking is a *Gedanken-gang* indicates that his thinking in *Contributions* is a thinking that occurs in the awareness of this overcoming character of the thinking of beyng. We are speaking of a thinking that occurs in its awareness of its occurrence out of *phusis* (*Aufgehen*), a thinking that occurs in the enactment of its own passage. What we discover here is that indeed, Heidegger's thought in *Contributions* is not a passage toward a horizon that awaits it, nor a nostalgic return to the Greeks. As Heidegger says in the "Preview," "We are already moving within an other truth, even as we are still in the crossing."[48] What beyng-historical thinking indicates is an overcoming motion that marks in its passage an opening, an inceptive moment that as such enacts the opening motion of a thinking saying that in its questioning keeps open the possibility of beyng out of its essential sway. The rest of this section will be devoted to further clarification of this statement.

In *Contributions* Heidegger speaks of "beginning" (*Anfang*). Furthermore, beyng-historical thinking is itself inseparable from the notion of beginning (*Anfang*), since this thinking occurs as an *anfängliches Denken* (inceptive thinking). Therefore, the issue is now how to understand Heidegger's notion of beginning. In a passage already cited, Heidegger says that "Beginning (*Anfang*) — understood inceptually — is beyng itself." This brings us to the second aspect of *Anfang*. In section 242 of *Contributions,* Heidegger says, the "truth [of beyng] as ground grounds originarily as ab-ground."[49] This means that the truth of beyng occurs as an ungrounded grounding motion. This also means that in order to understand *Anfang* we would have to seek it in the light of the essential sway of beyng in its truth in enowning (*Ereignis*).

Before going on we might keep in mind what is not implied by the word "ungrounding." We should be careful and not presuppose a "ground" that must be there first in order for the "ungrounding" to occur, and we should also be careful not to understand this ungrounding character of ground as an absence of grounding. In other words, "ungrounding" is being spoken of in the transition from metaphysics and is therefore not meant as a ground in the metaphysical or transcendental sense; at the same time, it is introduced in the concrete sense of a *geschichtliche Gründung*, a concrete living occurrence that is not an immovable ground but does occur as grounding in the full temporal and finite sense.

The ab-ground, or ungrounding of beyng, occurs as a twofold motion. It occurs as *Entrückung* and as *Berückung*.[50] *Entrückung* refers to the withdrawing aspect of the truth of beyng,[51] whereas *Berückung* refers to the rising or coming out that occurs in that withdrawal. As if "I" were to understand "my" being here, now temporally and spatially as a single passage constituted by this falling-rising, i.e., not as the being of an entity that can exercise its gravity by falling and react with astonishment,[52] not as an entity between death and life, but as the occurrence of being in single passage in coming to be in coming to pass. It is this falling-rising motion of beyng that characterizes beyng-historical thinking. It is in this motion in the occurrence of beyng that beyng-historical thinking appears as the thinking of beyng, a thinking from enowning (*vom Ereignis*).

It is in the resounding (*Anklang*) of this falling-rising of beyng in its essential sway that beyng-historical thinking occurs (*er-eignet*).[53] At the same time, this thinking is an enacting thinking because it occurs in this resounding in a time-space play in which beyng's essential sway is held open to its possibility. This double motion of being held in the sounding out of beyng and holding open in this attentiveness the possibility of its event is the way beyng-historical thinking can be understood from enowning (*Ereignis*).[54] Heidegger indicates this difficult play of beyng and beyng-historical thinking in section 21, "Inceptual Thinking (Projecting Open)," where he says, "The projecting-open unfolds the thrower and at the same time seizes it within what opens up."[55]

When Heidegger says that understood inceptually, beginning (*Anfang*) is "beyng itself" (*ist das Seyn selbst*),[56] he is pointing precisely to this double play, to the very occurrence of beyng in *Ereignis* (enowning) as the opening held fast by the insistence of a thinking questioning that in its remaining with the question is caught and held by the projecting open of beyng in its unfolding. The root of *An-fang* is *fangen*, a verb that means "capturing," "holding." *Anfang* is beyng itself as it occurs in the being held and holding in the openness of its essentially swaying un-grounded grounding occurrence. The word, beginning, understood inceptibly marks the passing falling-rising motion of beyng as held open in its possibility by beyng-historical thinking.

The character of beyng-historical thinking as inceptual thinking (*anfängliches Denken*) is therefore twofold. Beyng-historical thinking occurs out of the essential swaying in the truth of beyng. But as this truth occurs as enowning (*Ereignis*), in the falling-rising of its occurrence, beyng-historical thinking is a thinking enacting of this ungrounding motion, a thinking that would let resound in its openness a passing, rather than present a story about beings or any metaphysical or transcendental system.

"That where upon the leap, in opening up, leaps first becomes ground through the leap . . . the self becomes properly its own in the leap . . ." 57

If we were to think from *Ereignis,* in the occurrence (*Geschehen*) of beyng, if we were to think from within the motion of the passage of beyng, were we to think nothing, we would have to think in the face of the difficulty of the ungrounded character of beyng, and also therefore, in the awareness of the ungrounding character of its thinking, the thinking "of" beyng. This means that thinking would occur in utter play, in a free falling leap that would occur in its free-falling, both in and out of the very enactment of its ungrounded grounding. And, it would mean, almost at the end, that thinking would remain in that unbridgeable leap (*Sprung*) appearing in our speaking, making present and in that nothingness out of which, and in attunement to which, any speaking would occur. Beyng-historical thinking would then be this speaking in the passing sway of beyng.

Enactments "of" Beyng

The overcoming motion of beyng in its passing calls not for a story about beings[58] but for an enactment (*Vollzug*)[59] that as such would remain in the openness of this passing by undergoing the falling-rising of beyng in its occurring (*Geschehen*). *Contributions* occurs as such enactment. This is what Heidegger indicates when in the last sentence of the first page he says that the thinking-saying that belongs to the enowning of beyng is "the word 'of' beyng [*in das Wort 'des' Seyns*]."[60] In *The History of Beyng* Heidegger has more to say about the "of" beyng. He says,

    4. the word "of" beyng.
    5. the beyng-historical genitive (Not *genitivus "objectus"* and *"subjectus"*).[61]

"Of" is meant to indicate the openness of thinking in its enactment, in its attempting (*Versuch*) a thinking that in its passage is enowned by its coming to be in passing away in beyng. It is beyng-historical thinking that *Contributions* enacts with its fugal structure: a book written as a repeating of the "same" beginning in each of its six sections, or movements.[62] These movements are not gathered into a system. Rather, they remain in the open play of the temporality of the passage of beyng by giving these six variations. In understanding beyng-historical thinking in its temporality, one would think that *Contributions* is neither a system, nor a handful of meditations, but a work unified in its remaining in the very openness of the passing of beyng, in remaining in the awareness of a leap that would always be unreached in its own event.

But if, as I have suggested, *Contributions* enacts the temporalizing passage of beyng's essential sway, it does so concretely. This is primarily what "enactment" would suggest, a thinking-undergoing of beyng in its passing motion. Indeed, Heidegger indicates in the section of *Contributions* titled *Gründung* that it is with the holding open of the question of beyng in its space-time leeway (*Zeit-Raum Spiel*) that the decision (*Entscheidung*) "of" beyngs' essential sway would occur.[63] In speaking of beyng-historical thinking, we have been speaking in the configuring motion of beyng in its concrete occurring. This motion stands outside the material-ideal dualism of metaphysics and transcendental philosophies and at the same time places thinking in the very occurrence of beyng's essential sway in the configuring passing of words, works of art, things, bodies, identities, communities . . . all of which now remains to be thought.

Notes

1. GA 65, 3; CP, 3. For bibliographical information on the texts referred to here, see the introduction to this volume, note 1. When I use my own translation of entire passages or particular terms, I give the Emad/Maly translation in a note.

I have chosen to translate "Seyn" as "beyng" and not as "be-ing." This choice is in part a way of marking the leap Heidegger is making from "Sein" to "Seyn," where the terms although differentiated, still recall each other.

2. This is already announced in the same paragraph above, where Heidegger speaks of "the matter" that is already intimated by the title of the work: "Aber der öffentliche Titel entspricht auch insofern der 'Sache.'"

3. I have chosen to use Stambaugh's translation of *Historie* as "Historiography," and of *Geschichte* as "history." See Martin Heidegger, *Being and Time*, trans. Joan Stambaugh (Albany: State University of New York Press, 1996.) As Emad and Maly point out, differentiating these two terms is central to the reading of *Contributions*. The translators mark this difference by using "history" for both words, but they indicate "*Historie*" by writing it in parentheses following the English word "history" ("Translators' Foreword," CP, xxii–xxiii). I have also added

"occurrence" to Stambaugh's use of "history" for the German *Geschichte*. This I find helpful in at least two ways. First, this word refers to "event," "incident," and "episode." Thus the temporal and passing character of *Geschichte*, as well as its particularity as the occurrence of beyng are put into play. Also, "occurrence" relates *Geschichte* to *Ereignis* in the sense of the "opening of beyng in its particular givenness," and not only in terms of *Ereignis* as "Event," a word that already suggests the placement of the *Geschichte des Seyns* and *seynsgeschichtliches Denken* into a grand historiographical scale.

4. The translation of *Wesen* and *Wesung* requires careful consideration, given Heidegger's particular and various uses of these terms (see Emad and Maly's discussion in their foreword, CP, xxiv–xxvi). As Emad and Maly point out, the choice of "essential sway" and "essential swaying," respectively, is not ideal; but it does point both to the dynamic character as well as to the particular physicality of the occurrence of beyng. When I speak of "physicality," I mean the resonance of *phusis* that is always at play in Heidegger's beyng-historical thinking. How *Wesung* brings this physicality into play may be inferred, for example, from the fact that in German usage, *Wesung* is not identified with such an ontological determination of being as that indicated by *das Wesen*, a term traditionally used in German as analogous to *essentiae* and in direct contrast to a being's particular way of being or *Dasein*. *Wesung* instead recalls precisely the diverse configurings of particular living processes, as, for example, in the word *Ver-wesung*, which means "decay" or "decomposition."

5. Throughout this essay I speak of "presence" as the presence of entities at hand (*Anwesen*), and of "appearing" as the very occurrence of appearing.

6. GA 65, 3; CP, 3.

7. Ibid.

8. *Grundfragen der Philosophie*, GA 45, 133.

9. Martin Heidegger, *Nietzsche: Der europäische Nihilismus* (Pfullingen: Günther Neske, 1989), p. 25. Martin Heidegger, *Nietzsche*, vol. 3, trans. Frank A. Capuzzi, David Farrell Krell, and Joan Stambaugh, ed. David Farrell Krell (San Francisco: Harper San Francisco, 1987), p. 5.

10. *Ereignis* translated as "enowning" refers to the occurrence of beyng as thought in *Contributions*.

11. Heidegger, *Nietzsche*, ed. Brigitte Schillbach, vol. 1, GA 6.1 (Frankfurt am Main: Vittorio Klostermann, 1996), pp. 64–65; Heidegger, *Nietzsche*, vols. 1–2, ed. Krell.

12. Martin Heidegger, *Sein und Zeit* (Tübingen: Max Niemeyer Verlag, 1986), p. 6 (*Being and Time*, trans. Stambaugh, p. 5).

13. Martin Heidegger, *Die Geschichte des Seyns*, ed. Peter Trawny, GA 69 (Frankfurt am Main: Vittorio Klostermann, 1998), p. 173.

14. Ibid., p. 168.

15. In bringing together Heidegger's thought and Nietzsche's, we find a difficult double standard. On the one hand, Heidegger claims that Nietzsche's thinking remains metaphysical in the form of "the doctrine of the will to power." On the other hand, read otherwise, Nietzsche's thought seems to enact a self-overcoming motion that leads it beyond metaphysics, one that we find in Heidegger's thought in *Contributions*. It is then a question not only of Nietzsche as the "last metaphysician" and Heidegger as the thinker of the other beginning;

it is also, and more interestingly, a question of how much of a metaphysical reading Nietzsche's thought accepts and how much of a Nietzschean reading Heidegger's thought withstands. It is in each case a question of thinking at the limit. In other words, the question of the relation between these two thinkers belongs to the limit of thought in what gives itself to be thought out of the history of beyng (*Die Geschichte des Seyns*), and it would only be in coming to this beyng-historical thinking (*seynsgeschichtliches Denken*) that the question could be thought by us. We find Heidegger's own attempt in his 1943 lecture "Nietzsche's Word: God Is Dead," a lecture that brings together Heidegger's work on Nietzsche during the years of the composition of *Contributions*. (See Martin Heidegger, "Nietzsches Wort 'Gott ist Tod,'" in *Holzwege*, ed. Friedrich-Wilhelm von Herrmann, GA 5 [Frankfurt am Main: Vittorio Klostermann, 1977]; "Nietzsche's Word: God Is Dead," in *The Question Concerning Technology and Other Essays*, trans. W. Lovitt [New York: Harper, 1977]).

16. "The five main rubrics we have mentioned—'nihilism,' 'evaluation of the values hitherto,' 'will to power,' 'eternal recurrence of the same,' and 'over-man'—each portray Nietzsche's metaphysics from just *one* perspective, although in each case it is a perspective that defines the whole" (Heidegger, *Nietzsche* vol. 4, *Nihilism*, Frank A. Capuzzi, ed. David Farrell Krell (San Francisco: HarperCollins, 1987), p. 9; Heidegger, *Nietzsche: Der europäische Nihilismus*, vol. 2, p. 40.

17. See note 4 above.

18. See note 2 above. Cf. GA 65, 5; CP, 4: "Das übergängliche Denken leistet den gründenden Entwurf der Wahrheit des Seyns als geschichtliche Besinnung."

19. See note 17 above.

20. GA 65, 32; CP, 23. "Geschichte hier nicht gefaßt als ein Bereich das Seienden unter anderen, sondern einzig im Blick auf die Wesung des Seyns selbst."

21. *Historisches Wörterbuch der Philosophie*, vol. 3, ed. J. Ritter (Darmstadt: Wissenschaftliche Buchgesellschaft, 1974), p. 352.

22. Ibid.: "das momentane, zufällige Ereignis, der Anfang irgendeines Geschehens."

23. Ibid. The word that is translated into the Latin *eventus*, from which we get "event," is not *giskeht* but *anaskiht*. *Giskeht* is translated into Latin as *casus*.

24. Ibid.: "nicht nur die einmalige Tat und Sache, sondern auch ein größerer Ereigniszusammenhang."

25. Ibid., pp. 398–99. With regard to Dilthey, see section 77 of *Being and Time*.

26. Heidegger, *Being and Time*, trans. Stambaugh, "Introduction," part 2, section 69, p. 332; *Sein und Zeit*, p. 305. See also *Being and Time*, "Introduction," section 6, "The Task of Deconstructing the History of Ontology"; and, part II, chapter 5, sections72–77: "Temporality and Historicity."

27. Here it is a matter of taking Heidegger's words concerning *Being and Time* and the "turn" (*Kehre*) most rigorously. In 1949, for the second edition of "Vom Wesen der Wahrheit" (1930), Heidegger appends two final paragraphs to the earlier version. There Heidegger says, "Die Antwort auf die Frage nach dem Wesen der Wahrheit ist die Sage einer Kehre innerhalb der Geschichte des Seyns" (The response to the question of the essence of truth is the saying of a

turning in the history of beyng). Heidegger's language clearly places his think-ing in the thirties, and even in *Being and Time* (see the final paragraph of the 1949 edition, beginning, "Die entscheidende Frage [*Sein und Zeit, 1927*]"), within the question of "the history of beyng." Heidegger is not only saying this but he marks it by using *Seyn,* the archaic form of *Sein* that marks Heidegger's thinking in *Contributions.* It would then be possible, and perhaps necessary, not only to read Heidegger's thought as a motion from early to post-turn Heidegger, but to read backwards, i.e., for example, looking at *Being and Time* in the light of Heidegger's thought in the early thirties and in *Contributions.* (See "On the Essence of Truth," *Basic Writings,* trans. John Sallis, ed. David Farrell Krell [San Francisco: HarperCollins, 1993]; "Vom Wesen der Wahrheit" [1930], *Weg-marken* [Frankfurt am Main: Vittorio Klostermann, 1978].)

28. GA 65, 3–4; CP, 3–4: "Die Beiträge fragen in einer Bahn."

29. This translation keeps the sense of motion of the coming to be in passing of beyng. There is in Heidegger a crucial difference between the occurrence of the opening of beyng as given in Greek experience, *phusis,* and the metaphysical inter-pretation of this givingness through a logos of objective presence and calculation. This awareness of the double play of the truth of beyng in the Greek beginning is present throughout Heidegger's thinking concerning Greek philosophy.

30. "*Aletheia* (Heraklit, Fragment 16)" (summer semester, 1943), *Vorträge und Aufsätze* (Pfullingen: Günther Neske, 1985), pp. 163–66; "*Aletheia* (Heraclitus, Fragment B16)," *Early Greek Thinking,* trans. David Farrell Krell and Frank A. Capuzzi (New York: Harper and Row, 1975), p. 114. Cf. Martin Heidegger, "Der Anfang des abendländischen Denkens. Heraklit" (summer semester, 1943), in *Heraklit,* ed. Manfred S. Frings, GA 55 (Frankfurt am Main: Vittorio Kloster-mann, 1979), pp. 127–31.

31. GA 65, 3–4; CP, 3–5.

32. GA 65, 3; CP, 3.

33. We might think here of Heidegger's discussion of the bridge in "Building, Dwelling, Thinking": "The bridge gathers to itself in its own way earth and sky, divinities and mortals. . . . the bridge does not first come to a local to stand in it; rather a local comes into existence only by virtue of the bridge. . . . By this site are determined the places and paths by which a space is provided for." Even if thought were to enact a bridge, it would be this thinking that would occur as the gathering for past and future, and it would have to be thought as such. See "Building, Dwelling, Thinking," *Basic Writings,* ed. Krell, pp. 353–63; "Bauen Wohnen Denken," *Vorträge und Aufsätze,* pp.146–56.

34. GA 65, 5, translation mine; cf. CP, 4.

35. See sections 20-24: GA 65, 55–61; CP, 38–43. Cf. "Der Anfang der abendländischen Philosophie" (summer semester, 1932), GA 35. Throughout this essay, I have followed the Emad/Maly translation of *anfänglich* as "incep-tual" and *anfängliches Denken* as "inceptual thinking"; I have done so in order to point to the dynamic or passing character of the occurrence being thought and to the character of this thinking in what Heidegger calls the "leap" (*Sprung*).

36. GA 65, 58, translation mine; cf. CP, 41: "It is the essential swaying of *being* itself. But *this* beginning first becomes enactable as the *other* beginning when the *first* beginning is put into proper perspective. Grasped inceptually, the beginning is be-ing itself."

37. In section 117 of *Die Geschichte des Seyns* (GA 69), Heidegger also states, "The historical [*historisch*] never lets history itself [*Geschichte*] be experienced, let alone thought." This neither resolves nor eliminates but rather opens the question of the gathering of the historical in thinking. For a discussion of this issue, see, for example, Peter Warnek's "Reading Plato before Platonism (After Heidegger)," *Research in Phenomenology* 27 (1997).

38. Heidegger has already made this move in "On the Essence of Truth" (*Basic Writings*, ed. Krell); "Vom Wesen der Wahrheit" (1930), *Wegmarken*.

39. Hans-Georg Gadamer, "Plato," in *Heidegger's Ways*, trans. John W. Stanley (Albany: State University of New York Press, 1994); *Heideggers Wege* (Tübingen: J. C. B. Mohr, 1983).

40. Leonardo Samona, "L' 'Altro Inizio' della Filosofia," *Giornale di Metafisica*, New Series 12 (1990): 80.

41. *Die Geschichte des Seyns* (1938–1940), GA 69, 173. Cf. Heidegger, "The Anaximander Fragment," in *Early Greek Thinking*, p. 36; "Der Spruch des Anaximander" (1946), *Holzwege*, GA 5, 345–49.

42. Charles E. Scott, *The Time of Memory* (Albany: State University of New York Press, 1999).

43. We find a formulation of this motion already in *Being and Time*, where Heidegger discusses it as the "Destruktion der Geschichte der Ontologie," section 6, pp. 19–27.

44. GA 69, 168.

45. In speaking of passage and the truth of beyng, we are already approaching the motion of withdrawal that I discuss in the next section of this essay.

46. GA 65, 3, translation mine; cf. CP, 3.

47. In *Contributions*, Heidegger speaks of the *künftige Denken* (GA 65, 3) This does not mean the thinking of a future that lies ahead; rather, it refers to the *Zukunft* ("future") in its double sense of "coming to" and "arrival," *An-kunft*.

48. GA 65, 18; CP, 14.

49. GA 65, 383; CP, 267.

50. GA 65, 385; CP, 268.

51. Heidegger had already introduced this thought of the withdrawal of beyng in the thirties, in his discussions of the Greek term *a-letheia*, where the "lethic" element of truth is first brought to the question of the truth of being. See GA 65, 329; CP, 230–31.

52. The "astonishment" (*thaumadzein*) of the Greeks is for Heidegger the reductive event that grounds the first beginning, i.e., traditional ontology and metaphysics. Heidegger translates the Greek term as *Er-staunen* (GA 65, 20; CP, 15). This term can be contrasted with *das Erschrecken, die Verhaltenheit*, and *die Scheu*, the ground-attunements of thinking in the other beginning. See GA 65, 14; CP, 11.

53. GA 65, 385; CP, 267.

54. GA 65, 386; CP, 268.

55. GA 65, 56; CP, 39.

56. See note 39 above.

57. GA 65, 303; CP, 214: "This is grounded in the leap. That unto which the leap leaps in enopening is first grounded by the leap. . . . the self only becomes its own in the leap."

58. *Sein und Zeit,* p. 6; *Being and Time,* trans. Stambaugh, p. 5.

59. GA 65, 11; CP, 7.

60. GA 65, 3; CP, 3.

61. *Die Geschichte des Seyns,* GA 69, 170.

62. GA 65, 10–11; CP, 7–9.

63. See part V, GA 65, 371–88: "Die Gründung," "Der Zeit-Raum als der Ab-grund"; CP, 259–76: "Grounding," "Time-Space as Ab-ground." Cf. section 5, GA 65, 17; CP, 13. On *Entscheidung,* see GA 65 and CP, section 5; part III, "das Zuspiel" (Playing-Forth); part VIII, sections 266, 268.

4. Poietic Saying

Daniela Vallega-Neu

When *Contributions to Philosophy* first appeared in 1989 after having been announced by Otto Pöggeler and Friedrich-Wilhelm von Herrmann as Heidegger's second major work after *Being and Time*, the critical response seemed rather more disappointed than excited. What presented itself to critics was an apparently random collection of repetitive notes, aphorisms, fragments of texts, collections of questions, or lists of words and unfinished sentences that were utterly different from the systematic exposition of Dasein given in *Being and Time*. And even those sections with longer passages and "complete" sentences are marked by a strange abruptness. The reader finds herself deprived of linking elements providing continuity of thought in a smooth development from one question to the next. No "concepts" are systematically introduced and developed; no didactic considerations are provided. The reader is left alone, without support and eventually exposed to the power of naked words uttering the event of beyng.

The language of *Contributions* demands that the reader expose herself to a thinking that does not provide any support for familiar ways of thinking. For those who are not ready to engage in a journey along an unknown path with an uncertain destiny, *Contributions* must remain a random collection of fragments, a "private language" at most, cryptic in its content and unworthy of being taken seriously.

The way Heidegger speaks or writes in *Contributions* is intimately connected to what he wants to say—indeed so intimately that this distinction between what he says and how he says it collapses. One might say that what is in question reveals itself only and entirely in the "how," i.e., in the performativity of thinking. And we, as readers, need to participate in the performativity of Heidegger's thinking in order to understand it.

Contributions was written without any didactic considerations in the mere attempt to think (of) and say beyng as enowning (*Ereignis*). Its language arises out of the acknowledgment that our traditional metaphysical language is unable to articulate the core question of Heidegger's philosophy: the question of being. As long as we speak *about* being the way we speak *about* beings, we remain within the domain of metaphysical thought, where being is somehow regarded as an "other" to thinking and is taken to be like a being. Yet being can never become an object of thought because it is an event that precedes all reification.

In *Contributions*, Heidegger attempts not to speak *about* being but to let being eventuate in language. In other words, being occurs precisely in the language that articulates it. As he says in §1, "This saying does neither describe or explain, does not proclaim or teach. This saying does not stand over against what is said. Rather, the saying itself *is* the 'to be said,' as the essential swaying of beyng [*Wesung des Seyns*]."¹

Therefore, there are two main questions we need to consider: (1) the difference between propositional language (*Aussage*) and saying (*Sage*) (i.e., original [*ursprünglich*] or inceptive [*anfänglich*] language); (2) the original language as the open sway of beyng as enowning.

Proposition and Saying

According to what Heidegger says in the "Letter on Humanism," the main problem that led him to interrupt the itinerary of *Being and Time* and seek a new way of posing the question of being was a problem of language. Heidegger did not publish the third section of the first part of *Being and Time* ("The Explication of Time as the Transcendental Horizon of the Question of Being") "because thinking failed in the adequate saying of this turning [*Kehre*] [to understand being out of its temporal horizon] and did not succeed with the help of the language of metaphysics."²

In what sense does Heidegger still use the language of metaphysics in *Being and Time*? As he always says, metaphysics takes beings as a guiding thread and questions being itself as a kind of entity by thinking it in a presentative [*vorstellungshaft*] manner. Accordingly, metaphysical language is constituted by propositions that present that about which they speak in opposition to (or over against [*gegenüber*]) a thinking or presenting subject. A presentative statement always works within a distinction and opposition of thinking and what is thought that is formed according to our theoretical relation with things (beings).

In *Being and Time* Heidegger shows how presentative thinking is grounded in being which is disclosed in Dasein in the way that the disclosure of being is grounded in temporality. Thus, there appears to be a threefold foundational structure: temporality is the condition of the possibility for being as such, which is the condition for the possibility of Dasein. Yet, at the same time, this foundational structure dissolves at a level of a reading that attempts to think out of the finite temporality that is disclosed in Dasein's being towards death. The foundational structure dissolves in several ways. It dissolves if we think that the temporality of being as such (the sense of being) is disclosed *in* Dasein's being towards death, i.e., *in* Dasein's temporality and not beyond it or in distinction to it. The foundational structure dissolves also if we acknowledge that what seems to be an ultimate fundament, the temporality of being as such, is no fundament at all but is rather a finite disclosive event.

But still in some instances the language of *Being and Time* seems to reaffirm what it means to overcome, namely, metaphysical thought and language. This concerns particularly the notions of "transcendence," "horizon," and "condition of the possibility." When Heidegger says that Dasein always already transcends beings in the disclosure of being, he intends to say that the disclosure of being is more original than our relation to beings. But still the word "transcendence" implies that there is first something, a being, that is transcended, thus reinstating the primacy of our presentative relation to beings. Similarly the notion of a temporal *horizon* of being carries with it the connotation of an open space or landscape that presents itself in opposition to a presenting subject. Finally, the notion of "condition of the possibility" seems to refer back to Kant's transcendental thinking in his *Critique of Pure Reason* and thus to a metaphysical grounding that Heidegger's *Being and Time* intends to deconstruct.

This may also lead to a metaphysical (mis)understanding of the ontological difference. In *Being and Time* Heidegger states that the disclosure of being (*Seinserschlossenheit*) is the condition for the possibility for the discovery of beings (*Entdecktheit des Seienden*). This may lead to the representation of a permanent ontological structure at the basis of the disclosure of particular beings. Being and beings end up being represented as two different kinds of beings: a fundamental being and particular beings. Again, at another level of reading we find that the whole ontological structure of being as such is disclosed nowhere else than in Dasein's facticity, i.e., nowhere else than in Dasein's ontic-ontological being toward death into which it is factually thrown. And here beyng is disclosed as a temporal occurrence and not represented as a kind of being (*Seiendes*).

In *Contributions,* Heidegger is most critical about the possible misunderstandings of the ontological difference.[3] Even though he maintains the necessity of thinking the ontological difference in order to prepare a transition from metaphysical thought to a more original kind of thinking that would raise the question of being as such, at the same time, the ontological difference becomes a main obstacle for an attempt to think being as such in its truth, in and out of its temporal occurrence. Thus, in *Contributions* Heidegger thinks the necessity of "leaping over" the ontological difference and hence the necessity of "leaping over" transcendence in order to question inceptually *out of* (and not over against) beyng and its truth.[4]

The leap over transcendence is a leap into what in *Being and Time* is called the temporal horizon of being; in *Contributions* this temporal horizon is rethought as the truth of being. The leap into the horizon overcomes the very notion of horizon. As Heidegger says in a marginal note in *Being and Time*, referring to the withheld third section of the first part of the book, "The overcoming of the horizon as such. The return into the source [*Herkunft*]. The presencing out of this source."[5]

Heidegger's famous "turning" (*Kehre*) of the thirties occurs as this leap over transcendence and horizon into the truth of beyng as the original event out of which thinking and saying arise. This leap entails a transformation of language: the transformation from a propositional (presentative) language to a poietic (in the sense of the Greek word *poiesis*) saying. Whereas propositional language always addresses beings *about* which it speaks, poietic saying brings beyng forth in the saying *as* it finds itself enowned by beyng's event. Poietic saying thus is part of beyng's event as beyng's event occurs in the poietic saying. A certain blindness marks the origin of this saying since in the origin we do not have present to our mind that which the saying names, a presence that we are accustomed to when we think or speak propositionally. There is nothing already there to be signified. In this sense, poietic saying speaks about nothing. It simply says beyng in its historicality [*Geschichtlichkeit*].⁶ Its occurrence enacts the opening of the historicality of beyng.

This transformation of language from propositions to saying is difficult to achieve, first of all because it does not reside in the power of a human subject. The "human" part in poietic saying can be described at best as an inceptive response to beyng's call that first opens this call by echoing it in words. I will develop this point in what follows. Second, poietic saying requires a special kind of listening not only with respect to beyng but also with respect to uttered words.

The transformation of language does not mean that we necessarily need to find new words or a new grammar but rather that we are able to speak and listen in response to beyng's call. And since poietic saying occurs in words that arise in our tradition, it remains always in the danger of being misunderstood metaphysically. Heidegger points to this fact in §41 of *Contributions:*

> Every saying of be-ing⁷ is kept in words and namings which are understandable in the direction of everyday references to beings and are thought exclusively in this direction, [and as such can be misinterpreted as statements of beyng].⁸ Therefore it is not as if what is needed first is the failure of the question (within the domain of the thinking-interpretation of being), but the word itself already discloses something (familiar) and thus hides that which has to be brought into the open through thinking-saying.
>
> This difficulty cannot be eliminated at all; even the attempt to do that already means misunderstanding all saying of be-ing. This difficulty must be taken over and grasped in its essential belongingness (to the thinking of be-ing).⁹

The language of *Contributions* speaks in this difficulty: in an attempt to reach an original saying and in continuous reflection on possible metaphysical misunderstandings. The language of *Contributions* throughout is not original or poietic. As Heidegger says in the first section of the book, since the thinking and saying of *Contributions* ultimately depends on what beyng gives us to think and say (and does not depend on the thinker), it can only be an attempt at saying beyng's essential sway.[10] But even if it borrows from the metaphysical heritage (especially when Heidegger reflects on the transition from metaphysics to beyng-historical thinking), it always does this in a critical manner and in the struggle for a more original language.

This struggle is not just a sign of imperfection or failure. Rather, for Heidegger it belongs to the way in which beyng historically (*geschichtlich*) occurs. We may even take this problem back to the "failure" (*Versagen*) of language in *Being and Time*. Precisely this failure of language lets appear in a new and radical way the occurrence of beyng not just as a presencing but more originally as a withdrawal from and in presencing.[11]

It is not just a coincidence that the German word *Versagen*, which is commonly translated as "failing," appears in *Contributions* with respect to beyng itself: beyng occurs as "refusal," in German *Versagung*.[12] Heidegger was certainly aware that the root meaning of *Versagen* is *Sagen*, "saying." All this supports the interpretation of the *Versagen* ("failure") of language in *Being and Time* as indicating an incapability of saying beyng that arises out of beyng's own occurrence as refusal (or withdrawal). And it is certainly no coincidence that the thinking of *Contributions*—that attempts to articulate beyng's historical occurrence—is initiated through the experience of beyng's utter self-refusal at the end of metaphysics.

Beyng and Language

The first fugue of the six fugues that articulate in their unity the composition of *Contributions* is called *Anklang*, "echo." It starts with §50:

> Echo of the essential swaying of be-ing
> out of the abandonment of being
> through the distressing distress
> of the forgottenness of be-ing.[13]

The echo of beyng occurs in a need that arises in the abandonment of beyng. Beyng resounds in and as a lack, a lack which has very much to do with the lack of words, with an incapability of bringing beyng into a saying. The echo of beyng echoes no original sounds but rather an original withdrawal of its source. It is an echo without source, an echoing of silence, as it were. And it is only by staying with the silence that arises in the incapability of saying as well as by staying with the necessity of speech that arises in that incapability of saying that Heidegger explores and rethinks again and again the truth of beyng as enowning (*Ereignis*). The experience of a lack of words and the experience of the necessity of words that say beyng's occurrence go hand in hand. It is precisely the lack that compels thinking; it is in the lack that beyng's silent call resounds.

The question of language is so intimately connected with the question of the truth of beyng as enowning that it can hardly be regarded as a distinct question. In this respect it is interesting to look at §276 of *Contributions* which is titled "Be-ing [Beyng] and Language." After saying that beyng constitutes the ground of language, Heidegger questions the "relation" between beyng and language.[14] First he points to the inadequacy of asking "How does language relate to beyng?" or "How does beyng relate to language?" because both of these questions seem to imply that we take language as a given being in distinction to beyng. Then he reformulates the question more adequately: "How does the essence of language originate *in* the essence of beyng?" and "How does language sway *in* the sway of beyng?" (GA 65, 500, 501, translation and emphasis mine; cf. CP, 352). These questions already give some indication as to how we might think the relatedness of language and beyng: language originates in beyng, is of beyng, and occurs (sways) in beyng.[15] Thus, in order to understand how language occurs, we need to understand how beyng occurs. Let us rethink, then, how Heidegger thinks beyng in *Contributions,* namely as "enowning."

Let us recall the basic turning (*Kehre*)[16] that constitutes the core of the occurrence of the truth of beyng as enowning. The truth of beyng is initially experienced if thinking acknowledges the need that arises with the experience of the abandonment of beyng. To experience the truth of beyng as enowning requires that we let go of all metaphysical determinations of beyng and, as Heidegger says, that we undergo a "leap" into the truth of beyng.[17] Such an experience requires a leap into the opening of beyng as withdrawal, in an acknowledgment of the utter finitude of being. In the language of *Being and Time,* this opening occurs as the temporal horizon that is disclosed in Dasein's resolute being toward death.[18]

The letting go of all positive determinations of being in the leap into the truth of beyng as withdrawal does not mean that thinking gives itself to pure groundlessness and nothingness and that it ends there. Rather, in the leap one experiences a turning, one finds oneself enowned in one's thrownness, "given to one's own" (*er-eignet*) by already responding to a silent call. To be "given to one's own" means to be given to be, to come to be in passing away in original belongingness to beyng.[19] As Heidegger says in §122 of *Contributions,* the leap into the truth of beyng may be understood with reference to the language of *Being and Time* as Dasein's "opening projection" (*eröffnender Entwurf*) that in its very occurrence is experienced as being enowned. But whereas in *Being and Time* Heidegger thinks that Dasein's opening projection opens possibilities of being by coming back to possibilities of being in which Dasein finds itself thrown (thus prioritizing projection with respect to thrownness even though they occur simultaneously), in *Contributions* this thrownness is rethought as an enownment that enowns what is projected in Da-sein (thus prioritizing enownment, even though it occurs simultaneously with Dasein's opening projection). In the leap thinking experiences that it does nothing but take over the throw of beyng, that it does nothing other than respond to beyng's call (*Zuruf*). In such "taking over" or "responding," this call opens up. There is no enowning prior to Da-sein's being enowned, no call prior to the response; and yet in Da-sein thinking experiences the enownment of its projection in the very enactment of the projection (not in a theoretical reflection).

As noted earlier, the silent call of beyng resounds at first in an incapability of speech, it resounds as a necessity of speech in the failure of the word for beyng. One might say that at least for the thinker Heidegger, the truth of beyng as enowning is first experienced out of the necessity of saying the truth of beyng. And in an originary response, Da-sein's enowned projection would occur through a saying that lets the silent call of beyng resound. The incapability of saying beyng is due to beyng's occurrence as withdrawal; and as thinking lets go of all metaphysical determinations of being, as it leaps into the truth of beyng by acknowledging beyng's withdrawal, it experiences a turning event: Da-sein's enownment out of beyng's withdrawal *as* Da-sein opens the enowning event in response to beyng's call. Enowning occurs as a turning in-between beyng's enowning call and Da-sein's enowned belonging.[20] The words Heidegger uses[21] to say the turning that occurs in enowning point to the origin and sway of language in this turning. Not only does he speak of the call of beyng in which Da-sein is enowned, he also speaks of the *Zugehörigkeit* ("belonging") of Da-sein to the truth of beyng. The root meaning of "Zugehörigkeit," is "hören," "to listen." Thus we may translate "Zugehörigkeit" with "belonging in listening." This listening is a response to beyng's call in which this call at first resounds. This response is like an echoing, the source of which remains abysmal (*abgründig*). In this listening response language originates as the language of beyng.

Here language has a wider and more fundamental meaning than it has in traditional conceptions. It does not originate with speech but rather with speechlessness in the lack of the word of beyng that points to the silent abysmal source of beyng. This language arises in the thought of *Contributions* in the lack that compels Heidegger's writing, that compels his attempt to say beyng, even though Heidegger says that *Contributions* are not yet able "to join the fugue of the truth of beyng from itself" (§1), i.e., they are not yet able to say fully the sway of beyng. Human speech (words) is just one way in which language may be articulated (other articulations occur, for instance, in gestures, paintings, sculpture, music, etc.). Speech is grounded in the sway of language which originates in the opening of beyng as withdrawal. It is grounded in silence.[22]

Even though the origin and original sway of language is beyond (or more originary than) what we normally conceive as human speech, Heidegger nevertheless thinks of language as originally and essentially related to the essence of humans. The belonging together of beyng and language intrinsically means a belonging together of beyng, language, and humans.[23]

In *Contributions,* Heidegger speaks of "Da-sein" with a hyphen, which indicates a shift in his notion of Dasein as he conceived it in *Being and Time.* Da-sein now designates not primarily the essence of human beings but rather the open middle of the truth of beyng as enowning. Heidegger calls Da-sein the "in-between" and "the point of turn in the turning of enowning."[24] Da-sein occurs as a historical opening of the truth of beyng, an opening that occurs, as I said above, in a listening response to beyng's withdrawal. This composes a historical opening, thus one that is essentially abysmal (*abgründig*).[25] In this sense, Da-sein is the enowning ground of human being in which humans come to their proper essence. At the same time, Da-sein occurs as this ground, as the abysmal open middle of the truth of beyng as enowning, only in connection with humans. While the "Da" of "Da-sein" designates the opening of the truth of beyng, the "-sein" refers to human "insistence" [*Inständigkeit*][26] in this opening (which implicates, as will be shown in the third part of this essay, the sheltering of this opening in beings). Only through this insistence can the "Da" (t/here) be held open. With the word "insistence" Heidegger rethinks the "ec-static" being of humans. Whereas the word "ec-static," which we know from *Being and Time,* still suggests the language of transcendence and horizon, the word "insistence" is spoken from *within* the experience of the truth of beyng as enowning. Where the word ec-static (as it is used in *Being and Time*) says that in anticipatory resoluteness (*vorlaufende Entschlossenheit*), humans *stand out* in their being in the transcendent horizon of being as such, the word "in-sisting" says that in listening response to beyng as withdrawal, humans *stand in* the truth of beyng as it is opened in Dasein's enownment.

In order to say being originally (and not to make propositions about being that already have lost beyng's original occurrence), thinking needs to insist in Da-sein. And this means that we, too, as readers of *Contributions,* are called to insist in Da-sein if we want to think it originally. In order to do this, thinking needs to let itself be attuned by a ground-attunement, in which the truth of beyng as enowning is disclosed in

Da-sein. Heidegger mostly (not always) attempts to articulate this ground-attunement with the word *Verhaltenheit*, "reservedness," which implies a multiplicity of movements, intensities, and countermovements that he attempts to articulate in §5 of *Contributions*. Here, Heidegger names three guiding attunements: startled dismay (*Erschrecken*), reservedness, and awe.[27] Startled dismay articulates the sudden displacement (from a mode of being that does not feel any distress) that thinking undergoes when it is faced with the experience of the abandonment of beyng. With reference to language, this moment names the experience of the impossibility of saying beyng. Heidegger says that reservedness is the middle of startled dismay and awe. In it sways a "being turned toward [*Zukehr*] the hesitating self-denial [*zögerndes Sichversagen*]" which characterizes the occurrence of the truth of beyng. The experience of a hesitation in the withdrawal of beyng that allows a staying with this withdrawal is made possible in the reservedness (the German word "Verhaltenheit" includes the verb "halten," to hold, which points to the "holding-open" of the truth of beyng). With reference to language this articulates a staying with speechlessness, a staying turned toward the occurrence of beyng that denies language and at the same time compels thought to behold its own occurrence in language. Attuned by reservedness, insistent thinking stays with beyng's self-refusal (*Versagen*, "refusal of saying") by listening to beyng's compelling call, a call that is certainly beyond words and that Heidegger will rethink in his later works as *das Geläut der Stille* ("the gathered sounding of silence").

Within reservedness also occurs the third guiding attunement, "awe." Awe intensifies the "being-turned-toward" beyng's self-refusal. From awe especially arises the necessity of reticence (*Verschweigung*).[28]

As Heidegger says, reticence is the most original response human being can give to beyng's silent call. And in turn, only in reticence does beyng's silent call resound. A word related to reticence (*Verschweigung*) is *Er-schweigung*, which is, says Heidegger, the "'*logic*' [in the Greek sense of *logos*] of philosophy insofar as philosophy asks the grounding-question from within the other beginning,"[29] i.e., the question of beyng as enowning. In German, the prefix "er-" indicates a performative character, a process that either initiates an activity or brings it to an end. An attempt at a literal translation of *Er-schweigung* into English may be: "to bring forth and hold silence."[30] The "bringing-forth" of silence (*Erschweigung*) is the original enowned language in the thinking from enowning: "Silence springs forth from the swaying origin of language itself."[31] We might say that in the language of *Contributions* Heidegger attempts to bring forth the silence in beyng's refusal that echoes out of the failure of metaphysical language. Yet, he can achieve this only by speaking, by uttering words, poietic words that shelter beyng's silence and that open up—if they find the appropriate listening—beyng's occurrence as enowning.

Beyng's occurrence may exceed words, withdrawing into its abysmal ground; but this excess can never come forth without words or other "beings" that shelter in silence the occurrence of its abysmal truth.

Words

Humans' insistence in Da-*sein*—attuned by reservedness—is necessary in order to hold open the truth of beyng (in the "Da") and thus to let beyng as enowning originally occur. This insisting that holds open the Da of Da-sein requires that this opening is sheltered (*bergen*) in a being. This means that the truth of beyng occurs historically only if it is sheltered in a being. In the case of thinking such a being is the word of inceptive saying.

In *Contributions* Heidegger dedicates only five sections to the question of sheltering. In those sections he repeatedly refers to his essay "The Origin of the Work of Art,"[32] a work that may be seen as a supplement that develops this question in more detail. In this essay Heidegger shows how the original strife of the truth of beyng (its occurrence as concealment/unconcealment) needs to be transformed into the battle of world and earth and is opened up as such in the work of art ("poietic words").[33] Or to say it another way: the work of art puts into work (*ins-Werk-setzen*) the truth of beyng, and in this process the truth of beyng is transformed into the strife of world and earth. This also means that the work of art (the poietic word) is not able to place itself directly into the truth of beyng. The original self-withdrawal of beyng also withdraws *from* any word. But in contrast to words uttered in propositional speech, where any trace of the occurrence of beyng as enownment is covered up, poietic words are able to shelter the withdrawal of beyng by echoing it in the way they let appear the strife of world and earth. What initiates the creation of a work of art or the saying of a poietic word is precisely this withdrawal when a listening to this withdrawal occurs in the attunement of reservedness. Poietic words that arise in this attunement echo this withdrawal; they shelter the unspeakable as such in speech.[34]

We need to note, at this point, the difference between poietic words of a thinker and poietic words of a poet, although Heidegger does not thematize this difference in *Contributions*. The point also allows me to indicate the importance of Hölderlin's poetry (next to Nietzsche's thought) for Heidegger's thought from enowning. For Heidegger, Hölderlin is the one who not only experienced—as did Nietzsche—the end of metaphysics, but also (in contrast to Nietzsche) founded the possibility of another beginning in his poetry.[35] Heidegger understands himself as being responsive to beyng's historical occurrence *as* it comes to language in Hölderlin's poetry. For Heidegger, the poet is the one who *first* founds historical beyng by sheltering it in words. But it is the thinker who brings to light what is sheltered in poetic words through words that grasp (*begreifende Worte*) the truth of beyng as it is disclosed in the words of the poet and thus penetrate even deeper into the concealed essence of language.[36]

The origin of language occurs in beyng's enowning call out of beyng's original self-refusal (*Versagen*). Thinking can be responsive in poietic words only if the enowning call is opened up in a responsive (listening) belonging to it. Heidegger was convinced of the possibility of such an original poietic saying. He believed that in saying the flight of the gods in his poetry Hölderlin brought to word the historical occurrence of beyng, and he believed that in his own thinking he was responsive to this call. *Contributions* are Heidegger's attempt to think and articulate a historical experience of the coming to be and passing away of being in language in the performativity of his thinking and language.

Heidegger believed in the possibility of a thinking word that would arise purely from enowning and would simply say enowning in the most pure silencing.[37] This enowned saying would ground historically the truth of beyng in Da-sein, and by giving a historical site (the time-space of Da-sein) to the truth of beyng as enowning, it would contribute to an initiation of the other beginning of Western history. But according to Heidegger, this saying can be enowned only by beyng itself. And in our present era beyng occurs historically in such a way that it refuses a direct disclosure of its essence. This refusal resounds throughout *Contributions*. It is, one might say, the threshold through which Heidegger's thinking passes always anew in his attempt to think the truth of beyng.

One might doubt the possibility of a pure saying of beyng, or even denounce, like Derrida did, Heidegger's "hope" for a word that would purely say beyng in its truth as a metaphysical trait in Heidegger's thought; yet Heidegger's language of *Contributions* opens possibilities of thought and speech that allow for original transformations of thinking. The strongest points of his language seem to me to be his radical acknowledgment of the finitude and historicality of beyng in a language that moves away from transcendental and objective (or subjective) thought as he attempts to enact "what" is said in speech. The language of *Contributions* is a radical attempt to stay with the withdrawal and abysmal call that thinking experiences in its own historical (*geschichtlich*) originating event.

According to Heidegger there are only a few thinkers who are able to listen to beyng's silent call by facing and recognizing the abandonment of beyng. The others (the many) do not experience this abandonment. For them, beyng refuses the disclosure of its essential occurrence so radically that its silent call does not echo in the world. They do not think that a saying other than in propositions is possible. For them there is nothing but mere words, and no silence echoes in speech.

In Heidegger's own understanding, his struggle with language in *Contributions* has nothing to do with *his* "failure" (*Versagen*) to say beyng but rather with beyng's "failure" (self-refusal) in our present epoch. And yet, by acknowledging beyng's self-refusal, he already finds himself engaged by it. Doubtlessly Heidegger felt very much alone in his insight into poietic saying. His attempt to speak "from" (in responsive belonging to) the truth of beyng as enowning is, as he says, without precedent and without support from anything familiar.[38] In the fragmentary character of *Contributions*, in the silence surrounding the different sections, in the repetitions of the same words, in the continuous self-reflection upon and struggle with language, in all of this resounds an attempt to say beyng's historical occurrence that engages always anew the experience of beyng's self-refusal. This engagement requires that in each saying everything familiar is left behind. Thinking needs always to leap anew into a realm of thinking that has not been explored or said in this way before. This leap has always to be enacted anew because language tends to slip back into its metaphysical character: words tend to transform into mere words that make up propositions about given objects. And thus the performative character of these words, their enactment in an originating process of thinking (the echoing of their abysmal ground) gets lost.

This occurrence was certainly not totally unfamiliar to Nietzsche, as the opening sentences of the last section of his *Beyond Good and Evil* suggest:

> Alas, what are you after all, my written and painted thoughts! It was not long ago that you were still so colorful, young, and malicious, full of thorns and secret spices—you made me sneeze and laugh—and now? You have already taken off your novelty, and some of you are ready, I fear, to become truths: they already look so immortal, so pathetically decent, so dull! And has it ever been different?[39]

Notes

1. GA 65, 4; CP, 4. For bibliographical information on the texts referred to here, see the introduction to this volume, note 1.

2. See Martin Heidegger, "Letter on Humanism," in *Basic Writings,* ed. David Farrell Krell (San Francisco: Harper San Francisco, 1992), p. 231; "Brief über den Humanismus," in volume 9 of the Gesamtausgabe (hereafter GA 9) (Frankfurt am Main: Vittorio Klostermann, 1976), p. 328.

3. See *Contributions,* §§107, 132, 258, 266 (GA 65, 207, 250–51, 423–24, 466–69; CP, 144–45, 176–77, 297ff., 327–30).

4. *Contributions,* §132(GA 65, 250–51; CP, 176–77).

5. *Being and Time,* trans. Joan Stambaugh (Albany: State University of New York Press, 1996), p. 35; *Sein und Zeit* (Tübingen: Max Niemeyer Verlag, 1979), p. 39, note b.

6. For the difference between "Geschichtlichkeit" (historicality) and "Historie" (historiography), see in this volume Alejandro Vallega, "'Beyng-Historical Thinking' in Heidegger's *Contributions to Philosophy*."

7. Note that the translators of *Contributions* render *Seyn* with "be-ing" and not with "beyng." I prefer the latter, which renders the difference that Heidegger maintains between *Sein* (being in a transcendental perspective) and *Seyn* (being in the being-historical sense).

8. The material in brackets is my translation. Emad/Maly translate: "but which are misconstruable as the utterance of be-ing" [die . . . als Ausspruch des Seyns mißdeutbar sind]. It seems important to me to stress that "Ausspruch des Seyns" refers to propositional speech and stands in contrast to "Sagen des Seyns"; "-deuten" in the word "mißdeuten" does not have, in German, the sense of constructing but of interpreting or explaining.

9. GA 65, 83; CP, 58.

10. GA 65, 4; CP, 3.

11. See also Heidegger's reading of Stephan George's poem "Das Wort" in "Words" (*On the Way to Language*, trans. Peter D. Hertz and Joan Stambaugh (San Francisco: Harper San Francisco, 1982), pp. 139–56). In this reading, Heidegger shows how the essence of language and being appears precisely in the lack of the word of being.

12. See, for instance, §242, GA 65, 379; CP, 267.

13. GA 65, 107; CP, 75.

14. GA 65, 499; CP, 351.

15. If we read, in this context, Heidegger's famous expression in the "Letter on Humanism" — "language is the house of being" — we are brought to understand the "of" in terms of "belongs to." Being is not encapsulated in the house of "language"; rather, language is a sheltering (house) that belongs to being. In other words, being gives shelter through language.

16. This original sense of turning is to be distinguished from the so-called "turn" of Heidegger's thinking from *Being and Time* to his thinking of the thirties. Heidegger criticizes this talk about a turn in his thinking in the "Letter on Humanism."

17. See the passage from CP, §50, cited above.

18. See §202 of *Contributions*, in which Heidegger thinks being toward death in relation to the truth of beyng.

19. For a deeper understanding of this "coming into one's own," see especially §197 of *Contributions*.

20. §255, GA 65, 407; CP, 286–87.

21. See especially §255 of *Contributions*.

22. This differentiation, and with it a wider and more fundamental sense of language, is at play already in *Being and Time*, §§31–34 in the differentiation between discourse (*Rede*), interpretations (*Auslegung*), and statement (*Aussage*, implying speech). In §34 Heidegger emphasizes that discourse is equiprimordial with attunement (*Befindlichkeit*) and understanding (*Verstehen*), through which being is disclosed in Dasein. Discourse is understood as an articulation that is more fundamental than interpretation and statement (see *Being and Time*, trans. Stambrough, p. 150; *Sein und Zeit*, p. 161). This means that in *Being and Time*, Heidegger already understands language to constitute being's disclosure.

23. §276, GA 65, 499; CP, 351.

24. §§190 and 191, GA 65, 310–11; CP, 218–19.

25. The abysmal quality of Da-sein is stressed in §202 of *Contributions,* where Heidegger writes about the essential belongingness of *Weg-sein,* "being away," to Da-sein (literally translated: being here/there): "What here as ownmost shelteredness-concealedness advances into the t/here [*Da*]—the reciprocal relation of the t/here [*Da*] to the away that is turned toward the t/here [*Da*]—is the mirroring of the turning in the essential sway of being itself. The more originarily being is experienced in its truth, the deeper is the *nothing* as the abground at the edge of the ground" (GA 65, 325; CP, 228).

The translators of *Contributions* translate *Abgrund* with "abground." This allows them to keep a relation between "abground" (*Ab-grund*) and "ground" that Heidegger elaborates in, for instance, §242. According to the translators, the English word "abyss," which is the common translation for the German *Abgrund,* carries a too negative connotation and does not allow a relation to ground. Yet it seems to me that even if Heidegger maintains a relation between abyss and ground, in the sense that beyng as withdrawal calls for (enowns) a grounding (*not* a metaphysical ground), this grounding holds open precisely the groundlessness (in a metaphysical sense) of beyng, i.e., it holds open (in a beyng-historical sense) the truth of beyng as withdrawal. Thus, the German words "Abgrund," "Abgründigkeit," "abgründig," even in the relation to "Grund" and "Gründung," carry a meaning of radical "groundlessness" (in the metaphysical or everyday sense) that may be very well rendered with "abysmal."

26. The translators of *Contributions* translate *Inständigkeit* with "inabiding." I prefer to translate it with "insistence," because this word is a more literal translation. *Inständigkeit* carries the sense of *stehen in*: "standing in," and of *beständig,* "enduring." Further, "insistence" is used in common English (although in a slightly different sense) and carries a sense of struggle that is at play in Heidegger's thinking of the thirties.

27. GA 65, 14–15; CP, 11. The translators of *Contributions* translate *Scheu* with "deep awe." I do not think that the adjective "deep" is necessary here.

28. GA 65, 15; CP, 12. The necessity of reticence is stressed throughout *Contributions,* especially in reference to the "last God." This is an issue I can only point to here. Heidegger thinks of the Gods not as beings of any kind but rather in terms of their lack, a lack which the poet Hölderlin addresses. This lack dwells in beyng's self-refusal and in the call of beyng that compels humans to hold open and ground the truth of beyng in Da-sein. If we think of Da-sein as the open middle in this truth of beyng, Gods and humans are enowned, come to their own "essence" in their opposedness and at the same time in their encounter in this open middle. Da-sein provides the historical time-space for the differentiation (*Scheidung*) and encounter of humans and Gods. According to Heidegger, this encounter is still denied to us in the present era of technology, in which being refuses itself and remains forgotten. The grounding of Da-sein that Heidegger attempts to think and prepare in *Contributions* is meant to provide the time-space for this encounter. The *Augenblick* (moment) of this encounter occurs as what Heidegger calls the "passing of the last god" in the "great stillness."

29. §37, GA 65, 78; CP, 54–55.

30. The translators of *Contributions* render *Erschweigung* with "reticence in silence." The problem with this translation seems to me to be its loss of the verbal and executional character of the German word.

31. Emad/Maly translate: "Reticence in silence stems from the swaying origin of language itself" (§38, GA 65, 79; CP, 55).

32. In Heidegger, *Basic Writings*, pp. 139–212.

33. See §244, GA 65, 391; CP, 273; and §269, GA 65, 482–83; CP, 339–40.

34. See "The Origin of the Work of Art," in Heidegger, *Basic Writings*, pp. 198–99.

35. See Martin Heidegger, *Grundfragen der Philosophie. Ausgewählte "Probleme" der "Logik"* (winter semester 1937/38), ed. Friedrich-Wilhelm von Herrmann (Frankfurt am Main: Vittorio Klostermann, 1989), GA 45, 125–26, 133, 185–86.

36. See the Heidegger lecture that immediately preceded the elaboration of *Contributions* (*Hölderlins Hymnen "Germanien" und "Der Rhein"* (winter semester 1923/34), ed. Susanne Ziegler (Frankfurt am Main: Vittorio Klostermann, 1989), GA 39, 164, 286. See also Heidegger's later essay "Words," in *On the Way to Language*, especially pp. 155–56. For the importance of Hölderlin for Heidegger's transformation and thought on language in the thirties, see also Hans-Georg Gadamer, *Heideggers Wege. Studien zum Spätwerk* (Tübingen: J. C. B. Mohr, 1983), p. 23; Friedrich-Wilhelm von Herrmann, *Wege ins Ereignis* (Frankfurt am Main: Vittorio Klostermann, 1994), p. 228; G. Xiropaidis, "Einkehr in die Stille. Bedingungen eines gewandelten Sagens in Heideggers 'Der Weg zur Sprache,'" dissertation, University of Freiburg, 1991, p. 247.

37. §32, GA 65, 72; CP, 50.

38. GA 65, 8; CP, 6.

39. Friedrich Nietzsche, *Beyond Good and Evil*, trans. Walter Kaufmann (New York: Vintage Books, 1989), §296, p. 236.

5. The Event of Enthinking the Event

Richard Polt

What sort of thinking is Heidegger trying to carry out in *Contributions to Philosophy (From Enowning)*? Or should we rather say that the thinking at work here is carrying *him*—as a happening that sweeps him up in its force? Neither alternative seems right, for *Contributions* cultivates a way of thinking that tries to escape rigid distinctions between passivity and activity as well as between the thinking subject and the object of thought. Such thinking goes by various names: "inceptual thinking" (*das anfängliche Denken*, §§20–31), "ingrasping" (*Inbegrifflichkeit*, §27), "en-thinking" (*Er-denken*, §265), and even "philosophy" (e.g., §§14–17, 258–59).

The expression *Er-denken* is especially provocative. *Erdenken* ordinarily means "to think something up," "to invent it" (*erfinden*); by adopting the word *Erdenken*, Heidegger seems to imply a dimension of poetic inventiveness in his thought. But how—one might ask—is inventiveness compatible with truth? The conception of truth as correspondence (correct representation) tends to look upon inventiveness with suspicion: creativity must be subordinated to the way things are. This conception of truth has often been taken for granted in both the natural and the human sciences. As Heidegger puts it in "What Is Metaphysics?" all these disciplines interpret themselves as dedicated solely to representing beings themselves and *nothing else*—no inventions, no fantasies.[1] This sober dedication to *what is* may sound innocuous, but *Contributions* boldly asserts "the lack of truth in all science" (GA 65, 143; CP, 99).[2] The very word *Er-denken*, then, is part of Heidegger's assault on contemporary concepts of truth and thought, in which he accuses the apparently detached and neutral theories of modern research of imposing a domineering regime on beings by thinking of them only as "re-presented object[s]" (GA 65, 141; CP, 98).

However, Heidegger's enterprise of "enthinking" is more than just a reaction to modern research. According to him, the modern concept of representation is only one remote derivative of a fundamental event that shaped the "first beginning," or the early history of Western thought: the manifestation of being as presencing. In his "other beginning," Heidegger seeks a more radical understanding of being in terms of "be-ing" or "enowning." Enthinking forms part of this radical step beyond being as presencing and thus beyond *all* traditional theories of thinking and truth.

In order to understand the character and sources of enthinking, then, we must respond properly to enowning. But if Heidegger is right, we cannot do so by means of traditional, representational thought; we ourselves must engage in enthinking and thus allow enthinking and enowning to elucidate *themselves*. This makes it particularly hard to describe enthinking in accessible terms and nearly impossible to define it. However, I propose that we can approach enthinking as *the event of enthinking the event*. This implies that enthinking is not just *about* enowning but *is* enowning—if this claim is properly understood. In other words, enthinking is a happening that belongs inextricably to the happening of enowning itself, because enthinking is a crucial instance of the emergence and flourishing of meaning that is, in rough terms, what the word "enowning" indicates.

A fuller sense of enowning will emerge as we explore enthinking; before we go further, however, the following brief glosses of "enowning" and other key words may be useful. These glosses are intended not as self-evident definitions but as distillations of an interpretation of *Contributions* that I cannot fully justify in this essay. "Beings" (*das Seiende*, also translated by Emad/Maly as "a being") denotes all that shows up as making a difference to us, all that is revealed to us as other than nothing. "Being" (*Sein*) denotes the *meaning*[3] that beings in general have for us; Heidegger often emphasizes being's link to beings by speaking of it as "the being of beings."[4] "Dasein" denotes a condition in which the being of beings becomes a questionable issue for us, an issue that is at stake as a living problem.[5] "Be-ing" (*Seyn*) denotes the happening in which the being of beings is given to us as a questionable issue and we thus enter the condition of Dasein.[6] "Enowning" (*Ereignis*, formerly rendered by most translators as "appropriation" or "the event of appropriation") does not denote something beyond or separate from be-ing but rather the distinctive way in which be-ing holds sway or essentially happens (*west*).[7] Heidegger's question in *Contributions* is how be-ing holds sway, and his answer is: as enowning (GA 65, 30, 256, 260, 345; CP, 22, 181, 183, 241). Through enowning, the being of beings becomes our own, and at the same time, we are allowed to come into our own by entering Dasein.[8]

Even though enthinking can ultimately be understood only by engaging in enthinking itself, we can make some preliminary observations that should clarify what Heidegger is not and cannot be doing in *Contributions*—and so leave open the proper space for understanding what he *is* doing. We will begin, then, by taking a closer look at his criticism of traditional notions of truth, logic, and objectivity. In the first part of this essay, we will consider his critical genealogy of the conception of truth as correspondence, or correct representation; in the second part, we will turn to a Heideggerian critique of the conception of truth as an *identity* of knower and known. We will then be ready in the third part to understand in what sense enthinking can "be" enowning and, in the fourth part, to interpret both enthinking and enowning as *events*, and even as *one* event. The fifth and final part of the essay will investigate the prospects for enthinking.

From Be-holding to Representing

The first thing that enthinking is *not* is an exercise in *correspondence*, that is, an attempt to formulate and support judgments that correctly represent some object. Heidegger's objections to the concept of truth as correspondence emerge most clearly when we review his genealogy of this concept, which is also his story of the degeneration of the relation between thinking and being. The story is laid out clearly in *Introduction to Metaphysics* (1935), and rehearsed and elaborated in many subsequent texts, including *Contributions*. According to Heidegger, thinking and being were united in the pre-Socratics: these thinkers were not trying to represent being but were participating in a reciprocal relation between the self-manifestation of present entities (being as presencing) and the articulation of this manifestation (thinking). With Plato and Aristotle, however, thinking as the establishment of correct judgments seizes power and attempts to *determine* being.

Heidegger's readings of Parmenides and Heraclitus suggest an original unity of thinking and being. In Parmenides, Heidegger finds a way of thinking that is "the same" as its topic of thought, being (see Parmenides, fragment 3; fragment 8, lines 34–36). That is, in Heidegger's interpretation of Parmenides, thinking (or "apprehension," *Vernehmen*) and being belong together and need each other: "[a]pprehension happens for the sake of being. Being essentially unfolds as appearing, as stepping into unconcealment, only if unconcealment happens, only if a self-opening happens."[9] This self-opening takes place as apprehension.

Similarly, in Heraclitus, Heidegger finds a *logos* of thinking that is essentially responsive to the fundamental *logos* of being. The *logos* of being is the happening of primal *legein*—that is, "the originally gathering gatheredness that constantly holds sway in itself."[10] We might describe this as the way in which the cosmos arranges itself into a coherent articulation. The human activity of *legein* articulates this cosmic self-articulation in thought and speech—thus allowing cosmic *logos* to become manifest.

The pre-Socratic unity of thinking and being depends on an experience of being as coming to presence or presencing (*Anwesen*).[11] *Phusis*, which Heidegger interprets as the early Greek word for being, names presencing, that is, the self-display of beings as emerging and abiding.[12] The "sway" (*das Walten*) of this self-display requires primal gathering; thus primal *logos* is the same as *phusis*, or presencing.[13] Being as presencing requires the intimate participation of thinking, because in order for beings to present themselves, they must be "apprehended"—*perceived*, in a broad sense. In the first beginning, thinking is this gathering perceiving in which beings display themselves. Thinking, we might say, is a *be-holding* in which thought holds and is held by the potent manifestation of the coming to presence of beings.

Heidegger's accounts of pre-Socratic thought are easily mistaken for descriptions of what *he* considers to be authentic thinking. However, because being as presencing is not equivalent to be-ing as enowning, beholding is not enthinking; we cannot identify the thinking of the first beginning with the thinking that Heidegger is pursuing in the other beginning.[14] Nevertheless, his account of early Greek thought provides valuable *hints* of enthinking. (Similarly, presencing can provide an *indication* of the essential unfolding of be-ing as enowning, as long as we do not take it for granted as a final reference point.)[15] Like pre-Socratic beholding, enthinking will involve a reciprocity between thinking and that which it thinks.

But for now, let us follow Heidegger's story of the degeneration and loss of the original unity between being and thinking. According to *Contributions* and other writings of this period, the fatal step that initiates this degeneration is Platonism (§110). With Platonism, the happening of emerging into presence (*phusis*) fades into the background, while thought focuses on the beings that are present and on their distinctive, characteristic aspects (the *eidos* or *idea* of a being—its "form"). For instance, one might ask, "What is piety?" (as in Plato's *Euthyphro*) while neglecting to inquire into the way in which things, happenings, and people first emerge as holy or unholy, or indeed, as beings altogether. It is as if one became preoccupied with classifying and describing the patterns of foam on waves while forgetting about the waves themselves and the surging of the sea beneath them.[16]

The degeneration from *phusis* to *idea* entails a degeneration from an understanding of *logos* and truth as originary gathering to a notion of *logos* and truth as correct representation. "Because the *idea* is what really is, and the *idea* is the prototype, all opening up of beings must be directed toward equaling the prototype. . . . The truth of *phusis*—*aletheia* as the unconcealment that essentially unfolds in the emerging sway— now becomes . . . the correctness of apprehending as representing."[17] Before Platonism, truth was the coming-forth of beings as present within an open region; thinking was not correct representing but an acknowledgment of the sway of this coming-forth. Platonism, however, directs thinking toward grasping the *idea* correctly. Philosophy then loses sight of unconcealing as the *context* that allows present beings, their forms, and our representations of them to come forth.[18]

Heidegger's story goes on to explain how thinking comes to concentrate on forming correct *assertions* or *propositions*. That which can be correct or incorrect is taken to be an assertion, a judgment that attributes a predicate to a subject either appropriately or inappropriately.

In the inception, logos as gathering *is* the happening of unconcealment;

logos is grounded in unconcealment and is in service to it. But now, logos as assertion becomes the locus of truth in the sense of correctness. . . . Thus logos steps out of its originary inclusion in the happening of unconcealment in such a way that decisions about truth, and so about beings, are made on the basis of logos and with reference back to it—and not only decisions about beings, but even, and in advance, about being.[19]

What sort of decisions are these? First, philosophers now assume that in order for something to *be,* it must be amenable to representation in an assertion. This means that "logic," in the sense of the formal rules that govern what can and cannot be asserted, is taken to govern the being of beings itself. Furthermore, being is now conceived as beingness (*Seiendheit*)—the most general *idea,* the most universal characteristic of beings (see, e.g., §107). To think of being now means merely to establish correct propositions about beingness by means of logic.

Accordingly, when Aristotle tries to establish the basic characteristics of beings, he does so by way of the structures that distinguish what can be "said." The categories that characterize beings (such as substance, quality, and quantity) are "things said without combination," such as "horse," "white," and so on. Things said in combination—such as "the horse is white"—constitute an affirmation, and it is only in affirmations that truth or falsehood is possible.[20] Aristotle thus takes affirmations and their elements as indicators of the nature of beings as such, and assumes that truth primarily consists in the correctness of affirmations. What seems to have been lost is an appreciation of the happening of unconcealment.[21]

In the subsequent history of metaphysics, thinking no longer belongs to being but instead floats above it. The saying of the sway of being is supplanted by a kind of thought that supervises being and dictates to it.[22] Being itself is reduced to a few pallid, vacuous generalities that pretend to answer the question: What are beings as such? (the "guiding-question" of the first beginning, as Heidegger calls it [GA 65, 6; CP, 5]). These generalities (such as the categories) are then viewed as necessary, a priori structures, when in fact they are derivative—that is, these structures are abstracted from beings that are taken for granted as present and that are represented propositionally (GA 65, 183–84, 293, 458; CP, 128–29, 207, 322).

This story is assumed and briefly reviewed in the first part of §265 of *Contributions,* Heidegger's main discussion of enthinking. As Heidegger puts it here, philosophical thinking (inquiry into being) adopts, as its guideline, the propositional representation of beings (thinking in a narrow, representational sense). Thinking even becomes interpreted *exclusively* in terms of propositional representation (GA 65, 457; CP, 321–22). The consequences of this narrowing for Western philosophy are disastrous: we become incapable of a fresh experience of the disclosure of beings as such, and our thinking becomes inflexible and isolated from this event of disclosure. The consequences for human life in general are also disastrous, in Heidegger's view: modern research and "machination" operate according to this restricted mode of thinking, and under their sway, all beings tend to be reduced to mere objects to be inspected, measured, and exploited (see, e.g., §58).

The Identity of Knower and Known

If the domination of representational judgment has led to a fateful split between thinking and being, we might suppose that we should attempt to heal the split by seeking an original *sameness* of thinking and being. As the German idealists would put it, perhaps we could resolve the primal division (*Ur-teil*) by transcending representational judgments (*Urteile*) and finding a higher unity of knower and known, subject and object, thinker and what is thought. Truth would then be based not on a correspondence but on an identity.

But this, of course, would be nothing new in the Western tradition. If Heidegger's critique of the tradition is as radical as he intends it to be, then it must also apply to the notion of an identity of knower and known. In the third part of this essay, I will in fact argue that, in a sense, the event of enthinking *is* the event that it enthinks. However, this cannot be understood as any traditional identity of knower and known, any more than it can be understood as a case of correspondence. Heidegger's remarks on truth as identity are somewhat less extensive than his account of correspondence; however, he does give us the ingredients for a thorough critique.

First, let us briefly review the main appeals to an identity of the thinker and what is thought in Western philosophy. (We may leave aside the Parmenidean "sameness" of thinking and being, because in Heidegger's interpretation, as we have seen, this is not really an identity but a mutual dependence.) Aristotle's god is a pure act of self-beholding (*noesis noeseos*). The god is the most perfect of all substances because it is always a full performance of the most perfect activity (contemplation — an activity that requires no matter), and is contemplating that which is most perfect: itself.[23] The Cartesian *cogito* is a first-person analogue to this self-contemplation; it serves as the foundation of Descartes's metaphysics, just as Aristotle's god serves as the culmination of his. Kant strips the *cogito* of cognitive content and conceives of it as the transcendental unity of apperception — that is, as the ability of the subject to accompany all its cognitions with "I think" (*Critique of Pure Reason*, B131–32). However, this apparently empty ability turns out to be a necessary condition for all thinking and forms the basis of the legitimate employment of the categories (B143). Fichte conceives of self-consciousness as a *Tathandlung,* or primal, self-generating act. Hegel conceives of it as a much more inclusive and articulated process of externalization and re-internalization, or re-collection (*Erinnerung: Phenomenology of Spirit,* paragraph 808).

The Heideggerian critique of these moments in metaphysics has to begin by pointing out that they are all moments of more or less sophisticated *self-presence*—that is, moments in which the act of beholding is presented, or given, to itself. Even and especially the Hegelian system, with its elaborate deferrals, alienations, and mediations, is guided by *"the present that is present to itself"* (GA 65, 200; CP, 140) as a constant goal. In order to assess these moments, then, we must turn to Heidegger's critique of the interpretation of being as presencing.

Texts such as *Being and Time* and *The Basic Problems of Phenomenology* provide many elements of this critique, although they do not spell it out fully. If time is the "horizon" for being, then presence is only one mode of being, made possible by only one dimension of time.[24] Time cannot itself be understood in terms of presence, as a flux of momentarily present "nows." Instead, time must be interpreted in terms of the temporality of Dasein, whereby Dasein finds itself cast from a past that cannot be undone into a future that is subject to death. Because we are temporal, we are *engaged* in the past and the future: past and future are not mere absences but "ecstases" that lay claim to our own being, open up the present, and enable us to encounter other beings in their various modes of being, including presencing.[25]

Heidegger was unwilling to finalize this account, in part because it could be misunderstood as a transcendental project in the traditional sense. That is, it might seem that the limits of Dasein's being served as conditions of possibility for being itself, so that a fixed human nature would determine or "project" a circumscribed sense of being. In *Contributions,* he makes an effort to abandon all transcendental language in order to stress that "the enopening in and through [the] projecting-open [*Entwurf*] is such only when it occurs as the experience of thrownness [*Geworfenheit*] and thus of belongingness to be-ing" (GA 65, 239; CP, 169; cf. GA 65, 252, CP, 178). In other words, Dasein is not a fixed ground of meaning but finds itself already claimed by an inherited meaning and then (if it is properly Dasein) responds creatively to this inheritance. Thus, Dasein is "the preserver of the thrown projecting-open, *the grounded founder of the ground.*"[26] When Dasein properly takes up its thrown projection, the "there" (or "here") opens up. *Ereignis* is "the *appropriating event of the grounding of the there.*"[27] This grounding is not the establishment of a certain or absolute foundation, for be-ing can never be understood "definitively" (GA 65, 460; CP, 324)—be-ing can never be based on the perfectly correct representation of some perfectly present entity.

Despite the many differences between *Being and Time* and *Contributions,* the critique of the understanding of being as presencing still stands. Whether we think of time as a transcendental horizon or as "time-space" (§§238–42), the temporal opening of the "there" is prior to presencing.

How would this account apply to the identity of knower and known as a form of self-presence? For Heidegger, if such self-presence is taken as an absolute—as a moment that can function as a foundation or culmination of a system—then it violates the temporal character of both Dasein and be-ing. Dasein is more than present, because it is a radically temporal entity, at once having been and yet to be. Beings are present *to* Dasein only by virtue of temporality, which exposes Dasein to be-ing (the granting of the meaning of beings as such). Be-ing itself can never be present at all, because that would reduce it to an entity.[28] Instead, be-ing allows entities to be given to us as entities: it enables present beings to display themselves as present as well as enabling other types of beings to show themselves as such. This entire complex of Dasein and be-ing resists characterization in terms of presence or self-presence. It is not that there is no self-consciousness, but self-consciousness depends on enowning and cannot be the foundation of enowning.

Heidegger traces the importance of self-consciousness in modern philosophy back to the interpretation of philosophical thinking as such in terms of representational, propositional thinking (GA 65, 457; CP, 322). If we take representational consciousness as the guideline for philosophy, we naturally assign special importance to the consciousness of consciousness, the moment in which "I represent the representation [*die Vorstellung*—this could also mean the act or faculty of representing] and what it represents" (GA 65, 202; CP, 141). The extreme case of this trend is "[Hegel's] equating actuality (being) as [the] absolute with thinking as the unconditioned" (GA 65, 457; CP, 322). It seems clear that here we can find no model for the enthinking of be-ing: self-consciousness, as traditionally conceived, is too bound up with the narrow conceptions of being as presencing and thinking as representing. It appears that neither correct representation nor the identity of knower and known will work to describe enthinking.

The Reciprocity of Enthinking and Be-ing

Even though the notion of an identity of the thinker and what is thought seems to be fatally infected by traditional metaphysics, there are nevertheless some crucial passages in which Heidegger assimilates the thinking in which he is engaged to the topic of which he is thinking. The first section of *Contributions* says, "This saying does not stand over against what is [to be] said. Rather, the saying itself *is* the 'to be said,' as the essential swaying [*Wesung*] of be-ing" (GA 65, 4; CP, 4).[29] Later in part I, Heidegger writes, "the pathway of this enthinking of be-ing does not yet have a firm line on the map. The territory first comes to be . . . through and as the way of enthinking." This territory is where enowning takes place (GA 65, 86–87; CP, 60). Enthinking is not cartography—not the description of a given phenomenon—but an adventure; and this adventure is precisely what enthinking is "about." We can provisionally say, then, that the event of enthinking *is* the event that it enthinks. Enthinking *is* enowning as the essential swaying of be-ing.

But if enthinking cannot be conceived as an identity of the knower and the known, then what does it mean to claim that enthinking *is* enowning? The answer must depend on the unique character of this "is." It cannot express a conventional predication or identification or even a Hegelian "speculative proposition."[30] It indicates a distinctively Heideggerian theme, the reciprocal "turning" in which be-ing and Dasein come into their own (§§140, 141, 255)—the "[e]n-ownment of Da-sein by be-ing and [the] grounding [of] the truth of being in Da-sein" (GA 65, 262; CP, 184). Here, Dasein and be-ing attain the proper rapport that lets them flourish.

Our first clue to the character of the turning that joins enthinking and enowning is Heidegger's reading of the pre-Socratics. As we saw in the first part of this essay, the thinking of the "first beginning" is a beholding: it happens as a receiving of the self-manifesting, gathered presence of beings. Being as presencing needs beholding so that beings may appear; conversely, beholding needs being as presencing, because beholding *responds* to manifestation rather than supervising or dictating to it. We might suspect that enthinking and enowning, like beholding and presencing, must be inseparable. Heidegger even uses the word *Vernehmen* ("apprehension" or "*receiving*" [GA 65, 458; CP, 322]) to characterize enthinking, just as he had used it as a name for Greek beholding in *Introduction to Metaphysics*.

Still, enthinking is not the same as beholding, and enowning is not presencing. It is time for us to consider the differences more closely. The "guiding-question" of the first beginning is: "What is a being? [*Was ist das Seiende?*]" (GA 65, 75; CP, 52). In contrast, the "grounding-question" of the other beginning is, "*How does be-ing hold sway? [Wie west das Seyn?]*" (GA 65, 78; CP, 54). In other words, according to Heidegger, the Greeks were intent on beholding (and later, representing) *that which is, as such*. Their goal was to grasp the distinctive character of beings in general—"the being of beings" (GA 65, 75; CP, 52). His own question, however, asks how "be-ing" (*Seyn*) happens—that is, how the being of beings *is given to us* as an issue. He is trying to think of (or "from")[31] the radical happening that *enables the disclosure* of beings as such in the first place. "Be-ing [means] the ground in which all beings first of all and as such come to their truth" (GA 65, 76–77; CP, 53).

Contributions enthinks be-ing as enowning, or the event of appropriation. In this event, we are granted access to the being of beings as an issue; at the same time, we step into the condition of Dasein. To recognize enowning is to accept our mission as the thrown throwers (see GA 65, 304; CP, 214), to stand at our particular site and historical juncture, and creatively receive and wrestle with the meaning of what confronts us within our time-space. The happening of enowning enables presencing to take its place as *one* dimension of the being of beings. However, the fullness of be-ing as enowning can never be exhausted by presencing.

The Greeks, then, operated within a sense of being as presencing, without asking whether this was the only dimension of being, or how being becomes available to us in the first place. This means that Greek thought has certain limitations. For instance, at one point in his main account of enthinking, Heidegger argues that the Greek identification of that which *is* with that which is *one* is grounded in the primordial "gathering" that characterizes presencing (GA 65, 459; CP, 323).[32] As we saw in our review of the *Introduction to Metaphysics,* pre-Socratic thought responded to this gathering, or self-articulation of the cosmos. But if presencing is only "what is first and nearest [in] being's arising" (ibid.), then the thinking of Heraclitus and Parmenides is not enough. We need a kind of thinking that responds to the full happening of be-ing as enowning.

Despite this crucial difference from Greek thought, enthinking and be-ing, like beholding and presencing, belong together. First we will consider the way in which enthinking belongs to be-ing; this is the first aspect of the "turning." The "way of enthinking [is] attuned to and determined [*be-stimmt*] by be-ing itself" (GA 65, 86; CP, 60). In enthinking, "be-ing as enowning enowns thinking for itself" (GA 65, 464; CP, 327).[33] According to Heidegger, this distinguishes enthinking from the post-Platonic tradition of representational thought (GA 65, 458; CP, 322). Instead of attempting to form correct assertions about what is, in accordance with the logical rules that govern asserting, enthinking lets itself be drawn into the happening of be-ing. In this sense, enthinking casts aside every "'logical' interpretation of thinking" (GA 65, 460; CP, 324). Rather than following the canons of representation and imposing them on its "object," enthinking allows itself to be determined by the happening of be-ing.

We must not picture this as a slavish submission to some established *thing,* called "be-ing," that holds us in its grip—for the other aspect of the reciprocal "turning" is the dependence of be-ing on enthinking.

This dependence testifies to be-ing's "need" for Dasein (GA 65, 318; CP, 223). Dasein is required in order for be-ing to take place—for "Da-*sein* 'is' precisely [the] grounding [of] the truth of be-ing as enowning."[34] Dasein grounds be-ing through a *leap*, a free transition to the other beginning (GA 65, 460; CP, 324. Cf. §§115–24, 181). At the same time, this leap grounds Dasein itself, allowing it to own itself (GA 65, 303; CP, 214). Enthinking participates in this decisive event that grounds Dasein and be-ing: be-ing "must originarily and inceptually be opened up in a leap" so that be-ing can determine the character of enthinking.[35]

Here we should interpret the leap not as the arbitrary choice of a subject but as a venture that calls into question who the venturers are by exposing them to an event that is greater than they. Heidegger proposes that we can "open up the de-cision for ourselves in a leap"[36]—but here decision, strange as this may sound, is not a matter of choice (GA 65, 87; CP, 60). The hyphenated *Ent-scheidung* ("de-cision") indicates a division (*Scheidung*) that opens up a domain of unconcealment, separating it out from other such possible domains. The de-cision thus establishes both the mode in which beings are given and the way of being of Dasein—the one to whom beings are given. Choices, in contrast, are carried out by someone who is already an established self, and they concern "what is pregiven and can be taken or rejected" (GA 65, 100; CP, 69). De-cision, then, is prior to choice. It happens not within the will of a subject but as the essential sway of be-ing itself (GA 65, 92, 95, 103; CP, 64, 65–66, 71). The *leap* that opens up de-cision for us is neither an arbitrary choice nor a necessity that is forced upon us but a free venture in response to distress (*Not*).[37] Instead of surveying a set of given options and choosing one, we are motivated by an urgent plight that impels us to risk our own identity in a leap into the happening of be-ing, into a de-cision that will transform us and reveal beings in a new way. Leap before you look—Heidegger would say.[38]

Given the subtle fusion of daring and compliance in the leap, it seems clear that enthinking, as a form of leaping, can be neither a slave to be-ing nor be-ing's master. Instead, be-ing and enthinking are interdependent; they belong together because they both come into their own together. In this sense, enthinking "is" enowning.

The joint happening of be-ing and enthinking involves creativity—not as the willful imposition of a new form but as responsive engagement with the emergence of meaning. Be-ing is the happening in which meaning emerges; in other words, in the event of be-ing, the being of beings becomes a live issue for us. But this event cannot happen unless we dare to enthink it—that is, to leap into it as a possibility. It is not that we *make* be-ing but that we are needed as participants in the event of be-ing, the event that in turn affects how we, as thinkers, can think.

The process of drawing a landscape offers some parallels to the kind of "creativity" that is involved in enthinking. A landscape drawing, if it is a genuine work of art, not only represents a place—an entity—but also brings a meaning of this place (a facet of its being) to our attention. The artist elicits this meaning in the course of drawing. If the work of art succeeds, then a meaning of the landscape is brought to light. But this meaning was not simply "there" before the drawing was drawn, just waiting for someone to express it on paper; it was latent and vague, a possibility that was taken for granted. The meaning cannot come alive, then, cannot fully *happen,* until the drawing appropriates it—draws it out. At the risk of seeming to overemphasize creativity, we could say that the artist *in-vents* the meaning—as long as we use this word in its root sense of "coming upon" an opportunity in an innovative and illuminating way.[39] In-vention is not planning or willing; it is a venturesome openness to an experience in which the artist himself may be appropriated and transformed.

In-vention undercuts the opposition between creativity and truth. It is neither the discovery of a previously formed object nor the creation ex nihilo of a new form but the attentive cultivation of meaning. In-vention allows the meaning to flourish—and allows the finder of the meaning to flourish as well. Similarly, en-thinking (*Er-denken*) is the inventive finding (*Er-finden*) of be-ing, or the granting of the meaning of beings as such.

Enthinking *is* enowning. This "is" means that enthinking is one of the happenings that elicit the very upsurge of meaning that sustains invention. Enthinking is a signal way in which the truth of be-ing is fostered. Instead of functioning as a moment of self-presence, enthinking is a moment of thrown throwing in which we enown the event of be-ing that enowns us. In order to enter into Dasein—to awaken to beings as such and to stand steadfastly in the openness of the there—we must preserve and wrestle creatively with be-ing. Conversely, be-ing needs such preservation and struggle so that a site for be-ing may emerge. Dasein and be-ing thus happen together—and enthinking is central to this event.

Event and Uniqueness

We still have further to go, however, in exploring enthinking as a *happening,* as the event of enthinking the event of enowning. It is the event-character of enthinking and enowning that ultimately sets them apart from Greek beholding and presencing and constitutes the crux of *Contributions to Philosophy.*

One can imagine an immediate and serious objection to this claim: enowning is not an event at all. Enthinking may be an event, one might object—the occurrence of a particular human act—but enowning functions as the *precondition* for the emergence of all human acts; it first allows acts and happenings, along with other beings, to manifest themselves. Heidegger himself, more than two decades after *Contributions,* writes, "Appropriation . . . cannot be represented either as an occurrence [*Vorkommnis*] or [as] a happening [*Geschehen*]."[40]

Although I cannot respond fully to this objection in this essay, I believe Heidegger's late comments can be misleading as a guide to *Contributions.* It is true that *Ereignis* is not just an occurrence within the domain of beings, such as a sunrise, an auto accident, or a battle.[41] *Ereignis* is not a being but that which enables beings to manifest themselves as such. But what can serve as such an enabling ground? It cannot be a transcendental structure, a formal a priori framework that functions as a condition of the possibility of experience, if we take seriously Heidegger's rejection of transcendental thinking (see §§122, 184). It cannot be an essence or a universal, if we take seriously Heidegger's critique of the Platonic *idea* and all its avatars (§110). But if enowning is neither a particular entity nor a universal, how can we think of it? I propose that enowning, at least as it is thought in *Contributions,* can indeed be considered an event, or rather *the* event. My purpose in making this claim is not to reduce enowning to the familiar concept of event but to use some aspects of the familiar concept as an entry to enowning.

What is an event? In most cases, what we call events are interactions between entities, such as the heating of a stone by the sun. In more radical events, an entity comes to be or passes away—for example, a hawk kills a mouse. In still another kind of event, an entity's way of being is reinterpreted and thus transformed. For instance, a shy girl takes part in a school play, comes to present herself as outgoing, and thus becomes outgoing. We could call this a *reinterpretive* event.

Reinterpretive events cannot be reduced to a theoretical description of changes within a mathematicized space-time continuum, because they are essentially concerned with *meaning.*[42] We could take reinterpretive events as turning points, or critical junctures, in the unfolding of meaning. These junctures open up and close off ways of being-in-the-world—and thus of understanding oneself and other beings. A reinterpretive event heightens or resolves a tension that affects its protagonist's way of interpreting herself and her world—her way of being someone. Such events can happen only for an entity whose own being is "at issue" for it and who is thus essentially self-interpreting. According to *Being and Time* (§§4, 9), this entity is precisely Dasein.

Reinterpretive events hold promise as an initial approach to *Ereignis.* But if *Ereignis* can be understood as something like a reinterpretive event, then it would have to happen as *the* reinterpretive event—the event that makes possible interpretation itself.[43] *Ereignis* takes place as the critical moment in which Dasein and its "there" first emerge. In *Ereignis,* an order of unconcealment is in-vented (innovatively elicited). This happening of Dasein and its "there" ranks higher than all other reinterpretive events, which must take place *within* an established time-space.[44]

The event of enowning is not the sort of occurrence that is usually chronicled by historians and journalists—this, I take it, is what Heidegger is trying to distinguish from *Ereignis* in his late remarks. Enowning is marked by its *uniqueness.* Moments of enowning happen only once, for the first and last time. They can never be reproduced or represented, although they may serve as "beginnings" that *initiate* a domain of reproducibility and representability.[45] These moments can only be *retrieved* in a creative re-engagement: *"Only what is unique [das Einmalige, what happens once only] is retrievable and repeatable"* (GA 65, 55; CP, 39). Throughout *Contributions,* Heidegger insists on this historical uniqueness of be-ing. In §265, devoted to enthinking, he insists that be-ing has a "respective [or temporally particular, *jeweilige*] singularity and most originary historicity" (GA 65, 460; CP, 324). In the metaphysical tradition, beingness is a pale universal; but in the other beginning each happening of be-ing is richly unique, and for this reason it must strike us with a "unique estrangement and opacity," pervaded by the unfamiliarity of "the one-time-only and this-time-only" (GA 65, 463; CP, 326). The challenge is to experience "the nonderivable thrust [*Stoß*] of be-ing itself, which is to be seized in its purest 'that'" (GA 65, 464; CP, 326).

For more evidence of the event-character of enowning, one should consider the following passages together: "[O]nly the greatest occurrence [or happening, *Geschehen*], the innermost enowning, can still save us. . . . But now the greatest event [*Ereignis,* enowning] is always the beginning" (GA 65, 57; CP, 40). "The *beginning* is *be-ing itself* as enowning" (GA 65, 58; CP, 41). "All beginnings . . . withdraw from mere history [*Historie*], not because they are super-temporal and eternal, but because they are greater than eternity; they are the *thrusts* of time [*die Stöße der Zeit*]" (GA 65, 17; CP, 13). From these passages we can gather that enowning *takes place*—not as an ordinary process within time but as the inceptual happening of time itself.[46] We can think of time itself as "happening" only if we manage to separate the notion of happening from the notion of change within the framework of a timeline. Heidegger thinks of primordial happening not in terms of change but in terms of the play of belonging and estrangement, uniqueness and reproducibility.

We saw in the third part of this essay that the event of enthinking *is* the event that it enthinks. In other words, enthinking both elicits and depends on the emergence of the meaning of beings—and this coming-to-have-meaning is precisely the event of be-ing. Now, what implications does the uniqueness of such a happening have for the character of enthinking?

The implications are serious, for we are used to associating "thinking" with "the representation of something in general, and thus the representation of the unity of different [individuals] that are subordinate to a genus" (GA 65, 459; CP, 323, translation modified. Cf. GA 65, 63; CP, 44). In short, we assume that to think is to generalize—and philosophy is supposedly the most general, most abstract thinking of all. What would it mean to think uniquely about the unique? Surely this is not to limit ourselves to particular facts, such as "This apple is sweet." Every concept normally available to us is a generalization, so such a thought still traffics in universals—"apple," "sweet," and even "this," which, as Hegel argues, is the most indeterminate and thus most abstract concept of all.[47] Heidegger cannot intend to forbid us to think in broad terms, to look for deep connections, or to identify lasting grounds.

What matters is staying attentive to *how* we are finding these patterns. If we find them as simply given, as present, then we have not taken any essential step beyond Greek beholding. But if we experience the in-vention of the patterns, we can enter enthinking. Again, "invention" does not mean creating forms willfully, but cultivating and articulating meanings as they come forth. Meanings come forth in unique moments when enthinking and be-ing let each other happen.

Such moments of enthinking are rare, and they cannot be reproduced. As the happening of historically unique be-ing, a statement or word that is enthought should not be taken out of context and parroted; its sense lies in a move made at a particular moment and not in some conjunction of ahistorical concepts.[48] The only way to build upon a former achievement of enthinking is to retrieve it anew, letting it resonate in one's *own* place and moment. Thus Heidegger warns his readers: "[one] must be able to think what has been attempted *in such a way* that he thinks that it comes unto him from far away while still being what belongs closest to him" (GA 65, 8; CP, 7).

The Prospects for Enthinking

What we have said concerning enthinking may seem far too nebulous and far too arbitrary. Is there any evidence that enthinking can be *achieved*, that anyone can enable be-ing to take place in a way that guides thought? And what are the standards for judging an attempt at enthinking?

In response to this last question, Heidegger would say that there *are no* set standards. Whereas representational thought takes assertion and logic as its guidelines, in enthinking no guideline at all "comes into play" (GA 65, 458; CP, 322). If enthinking is truly originary, then it cannot be subjected to some criterion external to the topic that is in-vented in the event of enthinking. Enthinking is determined *only* by what is to

be thought (GA 65, 462; CP, 325). Be-ing attunes enthinking to itself, as
be-ing emerges in the event of enthinking; there is no external method
or test that can pass judgment on this event.

This may appear to be an irresponsible position; Heidegger's thought
cannot be verified or falsified by public standards, so it may seem arbitrary and illogical. However, he retorts that logic is "the *least* rigorous and
least serious procedure" when it comes to be-ing. By imposing a regime
of assertibility on be-ing, logical thinking wrongly presupposes that
assertion provides our primary access to be-ing (GA 65, 461; CP, 324).[49]
When we try to confront fundamental questions, there is no avoiding a
leap, a Promethean venture with no logical safety net; as Heidegger puts
it, there is no "essential view into philosophy which would not include
the 'titanic' in its view" (GA 65, 462; CP, 325).

En-thinking, in-ventive thinking, should no more be judged by a set
standard than a poem should be judged solely according to rules of
versification. However, this does not mean that enthinking is exempt
from all judgment. A poem can certainly fail even it conforms to formal
rules: it can fail to *find* its voice or its theme. There is, then, a kind of ap-
titude or appropriateness that sets a standard for the poem, beyond all
rules. Similarly, enthinking has to find its own appropriateness. The
"project" of enthinking is not subject to arbitrary whims, because it
must learn to adapt itself to the new dimension that it itself opens up
(GA 65, 56; CP, 39). Accomplished thinkers have a tact and sureness in
their performance, comparable to the sureness of a dancer or musician.
This "self-certainty" is what Heidegger interprets as *style* (GA 65, 69; CP,
48). In enthinking, as in art, there is a "stylistic" *rigor,* a demand for pre-
cision, that is not the rigor of representational propositions (GA 65, 65;
CP, 45).

We might grant this point but still wonder whether Heidegger is
actually *engaged* in enthinking. He often describes his thought as preparatory (cf. GA 65, 465; CP, 327) or transitional, on the way to "simple
doing" (GA 65, 463; CP, 325). *Contributions* claims to fall short of the status of "work": they are merely a premonition of a phantom text that
would be titled *Das Ereignis,* a text that exists only as a possibility
opened by this one (GA 65, 77; CP, 54).[50] At first glance, nearly all of
§265, and much of the book as a whole, may seem to be *about* enthinking rather than a "simple doing" of it. But if enthinking cannot be represented or judged by other modes of thought, this would be a waste of
time; a *representation* of enthinking would automatically *mis*represent it.

Such an assessment would be ungenerous, however. Heidegger does
find the words to describe his theme in an original and powerful way
(such as the word *Er-denken* itself). And enthinking may, above all, be
the art of *finding words,* the art of "naming" be-ing (GA 65, 460, 463; CP,
324, 326). As the name *Erdenken* suggests, enthinking is poetic; that is,

it practices the art of finding names. Poetic naming, unlike truth as correspondence, does not simply identify present aspects of present beings by correctly assigning pre-established predicates to them. In poetry, an inherited word is adapted to the unique exigencies of a moment. The word then *names* that which shows itself at this moment, instead of simply categorizing it. The name helps what it names to come forth in its singularity. Naming, then, is not a conventional use of concepts but an inceptual way of conceiving, perhaps the way indicated by Heidegger's word *Inbegriff* (§27).[51] In this happening, the name and the named become engaged: the named is elicited by the connotations of the name, but at the same time the connotations are transformed to fit the named. The name and the named come to own each other. This is a process of mutual adjustment and simultaneous emergence—a matchmaking and a marriage, we might say, rather than a representational correspondence. It is no wonder that Heidegger names a poet, Hölderlin, when he is impelled to say "what" is happening in enowning (GA 65, 463–64; CP, 326): poetic naming is the happening of enowning in language, and for Heidegger, Hölderlin is a master of such naming.

Heidegger does engage in enthinking, then, whenever he arranges an appropriate poetic engagement between name and named. Perhaps this essay, too, has engaged in enthinking, if its names (such as "be-holding" and "in-venting") have been appropriate. Names are appropriate when appropriation, or enowning, happens—that is, when naming and the thinking that abides in it happen reciprocally with the emergence of meaning.

But do we have words that are capable of naming *be-ing*? Heidegger's goal in *Contributions* is to enthink be-ing without basing it on beings (GA 65, 75–76; CP, 52–53). He wants to in-vent the event of giving without relying on the given. The problem for this project is that "all language is still the language of beings" (GA 65, 78; CP, 54). Our vocabulary, our repertoire of names, is so bound to beings that we may find ourselves at a loss for words when we try to speak the language of pure be-ing. "[W]herever and whenever en-thinking of be-ing succeeds, it reaches a rigor and keenness of historicity for the saying of which the language is still lacking, i.e., the naming and being-able-to-hear that is adequate to be-ing" (GA 65, 463; CP, 326). But if the language is lacking, can enthinking succeed at all? Do we have any hope of developing such a language?

In response to this problem, Heidegger proposes that we must "say the most nobly formed language in its simplicity and essential force . . . say the language of beings as the language of be-ing" (GA 65, 78; CP, 54). However, he does not explain how this "as" works—how we can shift words from naming entities to naming be-ing. I suggest that we should think of this not as a leap onto a wholly other plane, or a symbolizing of the unseen by means of the seen, but rather as a rediscovery of a happening that is already at work in our experience of beings themselves. We must appreciate not only given beings, but the *giving* of them *as* beings. Then the beings named are not simply taken for granted as more of the same—data, cases of "something." Instead, they come forth in their surprising uniqueness, in the wonder that beings are granted at all. This is perhaps what it means to "shelter" the truth of be-ing in beings (§§243–47).

While we should not confuse speaking of be-ing with representing facts about beings, the notion of a language of pure be-ing is probably a chimera. What *is* available is a way of speaking and thinking that describes beings while cultivating and attending to their coming forth as beings. Enthinking runs the risk of sterility or silence unless it keeps returning to the wealth of beings themselves in order to appreciate the unique ways in which they are given. This is not to fall again into the pedestrian inspection and labeling of what is present but to practice the art of finding appropriate names, the names that not only identify beings but also elicit the happening in which beings become manifest as such. What we need is not only a leap into be-ing but leaps that return repeatedly to make contact with beings. To leap and leap again, moving forward, is to run. To break into a run is to finish the transition from the pedestrian to the event of simple doing, the event in which the world breaks open for us and becomes our own as we open to it.

> He picks up speed and seems to lose his gangliness, the slouchy funk of hormones and unbelonging and all the stammering things that seal his adolescence. He is just a running boy, a half-seen figure from the streets, but the way running reveals some clue to being, the way a runner bares himself to consciousness, this is how the dark-skinned kid seems to open to the world, how the bloodrush of a dozen strides brings him into eloquence.[52]

Notes

1. "What Is Metaphysics?" in *Pathmarks,* ed. William McNeill (Cambridge: Cambridge University Press, 1998), p. 84.

2. For bibliographical information on the texts referred to here, see the introduction to this volume, note 1.

3. With the word "meaning"—which I will use frequently in this essay—I indicate the web of ways in which beings make sense to us. For example, beings make sense to us as people, as animals, as tools, as present-at-hand objects, as artworks, as gods, and as earth. These ways-of-sense (to coin a term) are inseparable from our dwelling in a world, an open region within which we can encounter beings and distinguish them from nonbeings. None of these ways in which beings make sense is itself *a being;* none of them can simply be reduced to what is given as and in the entity itself. Instead, these ways-of-sense are modes

of *access* to beings. Together, they constitute the *being* of beings: that is, they allow beings as a whole and as such to make a difference to us. We might also refer to the entire web of ways-of-sense as the *import* of beings. The word means both "importance" and "meaning." To say that something has meaning is also to say that it has some importance, even if it is almost negligible. An utterly unimportant thing goes utterly unnoticed; it is, for us, a nonbeing.

4. One particular way in which the being of beings has been interpreted in the tradition is as beingness (*Seiendheit*), or the most universal characteristics of beings (GA 65, 111–12, 293, 425, 458; CP, 78, 207, 299, 322). The being of beings can also be thought of in a way that allows for more flexibility and plurality (see note 3 above). However, this still does not address the question of *be-ing*.

5. Unlike *Being and Time, Contributions* presents Dasein as a *possibility* for human beings: see §§193–95, 201. Dasein, in *Contributions,* is roughly equivalent to what *Being and Time* called authentic existence. The being of beings is always given to humanity, but it is normally taken for granted. Only when we recognize this gift as a gift, and thus as worthy of question, do we enter into the condition of Dasein.

6. On *Sein* vs. *Seyn,* see GA 65, 436; CP, 307. Heidegger does not consistently follow the distinction; sometimes he uses *Sein* in a broad or unspecified sense that includes what I have described as *Seyn.* In this essay, however, I will maintain a consistent distinction.

7. Although the verb *wesen* calls for an interpretation of its own (see *Contributions,* §§164–67), for our purposes we can simply recognize it as a word for what be-ing "does"; *wesen* allows us to avoid the locution "be-ing is," which appears to reduce be-ing to an entity (however, on this locution, see also note 28 below).

8. Although in my view "enowning" is a successful coinage, my interpretation of *Ereignis* as a *happening* of ownness implies that the more traditional translation "event of appropriation" is also acceptable. On whether *Ereignis* can be said to happen, see the fourth part of this essay.

9. *Introduction to Metaphysics,* trans. Gregory Fried and Richard Polt (New Haven: Yale University Press, 2000), p. 106. My citations from this text follow the pagination of *Einführung in die Metaphysik* (Tübingen: Max Niemeyer Verlag, 1953); this pagination is provided in the margins of the translation. I have removed the capitalization from "being" in order to match Emad/Maly.

10. Ibid., p. 98.

11. Ibid., pp. 46, 54, 78, 96.

12. Ibid., p. 11.

13. Ibid., p. 100.

14. "With enowning, we are no longer thinking in a Greek way at all" (Mit dem Ereignis wird überhaupt nicht mehr griechisch gedacht): "Seminar in Le Thor 1969," in *Vier Seminare* (Frankfurt am Main: Vittorio Klostermann, 1977), p. 104.

15. "Without being grasped as such, essential swaying [*Wesung*] is presencing [*Anwesung*]" (GA 65, 189; CP, 132). In other words, presencing is one, but only one, dimension of enowning.

16. I must add that despite the possible merits of Heidegger's story as an

interpretation of Platonism, it is inadequate as an interpretation of Plato. Platonic dialogues, when read attentively, display both the limits of the search for the forms and the roots of this search in the concrete dramas of human life. In the *Phaedo*, for example, Plato's Socrates describes the "hypothesis" of the forms as a second-best way of trying to discover a basis for judgments of good and bad (99c); on his dying day, he insists that the hypothesis is still questionable (107b), and he remains open to myth and poetry as alternative ways of making sense of life (61a).

17. *Introduction to Metaphysics,* p. 141. Compare Heidegger's more extended discussion in "Plato's Doctrine of Truth" (1940), in *Pathmarks;* see esp. pp. 176–77. For *Contributions'* account of the Platonic origin of truth as correctness, see §§209–11.

18. Heidegger eventually abandoned the view that Plato was the turning point in the Greek conception of truth: see "The End of Philosophy and the Task of Thinking" (1964), in *On Time and Being,* trans. Joan Stambaugh (New York: Harper & Row, 1972), p. 70. But for our purposes, it does not matter whether his account of Plato is right; the point is to grasp the general distinction between thinking that belongs to being as presencing and thinking that is merely representational.

19. *Introduction to Metaphysics,* p. 142.

20. *Categories,* chapter 4, in *Aristotle: Selections,* trans. Terence Irwin and Gail Fine (Indianapolis: Hackett, 1995), p. 3.

21. For Aristotle's definition of a truth as "a statement of that which is that it is, or of that which is not that it is not," see *Metaphysics* Γ, 7, 1011b26 (*Aristotle's Metaphysics,* trans. Hippocrates G. Apostle [Grinnell: Peripatetic Press, 1979], p. 70). Aristotle does, however, recognize a secondary sense of truth that retains a connection to unconcealment: in the case of noncomposite things, such as "horse," "truth about each of these is to apprehend [*thigein*] it or to assert it (for affirmation [*kataphasis*] and assertion [*phasis*] are not the same), and ignorance of it is not to apprehend it": *Metaphysics* Θ, 10, 1051b24–25 (*Aristotle's Metaphysics,* p. 159). *Phasis* means the conceptual grasping of a being; *kataphasis* is a proposition, affirmative or negative. Aristotle adds, "the truth about each such [noncomposite] being is the conception [*noein*] of it, and there is neither falsity nor mistake about it but only ignorance": *Metaphysics* Θ, 10, 1052a2 (*Aristotle's Metaphysics,* p. 159). We could say that this sort of truth is a kind of unconcealment. However, Aristotle assumes that if noncomposite beings are unconcealed at all, they are fully and directly unconcealed according to their *eidos*. Heidegger would presumably object that the *eidos* emerges only within the context of the unconcealment of a world and that the emergence of this world also always involves a dimension of concealment.

22. One modern example of the subordination of ontology to logic is Kant's derivation of his categories from the logical forms of judgment; see *Critique of Pure Reason,* A79–81/B104–107.

23. See *Metaphysics* Λ, 9. Another type of identity between thinker and what is thought is found in the doctrine of *De Anima* that the human intellect becomes the same as the forms that it understands.

24. Heidegger refers to this enabling dimension as *praesens: The Basic Problems of Phenomenology,* trans. A. Hofstadter (Bloomington: Indiana University Press, 1982), p. 305.

25. On "ecstasis," see, e.g., *Sein und Zeit*, 7th ed. (Tübingen: Max Niemeyer Verlag, 1953), pp. 329, 350–51, 365.

26. "der Wahrer des geworfenen Entwurfs, *der gegründete Gründer des Grundes*" (GA 65, 239; CP, 169).

27. Emad/Maly translate the phrase "das *Ereignis der Dagründung*" as "*enowning the grounding of the t/here*" (GA 65, 247; CP, 174). In my opinion, passages such as this should retain the sense of a unique happening that the German naturally suggests. See section 4 below.

28. Heidegger does experiment with the formulation "be-ing *is*" (GA 65, 472–73; CP, 332–33); however, this is simply a new way of distinguishing be-ing from entities—for if be-ing *is*, then we must utter the paradox that entities are *not* (GA 65, 472; CP, 332).

29. Cf. *Introduction to Metaphysics*, p. 65: "philosophy has no object at all. Philosophy is a happening that must at all times work out [*erwirken*] being for itself anew." Similar statements appear in *Besinnung* (GA 66, composed 1938/39). "[The] word [of philosophy] never merely means or designates what is to be said, but rather is be-ing itself in the saying" (ihr Wort nie das Zusagende nur bedeutet oder bezeichnet, sondern im Sagen das Seyn selbst ist [GA 66, 51]). "Philosophy . . . *is* the imageless saying 'of' be-ing itself, a saying that does not express be-ing; instead, be-ing essentially unfolds as this saying" (Die Philosophie . . . *ist* die bildlose Sage 'des' Seyns selbst, welche Sage das Seyn nicht aussagt, als welche Sage es vielmehr west [GA 66, 64]).

30. In a speculative proposition, such as "substance is subject" or "God is love" (when understood in a Hegelian way), two concepts come to achieve a mutual determination. The "is" here functions, so to speak, as a transitive verb that allows each of the terms it joins to realize itself through the other. (See *Phenomenology of Spirit*, preface, paragraphs 60–62.) This is not completely unlike Heidegger's thought, but Heidegger would object that Hegel's speculative propositions are ruled by his *logic* and are thus part of the tradition of logical-representational thinking (cf. GA 65, 461; CP, 324–25). For Heidegger's explanation of the speculative proposition, see, for example, "Seminar in Le Thor 1968," in *Vier Seminare*, p. 63.

31. See Heidegger's explanation of the subtitle, or "essential heading," *Vom Ereignis:* "Vom Ereignis er-eignet ein denkerisch-sagendes Zugehören zum Seyn" (GA 65, 3). Curiously, Emad/Maly's rendition of this phrase obscures the evidence that supports their translation of the first word in the subtitle as "from" rather than "of" or "on." The translation reads: "a thinking-saying which is enowned by enowning and belongs to be-ing" (CP, 3). A more accurate translation would run: "From enowning there en-owns a belonging to be-ing, a belonging that thoughtfully says."

32. On gathering (*Sammlung, Versammlung*) as belonging to the first beginning, see GA 65, 264, 272; CP, 186, 191.

33. This phrase (*das Seyn als Ereignis sich das Denken ereignet*) suggests that the happening of be-ing involves the springing-forth of enthinking in such a way that be-ing and enthinking become each other's "own," or are intimately given to each other. Cf. GA 66, 357–58: "The term [enthinking] is meant to indicate that this thinking is en-owned by be-ing itself, and this en-owning constitutes what is ownmost to history" (Der Name soll anzeigen, daß dieses Denken vom Seyn selbst er-eignet ist, welche Er-eignung das Wesen der Geschichte ausmacht).

34. GA 65, 455; CP, 320; translation modified to reflect Heidegger's emphasis in "Da-*sein*."

35. GA 65, 458. I translate *"ersprungen werden"* as "be opened up in a leap" rather than "arise" (see CP, 323). Heidegger's word suggests that the leap enables be-ing to happen, and his emphasis on *er-* is probably meant to parallel *Er-denken*. Cf. *Introduction to Metaphysics*, p. 5: "the leap [*Sprung*] of this questioning attains its own ground by leaping, performs it in leaping [*er-springt, springend erwirkt*]. According to the genuine meaning of the word, we call such a leap that attains itself as ground by leaping an originary leap [*Ur-sprung*]: an attaining-the-ground-by-leaping."

36. The phrase is "uns die Ent-scheidung er-springen" (GA 65, 88), rendered by Emad/Maly as "give rise to de-cision" (CP, 61).

37. *Not* could also be translated as "urgency" or "emergency." Necessity (*Notwendigkeit*) is always based on *Not* (GA 65, 45, 97; CP, 32, 67). The *Not* at issue in the transition to the other beginning is *die Not der Notlosigkeit*, the distress of the lack of distress (GA 65, 11, 107, 119, 234–35, 237; CP, 8, 75, 83, 166, 168). The question of being has lost its urgency—and this situation is itself an emergency.

38. The German counterpart to our "look before you leap" is *erst wägen, dann wagen* (weigh before you dare). Heidegger, in contrast, writes: "Who leaps over this weighing and dares the unweighable and restores beings to be-ing?" (Wer überspringt dieses Wägen und wagt das Unwägbare und stellt das Seiende in das Seyn zurück? [GA 65, 238]). Emad/Maly translate: "Who surpasses this weighing and ventures the unweighable and defers beings to be-ing?" (CP, 168).

39. Compare Heidegger's suggestion that "imagination" (*Einbildung*) can be understood as enowning itself—the happening of the clearing (GA 65, 312; CP, 219).

40. "The Way to Language," in *On the Way to Language*, trans. Peter D. Hertz (San Francisco: Harper & Row, 1971), p. 127. Cf. *On Time and Being*, trans. Stambaugh, p. 20: "What the name 'event of Appropriation' names can no longer be represented by means of the current meaning of the word; for in that meaning 'event of Appropriation' is understood in the sense of occurrence and happening—not in terms of Appropriating as the extending and sending which opens and preserves" (Wir können das mit dem Namen "das Ereignis" Gennante nicht mehr am Leitfaden der geläufigen Wortbedeutung vorstellen; denn sie versteht "Ereignis" im Sinne von Vorkommnis und Geschehnis—nicht aus dem Eignen als dem lichtend verwahrenden Reichen und Schicken). Cf. also *Identity and Difference*, trans. Joan Stambaugh (New York: Harper & Row, 1969), p. 36: "The term event of appropriation here no longer means what we would otherwise call a happening, an occurrence" (Das Wort Ereignis meint hier nicht mehr das, was wir sonst irgendein Geschehnis, ein Vorkommnis nennen).

41. Thus, the thought of *Ereignis* is not "an interpretation of being as 'becoming'" (GA 65, 472; CP, 332). Heidegger routinely dismisses the usual notion of becoming as superficial (see, e.g., *Introduction to Metaphysics*, pp. 73–74). This might seem surprising in a philosopher who links being and time. However, Heidegger conceives of time not primarily in terms of change but in terms of phenomena such as thrownness and projection. Time as a medium in which things come to be and pass away is merely a framework for our representation

of entities; primordial temporality, the temporality of thrownness and projection, is deeper than all representation (cf. *Being and Time*, §§78-82; GA 65, 371, 382, 472; CP, 259, 267, 332). Of course, this does not mean that Dasein or being are static—simply that the concept of becoming is not powerful enough to interpret them adequately.

42. For this reason, reinterpretive events belong within dramas that call for *narrative* interpretation, not "objective" inspection. Paul Ricoeur has explored this problematic in his *Time and Narrative*, trans. K. Blamey and D. Pellauer (Chicago: University of Chicago Press, 1984 [vol. 1], 1985 [vol. 2], 1988 [vol. 3]). For a summary of Ricoeur's account of the narrative "refiguration" of time, see his "Narrated Time," in *A Ricoeur Reader: Reflection and Imagination*, ed. Mario J. Valdés (Toronto: University of Toronto Press, 1991), pp. 338-54.

43. One could make a case that the best translation of *das Ereignis* is *"the* enowning." The definite article suggests the uniqueness that, as we are about to see, Heidegger insistently ascribes to *das Ereignis*. It is even possible to argue that the enowning has never yet happened, and can happen only once—as the event that may come to pass in the transition to the other beginning. However, in what follows I will assume that enowning, even though it is not a universal *eidos*, can be discerned as a dimension of more than one event, as a happening that is shared by more than one "beginning," each of which nevertheless possesses its own unique, nonreproducible character.

44. Cf. *Introduction to Metaphysics*, p. 139: "appearing in the first and authentic sense, as the gathered bringing-itself-to-stand, takes space in; it first conquers space; as standing there, it creates space for itself; it brings about everything that belongs to it, while it itself is not imitated. Appearing in the second sense merely steps forth from an already prepared space, and it is viewed by a looking-at within the already fixed dimensions of this space."

45. On the "beginning," see especially §23. Emad/Maly argue somewhat cryptically that "'event' immediately evokes the metaphysical notions of the unprecedented and the precedent that are totally alien to *Ereignis*" (CP, xx-xxi). If an "unprecedented" event here means something like a traditional first cause, then I agree that this is not *Ereignis*. However, enowning *is* "unprecedented" in the sense that it is unique and nonreproducible. Presumably it is in this nonmetaphysical sense that the translators refer to the "unprecedented and monumental unfolding in the thinking of being that *is* the first beginning" (CP, xxiv).

46. Heidegger's earlier name for the happening of time was *Zeitigung*, maturation or "temporalizing" (*Sein und Zeit*, p. 304). In *Contributions* he speaks of the "thrusts" or shocks (*Stöße*) of enowning (GA 65, 463; CP, 326) as well as of time (GA 65, 17; CP, 13).

47. *Phenomenology of Spirit*, paragraphs 95-98. "This" is as abstract as "being" and "nothing"; see the opening of Hegel's *Science of Logic*. Hegel, like Heidegger, wants to think in a way that is neither bound to particulars nor dispersed into empty universals. However, the parallel is again misleading; Heidegger would insist that the logic by which Hegel proceeds cuts him off from the uniqueness and historicity of be-ing.

48. In Heidegger's words: "the projecting-open that does the experiencing here does not occur here in the direction of representing a general essence

(γένοζ) but rather in the originary-historical entry into the site for the moment of Da-sein" (GA 65, 374; CP, 261).

49. A parenthetical remark—"the so-called rigor of logical acumen (as the form for finding the truth, and not only as the form for expressing what is found)" (GA 65, 461; CP, 325)—suggests that Heidegger might concede that logic can play a legitimate role in organizing the *results* of enthinking. He generally does not address this issue.

50. For Heidegger's understanding of *Contributions* as preliminary or preparatory, see also GA 66, 427 and the editor's afterword.

51. Briefly, *Inbegriff* or "ingrasping" is a conceiving (inceiving?) that does not simply look for universals but stands rooted alertly and creatively in its historical site; it is *inständig*, "inabiding" or steadfast (GA 65, 64–65; CP, 45). (Enthinking, too, is a form of inabiding [GA 65, 462; CP, 325].) Because the word *Inbegriff* usually means "sum total," it also suggests a way of thinking that does justice to the fullness and richness of the unique.

52. Don DeLillo, *Underworld* (New York: Scribner, 1998), p. 13. My thanks go to Susan Schoenbohm and Charles Scott for their thoughtful and generous assistance with this essay.

6. *Contributions to Philosophy* and Enowning-Historical Thinking
Friedrich-Wilhelm von Herrmann

Anyone who sets out to interpret Heidegger's *Contributions to Philosophy* (*From Enowning*)[1] in a hermeneutically cogent manner should be guided in this task by two hermeneutic foresights.

The first is the challenge to forego seeking access to *Contributions* through Heidegger's later writings of the fifties and sixties—those writings which acquainted us with enowning (*Ereignis*) for the first time—and instead to render *Contributions* understandable out of *Contributions* itself. For it is in *Contributions* that Heidegger, for the first time, fundamentally and decidedly deals with enowning by opening the pathway of inquiry of being-historical or enowning-historical thinking. It is within this pathway of inquiry that Heidegger wrote his later works, without repeating or explicitly and thematically dealing with the pathway of inquiry into enowning. With that one already sees the unique importance of *Contributions to Philosophy* for being-historical thinking.

The second hermeneutic foresight that should guide the interpreter from the very beginning concerns the intellectual-historical fact that enowning-historical thinking originates from within the fundamental-ontological thinking of the question of being. Being-historical thinking becomes what it is from within a *transformation* (*Wandel*) of fundamental-ontological thinking—and *not* by turning away from that first pathway of the question of being, as if enowning-historical thinking would begin entirely anew and without precedent. Thus enowning-historical thinking, which is grounded in *Contributions to Philosophy*, will be sufficiently grasped only if this thinking is understood as emerging from within that transformation—i.e., when we see clearly and unambiguously what it is that Heidegger gives up and what it is that he retains in making the crossing from the fundamental-ontological pathway of the question of being into the being-historical pathway of this question.

Since it is in *Contributions to Philosophy* that Heidegger elaborates enowning as the perspective (*Blickbahn*) of being-historical thinking, a thinking appropriating of this treatise depends entirely on interpreting this perspective itself. For we can only co-inquire responsibly into the factual issues that are dealt with in *Contributions* if we allow co-enactment to shift into this guiding perspective from the outset. In order to accomplish this eminently hermeneutical task, we must draw upon and contextually think through those passages in *Contributions* which hold the key for gaining access to the pathway of questioning.

Contributions to Philosophy as the First
Full Shaping of the Jointure

Even as we read the first page of *Contributions*—where Heidegger elucidates the reason for the twofold title *Contributions to Philosophy* and *From
Enowning*, we realize that this treatise enacts "the truth of be-ing" as
"being-historical thinking" (GA 65, 3; CP, 3). In §12, "Enowning and
History," Heidegger explains what "history" means in the context of
being-historical thinking. The term "being-historical" indicates that
"be-ing's essential sway [*Wesen*] is grasped 'historically'" (GA 65, 32; CP,
23). That is why Heidegger does not experience *Wesen* here as *essence*
but as *Wesung*, i.e., as essential swaying; and essential swaying is what
he calls enowning. The statement "En-owning is originary history
itself" (GA 65, 32; CP, 23) clearly says that history of be-ing not only
encompasses the history of the metaphysical determination of the
beingness of a being but also includes the essential swaying of the truth
of be-ing as enowning.

Contributions to Philosophy, which for the first time enacts the being-
historical thinking of the truth of be-ing in its historical swaying as
enowning, is not "a 'work' of the style heretofore" (GA 65, 3; CP, 3).
This, of course, does not mean that *Contributions* is devoid of any work-
character. The work-character peculiar to *Contributions* is determined by
the matter of being-historical thinking. This thinking is not a "thinking
about" enowning. As the matter for this thinking and as the historical
essential swaying of the truth of be-ing, enowning does not stand "over
against" this thinking. Rather, enowning-historical thinking itself
belongs to the historical essential swaying of the truth of be-ing as
enowning because this thinking is itself "enowned by enowning" (GA
65, 3; CP, 3). The work-character of enowning-historical thinking consists in its being "underway," its being a pathway which is enowned by
enowning and leads into its essential swaying.

The thinking that goes on in *Contributions* understands itself as an
"attempt," which, although successful, remains an attempt because this
thinking is not yet able "to join the free jointure of the truth of be-ing
out of be-ing *itself*" (GA 65, 4; CP, 3). For the path of inquiry of *Contributions* begins only with a "crossing" *from* the metaphysical question of
being concerning the beingness of beings *to* the thinking of the truth of
be-ing itself—a crossing from the end of the history of the first beginning to the history of the other beginning, a "crossing" and not already
the other beginning in its fully unfolded swaying (see GA 65, 3–6; CP,
3–5). To join the "free" jointure of the truth of be-ing out of be-ing itself
could mean—and perhaps one day will mean—to join the essential
swaying of the truth of be-ing as the truth of the other beginning in
such a manner that "the jointure of the work of thinking" (GA 65, 4;

CP, 3) determines itself from within this free swaying. Such a work would have to be entitled "Enowning." But as the treatise that is preparatory to such a work, *Contributions* carries the title *Contributions to Philosophy* because it contributes to the becoming philosophy of the other beginning. However, because *Contributions* itself deals "only with the essential swaying of be-ing, i.e., with enowning, "this work receives the 'essential' and 'proper' title 'From Enowning'" (GA 65, 3; CP, 3).

In *Beilage zu Wunsch und Wille: Über die Bewahrung des Versuchten* (Appendix to will and testament: On preserving the attempted), which Heidegger wrote in 1937/38 and which has now been published in volume 66 of the Gesamtausgabe, he speaks of the "Endeavors Preliminary to the Work" (*Vorarbeiten zum Werk*) as well as of "'From Enowning' (Contributions to Philosophy)."[2] With regard to "Endeavors Preliminary to the Work" he points out that it is not the aim of these "approaches" (*Anläufe*) to complete *Being and Time* but rather that these approaches grasp "the entire questioning more originarily and shift it into corresponding perspectives" (ibid.). Immediately thereafter comes the revealing statement:

> Since the spring of 1932 the plan has been firmly established in its main features and it achieves its first shaping in the projecting-opening called "From Enowning." Everything moves toward this projecting-opening, including *Eine Auseinandersetzung mit Sein und Zeit*,[3] which also belongs to the domain of these mindful deliberations. (Ibid.)

Among the "Endeavors Preliminary to the Work," *Contributions* assumes the rank of a "first shaping" of the future "work"—a shaping which Heidegger characterizes when he says:

> In its new approach this *Contributions to Philosophy* should render manifest the range of the question of being. A detailed unfolding here is not necessary, because this all too easily narrows down the actual horizon and misses the thrust of questioning. (Ibid.)

This characterization of the textual shape of *Contributions* is important because it explains that what in this treatise has the appearance of being unfinished and provisional ensues from the deliberate decision that Heidegger made to renounce a "detailed unfolding" in favor of the task which in a unique way falls to *Contributions*. However, that *Contributions* is not yet the "work" itself but is only preparatory to the "work" is what comes through in the next sentence:

> But since the new style of thinking has to be revealed, even here *that* form has not yet been attained which, precisely at this point, I demand for a publication as a "work." (Ibid.)

The future "work" to which Heidegger alludes in this testament as well as in *Contributions*—and which must be entitled *Ereignis*—is not the treatise written in 1941/42 and later published as volume 71 of the Gesamtausgabe with the title *Ereignis*. That treatise as well as those of Gesamtausgabe 66, 67, 69, 70, and 72 all dwell in the domain that is preparatory to the future "work" as a work which first and foremost is able "to join the free jointure of the truth of be-ing out of be-ing *itself*" (GA 65, 4; CP, 3).

Although *Contributions* is only a "preparatory exercise" (GA 65, 4; CP, 4) for that future work, it nevertheless has its own rigorous structure that is called an "outline" (*Aufriß*) (GA 65, 6; CP, 5). Heidegger distinguishes the "outline" of *Contributions* from its "ground plan" or *Grundriß*. The outline is at the service of "preparing the crossing" from the metaphysical questioning of the essence of beings into the being-historical question concerning the essential swaying of be-ing itself. This outline "is drawn from the still unmastered ground plan of the historicity of the crossing itself" (GA 65, 6; CP, 5). The still unmastered ground plan belongs to the "future work." The outline of *Contributions* presents a sixfold division: "Echo," "Playing-Forth," "Leap," "Grounding," "The Ones to Come," and "The Last God." The sixfold structure of the outline presents "the first full shaping of the jointure" (GA 65, 59; CP, 42) of being-historical thinking, which is also called "inceptual thinking," because this inceptual thinking prepares for the other beginning of the history of be-ing by coming to grips with the first beginning of this history (see GA 65, 30; CP, 22).

As "the first full shaping of the jointure" (GA 65, 59; CP, 42) of enowning-historical thinking, *Contributions* is the first major treatise of being-historical thinking. *Contributions* is a major treatise because it articulates "the full shaping of the whole domain of jointure" (ibid.) of being-historical thinking. Heidegger distinguishes two "ways and directions for presenting and communicating the jointure of inceptual thinking" (ibid.). The first consists in "a uniform enopening and full shaping of the whole domain of jointure," and the second in "singling out individual questions" while renouncing "the uniform enopening and full shaping of the whole domain of jointure" (ibid.). Inversely, the full shaping of the whole domain of jointure must renounce a step by step unfolding of the individual thrusts of being-historical thinking. Both of these ways and directions for presenting and communicating being-historical thinking must complement each other.

Until *Contributions* appeared for the first time in 1989, the first enopening and full shaping of the whole domain of jointure of enowning-historical thinking was inaccessible to us. What was accessible until then was the "individual questions" that were singled out and elaborated by Heidegger, such as, for example, carrying out a being-historical inquiry into the origin of the work of art—an inquiry which he refers to specifically as an example. However, the publication of *Contributions* makes clear that it is only with this publication that we are in a position to examine the jointure of enowning-historical thinking, which was left unthematized when Heidegger singled out individual questions. Once we have this fact in mind, we face the challenge of thinking through anew, in the horizon of *Contributions,* all being-historical treatises which up until now we had read without the knowledge of *Contributions.*

Indeed, *Contributions* belongs to a group with another six treatises that will be published in the Gesamtausgabe; but since these six treatises are consequent upon *Contributions, Contributions* takes the first place amongst them. Such an ordering of rank justifies itself on the grounds that working out the history of be-ing requires holding fast to the "innermost jointure which is the projecting-opening called *Contributions"* (*Die Geschichte des Seyns,* GA 69, 173). To be sure, in §1 of *Die Geschichte des Seyns,* Heidegger says that *"Contributions* is the framework and not the jointure" (GA 69, 5). But "framework" and "jointure" here are related to each other in the same way as "outline" and "ground plan." *Contributions* establishes the framework for being-historical thinking—even though it is in the manner of an outline—because this treatise points ahead to the "innermost jointure," i.e., to the jointure of being-historical thinking. But this "innermost jointure" is still not the "jointure" in the sense of the "ground plan" that is to be mastered by the future "work."

If *Contributions* claims such an exceptional place in Heidegger's pathway of thinking, then it becomes clear to what extent this treatise can not only be designated but must also be received as a major treatise. Certainly *Contributions* is not *the* major treatise for inquiring into the essential swaying of be-ing itself. Rather, it is the *second* major treatise after *Being and Time,* which continues to be the *basic treatise* of the thinking of the grounding question of being as such. For even *Contributions* remains retro-related, in its own way, to the pathway of thinking which is enopened for the first time in *Being and Time.* It is along this pathway that Heidegger first inquires into the truth of being and its relation to what is ownmost to humans as Dasein. In the preliminary note that Heidegger added to the seventh edition of *Being and Time* in 1953, he pointed out that the pathway of the first half of the treatise "remains even today a necessary one, if our Dasein is to be moved by the question of being" (GA 2, vii).

Transcendence and Enowning

It is Heidegger himself who, in *Contributions,* addresses the relationship between the second pathway of elaboration of the question of being, which he takes in *Contributions,* and the fundamental-ontological path-way, which he takes in *Being and Time.* Numerous passages in *Contributions* are devoted to this relationship and have the power to elucidate the origin of being-historical thinking within fundamental-ontological thinking.

In §132, "Be-ing and a Being," Heidegger talks about the attempt "to overcome the first effort at the question of being in *Being and Time* and its emanations (*Vom Wesen des Grundes* and the Kantbook)" (GA 65, 250; CP, 176). Such an overcoming occurs when the relation of Dasein to disclo-sure as the truth of being is no longer determined as a surpassing or transcending of a being but when the transcendentally determined dif-ference of being and a being, and with it transcendence, is leapt over by a leap of thinking which is a "leaping into the enowning of Da-sein" (GA 65, 251; CP, 177). Moreover, what belongs to surpassing, as the "where-onto" of transcending, is horizon—the horizonal disclosure of being as the disclosure of the constitution of being of an innerworldly being, as well as the horizonal openness of the world. Along the fundamental-ontological pathway of the being-question, thinking is enacted within the transcendental-horizonal perspective. But this perspective proves to be inadequate when thinking experiences the historicity of be-ing and its truth (see GA 65, 306; CP, 215).

However, the leap by which transcendence is leapt over is not a leap-ing out of that pathway along which the essential swaying of be-ing as the truth of be-ing as well as Dasein is viewed for the first time—Dasein as what is ownmost to humans and as belonging to the essential sway of be-ing. The leap of being-historical thinking, by which it leaps over transcendence, is enacted from within a correctly thought *immanent transformation.* In this connection, §122, "Leap (The Thrown Projecting-Open)," offers elucidation:

> The leap is the enactment of projecting-open the truth of be-ing in the sense of shifting into the open, such that the thrower of the projecting-open experiences itself as thrown—i.e., as *en-owned by be-ing.* (GA 65, 239; CP, 169, emphasis added)

The deciding and all-determining experience, which from within transcendental-horizonal perspective opens the path to being-historical perspective, is the experience of *thrownness* of projecting-open as what is *enowned* by the enowning-throw of be-ing, i.e., by its call (*Zuruf*) (see GA 65, 33–34; CP, 24).

Accordingly, in §141, "The Essential Sway of Be-ing," we read: "En-ownment of Da-sein by be-ing and grounding the truth of being in Da-sein" (GA 65, 262; CP, 184) is enowning. Enownment of Da-sein by be-ing occurs as the enowning-throw and as Da-sein's being-thrown. But enownment of Dasein by be-ing occurs so that the truth of be-ing, as its enowning-throw, is grounded by Da-sein's enowned projecting-opening. The whole of enowned-projecting opening and enowning-throw occurs as enowning. Accordingly, enowning is the elemental word for the one-foldness of the relation of be-ing to Da-sein and the relatedness of Da-sein to be-ing. A *counter-resonance* (GA 65, 251; CP, 177) holds sway between enowned projecting-open and enowning-throw, that is to say, within enowning itself; Heidegger calls it *"the turning" (die Kehre)* (GA 65, 261; CP, 184). Turning reveals "the essential sway of being itself as the counter-resonating enowning" (GA 65, 261; CP, 184). Only now, when thrownness is experienced from within the enowning-throw as a historically self-transforming clearing-concealing-sheltering throw—only now does the possibility become manifest for thinking the historically self-transforming essential swaying of be-ing and its truth. Thinking along the fundamental-ontological pathway, Heidegger indeed thinks through the historicality of Dasein and its possibilities of being-in-the-world. But, in doing so, he does not yet think the historicity of disclosure of being. Thinking along the being-historical pathway, Heidegger determines the historicality of Da-sein from out of history (*Geschichte*), i.e., from out of the historical essential swaying of be-ing as enowning.

By thinking through the "turning in enowning," *Contributions* ultimately makes clear what Heidegger expressed literally for the first time in "Letter on Humanism" as "turning" (see GA 9, 327). Turning is "above all not a process in thinking-questioning" but "plays within the matter itself,"[4] i.e., within the historical essential swaying of the truth of be-ing as enowning. The insight into the turning-character of the essential swaying of be-ing amounts to experiencing the unfolding origin of thrownness of Dasein's projecting-open from within the enowning-throw—it is thus an insight into enowning itself. Only by taking this into account can we say that the thinking of the turning is a turning in Heidegger's thinking. Occurring on the pathway of the being-question, turning is a crossing from the transcendental-horizonal perspective into the enowning-historical perspective. It is a crossing that is brought about by the experience of the origin of thrownness of Dasein from within the enowning-throw of the truth of be-ing.

In the phrase "transcendence and enowning," *transcendence* is a word that guides us to the perspective in which the pathway of the first elaboration of the being-question unfolds; *enowning* is a word that guides us to the pathway of questioning which is intrinsic to the second elaboration of the question of being. In the systematic structure of fundamental ontology—and grasped as care—transcendence and its horizon constitute the perspective not only for the existential analytic of Dasein but, under the title "time and being," also for working out the question concerning the meaning of being in terms of fundamental ontology—and, further, for the turning of fundamental ontology to metontology (see

GA 26, 199ff.). The insight into thrownness of projecting-open and the realization that the latter is enowned by be-ing's enowning-throw initiates thinking's crossing from the perspective of transcendence and horizon toward the path of questioning which is intrinsic to enowning. But if we take into account that this crossing occurs from within a thrown projecting-opening toward an enowned projecting-opening and, furthermore, if we bear in mind that thrown-projecting-opening lies at the very core of the analytic of Dasein, then we realize that, by enacting such a crossing, Heidegger merely abandons the transcendental-horizonal interpretation of Dasein's relationship to the truth of being without giving up what is existentially ownmost to humans and is obtained through the analytic of Dasein.

In §34, "Enowning and the Question of Being," Heidegger points out:

> Enowning is that self-supplying and self-mediating midpoint into which all essential swaying of the truth of be-ing must be thought back in advance. (GA 65, 73; CP, 51)

With unsurpassable clarity this statement shows that the counter-resonance of enowning-throw and enowned projecting-open, and hence that enowning, is the prevailing perspective for all questions of being-historical thinking, just as transcendence and horizon were the perspective for the path of questioning which initiated the first pathway of being-question, i.e., all questions of fundamental-ontological thinking. That is to say, each sentence of *Contributions* should be interpreted according to the perspective of enowning, which is the midpoint of all essential swaying of the truth of be-ing.

The Outline of the Six Joinings of the One Jointure

Contributions is outlined as the enjoined jointure of six joinings: "Echo," "Playing-Forth," "Leap," "Grounding," "The Ones to Come," and "The Last God." Each of these six parts of the outline is a joining because each is determined from within the enjoined whole. Heidegger occasionally speaks of "jointure" instead of "joining," speaks of be-ing "in the joining of those jointures" (GA 65, 65; CP, 45) or of "joining its jointure" (ibid.). The first of these six joinings is preceded by that part of *Contributions* which, under the title "Preview," takes on the task of an extensive preparation. The first full shaping of the entire domain of jointure of being-historical thinking is followed by the part entitled "Be-ing." Here Heidegger "attempts to grasp the whole once again" (GA 65, 512; CP, 363). This part moves within the six joinings without repeating them in their enjoinedness at the same time as it presents very important complements, such as the eightfoldness of enownings in §267, "Be-ing (Enowning)."

Reflecting on the outline of *Contributions*, §1, "*Contributions to Philosophy* Enact the Questioning along a Pathway," states that this

> outline does not yield an arrangement of various observations about various objects. It is also not an introductory ascent from what is below to what is above. (GA 65, 6; CP, 5)

But how the enjoined-character of these six joinings joins them together in a way that being-historical thinking traverses the path that runs from "Echo" to "The Last God" is what the reader grasps by focusing on §39 in the "Preview," entitled "Enowning." Together with other sections upon which we have already drawn, §39 is one of the key texts in *Contributions;* once recognized as key, they open up the whole of the otherwise hermetic-sounding *Contributions* in such a way that we can infer from them the clearly and transparently structured perspective of enowning-historical thinking.

The key passage in §39 that makes us realize the enjoined character of the sixfold enjoined jointure of being-historical thinking reads as follows:

> Each of the six joinings of the jointure stands for itself, but only in order to make the essential onefold more pressing. In each of the six joinings the attempt is made always to say the same of the same, but in each case from within another essential domain of that which enowning names. (GA 65, 82; CP, 57)

This passage gives guidance to the reader and interpreter of *Contributions* on how to enact the sequence of the six joinings. Each of the six joinings, when held against any other joining, is a specific domain of the swaying of enowning. That is why each joining says the same from the swaying of the truth of be-ing as enowning. In each joining the same — not the identical — is said of the same. The same is that manner of swaying of enowning which is peculiar to each joining and belongs uniquely to it. To say in each joining the same of the same thus means always to unfold in thinking, a manner of swaying of enowning.

Guidance provided in this way requires that the interpreter heed how a specific manner of swaying of enowning always shows itself at first in "Echo," then in "Playing-Forth," "Leap," "Grounding," "The Ones to Come," and "The Last God." But at the same time this includes the knowledge of the basic structure of enowning that turns unto itself and counter-resonates. In each of the six joinings one must always heed the enowning-throw and the counter-resonating enowned projecting-open that is ownmost to each joining. Insofar as what is ownmost to being-historical thinking is not reflection, but rather — like fundamental-ontological thinking before it — explicitly accomplishes itself as a hermeneutically enacted thrown-enowned-projecting-opening, we can say that the enowned projecting-opening in each given manner of swaying of enowning of a joining is the manner of enactment of being-historical thinking. By keeping these factual interconnections in mind, the interpreter has access to the required hermeneutic pre-understanding for an interpretation of *Contributions* which extends into the matter itself.

Echo

Being-historical thinking begins with that experience which for the first time allots to this thinking *beings' abandonment by being* and *forgottenness of being* by the historically present humans. Through the allotted abandoment by and forgottenness of being, this thinking realizes the distress of the lack of distress. And this means that outside being-historical thinking, abandonment by and forgottenness of being is not experienced *as* distress. The being-historical thinking to which distress is allotted is attuned by shock or startled dismay which, together with deep awe, make up the grounding-attunement of reservedness as the grounding-attunement of this thinking. In and through this attunement a distressing occurs which sets thinking free to inquire into and to disclose what it experiences, namely the abandonment by, and forgottenness of, being. The enowning-throw is in play in the manner in which thinking is affected by the abandonment by and forgottenness of being, whereas questioning-disclosing of the allotted abandonment by and forgottenness of being gets accomplished as the enowned projecting-open of being-historical thinking that belongs to that enowning-throw. Accordingly, "echo" shows itself as the first essential domain of enowning with its counter-resonating structure.

But abandonment by being of a being means that a being has been forsaken [*abandoned*] by the sheltering and harboring possible to it — sheltering and harboring of the truth of what and how a being is. This abandonment is the historical manner of disclosure that is ownmost to a being. When thinking-questioning discloses the abandonment by being which is allotted to thinking, then the swaying of the truth of be-ing *echoes* in that disclosing and indeed in the manner of *refusal* of be-ing. The word refusal — a basic word of being-historical thinking — has many meanings, all of which belong to the one but manifold swaying-character of sheltering-concealing of be-ing. Here in "Echo" what shows itself in its refusal is the open swaying of the truth of be-ing as enowning — a truth to which refusal belongs as the origin of all clearing and unconcealing of be-ing. But the echo of the truth of being as a self-refusing truth is itself a manner of enowning by which enowning refuses itself in its open manner of swaying.

With regard to the manner of swaying of enowning, §141 of the "Leap," entitled "The Essential Sway of Be-ing," presents the possibility for making factual and terminological distinctions. Enowning-throw, which sways as refusal, reveals its essential character, namely *staying-away* (GA 65, 262; CP, 184), whereby the call for the open and not-refused manner of swaying stays away. The enowned projecting-open that corresponds to this staying-away does not have the basic thrust of belonging to the open swaying and thus leads to abandonment of a be-ing by being—and to humans' forgottenness of being. In two passages of *Contributions*, Heidegger speaks of a "dis-enowning" rather than an "enowning." In the first passage he says that a being which is aban-doned by being is "dis-enowned by being" (GA 65, 120; CP, 84), which, according to the second passage, corresponds to humans being "dis-enowned of being" (GA 65, 231; CP, 164). For our part, we shall talk of the staying-away of the call as a *dis-enowning-throw* and of forgottenness of being and abandonment by being as a *dis-enowned projecting-open,* to be distinguished from an enowned projecting-open that belongs to the open swaying. We shall terminologically grasp the resonating whole-ness of dis-enowning-throw and dis-enowned projecting-open with the word dis-enowning (*Enteignis*). Accordingly, echo is that domain of swaying of enowning wherein enowning resonates, but in the manner of dis-enowning, which leads into the possibility of enowning.

As allotted to being-historical thinking, being's abandonment of beings is being's historical and present manner of disclosure. As such, this disclo-sure is the present manner of swaying of what Heidegger calls machina-tion and machinational interpretation of beings. In the context of being-historical thinking the word *machination* does not mean a definite manner of comportment by humans but rather "a manner of the essential sway-ing of being" in accordance with which the beingness of a being is pro-jected-open and determined within the horizon of making, producing, and representing modernity (GA 65, 107ff.; CP, 75ff.). The machinational interpretation of beings as such commences already in antiquity, when ontological concepts are obtained in orientation to the producing com-portment. As long as the machinational way of looking at things supplies the orientation for interpreting beings, the open swaying of the truth of be-ing as enowning refuses itself in favor of an essential shaping of being-ness of a being to which belongs, as what is ownmost to humans, not Dasein, but the living being who possesses language and reason.

Insofar as abandonment by and forgottenness of being are experienced in the primary essential domain of enowning called echo, and inasmuch as abandonment by and forgottenness of being refer to the history of machi-national swaying of being, being-historical thinking must cross into that second domain of swaying of enowning which is called "Playing-Forth."

Playing-Forth

Coming from the echo of the truth of be-ing, which refuses an open swaying, the history of metaphysical inquiry into beingness of beings as

history of the first beginning *plays forth* into enowning-historical thinking, thus constituting the domain of swaying called "Playing-Forth." In
this playing-forth the resonating truth of be-ing is in play as the swaying of the other beginning. Separate and yet belonging together, the
first and the other beginning are two beginnings of the history of be-
ing. Playing-forth means

> Coming to grips with the necessity of the *other* beginning from out of the
> originary positioning of the first beginning. (GA 65, 169; CP, 119)

Since the swaying of the self-refusing truth of be-ing resonates in the
experience of beings' abandonment by being, and since this swaying as
dis-enowning points to an other possible beginning of the swaying as
enowning, the history of traditional thinking—from its early Greek
beginning to its present completion in modernity—enters the horizon of
a being-historical interpretation. No interpretation other than the being-
historical interpretation from out of the swaying of the truth of being
is possible within enowning-historical thinking, assuming that interpretation understands itself as a philosophizing and *not* as a *philosophical-
historical* (*philosophie-historische*) interpretation, which, of course, has its
own legitimacy. Since Heidegger interprets the history of the metaphysical question of being as an historical manner of swaying of the truth of
be-ing, he does not reject that history as the history of an aberration.
Instead, history of metaphysics receives its full appreciation when
Heidegger points out that

> history of the first beginning thus completely loses the appearance of fu-
> tility and mere errancy. Only now the great light shines on all the heretofore
> [accomplished] work of thinking. (GA 65, 175; CP, 123, interpolation
> mine)

This appreciative relationship to the history of metaphysics profoundly
separates being-historical thinking from *all* criticism of metaphysics.

To the domain of swaying of "playing-forth" belongs "everything involved in differentiating the guiding-question and the grounding-question" (GA 65, 169; CP, 119)—all being-historical interpretations of the
metaphysical guiding-question concerning the beingness of beings and
all related fundamental-ontological as well as being-historical discussions and presentations of the grounding-question concerning the truth
of be-ing. Hence all presentations, i.e., "all lectures on the 'history' of
philosophy" (GA 65, 169; CP, 119), belong to "playing-forth." This reference to the "historical" lectures is of great significance to readers who,
for decades, have been studying Heidegger's lectures on basic metaphysical positions; for this reference indicates how we should read these
lecture-texts within being-historical thinking by allocating to them the
place that they join within the jointure of enowning-historical thinking.

Since "playing-forth" is a domain of swaying of enowning, thinking receives, from within enowning-throw, that which shows itself from within the swaying of metaphysical beingness and from within being-historical truth of be-ing as something that this thinking questions and discloses in its enowned projecting-opening.

In §3 of "Preview," entitled "From Enowning," Heidegger indicates how, in crossing, "Playing-Forth" relates to the "Leap":

> The playing-forth is initially the playing forth of the first beginning, so that the first beginning brings the other beginning into play, so that, according to this mutual playing forth, preparation for the leap grows. (GA 65, 9; CP, 7)

Leap

If the other beginning, the swaying of be-ing itself in its own uncon-cealment, shows itself in the domain of swaying of playing forth, then being-historical thinking can go beyond its manner of enactment within the joining called "Playing-Forth"—can enact the leap into the self-throwing truth of be-ing. The third joining begins with a deciding elucidation of what the "leap" is all about:

> The leap . . . abandons and throws aside everything familiar [from out of the history of the first beginning], expecting nothing from beings immedi-ately [as in the history of the first beginning]. Rather, above all else it releases belongingness to be-ing in its full [open] essential swaying as enowning. (GA 65, 227; CP, 161, interpolations mine)

As an elemental word, *leap* characterizes projecting-thinking which, coming from within the first beginning as it plays forth into the other beginning, leaps into the truth of be-ing in such a way that this thinking now explicitly projects-open the truth of be-ing as constituted by enowning.

Now thinking experiences itself explicitly as an enowned projecting-open, which is capable of enopening, from the swaying of the truth of be-ing, only that which from within the enowning-throw hints at this think-ing as projectable. While, in counter-resonance to enowning-throw, thinking in "Echo" and "Playing-Forth" is still implicitly enacted as an enowned projecting-open, in the domain of the swaying of the "leap" thinking becomes translucent to itself in its belongingness to enowning.

Within the third joining, called "Leap," comes first "the leap into be-ing as enowning" (GA 65, 278; CP, 196). Only within the perspective thus enopened does the leap leap, i.e., project-open the truth as the ab-ground of the *cleavage* of be-ing. Heidegger tells us that what is called cleavage

> is the unfolding unto itself of the intimacy of be-ing itself, insofar as we "experience" it as refusal and turning-in-refusal. (GA 65, 244; CP, 172)

The manifoldness of be-ing in its truth, which is not granted to dis-enowning, i.e., to the swaying of be-ing as beingness of beings, breaks open in the projecting-opening-leap of thinking. What breaks open is, on the one hand, the manifoldness of modes of be-ing as distinct from only one mode of being, actuality and its modal variations, the modalities of being in the metaphysical question of being. (Along the transcendental-horizonal pathway this constitutes the third basic problem of phenome-nology.)[5] On the other hand, to the cleavage of be-ing belongs the breaking open of the difference which is the difference between ways of being and the "whatness" of a being, which is always determined in advance by these ways of being. (Along the transcendental-horizonal pathway this is the second basic problem of phenomenology.) Further-more, belonging to the cleavage of be-ing, the difference between be-ing and a being breaks open—now no longer in the manner of ontological difference as determined along the transcendental-horizonal pathway, where the truth of being is entirely other than a being (the first basic problem of phenomenology). Rather, through the cleavage of be-ing this difference breaks open in such a way that a being, as sheltering the truth of being, belongs to the full swaying of the truth of be-ing. This means that differentiation of be-ing and a being breaks open in the one-foldness of the swaying of the truth of be-ing. This is what "simultane-ity" (*Gleichzeitigkeit*) of be-ing and a being means as a simultaneity that replaces the a priori character of being: "enowning is the temporal-spatial simultaneity for be-ing and beings" (GA 65, 13; CP, 10). Finally, through cleavage of be-ing, belongingness of "nothing" and "not" to be-ing breaks open.

Prepared for by "Playing-Forth," the "Leap" in turn prepares for "Grounding." For, thinking as "leap"

> first of all opens up the ungone expanses [unconcealings] and conceal-ments of that into which the *grounding* of Da-sein, which belongs to the call of enowning, must press forth. (GA 65, 82; CP, 57, interpolation mine)

Grounding

Thinking as grounding grounds the truth of be-ing, which is enopened by the leap as enowning, *as* and *in* Da-sein. The truth of be-ing which sways as enowning needs this grounding. In accord with the turning in enowning, grounding occurs through enowning-throw and enowned projecting-open. Projecting-open is grounding only insofar as the throw is also grounding. This is an indication as to how grounding too occurs within the counter-resonating structure of enowning.

Section 187, entitled "Grounding," unfolds the counter-resonating structure of enowning. We are told that grounding is "two-fold in meaning" (GA 65, 307; CP, 216) because it occurs as grounding-throw and as grounding-projecting-open. Considering the enowning-throw, we are told that *"ground grounds,* sways as ground" (ibid.). This "grounding ground is gotten hold of and taken over as such" (ibid.) by Dasein's projecting-open. Since grounding of projecting-open is en-owned by the grounding-throw of be-ing, Heidegger calls this grounding an en-grounding (*Er-gründen*). The enowned projecting-open is an en-grounding because this projecting gets hold of and takes over the self-throwing grounding ground. Both the getting hold of and the taking over that en-ground occur by letting the grounding ground hold sway (*wesen lassen*) and by building on the grounding ground. Accordingly, the fourth domain of swaying of enowning is the counter-resonance of be-ing's grounding-throw and thinking's en-grounding-projecting-opening.

The question of truth lies at the very core of the fourth joining, which within enowning-historical thinking assumes the rank of a fore-question (*Vorfrage*) for the being-question. For the historical swaying character of be-ing emerges from clearing-sheltering-concealing of the essential sway of truth.

To the grounding truth as the truth for be-ing also belongs, as the question concerning the inner jointure of truth, the important question of time-space. Time-space names the co-originality of original time in its temporalizing as well as original space in its spatializing. Within the counter-resonating enowning, time-space holds sway as "the jointure of removal-unto and charming-moving-unto" (GA 65, 371; CP, 259). Temporalizing occurs as enowning-removal-unto of Da-sein, out of which Dasein temporalizes itself and into which Da-sein, as enowned, is removed. Spatializing occurs as enowning-charming-moving-unto of Da-sein, out of which Da-sein as a projecting taking-of-space is enowned and charmed-unto. Whereas in fundamental-ontological thinking truth of being is grounded in temporality, in enowning-historical thinking time-space unfolds within the truth of be-ing.

To the enowned-projecting-open as an en-grounding there belongs a disclosure of a being which in its unhiddenness *shelters* the throwing-projected-open truth of be-ing in a being as its manner of disclosedness. That is why the last part of the fourth joining deals with "Essential Swaying of Truth as Sheltering" (GA 65, 389–92; CP, 271–74). Whereas in fundamental-ontological thinking uncovering of a being is made possible by a disclosing-thrown projecting-open of the truth of being, in being-historical thinking, disclosing-letting-itself-be-sheltered (*entbergende Sichbergenlassen*) of the throwing-projecting truth of be-ing belongs to the full essential swaying of the truth of be-ing. This is to say that through en-grounding-projecting-opening and through letting-itself-be-sheltered of what is projected-open in disclosing a being, there occurs a restoration of a being *"from within the truth of be-ing"* (GA 65,

11; CP, 8)—after a being has been abandoned for so long by be-ing, i.e., abandoned by such a sheltering.

The Ones to Come

Coming from "Grounding," enowning-historical thinking advances into that domain of swaying of enowning where thinking projects-open the being of the ones to come as inabiding in Da-sein, which belongs to enowning. Inabiding is the being-historical name for "existence," i.e., for the being of the "t/here" (*Da*). Inabiding, too, manifests the threefold structure of "being- enowned," "projecting," and "disclosing" —a structure within which "the ones to come" comport themselves to be-ing's enowning-throw. Thus the fifth joining too becomes manifest as the domain of swaying of the turning-enowning.

They are called "the ones to come" because they experience the enowning-call of be-ing (the enowning-throw) as what comes toward them. They are those who knowingly take over the "belongingness to enowning . . . that has been awakened by the call" (GA 65, 82; CP, 57). They are "the lingering and long-hearing founders" of the "essential sway of truth" (GA 65, 395; CP, 277) as the truth for be-ing.

But "the ones to come" are also those "toward whom . . . the hint and the onset of distancing and nearing of the last god advances" (GA 65, 395; CP, 277). In this vein being-historical thinking crosses "the ones to come" toward the sixth joining "The Last God."

The Last God

In this joining the relation of be-ing to god, the relation of god to the truth of be-ing, the relation of god to humans, as well as humans' relation to god are thought enowning-historically.[6] The "last" god is the "utmost god," i.e., the one which both shows itself and withdraws from within the truth of be-ing. As the utmost god, the last god is not be-ing,

> is not enowning itself; rather, it needs enowning as that to which the founder of the t/here [*Da-gründer*] [the en-grounding Da-sein] belongs. (GA 65, 409; CP, 288, interpolation mine)

In contrast to first-ever-inceptual thinking, enowning-historical thinking of god thinks the difference between be-ing and god. Heidegger formulates the fundamental thinking of this difference as "not attributing being to 'gods'" (GA 65, 438; CP, 308). In the metaphysical thinking of god, god's determinations do not arise from "the divine-character of god, but rather from what is ownmost to a being as such" (ibid.). By contrast, enowning-historical thinking strives to think the godly god (*den göttlichen Gott*), whose divine-character this thinking experiences and determines solely from within what is ownmost to god itself. Enowning-historical thinking of god is a phenomenological thinking of god, which pursues the question concerning what is ownmost to god by following the maxim "to the things themselves."

A passage from "Preview" tells us how god's relation to humans and humans' relations to god inhere in enowning: "Enowning owns god over to man in that enowning owns man to god" (GA 65, 26; CP, 19). Here be-ing's enowning-throw above all proves to be an *owning-over* of god to humans and an *owning* of humans *to* god—indeed in such a way that enowning, which owns-over and owns-to, occurs within the counter-resonance of be-ing's enowning-throw and the enowned projecting-open. In order to unfold as such, the relation of Da-sein to god needs be-ing's enowning-throw as a throw that owns-over and owns-to. Thus the sixth joining, too, manifests itself as a specific domain of swaying of the counter-resonating enowning. And this shows that, without a hermeneutic pre-understanding of the counter-resonating turning enowning, an interpreting entry into the six joinings of *Contributions* would be without a reliable directive.

Jointure Instead of System

Having traversed the path of being-historical thinking through the six joinings of *Contributions*, we now attend to the specific joining-character of these joinings, which Heidegger calls *Fuge*, or jointure.

There are several significant passages in the "Preview" in which Heidegger distinguishes jointure, as the joining-character of being-historical thinking, from system as the structure of modern thinking of reason. Being-historical thinking unfolds its own "order" (*Ordnung*) from within the matter of this thinking. This order is not only *not* a system but also stands outside of the dichotomy of "system," and "lack of system." For in the strict philosophical sense (not in the loose sense of an extraneous collecting), system arises only "as a consequence of the mastery of mathematical thinking (in its widest sense)" (GA 65, 65; CP, 45). In the context of distinguishing being-historical jointure from the modern system of reason, Heidegger refers to two university lectures whose writing coincides with the beginning of the writing of *Contributions:* the lecture of the winter semester of 1935/36, *Die Frage nach dem Ding* (GA 41), and the Schelling lecture (GA 42) of the summer semester of 1936. In these university lectures Heidegger discusses the modern concept of system as well as modern thinking as a thinking which is oriented toward mathematics. In the Schelling lecture he demonstrates how, beginning with Descartes, modern thinking develops system as system of reason. Such a system arises when "system in its essence is determined by the conceivability and lawfulness of mathematical thinking" (GA 42, 57). Granting this, system as "the structure of be-ing must be a mathematical system at the same time that it is a system of thinking, of *ratio,* of reason" (ibid.). From Descartes to Hegel, modern system contains "representedness" as "the essential designation of beingness of beings . . . in modernity" (GA 65, 89; CP, 62). But being-historical thinking "is the crossing from modernity into the other beginning" (ibid.). And in this beginning, disclosure of a being is not thought from out of the representing relation of the subject but from within the swaying of the truth of be-ing as enowning.

Leaving reason behind as the measure for beingness of beings entails parting with the system of reason. But such a parting does not terminate in disorderliness; rather, it proceeds into a transformed inner order which traces out the swaying of the truth of be-ing as enowning. Such inner order is the jointure as the structure of the six joinings of *Contributions.* In the Schelling lecture we come upon a significant statement:

> And insofar as what is ownmost to be-ing as such has a joining-character . . . every philosophy, as an inquiry into be-ing, is oriented toward jointure and joining, i.e., toward system. Every philosophy is systematic but not every philosophy is a system. (GA 42, 51)

Here Heidegger uses the word systematic not only as an adjective of the noun "system" but also in the broad sense of an inner order. Being-historical thinking of *Contributions* is not systematic in the sense of belonging to a system but *is* systematic in the sense of an order that accrues from a jointure.

Heidegger distinguishes three characteristics of the jointure of being-historical thinking. The first characteristic concerns *the rigor of jointure.* Although *Contributions* is preparatory to the future work, *Contributions* in its structure leaves out "nothing of the rigor of jointure[,] . . . as if what counts" in *Contributions* is "to grasp the truth of be-ing in the completely unfolded fullness of what is ownmost to it in its groundedness" (GA 65, 81; CP, 56). The inner joining-character of enowning-historical thinking cannot be characterized more penetratingly than this. This challenges the interpreter in the course of interpreting *Contributions* to take seriously the rigor of jointure.

The second characteristic concerns the *access* in thinking. For the shaping of the jointure of being-historical thinking allows

> only the *access* to *one* way which an individual can open, foregoing a survey of the possibility of other perhaps more essential ways. (ibid.)

Here access does not mean having something at one's disposal and doing with it as one pleases. Rather, access refers to questioning-thinking-projecting-open, which sustains the jointure of the six joinings of *Contributions.* Such an access (*Verfügen*) could also be called an en-joining (*Er-fügen*) because access is the en-owned joining out of an en-owning fore-indicating (*er-eignende Vor-zeichnung*) of the joinings. With this we touch upon the third characteristic of the jointure.

The third characteristic concerns be-ing itself in its *joining*. Looking at both the first and the second characteristics together—that is, at the structure of jointure of six joinings and at the access in thinking—we realize that "both the jointure and access, remain an *endowment* of be-ing itself" (ibid.). Jointure and access in thinking become possible only by a joining-throw, which at the same time is both a hint and a withdrawal of the truth of be-ing. What incessantly throws itself forth (*das Zugewor-fene*) is never "something finished and settled" (*ein Fertiges*), which thinking has to accept without its own enopening enactment. What incessantly throws itself forth has the character of a disclosing and self-withdrawing hint, which releases thinking as projecting-opening. What is in play in such a thinking is freedom of thinking, which is surely not a freedom which grounds itself out of itself but is a freedom which, as en-owned freedom, is brought to itself by the hint. This would be the juncture for dealing with the issue of "freedom and history."

Over against the rigor of "system-thinking," being-historical think-ing, as it crosses the end of the history of the first beginning into the his-tory of the other beginning, "has a rigor of another kind" (GA 65, 65; CP, 45). Heidegger characterizes this rigor as "the freedom of joining its jointures" (ibid.)—a joining in thinking which is accomplished "accord-ing to the mastery of the questioning-belonging to the call" (ibid.). Here again being-historical thinking is grasped as enowned projecting-open, which belongs to the enowning-throw in such a manner that, from within the swaying of the truth of be-ing, this thinking can only pro-jectingly enopen that which from within the hinting-call is offered to this thinking as projectable.

This fore-giving from within the enowning-hinting-throw is the herme-neutic fore-having of being-historical thinking. To fore-having also belongs the hermeneutic fore-sight as well as the hermeneutic fore-conception. This shows that, as fundamental-ontological thinking gets transformed into enowning-historical thinking, hermeneutic phenomenology—initially shaped fundamental-ontologically—gets transformed into a hermeneutic phenomenology which is determined being-historically.

This is unequivocally supported by what Heidegger says in a text of the fifties entitled "A Dialogue from Language" (GA 12, 79–146). There Heidegger specifies the ἑρμηνεύειν of hermeneutic phenomenology as a thinking "that brings tidings inasmuch as that thinking is capable of listening to a message" (GA 12, 115). Such a "bringing of tidings" is what Heidegger calls "the hermeneutic relation" of the thinking of being (GA 12, 116). It is not difficult to glean from this phrase the structure of enowning. In "bringing tidings" there lies the structure of projecting-open while "listening to a message" indicates the structure of enowning-throw.

The fact that thinking of be-ing and of its truth can think only what this thinking, in listening to a message, is able to bring each time as tidings from this message, means that thinking as projecting-opening is an enowned projecting—enowned by be-ing's enowning-throw. But this is the fundamental hermeneutic thrust of being-historical thinking, which has its fore-having in hinting-enowning, gets enacted in an enowned projecting-open as hermeneutic fore-sight, and maintains itself in hermeneutic fore-conception within the sheltered wording of each enowned projecting-open.

But being-historical thinking as a thinking which is hermeneutical in the already elucidated sense is at the same time a phenomenological thinking. For, as projecting, this thinking can disclose from out of the truth of be-ing only what shows itself out of the hermeneutic fore-having as discloseable for a hearkening understanding. What always hints in the hinting-throw is what is manifest for thinking-projecting as a being-phenomenon. Thus thinking-projecting gets enacted as the enopening-letting-be-seen of what shows itself, the manifest.

Section 27 of *Contributions,* entitled "Inceptual Thinking (Concept)," contains significant statements about being-historical conceptuality. Enowning-historical thinking has its own "keenness of saying" and "simpleness of the shaping word" (GA 65, 45; CP, 45). Saying and the words of being-historical thinking have their own "conceptuality" by which "be-ing" is always grasped "in the joining of those jointures" (ibid.). Heidegger calls the being-historical concept an "in-grasping." What is ownmost to the in-grasping of the being-historical concept is its "accompanying co-grasping of the turning in enowning" (ibid.). What is grasped by being-historical concept as in-grasping is determined from out of the turning of the enowned projecting-open and the enowning-throw.

Prospect

Under the title "Contributions to Philosophy and Enowning-Historical Thinking," we attempted to interpretively articulate the major thrusts of the all-determining perspective and path of questioning of *Contributions.* Can this being-historical perspective, which is worked out between 1936–1938, still claim to be decidedly significant for the later pathways of Heidegger's thinking? Doesn't topological thinking replace being-historical thinking?

We find the response to these questions in a passage from the summary of the seminar of 1962, which was devoted to the lecture "Time and Being." There Heidegger points out:

> The relations and interconnections that make up the essential structure of enowning were worked out between 1936 and 1938.[7]

In thinking through the lecture text "Time and Being"—one of Heidegger's most recent texts—he refers to *Contributions* of 1936–1938 where "the essential structure of enowning" is worked out. This means that in the text of the 1962 discussions concerning enowning take place within the perspective of "the essential structure of enowning" as worked out in *Contributions*. Although "Time and Being" unfolds a manifold of relations within enowning, the essential structure of enowning is not treated thematically in that lecture. But because this text is thought within the perspective of the essential structure of enowning, this text becomes hermeneutically translucent only when it is interpreted with a knowledge of *Contributions*.

Being-historical thinking is a thinking of the truth of be-ing. In the seminar he held in Le Thor in 1969 (GA 15, 326–71), Heidegger did in fact talk about a topology of being and of topological thinking; but he never suggested that topological thinking succeeds being-historical thinking of the truth of be-ing. Rather, what he said in that seminar was only that the phrase "truth of being" is "elucidated" by the phrase "place of being" (*Ortschaft des Seins*). Because "place of being" is solely an elucidation of the "truth of being," topological thinking too belongs to being-historical thinking and is itself enowning-historical thinking.

A hermeneutically cogent interpretation of *Contributions* should hold open the being-historical perspective, which is worked out in this treatise, as a perspective which is indispensable for an interpretation of Heidegger's later writings of the fifties and sixties, which include *Zur Erörterung der Gelassenheit, Bauen Wohnen Denken*, and *Der Satz der Identität*. For all of Heidegger's later writings are thought from within the perspective which is worked out for the first time in *Contributions*.

Translated by Parvis Emad

Notes

Translator's note: Terminology used in this essay presupposes that the reader is already thoroughly familiar with what is said in the "Translators' Foreword" to *Contributions to Philosophy (From Enowning)* regarding the English renditions of key words in Heidegger's *Beiträge zur Philosophie (Vom Ereignis)*. In addition to the words discussed in that "Foreword," note the following:

The two independent words, *Blick* and *Bahn*, come together in the German word *Blickbahn*, rendered here as "perspective." Composed of *Blick*, meaning "glance," and *Bahn*, meaning "path" or "track," *Blickbahn* indicates the path to be taken by hermeneutic-phenomenological thinking. In the context of hermeneutic phenomenology, this meaning of *Blickbahn* is central to what this paper has in mind as enacting of "inquiry" and "questioning."

The English word "perspective" comes close to *Blickbahn* if we focus on its Latin roots *per* (through) and *specere* (to see). Thus the word *perspective* used here as a rendition of *Blickbahn* has solely to do with glancing and looking at things according to the path which is appropriate to them. Hence "perspective" should not be confused with what is adopted by the "will to power" for its own intensification and unfolding in Nietzsche when he talks about perspective and perspectival thinking.

Finally, the word *foresight* (without a hyphen) is a rendition of *Voreinsicht* and should be kept distinct from fore-sight as a translation of *Vor-sicht,* which is a technical term of hermeneutic phenomenology. *Voreinsicht* refers to an insight with futural implications and possibilities, whereas *Vor-sicht,* achieves its full meaning as *fore-sight* in conjunction with fore-having, *Vorhabe,* and fore-conception, *Vor-griff.*

1. For bibliographical information on the text referred to here, see the introduction to this volume, note 1. See also Friedrich-Wilhelm von Herrmann, *Wege ins Ereignis: Zu Heideggers "Beiträgen zur Philosophie"* (Frankfurt am Main: Vittorio Klostermann, 1994), pp. 5–84. See also the "Translator's Note" preceding note 1 of this essay.

2. Cf. Martin Heidegger, *Besinnung* (GA 66, 424), ed. Friedrich-Wilhelm von Herrmann (Frankfurt am Main: Vittorio Klostermann, 1997), pp. 419–28.

3. To be published in volume 82 of the Gesamtausgabe.

4. Martin Heidegger, "Preface," a letter to William J. Richardson, in *Heidegger: Through Phenomenology to Thought* (The Hague: Martinus Nijhoff, 1967), pp. viii–xxiii.

5. Regarding the third basic problem of phenomenology, see Martin Heidegger, *The Basic Problems of Phenomenology,* trans. Richard Hofstadter (Bloomington: Indiana University Press, 1988), p. 40, as well as Friedrich-Wilhelm von Herrmann, *Heideggers "Grundprobleme der Phänomenologie": Zur "Zweiten Hälfte" von "Sein und Zeit"* (Frankfurt am Main: Vittorio Klostermann, 1991).

6. Regarding the last god, see Paola-Ludovica Coriando, *Der Letzte Gott als Anfang: Zur ab-gründigen Zeit-Räumlichkeit des Übergangs in Heideggers "Beiträge zur Philosophie (Vom Ereignis)"* (Munich: Wilhelm Fink Verlag, 1998).

7. Martin Heidegger, *Zur Sache des Denkens* (Tübingen: Max Niemeyer Verlag, 1969), p. 46. For an English translation of the passage cited, see *On Time and Being,* trans. Joan Stambaugh (New York: Harper & Row, 1972), p. 43.

Part 2. Readings

7. The Time of *Contributions to Philosophy*
William McNeill

In memory of Hillary Johnson, 1975–1999

Chronologically reckoned, Heidegger's *Contributions to Philosophy (Of Ereignis)*[1] date from 1936–1938, an extremely rich and productive period of his work that is commonly regarded as marking a fundamental "turning" in his thought. To the most important works of around that period—works that at once attune, and are in turn attuned by, *Contributions*—there are the lecture course on *Hölderlin's Hymns "Germania" and "The Rhine"* (1934/35); the lectures entitled *Introduction to Metaphysics* (1935); the lecture courses on *Nietzsche* (1936–1939); and the essays "The Origin of the Work of Art" (1935/36), "Hölderlin and the Essence of Poetizing" (1936), and "The Age of the World Picture" (1938). Of these, all but the lectures on Hölderlin's "Germania" and "The Rhine" (which have since appeared as volume 39 of the Gesamtausgabe), and of course *Contributions* itself, were published by Heidegger himself during his lifetime. Taken together, these works point to a formidable breadth and depth of philosophical activity in the space of just a few years. And *Contributions* should, of course, be read critically within the context of the other works of this period, as well as within the scope of the thinker's work as a whole.

Nevertheless, the true time of *Contributions* is not that of a particular historical period as commonly understood by our historiographical representation of events, nor does it belong within a chronological ordering of the thinker's biography. As with all of Heidegger's thinking from the early 1920s on, the time of *Contributions* is that of the *Augenblick:* the "glance of the eye" or moment of authentic presence that at once sustains and is sustained by the authentic action of the thinker, his thoughtful work. The time of the *Augenblick* is not that of a "now" or point in time that can be set before us or represented as one "moment" in a linear sequence of events. It no more belongs to such a sequence than does the associated event of *Ereignis*, or coming into one's own, that is the proper topic of *Contributions*. This is not to say, however, that the *Augenblick* is not also historical; rather, it belongs to the *Ereignis* or event of the "history of being," that is, to the way in which being happens and is destined to historical human beings. Human beings, on Heidegger's account, first become historical and come to belong to a history through the happening of this event that is the address—the speaking—of historicality itself. The *Augenblick* or moment of authentic presence is the temporal moment in which we thoughtfully respond to the way in which being addresses us. Whether thoughtful or thought-less, our response to the address of being is the essence of all human action. The time of the *Augenblick,* as the time of thoughtful action itself, is a time of genesis, creation, and passing away, of both natality and mortality: a time in which and out of which an action or a work first emerges that can then, subsequently, be taken up into a history or ordered within a chronology. Such, as I shall try to show, is the time of *Contributions.*

Before proceeding to look at *Contributions,* and in particular at part II, entitled *Der Anklang,* I should first like to recall some of the key characteristics of the *Augenblick* that emerge from Heidegger's early phenomenological analyses.[2]

The Augenblick as the Site of Human Action: Heidegger's Reading of Aristotle and the Phenomenology of Dasein

Heidegger's early phenomenological analyses of Aristotle, as presented particularly in the 1922 treatise "Phenomenological Interpretations with Respect to Aristotle"[3] and in the 1924/25 lecture course on Plato's *Sophist,*[4] are of pivotal importance for his subsequent understanding of the *Augenblick.* For it was in these early encounters with Aristotle, as his student Hans-Georg Gadamer reports, and in particular through his discovery of the intellectual virtue of *phronesis* in Book VI of the *Nicomachean Ethics,* that Heidegger "took his first, decisive distance from 'phenomenology as a strict science.'"[5] In Aristotle's analysis of *phronesis,* Heidegger found a kind of knowing and understanding that was fundamentally different from—and indeed more primordial than—any form of theoretical or "scientific" knowledge and yet absolutely decisive for the apprehension and conduct of human life. Aristotle's analyses of the dianoetic virtues as modes of the disclosure of truth (*aletheuein*) in Book VI of the *Nicomachean Ethics* had, as Gadamer notes, "for Heidegger the following significance above all: that the primacy of judgment, of logic, and of 'scientific knowledge' hit a decisive limit with regard to understanding the facticity of human life."[6] That limit became manifest above all through the analysis of *phronesis,* practical wisdom regarding the accomplishment of factical life. As an intellectual virtue, *phronesis* is concerned with deliberating well (*euboulia*), with finding the best action (*eupraxia*) in a given situation, the action most conducive to accomplishing the good life or living well as a whole (*to eu zen holon*). As such, *phronesis* is not theoretical or formal knowledge—even though it must be informed by a *theoria* or contemplation of the whole, that is, by *sophia,* philosophical knowing—nor is it a kind of technical know-how (*techne*) that possesses the form, or *eidos,* of its action in advance. What is decisive, rather, is that *phronesis* must be attuned to the particular situation, to the here-and-now circumstances of action that cannot be seen or known in advance. The situation of action can be seen only in the moment of action itself, in the moment in which one finds oneself faced with having to act, that is, to participate in disclosing the truth of one's worldly being as best one can, and to act accordingly. *Phronesis* is concerned with the disclosure and accomplishment of the truth of being—for Aristotle, of one's own finite and temporally determined being in the situation of action—and not with the discovery or knowledge of an already existing truth. For one's own, thrown being is that which is factically otherwise at every moment, futural in the sense that it not only already is but has always yet to come, so long as one continues to exist.

In Book VI of the *Nicomachean Ethics,* Aristotle identifies the kind of practical seeing that belongs to *phronesis* and is attuned to the situation of action as a kind of *nous* or *aisthesis.* It is a sheer seeing or apprehending of the circumstances as a whole in the light of one's ends and one's general orientation toward the world. In both the 1922 treatise and the 1924/25 course, Heidegger translates this practical *nous* as the *Augenblick* of action, as that moment of presence in which one's ownmost, worldly being is held open for a possible decision. As he puts it in the *Sophist* course:

> *Phronesis* is *a catching sight of the here-and-now,* of the concrete here-and-now character of the momentary situation. *As aisthesis it is the glance of the eye, the momentary glance* [der Blick des Auges, der Augen-blick] *at what is concrete in each specific case and as such can always be otherwise.*[7]

What is decisive in *phronesis* is the *Augenblick* itself. It is decisive in the sense of being that starting from which and toward which the entire deliberation and practical judgment of *phronesis* proceeds, its *arche* and *eschaton.* Practical deliberation, although crucially informed by a wider context that goes beyond the particular situation of action (most notably, it is informed by one's ethical dispositions or *hexeis;* by one's goals, both immediate and general; and by one's view and understanding of the whole of life), has the task of responding appropriately to whatever is given in the situation itself, that is, of responding to that which is disclosed in and through the *Augenblick,* and of determining the *kairos* of the *Augenblick.* The *kairos* refers to the opportune moment of action: it is the "most extreme" point or *eschaton* in which the *Augenblick* of *phronesis* culminates or peaks, the decisive moment in which an action engages.[8]

The time of the *Augenblick* as the moment of genuine *praxis* informed by *phronesis* is thus a moment of knowing and seeing oneself—one's own being—as addressed and called to decision by one's worldly situation as a whole. It entails an authentic understanding of the being of oneself as *praxis,* that is, of one's being futural in such a way that one's own having-been—who and what one has been up to that moment—is not left behind as a past that can never be retrieved except by recollection,

but approaches one as that whose being is now to be decided, held open
for decision. As the time of authentic action, the *Augenblick* as the moment of authentic presence is distinguished from the ordinary representation of the "objective" time of nature (conceived as a linear sequence
of homogeneous "now"-points unfolding before an independent or outside observer) in being finite and unrepeatable, unique and singular,
bound to the finite being of the individual in these particular circumstances and at this particular place and time, and—as this protoethical
moment—essentially inaccessible to others. The phenomenon of the
Augenblick has certainly been seen in the history of philosophy, yet according to Heidegger not fully appreciated in its radical implications, in
large part because of the dominance of the theoretical view of the world.
Indeed, even Aristotle, "the last of the great philosophers who had eyes
to see,"[9] and who saw most clearly here, did not fully fathom the temporality that announces itself in this phenomenon. As Heidegger remarks in his lecture course *The Basic Problems of Phenomenology* (1927),
"Aristotle already saw the phenomenon of the *Augenblick,* the *kairos,* and
delimited it in Book VI of his *Nicomachean Ethics,* although without suc-
ceeding in connecting the temporal character specific to the *kairos* with
what he otherwise knows as time (the *nun*)."[10] Similarly, Heidegger acknowledges the significance attributed to the *Augenblick* in Kierkegaard's
thought but emphasizes that Kierkegaard understands the moment only
as the "now" of the ordinary concept of time, that is, he does not explicate the originary temporality specific to the *Augenblick.*[11]

In the hermeneutic of Dasein presented in *Being and Time,* Heidegger
attempts to explicate phenomenologically the originary and authentic
time of the *Augenblick* in terms of the "ecstatic" temporality proper to it,
by contrast to the ordinary concept of time that issues from an "inau-
thentic" self-understanding of Dasein. Indeed, ordinary understanding
too "sees" the *Augenblick,* but sees it only as an instant, as a fleeting
moment that is simply present-at-hand, and not as the decisive time of
action itself.[12]

Just as it interprets the being of the self inauthentically, in a manner
phenomenologically inappropriate to it, by regarding it as something
present-at-hand or ready-to-hand, so too it misinterprets the originary
time and presence of human existence—the moment—as something
objectively and independently present, thus failing to see it fully or per-
spicuously, in the degree of transparency possible with regard to the
phenomenon itself. The authentic presence of Dasein's existence, however, as Heidegger elucidates in *Being and Time,* is neither a fleeting
instant nor an objectively ascertainable "now":

> That *presence* [Gegenwart] which is held in temporality proper and which is
> thus itself authentic, we call the *Augenblick.* This term must be understood

in the active sense as an ecstasis. It means the rapture of resolute openness [*die entschlossene Entrückung*] in which Dasein is carried away toward whatever possibilities and circumstances are encountered in the situation, but a rapture that is *held* in this resolute openness. The *Augenblick* is a phenomenon that *in principle* can *not* be clarified in terms of the "now." The "now" is a temporal phenomenon that belongs to time as within-time-ness: the "now" "within which" something arises, passes away, or is present-at-hand. Nothing can occur "in the *Augenblick*"; rather, as authentic presence or waiting-toward [*Gegen-wart*], the *Augenblick* lets us *first encounter* whatever can be "in a time" as ready-to-hand or present-at-hand.[13]

The *Augenblick* is not a formal, already-existing framework within which events then occur or phenomena appear; it is, rather, the moment of concretion, of the coming-into-presence of an event or action itself and thus *is* the presence of that event or action in its very unfolding. Such presence is not only not that of a fleeting moment or instant, inasmuch as it is "held" within future and having-been and thus has a certain duration (again, one that cannot be formally determined in advance, since it pertains to the finite situation of action), but is a presence that is held in an openness to the authentic future, that is, to the originary closure that enables it to exist as the thrown "ground" of a nothingness or nullity.[14] As such, the *Augenblick* is a "waiting toward"—as the German *Gegen-wart* (presence) suggests when hyphenated —the unforeseeable that may be encountered in a given situation, a being held ready and open for whatever may be encountered. Such being held at the ready is the accomplishment of the fundamental attunement of anxiety or *Angst*. In such an attunement, which first brings it before the world as world and before the fundamental possibilities of its being,[15] Dasein has always already anticipated, and thus is opened to the authentic possibility of understanding itself from out of, the "most extreme" possibility of its ownmost being. Such is a possibility that cannot itself be determined in advance (in the sense of "outstripped" or "bypassed" [*überholt*]), the possibility whose moment or *Augenblick* cannot be known, except as "indeterminate," "possible at any moment [*Augenblick*]," the possibility of the impossibility of any retrieval (*Wiederholung*) of the possibility of being-in-the-world as such and as a whole. Yet this means that this anticipatory being-toward-death, in which Dasein holds itself in resolute openness (*Entschlossenheit*) and in readiness for the retrieval of its ownmost, singular and individuated being (that is, for "action"), is always already exposed to a "decision" or closure within the happening of being itself, namely, that closure that belongs to (and indeed "is") the action or accomplishment of the originary future, the closure of that which is and has been, of that which is now present, the closure that is the opening of the moment itself, the possibility of the new, of origination. The *Augenblick*'s proceeding toward, or unfolding into, the absolute *eschaton*, the moment of an open decision (*Entschluß*) in which an action engages, itself responds not only to the necessities of the situation of action, but to a more originary necessity and decision within being itself. And this in itself tells us that human existence or being as "action" is not reducible to "the decided action of a subject," as Heidegger later emphasized,[16] since being itself gets decided whether or not we "act" as subjects or as individuals, whether or not we (Dasein) choose to take action or not. For being is that which has not only always already been decided, but, at one and the same moment, has always yet to be decided. And how being comes to be decided is indeed a matter of indifference, one might say, to being—though not, presumably, to us. While as human beings we cannot but "care" about our being, fundamentally and in the sense of *Sorge* outlined in *Being and Time*, so that we cannot fundamentally be indifferent to it, there is nevertheless something about being itself, about its very event, its happening or unfolding, that strangely fails to touch us, that withdraws from us, that remains indifferent to us. We, as human beings, are those who stand and are held in the moment of being's decision, whether authentically and knowingly or not. The *Augenblick* is not itself something that is decided by the human being's power of thought or decision alone, nor indeed in the first instance. For even in the situation of human action guided by *phronesis*, human judgment can only respond to what already presents itself in the situation, that is, to the *Augenblick* itself.

What is especially significant here is the way in which these provisional phenomenological analyses of Dasein—provisional with respect to the interpretation of authentic time as the horizon of any understanding of being in general (not merely of the being of Dasein)—already point back into the originary dimension of presencing (of the presencing of a world) in which Dasein is held and to which it remains exposed in advance of any action or activity of its own. All activity on the part of Dasein—whether that of ethical or political action, or that of thinking, knowing, or judging, or indeed that of making or producing—all such activity as in each case a mode of coming-into-being is shown to be primarily *responsive* in its very origination. This does not mean, of course, that Dasein or the being of the human being is thereby reduced to a mere passivity that would stand over and against the activity or action of "being itself" conceived as a subject. "Being itself" is neither a hypostatized "subject" nor something that stands opposite to and independent of human being, but refers to the worldly horizon or field of presencing, the open expanse in which beings first show themselves and appear as such. The primordial responsiveness of all human existing and action to the openness of being does, however, mean that human action of whatever kind cannot be adequately conceived as having its originating ground in an already existing self or subject, or in human understanding or judgment alone. Rather, human action first comes into its own (*eigenes*), authentic being in response to the more originary happening or event (*Er-eignis*) of being itself, in response to a necessity and decision within being. There is, in this sense, not a logical or hierarchical priority of being over beings, but a *precedence* of being itself, a precedence that is the happening in which being "sends" or destines itself, a precedence that is the history or historicality of being. Such precedence unfolds as an event of difference, of the originary differentiation of the "ontological" difference whereby beings are, in their coming into being and passing away, differentiated from this very event of their presencing.

We may briefly consider the significance of Heidegger's phenomenological recovery of the originary time or Temporality (*Temporalität*) of being itself from two sides: with respect to Aristotle's ontology, and with respect to the so-called "turning" within Heidegger's own thinking that leads from his work of the 1920s into the more mature work of the 1930s and beyond. First, with regard to the basic distinction between *phronesis* and *sophia* that guides Aristotle's ontology of factical human life, it is especially important to note how Heidegger's analyses integrate the phenomenon of world into the radical temporality disclosed in the phenomenological analysis of *phronesis*. The world is no longer seen as that which is permanent (*aei*), as that which always is as it is, which can be disclosed in its being only via the pure, untroubled, contemplative gaze of *theorein*, and which is thus to be contrasted with the being of that which can be otherwise than it is, the factical life of human concerns that is disclosed in *phronesis*. The being or Dasein of the human being and of the realm of human affairs is not to be contrasted with the being of the *kosmos* or of nature in its presence-at-hand; rather, the world is that which, insofar as it can be disclosed at all, is only ever disclosed within and through the temporality of factical human existence: it is temporalized in that very temporality as its "horizon." Dasein's being is intrinsically "being-in-the-world" and not that of an individual subject or knower that stands opposite the "world," conceived as the totality of what is permanently present-at-hand and simply there as a potential object to be known or disclosed scientifically or philosophically. On the other hand, a corollary of this is that Aristotle's focus in the *Nicomachean Ethics* on human beings insofar as they can be regarded as the origin (*arche*) of their actions, the focus of the analyses of action on the importance of judgment, knowledge, and *proairesis* (prior choice or "intention"), and thus the bringing about of an individual "subject" of action, while not simply opposed by Heidegger (since Dasein's projective or "proairetic" understanding plays a crucial role in the disclosure and happening of the self), is likewise complicated by the orientation of the analysis of Dasein toward the worldly and thrown character of Dasein's temporal individuation. Dasein's actions and decisions are determined much more by its coming toward itself from out of its already having been thrown into the happening of a world and finding itself in the midst of that world than by any "subjectivity." The *Augenblick* as ecstatic presence in each case designates the authentic and originary presence of world in the midst of the factical situation of action. As Heidegger elucidates in *The Basic Problems of Phenomenology*, it names the way in which the world is authentically disclosed in the resolute openness of Dasein for action:

> In the *Augenblick* as an ecstasis, the Dasein that exists as openly resolved is transported on each occasion into the factically determinate possibilities, circumstances, and contingencies of the situation of its action. The *Augenblick* is that which, springing from resolute openness, first and solely has an eye [*Blick*] for what comprises the situation of action. It is that mode of existing in resolute openness in which Dasein as being-in-the-world holds and keeps its world in view [*im Blick*].[17]

This phenomenological retrieval of world as the temporally determined, open horizon of the presence or being of beings as a whole as that starting from which factical Dasein first comes to be, that is, to enact itself in each instance, not only dislodges theoretical contemplation from its privileged position as granting primary access to the world, however. It also means that, while the temporal being of Dasein that finds its pivotal focus in the *Augenblick* must indeed be understood as action (*Handeln*) or *praxis*, such *praxis* must be taken in an originary sense that encompasses or underlies all of Dasein's modes of being. It should not, as in Aristotle, be restricted to ethical or political *praxis* understood in a narrow sense as contrasted with the *praxis* of theoretical contemplation or philosophizing.

With regard to the second question, that of the transition of Heidegger's own thinking from the preparatory, hermeneutic phenomenology of the being of Dasein in the 1920s into the thinking of being itself that gains ascendancy from the early 1930s on, a twofold shift occurs. The first aspect concerns the manner of thinking; the second, the issue or *Sache* that becomes the focus of thought. On the one hand, what is left behind as inadequate to the issue or matter itself (the question of being) is the conception of phenomenological ontology as a science—as "the science of the being of beings"[18]—that is, the entire venture of a theoretical representation and thematization of the being of beings, the objectification of being upon the horizon of its givenness.[19] For this very aspiration to develop a science of being soon showed itself, as Heidegger would concede in the "Letter on 'Humanism,'" to be "inappropriate."[20] The horizon of givenness of the being of beings showed itself phenomenologically to be neither a stable entity (the "subject" as ground of the act of presentation or theoretical objectification), nor the permanent presence (*nous*) of the world, but the temporal event of the presencing of world whose horizon, as originary and futural, and thus essentially open, is simultaneously one of the closure and concealment of being itself. This event of presencing is the way in which being is originarily "given" or destined; as in each case singular and finite, bound to a particular worldly context and showing itself only in the *Augenblick*, it cannot by its very nature become the object of theoretical contemplation or thematization. Commensurate with this, the *Sache* or issue of this thinking has also changed accordingly. In place of the attempt in the 1920s at a thematic and scientific objectification of being starting from the analytic of Dasein, where being is conceived metaphysically as the horizon of givenness belonging to beings—an attempt that, at least in its scientific and methodological aspirations, is itself already historically determined by subjectivity—Heidegger's work of the 1930s and beyond constitutes the continually renewed endeavor to stand thoughtfully within and to think from out of the event or *Ereignis* of being as presencing, that is, to assume a stance within the *Augenblick* as the originary "site" of this event. It emerges from the attempt to think this very event, and indeed, to understand thinking itself—the most proper action or activity of the thinker—as nothing other than a finite response to this event. The resolute openness of the *Augenblick* is from here on seen not so much as belonging to the being of Dasein conceived as one particular, albeit distinctive entity among others; rather, the being of Dasein, as of all other entities, is now understood as belonging, always already and in advance, to the *Augenblick* as the site of the disclosure of a world and of the historical destining of the event of being. Furthermore, the *Augenblick* itself is now seen to be historically determined, not primarily by the historicity of Dasein, as it was in *Being and Time*, but by historicality understood as the happening of being itself, to which human actions are responsive.

The so-called "turning" within Heidegger's thinking is thus itself a response to a turning within being itself, that is, to a change in the way in which being shows itself and addresses itself to the thinker. No longer showing itself as a temporal horizon whose temporal character (*Temporalität*) was to be thematically illuminated and objectified by theoretical-scientific study—as though this kind of thinking were itself fundamentally untouched by its object; as though such contemplation were not itself already a response to a historical address and destiny of being—being now appears in its historical precedence as the event of presencing that announces itself in the *Augenblick* in its finitude and singularity and which, precisely as this singular and finite event in each case, cannot itself become something present. It thus remains inaccessible to theoretical apprehension, which for its part can contemplate only that which already *is*, that which is already present, and whose being, moreover, always is as it is (*aei*): that which is constantly present in its sameness. Accordingly, Heidegger indicates in *Contributions:*

> [T]he task was . . . above all to avoid an objectification of beyng, on the one hand by *holding back* the "Temporal" [*temporalen*] interpretation of beyng, and at the same time by attempting to make "visible" the truth of beyng independently thereof. . . . Thinking became increasingly historical. . . . Beyng itself announced its historical essence.[21]

A key transitional text in this respect, on the way from Heidegger's early phenomenology to the thinking of *Contributions*, is the last lecture course of the 1920s, the course of winter semester 1929/30, entitled *The Fundamental Concepts of Metaphysics: World, Finitude, Solitude*. Toward the end of that course, Heidegger raises the critical question of the appropriate "dimension" for thinking the ontological difference, that is, for thinking the distinction between being and beings. It is inappropriate, he now insists, to think this distinction in the manner of objectifying thinking, as though we could simply place "being" and "beings," and the difference between them, all before us on the same level, as though they simply lay independently there to be contemplated by our theoretical gaze. For metaphysical thinking has in essence always represented being and beings in this manner, in their difference, although without thinking this difference radically enough (and thereby tending to reduce being to what Heidegger calls "beingness," an existent quality or ground of beings) or paying heed to the difference as such. Not only does the ontological difference not lie before us as an object that lies present-at-hand within the field of presence; it is also, Heidegger emphasizes, not something first created by a particular way of thinking (philosophy). Rather, "we are always already moving *within* the *distinction as it occurs. It is not *we* who make it, rather, *it* happens *to us* as the fundamental occurrence of our Dasein."[22] Furthermore, not only is this differentiation of being (presence) from beings (that which is present) something that happens constantly, whether with or without any explicit intervention or conscious action on our part, but it must, Heidegger stresses, "*already* have occurred" simply for us to be able to apprehend beings in their being such and such. "In a metaphysical sense, therefore, the distinction stands at the origin [*Anfang*] of Dasein."[23] In these statements we see at once an explicit recognition of the precedence of the event of presencing as an event of differentiation, and an insight into this event as lying at the origin of the being of Dasein, as that starting from which Dasein can first be open for the approach of beings themselves. Finally, and most importantly, Heidegger here makes the decisive call to set aside the thematic coining of the distinction and to "venture the *essential step* of transposing ourselves into the *occurrence of this distinguishing* in which the distinction occurs,"[24] that is, into the dimension of the happening of world, the occurrence in which world is "formed." This is, in effect, the first formulation of what Heidegger would later refer to as the call for the "step back" out of metaphysics (founded on this distinction) into the "essence" of metaphysics as the dimension from which the distinction first arises.[25]

The *Augenblick* as the Time of *Ereignis:*
From Phenomenology to *Contributions*

When Heidegger alludes to *Contributions* in a marginal note to the "Letter on 'Humanism,'" as "a path begun in 1936, in the *'Augenblick'* of an attempt to say the truth of being in a simple manner," his highlighting of the *Augenblick* here indicates that it is central to the very stance of this thinking and not to be understood in the ordinary sense of a chronological moment. On the other hand, as I have tried to indicate, while chronologically speaking, the said path may have its immediate beginning in 1936, its true origins and commencement lie much earlier in the chronology of the thinker's work. Indeed, on Heidegger's self-understanding, the true origins of this new endeavor of thinking lie in the history of being itself that unfolds in a destinal and epochal manner from out of the first beginning or commencement (*Anfang*) of Western philosophical thought, the beginning of metaphysics itself. The transition in Heidegger's thinking outlined above corresponds, in effect, to the historical transition that thinking now finds itself called upon to accomplish, the transition from this first beginning to what Heidegger calls an "other beginning." The *Augenblick* of thinking must therefore understand itself as "historical" in precisely this sense, namely, that of belonging to the way in which being itself unfolds or "happens." Thus, in the opening sections of the *Beiträge* Heidegger writes that "the historical *Augenblick* of transition must be accomplished from out of the knowledge that all metaphysics . . . remains incapable of placing the human being into any foundational relations toward beings."[26] For insight into the essence of metaphysics, founded on the ontological difference, has shown that metaphysical thought itself fails to think back into or from out of that very dimension that first founds it: it remains closed off in advance from the originary happening of being and thus remains condemned to think and to relate toward beings themselves in a reductive manner.[27] Similarly, writing the archaic "beyng" (*Seyn*) to indicate that being (*Sein*) is here thought otherwise than in metaphysical representation, Heidegger emphasizes that:

> The thoughtful question concerning the truth of beyng is the *Augenblick* that carries the transition. This *Augenblick* can never be ascertained as something actual; still less can it be calculated. It first establishes the time of *Ereignis.*[28]

The question concerning the truth of the happening of being, as *Ereignis,* itself occurs as the *Augenblick* of a historical transition to another thinking of being, a thinking whose time is that of its own enactment, of its coming into its own being, of its being "enowned." The "singular simplicity" of this transition, Heidegger goes on to say, can never be grasped historiographically or by our ordinary concept of history—since these merely represent objectively what has already occurred and lies present. They belong to metaphysical thinking. The transitional thinking of *Contributions,* by contrast, belongs to a time that can never become present as such, to what Heidegger calls "the concealed moments [*Augenblicke*] of the history of being."[29] On the other hand, is it not only by virtue of its becoming misrepresentable as a possible object of metaphysical or historiographical representation that this *Augenblick,* as Heidegger puts it, "has a long future in store for it"—granted, he adds, that being's abandonment of beings can once more be ruptured? The *Augenblick* of this thinking, which first "sets" or establishes (*setzt*) the time of *Ereignis,* is also the *Augenblick* of this thinking's being established within being, that is, becoming a *work* that itself henceforth *is* and remains to be read—a work whose time has always yet to come. Such thinking becomes a being (*Seiendes*) that "is," not in the sense of being a fixed entity, but of being a work, that is, of being something at work, something that manifests the event of its own coming into being as an event that precedes and carries it, that remains always yet to occur. The thinking "of," that is, from out of *Ereignis* that is the work of *Contributions,* has thus, in this sense, always yet to happen, always yet to be accomplished—which accomplishment (*Vollbringen*) of being is the authentic action of thinking.[30] The event or *Ereignis* of this thinking is thus, astonishingly enough, an event that demands its own faithfulness, that calls for its own historical *Augenblick* as something that, in all its simplicity, remains singular, unique, repeatable only in the singularity of its unrepeatability (or untranslatability—and this is at once this thinking's resistance to translation *and* its necessity of being translated). What is at issue here is, therefore—and this is something Heidegger stresses throughout *Contributions*—not at all a thinking of being or beyng in its difference from beings (thus not at all a thinking from out of the ontological difference), but a "saving" or rescuing (*retten*) of *beings themselves,* a bringing of (our experience of) beings themselves back into the "truth of beyng." The task is that of preparing "the time of building the essential shape of beings from out of the truth of beyng,"[31] of *"the restoration of beings from out of the truth of beyng."*[32] This entails "letting Dasein become possible for human beings and thus rescuing a steadfastness in the midst of beings, so that beings themselves may undergo restoration in the open of the strife between earth and world."[33] The site of this possible steadfastness in the midst of beings, in contrast to the marked lack of steadfast abode that characterizes the fleeting existence of "living for the moment" in the contemporary epoch, is the *Augenblick* as the site (*Stätte*) of the strife between earth and world—here, the site in which the work of the thinker can first come into its own and thus authentically be the work that it is. Thus, throughout *Contributions* the site of the *Augenblick* is identified as the "time-space" of the strife between earth and world, and, as such, as the site of *Ereignis* itself.[34] The *Augenblick*, as the originary time of the event of being itself in which the being of beings attains possible steadfastness in being set to work, is in this sense *"the time of being."*[35]

The originary, authentic being of Dasein as a being held in the *Augenblick* of resolute openness is now to be thought from out of *Ereignis*. The fundamental, thoughtful attunement of such being held (*gehalten*) — an attunement that is presumably already intimated within the *Angst* that in *Being and Time* opens Dasein onto its world as world and is said to "hold the *Augenblick* at the ready"[36]—is now understood as that of restraint or reservedness (*Verhaltenheit*).[37] Restraint is, as Heidegger articulates it, "the distinctive, momentary [*augenblickliche*] relation to *Ereignis* in having been called by the address of *Ereignis*."[38] It attunes the *Augenblick* in the manner of a "deep stillness."[39] Dasein's being-a-self or selfhood—the originary dimension of being-a-self that is to be "retrieved" for the human being[40]—indeed consists in its being "the site of the *Augenblick* of this address and belonging [to *Ereignis*]."[41] Dasein, as "the fundamental occurrence of future history," "springs from *Ereignis* and becomes the site of a possible *Augenblick* for the decision concerning man—his history or non-history [*Ungeschichte*] as its transition unto downgoing."[42] In emphasizing that "decision" here, in the context of *Contributions*, is not to be understood as the action or activity of the human being, but in the first instance as the decision that belongs to the happening of being itself and that addresses itself to humans in calling for their possible response, Heidegger concedes that *Being and Time* was, in this respect, open to the danger of misinterpreting Dasein's resolute openness in the *existentiell*-"anthropological" sense of "moral resolve," rather than "the other way around," as "the temporalizing-spatializing of the free play of the time-space of beyng."[43] The "turning" in which being shows itself as the historical or destinal happening of *Ereignis* responds to this danger.

In seeking to understand the historical *Augenblick* of this transition I would like to call attention once again to the lecture course of winter semester 1929/30 as an important intimation of the thinking attempted in *Contributions*. In part II of *Contributions*, concerned with the intimation (*Anklang*) of beyng from out of the refusal that announces itself in being's abandonment of beings,[44] which the consummation of metaphysics in the epoch of planetary technology itself institutes as an oblivion of being, Heidegger writes of the kind of knowing (*Wissen*) appropriate to such intimation. It is a knowing that is itself *augenblicklich:* a knowing of the *Augenblick* that is enacted from out of and as the *Augenblick* of this historical transition:

> because in the other beginning beyng becomes *Ereignis,* the intimation of beyng also must be history, must pass through history by an essential disruption, and must at the same time know and be able to say the *Augenblick* of this history. (What is meant is not a characterization or description according to a philosophy of history, but a knowing of history from out of the *Augenblick* and as the *Augenblick* of the first intimation of the truth of beyng itself.)[45]

If the history of being as metaphysics can justifiably be seen as the history or happening of the oblivion of being, then the first intimation of beyng—as the intimation of this oblivion as such—itself emerges from, and in this sense belongs to, that history as what is withheld in it in and throughout its epochal destinings. The intimation itself, however, thus also passes through that history in disrupting it, in rupturing the concealment of the oblivion of being and thereby first letting it be seen as such, indeed first letting that history be seen as what it has been in this regard. The intimation of beyng, in and as this historical *Augenblick,* is that very disruption.[46]

The intimation of beyng unfolds from out of a "compelling need" (*nötigende Not*) that issues from the oblivion of beyng and demands to be recognized and acknowledged as such in its highest instance: the "need of needlessness" (*Not der Notlosigkeit*).[47] Being's abandonment of beings is an "emptiness" (*Leere*), a "telling refusal" (*Sichversagen*) that, as originarily both recollective and awaiting, opens up a presence that is directed toward the decision of beyng itself, the presence that is the *Augenblick.*[48] In the 1929/30 course, such need and refusal were already recognized by Heidegger as the absence of any essential oppressiveness or distress (*Bedrängnis*) of contemporary Dasein as a whole. Dasein's ordinary, everyday understanding, itself historically conditioned, suppresses the profound boredom that underlies it in its continual haste to attend to every social, political, and cultural need of the day through its organizations and programs.[49] As such, it fails to let any essential need as a whole emerge, that is, to direct its view toward what is happening fundamentally in the midst of the being of beings as a whole, namely, being's abandonment of beings that, in profound boredom, lets all beings recede into an indifference.[50] In profound boredom—which contemporary existence precisely does not let arise as such—Dasein is left empty in being delivered over to beings' refusal of themselves as a whole, in being refused any essential possibilities of engaging with or attending to beings themselves.[51] Yet such refusal, Heidegger emphasizes, is intrinsically a "telling refusal" (*Versagen*) that impels and holds Dasein toward that which originarily makes it possible, enabling its existence in the midst of beings as a whole as a potentiality for being, carrying and sustaining all its essential possibilities. And that is: the *Augenblick* as "that which is most extreme [*Äußerste*]," enabling all the possibilities of Dasein as possibilities,[52] and which, as "the *Augenblick* of essential action," ruptures the temporal entrancement attuning us in the manner of the "long while [*Lange-weile*]" or "long time" that profound boredom originarily is.[53] Yet which *Augenblick*, Heidegger asks, announces itself and can thereby be intimated in this telling refusal of beings as a whole?[54] To what must Dasein, entranced by the need of the absence of any distress as a whole, openly resolve itself so as to rupture such entrancement and to be open for such need?

> To this: namely, first *bringing about* for itself once again a *genuine knowing concerning that wherein whatever properly makes Dasein possible consists.* And what is that? The fact that the *Augenblick* [emphasis Heidegger's] in which Dasein brings itself before itself as that which is properly binding must time and again stand before Dasein as such. . . .
>
> What, therefore, is demanded by the *Augenblick* simultaneously announced in this absence of any distress as a whole? That the *Augenblick* itself be understood, and that means seized upon, as the *innermost necessity* [Notwendigkeit] *of the freedom of Dasein.*[55]

What is needed above all is a genuine knowing (*Wissen*) and understanding of the *Augenblick* itself as the ground of Dasein's freedom, that is, as that wherein the possibility of all its possibilities is gathered in each case. Yet this knowledge of the *Augenblick* is here already seen as a knowledge that is called for by the "need" of the contemporary situation itself, of the historical moment in which Dasein finds itself. And this entails, as Heidegger had expressed it in 1928, a "historical recollection." The activity of philosophizing, he insisted in *The Metaphysical Foundations of Logic,* must itself respond to the "necessity of the *Augenblick.*"[56] And this means that it must understand itself in terms of the historicality of its own being. Historical recollection of the history of philosophy occurs not in a theoretical or speculative-dialectical seeing but "thrives only in understanding oneself in terms of the *Augenblick*" (*im augenblicklichen Sichselbstverstehen*). It is "at once recollective and *augenblicklich,*" grounded in the "originary unity . . . of the temporality of the factical Dasein that is philosophizing."[57] What Heidegger in *Contributions* names "the concealed moments [*Augenblicke*] of the history of being"[58] is, toward the end of the 1928 course, foreshadowed in his remarks on the significance of Kant's discovery of the productivity of the transcendental imagination—a productivity that, from Heidegger's perspective, belongs originarily not to the "subject" but to the temporalizing of ecstatic temporality itself, in which what is "produced" or brought forth is not a being or entity but nothing less than the *nihil originarium* of the phenomenon of world, the unity of the ecstatic horizon, that is, of the Temporality of being. In the 1929/30 course this productivity will be thought as the event of world-formation (*Weltbildung*). Kant's discovery of the productivity of the transcendental imagination, the temporal significance of which is not fully fathomed by Kant himself, is, Heidegger comments, "the first *Augenblick* in the history of philosophy in which metaphysics attempts to free itself from logic." And yet, he adds, "this *Augenblick* passed." "Perhaps the true happening in the history of philosophy is always only a temporalizing of such *Augenblicke*, moments that, irrupting and cast at distant intervals, never actually become manifest in what they properly are."[59]

In view of Heidegger's growing recognition of the inappropriateness of understanding the phenomenological thinking of being as the science of the being of beings, §76 of *Contributions*, in which Heidegger presents a number of theses concerning "science," is especially significant. Heidegger here not only acknowledges that "science" (*Wissenschaft*) does not constitute genuine knowing (*Wissen*) but, alluding to the 1929/30 course, identifies the implicit oblivion and abandonment of being that announces itself in profound boredom as being the "concealed end" or goal of modern science — even though science itself has not the slightest intimation of this state of "complete boredom" toward which it rushes in bringing about being's "yawning abandonment of beings."[60] The science referred to here is presumably that of the ontic sciences that determine the historical era of modernity (since philosophy in the form of Heidegger's attempted grounding of a phenomenological science of being precisely leads to an intimation of this concealed end): those sciences that objectify beings upon the horizon of their being (subjectivity). But Heidegger's critique of science also extends to his own conception of ontology as an objectifying science of being. In §73, he concedes that, with regard to any attempt to theoretically lay the ground or foundations of science, or in other words to thematically and theoretically account for the activity of science as such, "Every kind of theoretico-scientific (transcendental) attempt to lay the ground has become impossible." Commensurate with this comes the insistence that the very notion of "science" must be "freed from its historical indeterminacy" and ascertained with respect to its specifically modern essence.[61] In short, the activity of science itself must be seen in terms of its own historicality, as determined by the history of being; the very horizon of the thinking of being is itself historical and as such cannot be theoretically ascertained, but only apprehended in a recollection that is *augenblicklich*.

Being's abandonment of being, according to Heidegger, constitutes a "unique era" in the history of the truth of beyng, the era of "the long time" in which the truth of beyng hesitates to bestow its essence clearly.[62] But this long time, which is that of the concealed, profound boredom that draws back and forth in the abysses of contemporary Dasein, is not that of a genuine steadfastness in the midst of things. It goes hand in hand with the modern phenomena of speed, acceleration, and rapidity that entail "fleetingness," "rapid forgetting," and "losing oneself" in the next newest thing—in short, with the entire ethos of "living for the moment" which, Heidegger reminds us, is in truth only "a blindness toward what is truly *augenblicklich*, that which is not fleeting, but opens up eternity."[63] The "eternity" in question here is not that of the *nunc stans*, the vision of a divine *praesens intuitus*, but that of the *Augenblick* itself: the "eternal," as Heidegger later indicates, does not refer to that which is ceaselessly prolonged but to "that which can withdraw in the *Augenblick*, so as to return once again . . . not as the *identical* [das Gleiche], but as that which is transformed ever anew, this one and singular thing: being [*Seyn*]."[64]

That which can thus return remains, to be sure, a child of its time— but a child, nevertheless. Of Mnemosyne, perhaps.

Notes

1. For bibliographical information on the texts referred to here, see the introduction to this volume, note 1. In this essay, all translations of texts by Heidegger are my own or modifications of the translations cited. Pagination cited refers in each case to the German edition. Where divergences from existing translations concern substantive issues of interpretation, rather than questions of style, I have added a note of clarification. With regard to *Contributions* in particular, I have chosen to retain for the most part the German words *Augenblick* ("moment") and *Ereignis* ("enowning"), since the aim of the present essay is to clarify the meaning of these terms in the context of Heidegger's thought with particular reference to *Contributions*.

2. For a more extensive account of Heidegger's thinking of the *Augenblick*, see my remarks in *The Glance of the Eye: Heidegger, Aristotle, and the Ends of Theory* (Albany: State University of New York Press, 1999).

3. "Phänomenologische Interpretationen zu Aristoteles (Anzeige der hermeneutischen Situation)," *Dilthey Jahrbuch für Philosophie und Geschichte der Geisteswissenschaften* 6 (1989): 235–74. Translated by Michael Baur as "Phenomenological Interpretations with Respect to Aristotle: Indication of the Hermeneutical Situation," *Man and World* 25 (1992): 355–93.

4. Gesamtausgabe, vol. 19: *Platon: Sophistes* (Frankfurt am Main: Vittorio Klostermann, 1992) (henceforth GA 19). Translated by Richard Rojcewicz and André Schuwer as *Plato's Sophist* (Bloomington: Indiana University Press, 1997).

5. *Gesammelte Werke*, vol. 3, pp. 286–87. Translated by John W. Stanley as

Heidegger's Ways (Albany: State University of New York Press, 1994), p. 141 (translation modified).

6. *Gesammelte Werke*, vol. 3, p. 312; *Heidegger's Ways*, p. 172 (translation modified).

7. See GA 19, 163–64.

8. See *Glance of the Eye*, pp. 39–47, for a more detailed discussion of the *Augenblick* and *phronesis*.

9. See Gesamtausgabe, vol. 24: *Die Grundprobleme der Phänomenologie* (Frankfurt am Main: Vittorio Klostermann, 1975) (henceforth GA 24), p. 329. Translated by Albert Hofstadter as *The Basic Problems of Phenomenology* (Bloomington: Indiana University Press, 1984).

10. See GA 24, 409.

11. GA 24, 408. See also *Sein und Zeit* (Halle an der Saale: Max Niemeyer, 1927) (henceforth SZ), p. 338, note 1. Translated by John Macquarrie and Edward Robinson as *Being and Time* (Oxford: Blackwell, 1987). For a more charitable affirmation of Kierkegaard, see Gesamtausgabe, vol. 29/30: *Die Grundbegriffe der Metaphysik: Welt-Endlichkeit-Einsamkeit* (Frankfurt am Main: Vittorio Klostermann, 1983) (henceforth GA 29/30), p. 225. Translated by William McNeill and Nicholas Walker as *The Fundamental Concepts of Metaphysics: World, Finitude, Solitude* (Bloomington: Indiana University Press, 1995). Karl Jaspers's analysis of the *Augenblick* in his *Psychology of Worldviews* is also acknowledged in SZ, p. 338, note 1, although without further comment. Finally, the significance of the *Augenblick* in Nietzsche's thought would become central to his reading of Nietzsche in the 1930s and beyond. See in particular the lecture course on "The Eternal Recurrence of the Same" in *Nietzsche*, vol. 1 (Pfullingen: Günther Neske, 1961). Translated by David Farrell Krell as *Nietzsche*, 4 vols. in 2 (New York: HarperCollins, 1991).

12. GA 29/30, 427.

13. SZ, 338. I have translated the German *Gegenwart* as "presence" rather than as "the present" since "the present" misleadingly suggests a fully constituted, determined presence, whereas Heidegger understands *Gegenwart* as entailing an essential openness in the direction of the future, an openness toward the event of presencing, and thus also an essential indeterminacy.

14. SZ, 330.

15. SZ, 187–91.

16. *Der Ursprung des Kunstwerkes*, in *Holzwege* (Frankfurt am Main: Vittorio Klostermann, 1950), p. 55. Translated by Albert Hofstadter as "The Origin of the Work of Art," in *Poetry, Language, Thought* (New York: Harper & Row, 1971), p. 67 (translation modified).

17. See GA 24, 407–408.

18. See SZ, 37.

19. On thematization and objectification as central to the method of scientific phenomenology, see SZ, §69b, and GA 24, §20b, and my remarks in chapter 3 of *Glance of the Eye*.

20. Gesamtausgabe, vol. 9: *Wegmarken* (Frankfurt am Main: Vittorio Klostermann, 1976), p. 357 [1st ed., p. 187]. Translated as *Pathmarks* by William McNeill, ed. (New York: Cambridge University Press, 1998).

21. GA 65, 451; CP, 317–18. In the present essay, I have preferred to render

the German *Seyn* by the corresponding Old English archaism "beyng" rather than by the neologism "be-ing." However, in keeping with Heidegger's own practice in the *Beiträge*, I have used "being" and "beyng" somewhat interchangeably. Here I have let the context decide the usage, sometimes preferring to emphasize the nonmetaphysical thinking by "beyng," at other times leaving the accent on continuity by using "being" where it should be clear from the context that "being" is here understood in a nonmetaphysical way.

22. See GA 29/30, 519.

23. See ibid. (translation modified).

24. See GA 29/30, 524.

25. On the "step back" into the happening of the ontological difference, see "The Onto-Theo-Logical Constitution of Metaphysics" (1957) in *Identität und Differenz* (Pfullingen: Günther Neske, 1957), pp. 39ff. In the same lecture, Heidegger remarks that we can enter the destinal clearing or event of being in its epochal significance only through *die Jähe des Augenblickes eines Andenkens:* only through a sheer or abrupt (thus unpredictable) *Augenblick* of commemorative thinking or remembrance (p. 59). On the association of "suddenness" or "abruptness" with the *Augenblick*, see my remarks in *Glance of the Eye* and note 46 below.

26. GA 65, 12; CP, 9.

27. On this point, see especially §266 of the *Beiträge* (GA 65, 465–69; CP, 327–30).

28. GA 65, 20; CP, 15.

29. GA 65, 92; CP, 64.

30. See the opening of the "Letter on 'Humanism'" (GA 9, 313).

31. GA 65, 5; CP, 4.

32. GA 65, 11; CP, 8.

33. GA 65, 7; CP, 6.

34. GA 65, 29–30; CP, 21–22. See also GA 65, 96–99, 260–61, 310–11, 349, 371, 391, 506–10; CP, 66–69, 183–84, 218–19, 244, 259, 273, 356–59. In later works, Heidegger underlines the intrinsic belonging together of *Ereignis* and the *Augenblick* by pointing to the original root of *Ereignis* as *Er-äugnis* (from *Auge*, the eye, as in *Augenblick*). *Ereignis* as *Er-äugnis* is being's catching sight of human beings, catching our eye, looking upon us in the *Augenblick*. See *Glance of the Eye*, p. 217, for further details. Regarding the strife between world and earth in relation to the work, see "The Origin of the Work of Art" and my remarks in *Glance of the Eye*, chapter 8.

35. GA 65, 508; CP, 358.

36. SZ, 344. On the difficult relation between the held presence of *Angst* and that of the *Augenblick*, see *Glance of the Eye*, pp. 132–34.

37. Note that the term *Verhaltenheit* is used by Heidegger as early as the 1929/30 course to characterize the essence of human action and selfhood: all "comportment" (*Verhalten*), by contrast with animal "behavior," is possible only where there is *Verhaltenheit*; a stance or *Haltung* is found only where there is selfhood. See GA 29/30, 397–98.

38. GA 65, 31; CP, 23.

39. GA 65, 34; CP, 24–25.

40. GA 65, 31; CP, 23.

41. GA 65, 52; CP, 37.

42. GA 65, 32; CP, 23.

43. GA 65, 87–88; CP, 60–61.

44. I have preferred to translate *Anklang* as "intimation" rather than as "echo," since the German word has more of a sense of the arrival or advent of a discernible trace or resonance, of a ringing or sounding, while the English "echo" tends to suggest the sounding of something already past. Heidegger's usage of *Anklang*, it seems to me, is very much intended to convey the sense of an opening up, an initial breaking forth or arrival (in German, *Ankunft*). See also my remarks in note 54.

45. GA 65, 108; CP, 76 (translation modified).

46. On the "abruptness" or suddenness (*Jähe*) of the *Augenblick* as a "historical" disruption and decision in the sense of an event of beyng, see the important reflections in §39 of *Besinnung* from 1938/39 (Gesamtausgabe, vol. 66 [Frankfurt am Main: Vittorio Klostermann, 1997]).

47. GA 65, 107; CP, 75.

48. GA 65, 383–84; CP, 268. For a discussion of these important pages, see Daniela Neu, *Die Notwendigkeit der Gründung im Zeitalter der Dekonstruktion* (Berlin: Duncker & Humblot, 1997).

49. GA 29/30, 238, 243–45.

50. GA 29/30, 215.

51. GA 29/30, 210–11.

52. GA 29/30, 215–16.

53. GA 29/30, 226–30.

54. Heidegger does not speak of an *Anklang* of being in GA 29/30, but he does speak of the *Augenblick* and its extremity as something that can be *geahnt*, "intimated," by Dasein in the temporal entrancement of profound boredom (GA 29/30, 227). Whereas *Ahnung* is here understood as a responsive activity on the part of Dasein, *Anklang* refers to the intimation that is addressed to us from beyng itself.

55. See GA 29/30, 247.

56. Gesamtausgabe, vol. 26: *Metaphysische Anfangsgründe der Logik im Ausgang von Leibniz* (Frankfurt am Main: Vittorio Klostermann, 1978) (henceforth GA 26), p. 11. Translated by Michael Heim as *The Metaphysical Foundations of Logic* (Bloomington: Indiana University Press, 1984).

57. See GA 26, 9–10.

58. GA 65, 92; CP, 64.

59. See GA 26, 272–73. The sentence, "Yet this *Augenblick* passed" (*Aber dieser Augenblick ging vorüber*), appears to be omitted from the English translation.

60. GA 65, 145, 157; CP, 101, 109.

61. GA 65, 142; CP, 99. As I indicate elsewhere, this concession concerning the limits of science should also be seen in the context of Heidegger's political involvement with the university. See *Glance of the Eye*, pp. 162–64.

62. GA 65, 120; CP, 84.

63. GA 65, 121; CP, 84–85.

64. GA 65, 371; CP, 259. This remark, which goes on to contrast beyng as "the Same" (*das Selbe*) with *das Gleiche*, the "identical," presents itself as an apparent repudiation of Nietzsche's thinking of the eternity of the *Augenblick* in

his formulation of "the eternal return of the same" (*die ewige Wiederkehr des Glei-chen*). Yet Nietzsche's thought of the *Augenblick* of eternal return—as Heidegger's 1937 reading of Nietzsche well shows—itself enacts and thereby manifests the impossibility of thinking being in terms of *das Gleiche*. See Heidegger's 1937 lecture course "The Eternal Recurrence of the Same" in *Nietzsche*, and my commentary in *Glance of the Eye*, chapter 7.

8. Turnings in Essential Swaying and the Leap
Kenneth Maly

Within the context of the joining called "Leap" (*der Sprung*) in *Contributions to Philosophy (From Enowning)*, one of the first things that we can say is that, however the "turning" (*die Kehre*) in Heidegger's thinking has been read/interpreted to this point, it now calls for a rethinking. What the turning means must be thought to a new level. To begin with, all talk of a shift from "Heidegger I" to "Heidegger II" — along with the rather simplistic idea that Heidegger's thinking moved *from* "Dasein-oriented" *to* "being-oriented" (at times even more misunderstood by calling that shift a "reversal") — is, once and for all, obsolete.

A first and strong hint, which might have grounded thinking of the turning even then, can be found in Heidegger's letter to William Richardson. Writing in 1962, Heidegger in that letter offers several "warnings": (1) Thinking being cannot be a "from . . . to" but is always rather a "through . . . to" — thus *not* leaving anything behind. (2) Be-ing (*Seyn*) will always need a properly responsive thinking — thus thinking is never abandoned. (3) The turning involves a dynamic and a bearing that took his thinking years to clarify. (4) Whereas thinking the turning *is* a shift in his thinking, it is not a new standpoint, nor does it abandon the grounding of the questioning of *Being and Time;* rather, it happens because his thinking *stays with* the matter for thinking in *Being and Time*. (5) The turning, then, is in play in the dynamic itself (the very bearings of the issue) — neither invented by Heidegger nor applicable only to his thinking. (6) Since from the beginning the movement of thinking in *Being and Time* takes place outside the domain of subjectivity, since the being that is thought therein is neither posited by human subjectivity nor in any way substantial, and since that being comes into play for Dasein and gets thought from within being's character as time, as temporal, in coming-to-presence (*An-wesen*) — thus from the beginning of the being-question in *Being and Time* a kind of thinking is called for and enacted that matches the movement of the turning that is *in play in the dynamic itself (in the very bearing of the issue)*. (7) Far from *abandoning* the question begun in *Being and Time*, thinking the turning enhances it. (8) This enhancement of the question of *Being and Time* with the thinking of the turning actually gives for the first time a sufficient and adequate determination of Da-sein as what is ownmost to the human being *thought in terms of the truth of being* (truth as concealing unconcealing).[1]

The whole discussion of the turning in his letter to Richardson culminates as Heidegger quotes his own text, a text belonging to the first draft of his lecture course *Grundfragen der Philosophie* (GA 45), written at the same time as *Contributions:*

Over and over again one must be enjoined: In the question of truth that is asked here, what is at stake is not merely an altering of the traditional/inherited concept of truth. . . . What is at stake is a transformation of being-human. New psychological or biological insights do not require this transformation. The human being here is not object of some kind of anthropology. [Rather] the human being is in question here in the most profound and far-reaching—in what is really the grounding—perspective: Humans in their relation to being—i.e., in the turning. Be-ing and its truth in relation to humans.[2]

Given all these warnings regarding the turning, given that with the publication of *Contributions* in 1989 the old ways of thinking the turning are obsolete, and given that a rethinking of the turning is called for, to a new level, what are the ways that *Contributions* shows us? One pathway, the one that I take here, is to move through several radical openings that are thought in *Contributions*, thought within the joining called "Leap":

a. the turning as it sways in the "whereunto" of the leap—leap into the encleaving midpoint of the turning in enowning (*der Sprung in die erklüftende Mitte der Kehre des Ereignisses*);

b. the turning-in-relation of and in be-ing (*der kehrige Bezug des Seyns* or *im Seyn*) told also in be-ing's need (*Brauch*) of humans and humans' belonging-to and taking-part-in be-ing (*Zugehörigkeit*);

c. be-ing-history and be-ing-historical thinking (*die Geschichte des Seyns* and *seynsgeschichtliches Denken*);

d. essential swaying and the leap (*die Wesung* and *der Sprung*).

The Turning as It Sways in the "Whereunto" of the Leap

A few remarks are in order on how the thinking enacted in *Contributions* "leads up to the leap." The first joining, "Echo" (*Anklang*), opens up how being refuses the en-ownment (or be-ing as enowning), how this abandonment of beings by being holds sway (in machination and constant presence), but also how this refusal and this abandonment can become and be thought as itself a remote enowning—can "echo" be-ing as enowning. When Dasein grasps, takes part in, and thinks this not-granting, the very "loss" or "forgottenness" carries within it an echo of be-ing.

This is manifest (a) in how humans have lost their power to hold fast to Dasein, (b) in how humans are forgetful of being, but also (c) in how, abandoned by being, beings still manifest (are disclosed), (d) in how the grounding-attunement of reservedness (*Verhaltenheit*) lets the echo become audible for thinking.

Within this kind of gathering, we can better hear the opening words of this joining:

Echo of the essential swaying of be-ing
from within the abandonment of being
through the distressing distress
of be-ing's having been forgotten. (GA 65, 107; CP, 75)[3]

Or: Be-ing's echo is heard in how being (in metaphysics) has abandoned beings and in how humans have forgotten be-ing (as enowning). Since humans seldom shift into this truth and are quickly content with beings, humans thus continue to be dis-enowned (*enteignet*) of be-ing. In all of this the echo of the essential swaying of be-ing reverberates for thinking, since this abandonment or disenownment is enowned.

The second joining, "Playing-Forth" (*Zuspiel*), opens and reveals how the history of thinking up to now (history of metaphysics) plays forth as the *first beginning*, but in such a way that an other beginning also plays itself forth. The other beginning is played forth when this refusal (*Verweigerung*) that happens when being abandons beings and humans forget be-ing in the first beginning gets experienced as dis-enownment (*Enteignis*) within the thinking of be-ing as enowning.

The second joining begins with these words: "Playing-forth [is] coming to grips [*Auseinandersetzung*] with the necessity of the *other* beginning from within the originary positioning of the first beginning" (GA 65, 169; CP, 119). *Auseinandersetzung* is to be thought and understood here in its hermeneutic-phenomenological import. Thus and first of all, it has nothing to do with a normal meaning of "discussion" or "debate." Second, it goes deeper than a mere "putting into perspective" or the "coming to grips with" that humans might do. Rather, and within the phenomenological thinking that enacts and engages with the essential swaying of be-ing as enowning (what *Contributions* turns toward and into), this word *Auseinandersetzung* says: encounter (the two beginnings coming to each other), setting out (the two beginnings being set apart and set out in their relation to each other), joining issue with each other—playing off, taking part in, lending to each other.

Thus in this deeper sense, *Auseinandersetzung* says and enacts what is in the dynamic or bearing of this joining, "Playing-Forth." This deeper sense is said in §3 of the "Preview" of *Contributions*, where Heidegger writes: "Playing-forth is initially playing-forth of the first beginning, so that the first beginning brings the other beginning into play and from within this mutual playing-forth (*Wechselzuspiel*) preparation for the leap grows" (7).

Thus the second joining, "Playing-Forth," shows (a) how there is an interplay (*Wechselzuspiel*) of the first and the other beginning; how coming to grips with (*Auseinandersetzung*) the first and the other beginning is also a setting out—the play of each beginning against the other, each partaking in the play of the other, playing off each other, lending to each other; (b) how in *Contributions* the first beginning and its history get thought in such a way as to let an other beginning emerge and shine forth from within the first beginning; and (c) how playing-forth unto an/the other beginning leads to the third joining, "Leap."

How the first beginning gets thought is within be-ing-history (*Seyns-geschichte*) and be-ing-historical thinking (*seynsgeschichtliches Denken*). For now we can say that be-ing-history is not history as historiography (the discipline of writing history, of lining up events and identifying them within a common thread), but history as unfolding, issuing, proffering.[4]

Heard and thought in this sense, the history of the first and the other beginning is an interplay within be-ing. In §28 of *Die Geschichte des Seyns* (GA 69), which (section) is entitled "The History of Be-ing," there is a diagram that shows both beginnings as part of be-ing.[5] There Heidegger writes: "It is not a matter of going from one to the other beginning [of going between beginning and beginning]."[6] Rather, each beginning is thought be-ing-historically, within the domain of each beginning. When thought *historically* (*geschichtlich*) rather than historiographically (*historisch*), beginning is enowned as beginning.

Thus one can say: (a) letting the first beginning play forth in accord with what is its ownmost—abandonment of beings by being, i.e., as refusal—brings on an other beginning; but (b) since this first beginning is enowned within be-ing-history, the first beginning is what it is only from within the other beginning: *"Erst aus dem anderen Anfang—der erste."*[7]

Now, after this brief excursus into *Die Geschichte des Seyns*, we turn to the leap: What is the turning that sways and is enacted in the leap? What does the leap turn to?

In the opening section of the third joining, "Leap," Heidegger writes: "The leap . . . above all else releases belongingness to be-ing in its full essential swaying as enowning" (GA 65, 227; CP, 161)—and *not* any longer in terms of beings at all! Not held captive or informed solely by the history of metaphysics in the first beginning, no longer *guided* by beings but rather thinking their groundedness in the truth of be-ing, where the projecting-open that Dasein enacts "is itself [first] experienced and sustained as occurring from within [be-ing as] enowning" (GA 65, 231; CP, 163)—this is thinking the other beginning. With this thinking, the *leap* is into the "encleaving mid-point of the turning of enowning" (GA 65, 231; CP, 163–64). This means that the leap is not shaped/oriented in terms of beings but held within the free-play of be-ing itself—as enowning.

In the first beginning being is thought for the sake of manifesting *beings*. Thus being or beingness is that by virtue of which beings emerge or come forth. "And so, be-ing holds sway for the sake of beings" and "being is in service to beings" (GA 65, 229; CP, 162). This relationship of beings to being carries two levels of meaning: being as *summum ens*, highest being, transcendent being, *and* being as *essentia,* as objectivity. In the first beginning, being is thought as what is in service to beings.

In the leap into the other beginning this no longer happens. Beings give way to be-ing as the issue for thinking. And "be-ing holds sway as enowning" (GA 65, 230; CP, 163). This is what first sways as "turning" in the leap—where thinking takes hold, where thinking the leap "begins." The guiding question of the ontological difference (being-beings) provided a first step away from thinking being in terms of beings. The leap into be-ing as enowning—and thus into an/the other beginning—frees up and accomplishes the removal from "beings" as what "sets the standard" (GA 65, 258; CP, 182). The ontological differ-ence of the guiding question gives way to enowning. It is a leap into "the encleaving mid-point of the turning of enowning" (GA 65, 231; CP, 163–64)—working from within the truth of be-ing (as enowning).

This issue of how Heidegger's thinking moved through the opening to being that he named "ontological difference" (e.g., in *Being and Time*) to arriving directly at the question of be-ing that he named enowning, or be-ing as enowning (in *Contributions*)—this issue is com-plex and subtle, allowing for thinking to easily lose its way. For on the one hand the distinction named and grasped as "ontological differ-ence" (since *Being and Time*) was necessary, providing a clarification and in its origin opening up the issue of the truth of *being* over against beings. On the other hand, the distinction named in "ontological dif-ference" is shaped and "defined" by its orientation toward *beings,* thus holding thinking back from letting be-ing hold sway as what it "is," "as such." In other words: Whereas the thinking of "ontological differ-ence" thinks being over against beings—and thus begins to clarify the issue of the first beginning—it still thinks being as beingness, i.e., the thinking of being is held within the *distinction.* But now Heidegger wants to think this differently, namely, from within the truth of be-ing as enowning. The question becomes: Is the term "ontological differ-ence" a help or a hindrance here?

Because this issue is so important for understanding "the whereunto of the leap," I choose now to quote §132 of *Contributions* at length:

> This distinction [between be-ing and a being] is grasped since *Being and Time* as "ontological difference"—with the intention of safeguarding the question of the truth of be-ing from all confusion. But this distinction is immediately pushed in the direction from which it comes. For here being-ness is claimed as οὐσία, ἰδέα; and following these, the objectness is claimed as *condition for the possibility* of the object. Therefore, in attempting to overcome the first effort at the question of being in *Being and Time* and its emanations (*Vom Wesen des Grundes* and the Kantbook), varying attempts were needed to master the "ontological difference," to grasp its very origin and that means its genuine *onefold.* Therefore, the effort was needed to

come free of the "condition for the possibility" as going back into the merely "mathematical" and to grasp the truth of be-ing from within its *own* essential sway (enowning). Hence the tormenting and discording character of this distinction. For as necessary as this distinction is (to think in traditional terms), in order to provide at all a preliminary perspective for the question of be-ing, just as disastrous does this distinction continue to be. For this distinction indeed *does* arise from a questioning of beings as such (of beingness). But in this way one never arrives directly at the question of be-ing. In other words, this distinction *itself* becomes the real barrier which misplaces [waylays] the inquiry into the question of be-ing, insofar as, by presupposing this distinction, one attempts to go further than this distinction and to inquire into its onefold. This onefold can never be anything but the mirroring of the distinction and can never lead to the origin, in view of which this distinction can no longer be seen as originary. . . .

But in thinking in the crossing, we must sustain this ambiguity: *on the one hand* to begin an initial clarification with this distinction and *then* to leap over this very distinction (GA 65, 250–51; CP, 176–77).

On the one hand the distinction helps to break free of a beings-oriented way of thinking (metaphysics). On the other hand it becomes a barrier to the truth of be-ing, to what is originary. Thus "the tormenting and discording character of this distinction." The ambiguity must be sustained and brought along — but *then* thinking needs "to leap over this very distinction" (GA 65, 251; CP, 177). For, as Heidegger says later (GA 65, 258; CP, 182), "the notion of 'ontological difference' is only preparatory, as crossing from the guiding-question [of the first beginning] to the grounding-question [of an/the other beginning]."

Thus a first way to think the turning that happens within the matter itself of the third joining is to see how thinking turns to be-ing itself and thinks this directly — no longer in service to beings, no longer guided by and shaped (as a question) from within beings.

In the other beginning thinking thinks be-ing as enowning — *as it shows itself from out of itself!* No longer guided by, in service to, or using the standard of beings. Heidegger writes:

> In the other beginning a being can no longer supply the measure for be-ing — neither a specific domain and region, nor a being as such. Here one must think so far ahead — or better: so far into — the t/here [*Da*] that the truth of be-ing lights up originarily. (GA 65, 248–49; CP, 175)

It is no longer an issue of moving "from" or "beyond" beings to the question of be-ing. Rather be-ing as enowning (the essential swaying of truth, the truth of be-ing) "bears up every relation to a being" (GA 65, 248; CP, 175). Thus Heidegger writes how the essential swaying of be-ing must be attained "in its full estrangement over against [from] beings" (GA 65, 258; CP, 182).

Finally, with the leap into the "mid-point of enowning," with the turning away from beings to be-ing, a turning inherent in the matter itself of the "Leap," with the understanding that be-ing as enowning bears up and carries whatever beings are or become, with the estrangement from beings in the look of be-ing—with all of this the distinction named in transcendence collapses and no longer has any bearing. Heidegger writes:

> Therefore the task is not to surpass beings (transcendence) but rather to leap over this distinction and thus over *transcendence* and to inquire inceptually into be-ing and truth. (GA 65, 250–51; CP, 177)

So in crossing to the other beginning, thinking is to prepare for the leap—a leap into the mid-point of enowning, a leap that, "expecting nothing from beings immediately . . . releases belongingness to be-ing in its full essential swaying as enowning" (GA 65, 227; CP, 161). This be-ing as enowning is not self-evident, but rather: unique (as enowning), unrepresentable (is not an object), extremely strange and estranging, and essentially hiding itself (cf. GA 65, 252; CP, 178). The turning in the leap to be-ing itself, directly and no longer guided by or in service to beings, evokes these aspects of be-ing. But—and this is of paramount importance for understanding this turning that is within enowning itself—be-ing's uniqueness, unrepresentability, strangeness, and self-sheltering *inheres within the very turning-relation* (kehriger Bezug) *of and in be-ing*. The turning-relation emerges, not from within the first beginning (metaphysics) or from within knowing awareness of what metaphysical thinking up to now did *not* take up (the ontological difference), but rather from *within the very core of* what is at stake in be-ing as enowning: "the leap into the encleaving mid-point of the turning of enowning" (GA 65, 231; CP, 163–64).

A very important question emerges here: Granting that thinking in the leap leaps into the sway of be-ing directly, is this "turn" the same as the "turning" of enowning, that thinking the leap "turns to"? If thinking "turns to" be-ing, this "turn" is not identical with the turning (*Kehre*) of enowning as such—which cannot be something that thinking "does" by itself. This is a quandary *of* language, which is always already showing what is. None of this occurs outside language. Language is essentially there!

One option is to reserve the word *turning* for what is said in *die Kehre des Ereignisses*—the turning that we will focus on in the second part of this essay and that we will call, with Heidegger, "originary turning." Then this "turning" directly to the sway of be-ing that is thought in the "Leap" would be called a shift, a change, or even a crossing. Another option is to allow for turnings (in the plural), none of which is separable from "originary turning" of enowning—but which are fully distinguishable for the sake of *thinking*. However, it is of utmost importance to remember that the turning that happens in thinking is grounded in originary turning of enowning. And the originary turning that belongs to enowning is *always in play in other turnings*.

The Turning-Relation of and in Be-ing

> Enowning has its innermost occurrence [*Geschehen*] [happens in its core] and its widest reach [outreach] in the turning. The turning that holds sway [sways deeply] in enowning is the sheltered ground of the entire series of turnings, circles, and spheres—[each one] which are of unclear origin, remain unquestioned, and are easily taken in themselves as the "last" [turning] (consider, e.g., the turning in the jointure [whole complex] of the guiding-questions and the circle of under-standing). (GA 65, 407; CP, 286, interpolations mine)

Thus begins §255: *Die Kehre im Ereignis:* Turning in Enowning. Immediately thereafter Heidegger asks: "What is this originary turning in enowning?" With that Heidegger distinguishes between "other" turnings and the "originary" turning-relation in be-ing as enowning.

First, originary turning is not what happens in the turning from (within) the guiding-question in the first beginning (metaphysics) to the grounding-question in the other beginning. The turning "from the guiding-question, through its full unfolding, to the leap into the grounding-question" (GA 65, 233; CP, 165) holds sway within originary turning.

Second, whether it is the turning of the hermeneutic circle (in under-standing) or the turning in the analytic of temporality of being (the "third part" of *Being and Time*) or the transformation of fundamental-ontological thinking into be-ing-historical thinking (in *Contributions*)—or even the turning directly to be-ing itself as enowning, no longer guided at all by beings or the ontological difference (see the first part of this essay)—in all of these cases the turning that is at issue is grounded in the originary turning relation of and in be-ing.[8]

So let us turn directly to thinking the "originary" turning in enowning. I will do this by (a) an initial gathering of the moments of this turning, which in their onefold make up the "innermost occurrence" of enowning, make up what happens in the core, deep essential sway of enowning, (b) a careful reading of key passages from §§122 and 182 of *Contributions*, and (c) a brief look, from within this originary turning-relation in and of be-ing, at what in the leap is ownmost to Da-sein.

a. *Initial gathering of the moments of the turning.* The "unfolding of be-ing as enowning" *is* the "turning in enowning." The "turning in enowning" *is* "be-ing as enowning." However be-ing holds sway, deeply and essentially, i.e., as enowning, it does so "within the turning." The two moments of this "turning" are named as follows: (1) "Enowning must need Dasein and, needing it, must place Dasein into the call" (GA 65, 407; CP, 287); (2) "in the inabiding of Da-sein, [i.e.,] in the experience of thrownness into the t/here [*Da*] from within belongingness to the call of enowning" (GA 65, 233; CP, 165).

In one of many formulations of this originary turning-relation in enowning, Heidegger writes: "[Originary] turning holds sway between the call (to the one belonging) [by and from be-ing as enowning] *and* the belonging (of the one who is called). Turning is counter-turning" (GA 65, 407; CP, 287, interpolations mine).[9]

A seemingly simple formulation from §133 notes: "Be-ing needs [*braucht*] man in order to hold sway; and man belongs to [*gehört*] be-ing, so that he can accomplish his utmost destiny as Dasein" (GA 65, 251; CP, 177). But what seems here to be "simply" two sides of a phenomenon must be thought more deeply in the onefold of its counter-resonance. In his book *Wege ins Ereignis: Zu Heideggers "Beiträgen zur Philosophie"* Friedrich-Wilhelm von Herrmann writes:

> Da-sein is enowned as one who, projecting-open, stands in its turn in [inabides] the t/here [*Da*] as the enowned truth of be-ing. But the essential swaying of being happens, not only as that en-owning of Da-sein, but also and at the same time in the enactment of the enowned projecting-open that Da-sein enacts. Because be-ing "needs" man as Da-sein for its [be-ing's] essential swaying, it [be-ing] en-owns Da-sein, i.e., it opens [up] Da-sein to itself as projecting-open inabiding in its [be-ing's] clearing. Da-sein for its part, then, belongs, with its enowned projecting-open, in the essential swaying of be-ing. Thus Heidegger (in §133) can say: "Be-ing needs man in order to hold sway; and man belongs to be-ing, so that he can accomplish his utmost destiny as Dasein" ([GA 65, 251; CP,] 177). He grasps the relationship of *needing* and *belonging-to*—of the enowning call and the enowned projecting-open—as "counter-resonance." "*This counter-resonance of needing and belonging* makes up be-ing as enowning" (ibid.). Thus *enowning* is the essential swaying of be-ing—not in being over against Da-sein, but rather including Da-sein in its ownmost as enowned and projecting-open. . . .
>
> This *counter-resonance* of enowning call and enowned projecting-open Heidegger calls: *die Kehre*/the turning. The [originary] turning is nothing that gets added to enowning, but rather, as essential swaying of be-ing, enowning is in itself counter-resonating, is in itself turning, is the turning. . . . [Thus in §255, already quoted]: "Enowning has its innermost occurrence [*Geschehen*] and has its widest reach [outreach] in the turning" ([GA 65, 407; CP,] 286). Thus: *In its turning-relation,* enowning is the be-ing-historical path or point of view for all questions in be-ing-historical thinking.[10]

It is this *onefold* of originary turning of and in be-ing that is enacted in be-ing-historical thinking. For, Heidegger writes, "turning in enowning is contained neither in the call [by be-ing] . . . alone nor in the belonging-to [of Da-sein] alone, nor in both together. For this 'together' and the 'both' resound, in their turn, first in enowning" (GA 65, 262; CP, 184–85). The "together" and the "both" are subordinate to the originary turning relation, to the counter-resonance. Enowning is this counter-resonance. Be-ing-historical thinking brings this into knowing awareness.

Our task, then, is first to look more closely at this onefold of the turning-relation of and in be-ing in the leap. For, as von Herrmann writes, "It is in this leap that thinking first of all en-springs—i.e., projects-open, opens up—the essential swaying of the truth of be-ing as enowning, as the turning between the enowning calling-to [of and by be-ing] and the enowned projecting-open [by and of Da-sein], which as such belongs to the *undissembled* essential swaying."[11] We will take this closer look in what follows.

b. *Reading the texts.* As we enter into readings of key passages from §§122 and 182 of *Contributions,* it is useful to heed several points: (1) the turning-relation is to be thought from within the matter itself; (2) thinking must stay with the matter that gets said in the text and shows itself and is thus important hermeneutically-phenomenologically; (3) something shows itself, from out *of itself,* not by human agency or subjectivity; (4) thinking lets this self-showing, which gets revealed in the text, be brought into knowing awareness; (5) such thinking is enactment; and (6) this enacting thinking, reading the text and letting it resound unto the matter, the phenomenon in its self-showing—using Heidegger's words to Richardson—"sets into motion the manifold thinking of the simple matter *for* thinking, which, by virtue of its very simplicity, abounds in hidden fullness."[12]

Section 122 is entitled "Leap (the Thrown Projecting-Open)." It begins:

[The leap] is the enactment of projecting-open the truth of be-ing in the sense of shifting into the open, such that the thrower of the projecting-open [Da-sein] experiences itself as thrown—i.e., as en-owned by be-ing. The enopening in and through projecting-open is such only when it occurs [happens, *geschieht*] as the experience of thrownness and thus of belonging-ness to be-ing. [Be-ing enowns Da-sein. Enowning is the turning-relation of enowning throw (by be-ing as enowning). Within that turning Da-sein is enowned and, *as enowned*, projects open.] That is the essential difference from every merely *transcendental* way of knowing with regard to the conditions of possibility (cf. Leap, 134: The Relation of Da-sein and Be-ing) [not as in subject-object, not as in objectifying subjectivity, not as in objectifiable, not as in conceivable/conceptual or representable—and finally not as in service to or guided by beings as such]. . . .

In that the thrower projects-open and speaks thinkingly "from enowning" [not "about" enowning but "from within and out of"] [from the enowning throw or call of/by be-ing, as the "matter" that shows itself], it

becomes manifest that, the more the thrower projects-open, the more the
thrower as thrower is the thrown one [is *enowned* projecting-open]. (GA
65, 239; CP, 169, interpolations mine)

Section 182, entitled "Projecting Be-ing Open: Projecting-Open as
Thrown," begins with a sentence that parallels the opening sentence of
§122: "What is meant is always merely the projecting-open of the truth
of be-ing. The thrower itself, Da-sein, is thrown, en-owned by be-ing"
(GA 65, 304; CP, 214).

In both passages, "thrown" says "enowned." Also, the projecting-open
of the truth of be-ing happens as Da-sein, even as Da-sein essentially
always already "projects-open," i.e., is enowned by be-ing. Gathering up
the core significance of this matter, von Herrmann writes:

> The experience of thrownness as being-enowned from within and out of
> the enowning call of be-ing is the *primary experience* for be-ing-historical
> thinking and draws and traces out from itself the immanent transformation
> of the being-question that was initially asked transcendentally. Therefore,
> the thinking that gets enacted as leap is "leaping into the enowning of Da-
> sein" ([GA 65, 251; CP,] 177), i.e., into Da-sein's being-enowned from
> within and out of the en-owning of be-ing."[13]

c. *A brief look from within this originary turning-relation in and of be-ing.*
What in the leap is ownmost to Da-sein? What "role" does Da-sein play?
Da-sein does not conceive or define, nor does Da-sein provide "from
itself," anything like "categories" by which to understand. So what does
Da-sein "do"?

Section 122 ends: "In opening up the essential swaying of be-ing, it
becomes manifest that Da-sein does not accomplish anything [*nichts
leistet*], unless it be to get hold of [*auffangen*] the counter-resonance of en-
ownment, i.e., to shift into this counter-resonance and thus first of all to
become itself: the preserver of the thrown projecting-open, *the grounded
founder of the ground* [der gegründeter Gründer des Grundes]" (GA 65,
239; CP, 169). Section 182 ends with a very similar sentence: "In that the
thrower projects-open and enopens openness, the enopening reveals
that the thrower itself is the thrown and does not accomplish anything
other than getting hold of the counter-resonance in be-ing, i.e., shifting
into the counter-resonance and thus into enowning and thus first
becoming itself, namely the preserver of the thrown projecting-open"
(GA 65, 304; CP, 214).

Reading these two sentences together and interpreting them phenomenologically, one might say as follows: The thrower, Da-sein, is
itself thrown. In opening up (projecting-open) the essential swaying of
be-ing, Da-sein does not so much "accomplish" anything (*leisten*) as
"get hold of" (*auffangen*) the counter-resonance of be-ing's enowning

Da-sein and Da-sein's being-enowned and *as such* projecting-open the truth of be-ing—as enowning. The counter-resonance is (in) be-ing and is enowning. Getting hold of the counter-resonance means (1) shifting into it, i.e., (2) shifting into enowning and *thus* (3) Da-sein's becoming itself, becoming what is its ownmost to be. The thinking-saying in *Contributions* shows that Da-sein's ownmost way of being (its *Wesen*) is as preserver/tender/herder of the thrown projecting-open, i.e., of the enowned projecting-open. Since *what* is projected open by Da-sein, the tender, is the essential swaying of be-ing as enowning, what Da-sein preserves or tends is be-ing's enowning of Da-sein. Or, better said: Da-sein tends or preserves the counter-resonance of be-ing that en-owns and Da-sein who, enown*ed*, projects-open this counter-resonance.

The leap is turning into be-ing (1) directly and not guided by or in service to beings (2) as the counter-resonance of enowning, be-ing's enowning Da-sein and *enowned* Da-sein's projecting be-ing open. The first turning (1) is subordinate to the second, originary turning (2). Inceptual thinking springs off the echo and playing-forth "to the *leap* into the essential swaying of be-ing" (GA 65, 82; CP, 57).

Inceptual thinking dares the leap; "leaping into preparedness for belonging to enowning . . . cannot be forced by thinking . . . but thinking can make or hold ready the open" (GA 65, 235; CP, 166–67). What *seems* to be accomplished *by* human thinking actually happens as "historical in and through en-ownment that fosters Da-sein" (GA 65, 235–36; CP, 167).

If the leap is enacted, that is what Heidegger calls "enthinking of be-ing" (*Erdenken des Seyns*). And that enthinking "has its ownmost [*eigenes Wesen*] as 'thinking' from within that which be-ing as en-owning enowns, from within Da-sein" (GA 65, 452; CP, 318).

Who can go this path? Heidegger says: Only the few, who found Da-sein as preserver/tender of the truth of be-ing. And, since be-ing "is always in utmost sheltering-concealing and is removal-unto the incalculable and unique . . . [and is] the 'alongside' for the ab-ground," Da-sein and thinking can never "make" be-ing in to an object of "knowledge" or of "representation" (GA 65, 236; CP, 167).

Gathering up the "role" or "place" of Da-sein or thinking within the third joining, "Leap," Heidegger says: "The leap is knowing leaping-into the momentariness of the site for the onset [of be-ing as enowning]; the leap is that which comes first and ensprings the sheltering of en-ownment in the directing [showing] word (cf. the essential swaying of be-ing)" (GA 65, 237; CP, 168, interpolations mine).

Da-sein's thinking gets hold of, is knowing awareness, is needed by be-ing as it (be-ing) enowns, holds in preparedness, opens up the between of enowning and being-enowned, belongs to be-ing. But *this* matter is in truth the matter of the fourth joining: Grounding.

Leaping into Be-ing-History and Be-ing-Historical Thinking

In the opening section of the "Leap," Heidegger speaks twice of daring. First, the leap directly into be-ing and its full essential swaying as enowning (the turning of the first part of this essay) is "the most daring move in proceeding from inceptual thinking" (GA 65, 227; CP, 161). Secondly, "the leap is to dare an initial foray into the domain of *being-history*" (ibid.). This history is grasped "solely with a view to essential swaying of be-ing itself," where "en-owning is originary history" (GA 65, 32; CP, 23). What is ownmost to history is enacted from within essential swaying of be-ing (GA 65, 33; CP, 24).

In *Die Geschichte des Seyns,* Heidegger writes that *when* philosophy genuinely is what it is to be, it is "leaping-into the be-ing-history, which leap engrounds the truth of be-ing more inceptually."[14]

Thus we see the inherent and essential connection of be-ing-history to this third joining. We also see how be-ing-history (*Seynsgeschichte*) is essentially bound to what en-owning is/does, how en-owning is the "origin of history" (GA 65, 453; CP, 319).

Thinking what is enacted in the *Geschichte des Seyns* in German, Heidegger has at his disposal the richness of the German language, in which (a) *Geschichte* can be distinguished from *Historie,* (b) *Geschichte* has an essential connection with the German words *schicken, Geschick, Schickung,* and (c) *Geschehen* (happen, take place, go on/forth) is etymologically related to *Geschichte* (history, historical action, shaping-history). None of this is available to us in English. This fact makes *Seynsgeschichte* and *seynsgeschichtliches Denken* among the most difficult words to translate in *Contributions.*

How can we say/think in English what this *Geschichte* is? As translators, Parvis Emad and I found it impossible not to translate *Geschichte* as "history." To distinguish history as *Geschichte* from history as *Historie,* we chose to indicate history as *Historie* by adding the words "as a discipline" — history "as a discipline." One might name this history "historiography." One must keep clear when Heidegger is speaking of *Historie* as the systematic account of events in the past — historiography as the compilation of past events — and when he is speaking of *Geschichte.* When used without the qualification of "as a discipline," the English word *history* wants to say the richness of the German word *Geschichte* as well as its essential connection with other German words like *schicken, Schickung,* and *Geschick.*

Carefully reading §273 (GA 65, 492–94; CP, 346–48), entitled *"Geschichte,"* we can make the following observations regarding *Geschichte* and *Historie:* (1) the essential sense of *Geschichte* has never been enacted within metaphysics; (2) in order to come to know "the essential swaying of *Geschichte,"* what is ownmost both to humans and to being must become questionable; (3) *Geschichte* can be grounded solely in the essential sway of be-ing and its relation to Da-sein (the originary turning-re-lation in and of be-ing); (4) whether thinking can attain *Geschichte* in this essential sense and thus bring *Historie* to naught rests with be-ing it-self; (5) modernity has raised *Historie* to the highest priority, thus mak-ing any clarifying of these questions most difficult; (6) "Historie" means the "ascertaining explaining of the past from within the horizon of the calculative dealings of the present. Beings are hereby presupposed as as-certainable (ἰδέα)"; whereas (7) on the other hand, *Geschichte* is "be-ing as en-owning. It is from this perspective that what is ownmost to history must be determined, independently of the representation of becoming and development, independently of historiographical observation and explanation" (GA 65, 494; CP, 348).

How, then, can we get a clearer focus on what *Seynsgeschichte* and *seyns-geschichtliches Denken* say? Using the English word *history,* how shall we open up that *English* word to embrace and say what Heidegger says in the *German* words *Seynsgeschichte* and *seynsgeschichtliches Denken?*

To begin this journey, let us take a look at some other texts where the question of *Seynsgeschichte* and *seynsgeschichtliches Denken* is taken up. In *Was ist das—die Philosophie?* Heidegger says that the deep question What is philosophy? is "eine geschichtliche, d.h. geschickliche Frage."[15] How do we render that into English?

In the lecture "Time and Being" Heidegger says:

Being-history means the handing-over or sending from being [that being does], in which handings-over [gathering-throws, shapings] both the handing-over [sending, carrying-forth] and the it that does the handing over hold to themselves, even as they manifest themselves.

Seinsgeschichte heißt Geschick von Sein, in welchen Schickungen sowohl das Schicken als auch das Es, das schickt, an sich halten mit der Bekundung ihrer selbst.[16]

Geschichte is in play in *Geschehen, Geschick, Schickung*—a handing-over in be-ing as enowning, be-ing enowning throw, a sending that inheres in the essential swaying of be-ing.

In *Der Satz vom Grund,* Heidegger says that *Geschichte* is "not some-thing past [from the past], but history [*Geschichte*] as a handing-over or shaping [*Geschick*] that still endures and motivates us today as hardly ever before."[17] Toward the end of that lecture course Heidegger says:

The crossing . . . as leap is not under any force. The leap remains thinking's free possibility—and this so decidedly that it is only with the domain of the leap that the essential region of freedom is opened. It is precisely because of this that we are bound to prepare for the leap. . . . The springboard [for the leap] is the history of Western thinking experienced as the gathering-throw or handing-over or carrying-forth, or sending-shaping [*Geschick*] of being. Therefore the history of being is not an uncoiling process of the changes of a being that has let loose even as it stays independent. The history of being is not an objectively representable process, about which one could tell "stories of being." The gathering-throw or shaping-sending of being remains inherently the ownmost history of Western man insofar as the one who is historical is in the employ of the building-dwelling of the clearing of being. As withdrawal that belongs to this handing-over or gathering-throw, being is inherently already relation to what is ownmost to man. However, being is not human-ized ["made human"] by this relation; rather by this very relation man's way of being [what is ownmost to man] remains housed at the site of being.[18]

Thus thinking that is *seynsgeschichtlich* thinks the handing-over or send-ing, gathering-throw, shaping-sending, carrying-forth that is be-ing as enowning. This handing-over, which en-owns Da-sein, inseparable from Da-sein's projecting-open, is what be-ing is in its truth.

Thinking comes full circle when it, exigently, thinks *Geschichte/Geschick* within the context of be-ing's turning-relation (*kehriger Bezug*) to Da-sein. The essential swaying of be-ing as enowning (the elemental enact-ment of *Contributions*) is in its truth this encircling (counter-resonance) whereby *in one stroke* be-ing enowns Da-sein, *and* Da-sein, enowned by be-ing, projects be-ing open.

Gathering *Geschichte, Ereignis,* and *Kehre*—history, enowning, and the turning—*in order to say the "between"* of be-ing and Da-sein *as a onefold,* Heidegger writes:

> What is ownmost to history in the deepest sense rests in the encleaving (truth-grounding) enownment which lets all those first emerge who, needing one another, mutually turn to and away from one another only in the enowning of the turning. (GA 65, 311; CP, 219)

And what is Da-sein? *"Da-sein is the occurrence* [Geschehen] *of the encleaving of the turning-midpoint of the turning in enowning"* (GA 65, 311; CP, 218). And, "Dasein is: enduring the essential swaying of the truth of be-ing" (GA 65, 311; CP, 219).

The English word *history* cannot say all of the richness of the German word *Geschichte*. And yet it must! Can we open up what "history" says beyond and deeper than its "normal" meanings: systematic account of past events, compiling and recording, or the recorded past itself? *Ge-schichte, Geschehen, Geschick:* something happens, is carried forth, is set to work (*Geschichte* as *Begebenheit*). *Seynsgeschichte:* the getting going or set-ting to work of be-ing that *is* be-ing.

English usage intimates something of this "deeper" sense of history when we speak of "family history" or "medical history." Neither means simply or only a systematic account or the recorded past. Rather, the phrases "family history" and "medical history" imply how things unfold, what comes "their" way, how things take shape or get shaped—a setting forth of the family or of one's medical "history," a setting to work. This is also implied in the phrase "historical character"—historical: dramatic, "making history."

It is perhaps more useful to keep in mind two images with which Heidegger opens the volume *Die Geschichte des Seyns*: (1) "'History of be-ing' is the name for the attempt to bring the truth of be-ing as enowning back into the word of thinking," and (2) the attempted saying "belongs to enowning itself."[19]

Gathering from *Die Geschichte des Seyns,* we can say the following:

1. Be-ing-historical thinking "thinks forth into be-ing and is in every-thing determined by be-ing as the only thing that attunes."[20]
2. Be-ing-historical thinking is "not describing or exhibiting, not deducing from highest principles, but rather enowned *saying* of the *en-ownment* of history as *Da-sein*."[21]
3. "Be-ing as enowning calls for the *word* and for *listening*. . . . Listening—not as another 'sense' but rather, in accord with *en-ownment*, the awaiting finding of what is coming—i.e., of his-tory."[22]
4. ". . . history [is] as essential swaying of the truth of be-ing."[23]
5. ". . . thrownness is experienciable only from within the history of be-ing."[24]
6. In be-ing-historical thinking, "be-ing is thought as en-ownment of a carrying out [*Austrag*]."[25]
7. "History is the entemporalizing of the space of carrying out [carry-ing forth, *Austrag*]."[26]

Be-ing-historical thinking is thinking that enacts be-ing's carrying out, enacts the setting to work of be-ing, the play of be-ing in the "turn-ing of en-owning."

Taking all of those word-images in thinking back to *Contributions*, we can perhaps get a better hold on what history as *Geschichte* says in *Con-tributions*. Heidegger addresses directly what *Geschichte* is/says/does *most often* in the part entitled "Be-ing," the last major section of the entire work, after the preview and the six joinings:

In §258 he writes: "'Historical' [*geschichtlich*] here means: belonging to the essential swaying of be-ing itself, enjoined unto the distress of the truth of be-ing and thus bound into the necessity of that decision which on the whole has at its disposal what is ownmost to history and its essential swaying" (GA 65, 421; CP, 297).

In §265 he writes: "From now on everything that reads beingness from out of and off beings remains outside *that* history in which be-ing as enowning enowns thinking for itself, in the shape of what accords to and belongs to Da-sein" (GA 65, 464; CP, 327).

Finally, at the beginning of that same section, Heidegger writes that "en-thinking be-ing" (the title for §265) perhaps names decisively a way "by which Western man in the future takes over the essential swaying of the truth of be-ing and *thus first becomes historical*" (GA 65, 456; CP, 321, italics added).

There is some danger in working the notion named in the German word *Geschichte* by evoking its ties with the German word *Geschick/schicken/ Schickung*.[27] *Geschick* as it is said/thought in *Der Satz vom Grund* is not the same as *Geschichte* in *Contributions*. However, if we think these connections among these words in German, if we think how Heidegger struggled with the word-image as well as the matter itself, if we think their connection in German unto a deeper saying in the English words, then we can go back to *Contributions* with more light shed on what happens in that work. For what *Geschichte* says in *Contributions*, within the whole dynamic of be-ing's enowning Da-sein and enowned Da-sein's projecting be-ing open, is the key for understanding both *Die Geschichte des Seyns* as well as *Der Satz vom Grund*—and not vice versa. Thus be-ing's enowning Da-sein and Da-sein's being enowned by be-ing and projecting be-ing open is not the same as *Geschick*. Rather, the projecting-open of be-ing's enowning, the essential swaying of be-ing, is what "holds" or "bears up" *Geschick*.

This is to reconfirm how the thinking of enowning and being-history in *Contributions* must be thought from within *Contributions* itself. To think the handing-over or sending (*Geschick*) helps to think how be-ing enowns Da-sein. However, be-ing-historical thinking thinks this enowning-enownedness within the originary turning in enowning; *and this thinking takes place in* Contributions. Be-ing-historical thinking enacts the setting-to-work of be-ing, which includes the projecting-open that Da-sein enacts, itself enowned by be-ing—projecting-open this very enownment that includes Da-sein's projecting-open.

Thus it is that the leap that prepares for "belonging to enowning" cannot be forced *denkmäßig:* with thinking as measure, in accord with thinking. No thinking of *any* kind can delineate, outline, or otherwise capture in concepts the web of be-ing's "enowning-throw"[28] and Da-sein's projecting-open the essential swaying of be-ing, all of which—be-ing's "enowning-throw," Da-sein's being enowned, Da-sein's projecting open the enowning and the enowned, the *Da* (t/here) as the site of be-ing, the site of be-ing's enowning and Da-sein's projecting-open this be-ing— is in play in/as the turning of enowning. But the open for all of this can be held ready *denkerisch:* in thinking (cf. GA 65, 234; CP, 167).

Be-ing-historical thinking draws its character as thinking from within be-ing as enowning. Be-ing-historical thinking "thinks forth" and leaps into be-ing, into enowning, into be-ing as enowning. It is the "enowned saying" of that enowning. It enacts history as the essential swaying of the truth of be-ing. It is a "carrying-out" that places into the open the enowned-projecting-open (*ereigneter Entwurf*).[29] It is the thinking by which thinking first becomes historical.

Thus Heidegger says: "Thinking's leap 'into' the truth of be-ing must at the same time leap into the essential sway of truth and establish itself and become inabiding in the throw of a single projecting-open" (GA 65, 446; CP, 314). Thinking that is *denkmäßig* (using itself as measure) may have worked in the time of "system" of logical and conceptual philosophy. But thinking that is *denkerisch*—where something unfolds *in* thinking—cannot work in systems. "The time of 'systems' is over. . . . In the meantime . . . philosophy has to have achieved one crucial thing: projecting-open, i.e., grounding enopening of the free-play of the time-space of the truth of be-ing" (GA 65, 5; CP, 4).

Essential Swaying and the Leap

As this essay comes to a close, I will return to those two "darings" at the very beginning of the joining "Leap": the daring to think be-ing directly (not guided by or in service to beings, not guided by the ontological difference) and the daring to make a foray into the domain of be-ing-history. The "turning" in the first daring, to leap over ontological difference and to leap directly into be-ing as en-owning (in the first part of this essay) is embedded in and grounds the "*mid-point* of the turning of enowning," i.e., the turning of be-ing's enowning Da-sein and enowned Da-sein's projecting be-ing open—originary turning (in the second part of the essay). Since the leap is leaping into enowning and since "enowning is originary history" (GA 65, 32; CP, 23), our path took us directly into be-ing history and be-ing-historical thinking (in the third part).

Here at the end, these three moments can be gathered into something like a onefold of "turnings in essential swaying and the leap":

1. Thinking as leap leaps "into be-ing" (GA 65, 7; CP, 6).
2. To take this leap is "to grasp the truth of be-ing from within its *own* essential sway (enowning)" (GA 65, 250; CP, 176).
3. Da-sein is enowned by be-ing, as it [Da-sein], enowned, projects be-ing open—thus the projecting-open that is Da-sein's projects open the very enowning of Da-sein by be-ing, along with enowned Da-sein's projecting-open.
4. Da-sein's "role" is to get hold of this happening in the essential swaying of be-ing.
5. The onefold of be-ing's enowning Da-sein (be-ing's need) and of enowned Da-sein's projecting be-ing open (Da-sein's belonging), which Heidegger calls "counter-resonance, *makes up be-ing as enowning*" (GA 65, 251; CP, 177, italics added).
6. This counter-resonance is what Heidegger calls "the turning in enowning—*die Kehre im Ereignis*" (GA 65, 407; CP, 286).

7. The leap into the turning in enowning is a leap into be-ing-history, and Da-sein is historical as it gets hold of this be-ing (turning in be-ing).

Writing in 1962 to William J. Richardson, Heidegger says that the turning is "be-ing and its truth in relation to human being," that it happens because his thinking *stays with* the matter for thinking, that the turning is in the dynamic itself and not just some new way of thinking/ conceiving, that *enhancing* the question of being in *Being and Time* by thinking the turning "furnishes for the first time a sufficient [adequate, full, whole] determination of Da-sein, i.e., of the essential way of [way of being of, what is ownmost to] man [as] [because it is] thought from out of [in terms of, from the perspective of, from within] the truth of being [be-ing] as such."[30] This turning is now roundly unfolded as the turning in the midpoint of enowning: the enowning throw of and by be-ing and the enowned projecting-open by and of Dasein—what the thinking in *Contributions* enacts.

Finally, let me reflect on the temptation to "translate" Heidegger into a "fully accessible language." I would offer that the "urge" for a "fully accessible language" is not the issue. It is not about being totally "correct" in interpretation or in translation, nor is it about an "orthodox" reading. Rather it is about "getting hold of" what is at issue, about "shifting-into" what is at issue. This requires circling around be-ing as enowning, a circling that sometimes appears repetitious and even tautologous. But repetition and tautology *belong* to this thinking. I would apply to the work of thinking en-owning and be-ing as en-owning in *Contributions* the words that Heidegger used to describe the words of Parmenides:

> In this regard it must be fully acknowledged that tautology is the only possibility of thinking that which dialectic can only mask, gloss over, darken, ill-define.[31]

And [when we think "this way"] we immediately land in front of a new difficulty. We stand in front of an evident and notorious *tautology.* However, in front of a *genuine* one. It does not enumerate twice what is identical. It names only once the same, and indeed it itself.[32]

Notes

1. All of these "warnings" have been gleaned from the letter to Richardson, published as the Preface/*Vorwort* to William J. Richardson, *Heidegger: Through Phenomenology to Thought* (The Hague: Martinus Nijhoff, 1967), pp. xvi–xxi.

2. Ibid., pp. xx–xxi, translation modified. Appears also in Martin Heidegger, *Grundfragen der Philosophie,* GA 45 (Frankfurt am Main: Vittorio Klostermann, 1984), p. 214.

3. Page references for *Beiträge* are included with references to the Emad/

Maly *Contributions*. For bibliographical information, see the introduction to this volume, note 1. The "Translators' Foreword" to *Contributions* deals with a number of specific words whose refined subtlety is difficult to render into English, as well as with more general translation-issues in this volume.

4. See Translators' Foreword to *Contributions to Philosophy (From Enowning)*. The issue of be-ing-history and be-ing-historical thinking will be taken up in the third part of this essay.

5. Martin Heidegger, *Die Geschichte des Seyns*, GA 69 (Frankfurt am Main: Vittorio Klostermann, 1998), p. 27.

6. Ibid., pp. 27–28.

7. Ibid., p. 28.

8. Cf. Friedrich-Wilhelm von Herrmann, *Wege ins Ereignis: Zu Heideggers "Beiträgen zur Philosophie"* (Frankfurt am Main: Vittorio Klostermann, 1994), pp. 67–68, where von Herrmann shows various ways in which Heidegger thinks *Kehre* and how all these subordinate ways rest in the turning-relation in and of be-ing—in the "originary" turning.

9. Then Heidegger writes: "The *call-unto* [*Anruf auf*] leaping-into enowning is the grand stillness of the most sheltered and concealed self-knowing." This is where all language of Da-sein originates—and is essentially "stillness" or "silence," which belongs to "reservedness, enowning, truth, and language." In this essay I will not pursue this very important trail.

10. Von Herrmann, *Wege ins Ereignis*, pp. 18–19, italics added. Here is manifest the connection between *Geschehen* and *Geschichte*, whereby be-ing-history and be-ing-historical thinking need to be thought. See the third part of this essay.

11. Ibid., p. 61, italics added.

12. Richardson, *Heidegger*, pp. xii–xiii.

13. Von Herrmann, *Wege ins Ereignis*, p. 18.

14. *Die Geschichte des Seyns*, p. 15.

15. Martin Heidegger, *Was ist das—die Philosophie?* published in *What Is Philosophy?* (New Haven, Conn.: College and University Press, 1956), p. 40. (This text is from a lecture that was originally given in Normandy, France, in August 1955.) See also my "Soundings of *Beiträge zur Philosophie (Vom Ereignis)*," in *Research in Phenomenology* 21 (1991): 172ff.

16. Martin Heidegger, *Zur Sache des Denkens* (Tübingen: Max Niemeyer, 1969), p. 9. (This lecture, "Time and Being," was originally given at the University of Freiburg in 1962.)

17. Martin Heidegger, *Der Satz vom Grund*, GA 10 (Frankfurt am Main: Vittorio Klostermann, 1997), p. 30. (This lecture course was given at the University of Freiburg during the winter semester of 1955/56.)

18. Ibid., p. 139.

19. *Die Geschichte des Seyns*, p. 5.

20. Ibid., p. 167.

21. Ibid., p. 170.

22. Ibid., p. 222.

23. Ibid., p. 20.

24. Ibid., p. 23.

25. Ibid., p. 115.

26. Ibid., p. 116.

27. If the English language were not so destitute when it comes to thinking/ saying this phenomenon, I would not have turned to this connection. However, English *is* destitute here: The word *history* is flat; the inherent connection in German between *Geschichte* and *Geschehen* is totally lacking in English; and the kinship in German of *Geschichte* and *Geschick/schicken/Schickung* is absent in English as well.

28. See von Herrmann, *Wege ins Ereignis,* p. 92 and passim.

29. Ibid.

30. Preface/*Vorwort* to Richardson, *Heidegger,* p. xxi.

31. Martin Heidegger, *Seminare,* GA 15 (Frankfurt am Main: Vittorio Klostermann, 1986), p. 400. Heidegger used these words in the seminar held in Zähingen in 1973.

32. Ibid., p. 405.

9. Da-sein and the Leap of Being

Walter A. Brogan

Martin Heidegger's *Beiträge zur Philosophie,* or *Contributions to Philosophy,* is a sustained meditation on the problem of thinking about what had not previously been thought in metaphysics, or even in Heidegger's earlier major work, *Sein und Zeit* (*Being and Time*). The matter in need of thinking is *Ereignis,* the enowning event of the truth of being. This book, written ten years after *Being and Time,* promises only to *attempt* to get underway toward this needed originary thinking and to think (and discuss) the matter in a manner that assists (as in *Zu-spiel*) in its enactment. It is noteworthy that Heidegger does not pose this treatise as an "example" of such thinking. To the contrary, a central theme of this work is the peculiar philosophical character and methodology of a book whose task is to prepare for something it cannot itself claim ever to have accomplished.

As Parvis Emad and Kenneth Maly, the translators of the English text, point out, the ambiguous status of the book's relationship to that of which it speaks is coded in the subtitle: *Vom Ereignis.* The preposition here is indeed difficult to translate. Emad and Maly opt for "from" *Ereignis,* trying to capture the sense that this is a "thinking that is enowned by being" (CP, xxii) rather than a thinking "about" *Ereignis,* which would demand the alternative translation "on," indicating that *Ereignis* is the topic of the volume. But Heidegger does not pretend that *his* thinking in this work comes *from* the enowning event of the truth of being. It is more the case that even this thinking needs to "go under" (GA 65, 7; CP, 6),[1] that is, to enact its own unthinking of itself so as perhaps to leave open a space in the interstices for the enowning event. Similarly, Heidegger speaks of the reticence of his words and the need for a saying that becomes silent as a way of expressing the peculiarity and difficulty of discussing the task he is undertaking in this project.

Were this book to have a genuine title, Heidegger says, it would necessarily be called *Ereignis* (GA 65, 3; CP, 3). But in fact it is impossible to successfully write of *Ereignis* except in a way that unwrites itself, just as it is impossible to write such a text that in turn can be authored and titled in a traditional manner. This work does not enact the thinking of the enowning event; rather, it enacts an attempt, a searching-questioning that is provisional, an attempt at responding in words to the gift of be-ing (*Seyn*) that enjoins inceptual thinking (GA 65, 81; CP, 56). *Ereignis* is an originary enowning and belonging (*Zugehörigkeit*) that cannot be possessed or owned or "gotten." It is in this sense belonging itself, and never something that belongs. Thus, Heidegger argues, his "contribution" has a transitional character; it performs a kind of transitioning-crossing

(*Übergang*), but its being-underway is not in transition *to* something. It is no longer caught up in a teleological or transcendental schema or focused on a solution to the problems and questions of philosophy. This new Heideggerian attempt at thinking, this *Besinnung*, does try to transcend metaphysics, but it does so by turning this transcendence back to the earth, remaining faithful to the earth that the gods call forth; and therefore it is a transitioning-questioning that is appropriate for one who would attempt to listen to the earthly echoing of the intraversably distant singing of the gods.

This essay will focus on a chapter of this work in which the difficulty of such thinking and writing is most evident, part IV, the central one in the book, entitled "Der Sprung" (The Leap). But I want to acknowledge at the outset the limitations of approaching *Contributions* in this piecemeal manner. This is Heidegger's most Nietzschean book, both in terms of content and style. The fact that this relatively short chapter has fifty-two sections is an indication of its fragmentary and aphoristic form. The sections circle around each other and build up an intensity by returning again and again to the question of the leap, beginning anew each time to say what cannot be said in the manner of an extended and sustained discussion. I will try to show that the interruptive style is appropriate to the thinking of the leap attempted in this chapter. But it is also the methodology of the entire work.

It is impossible to read this disturbing work in the usual, sequential manner as if it were a book that proceeds from beginning to middle to end, and goes from thesis to conclusion. The book's chapters are more like the movements of a peculiar type of musical composition. Heidegger expresses early on in the text an awareness of his own limitations in the face of originary thinking, and he promises only to produce "a fugue [*Fuge*] of this thinking" (GA 65, 81; CP, 56). *Die Fuge* in German can mean the fugue, the musical composition itself, and also the jointure, the interplaying structure that hinges together the parts of such a composition. "Following a simple *shift* [Ruck] of essential thinking, the happening of the truth of be-ing must be transposed from the first beginning into the other, so that the wholly other song of be-ing sounds in the playing-forth [*Zuspiel*]" (GA 65, 8–9; CP, 7). But the point and counterpoint between the first and other beginnings is intertwined so that it is not a matter of one answering the other, but rather an echoing, playing back and forth, and leaping across that lets play the abysmal grounding of be-ing in its withdrawing from beings.

Thus, this book is written like a musical fugue whose score requires one to listen to each of the six parts of the text in the way they mutually pursue and alternately duplicate each other. It is important to hear the episodes of the text not only as they appear alongside each other but also in their interplay. Reading this text requires not only that we follow its linear and vertical progression but also—as in a fugue—that we follow each part horizontally as it is addressing and being addressed by the other parts. This requires attentiveness to the multilayered character of the composition. Heidegger structures each of his chapters in this fugue-like way in order to begin to attune us to the kind of listening required of one who would attend to the unique timing and spacing in the event of the truth of being. "Every joining stands for itself, and yet there is a hidden inter-resonating and an enopening grounding of the site of decision for the essential *Übergang* into the still possible transformation of Western history" (GA 65, 82; CP, 57). The site of decision, wherein Western history is not left behind but transformed, occurs precisely as the interjoining of these jointures that are named in the titles of each of the chapters in this volume. Heidegger's *Contributions* is written to prepare our ears to hear the interplaying resonance, the *Anklang*,[2] of the other beginning, which from our present position can mostly be heard in the mournful tonality of the abandonment and forgottenness of being (GA 65, 110; CP, 77).

But what needs to be heard by one who would engage in this kind of originary thinking, and by one whose ear is attuned to and appropriated for this event, is something never before able to be heard, namely the great stillness (GA 65, 34; CP, 24). It is this silence that inter-resonates in the "joinings" of which Heidegger speaks (GA 65, 82; CP, 57). Heidegger says that this stillness and reservedness (*Verhaltenheit*) preserves the truth of being. The truth of being, therefore, cannot be heard in ordinary discourse and presumably cannot be exposited in ordinary discursive writing, both of which fill in and fill out the space of this silent sounding of being.

One might well ask how one can hear what is essentially silent and hidden and in principle unable to be extended in the manner which makes ordinary sound and space and time possible. This silent saying of the event of the truth of being, Heidegger says, occurs in the space/time of the moment (*Augenblick*) (GA 65, 108; CP, 76). There is no time to hear the instant because the moment interrupts the flow of time. Likewise, there is no space in which to locate the occurrence of this enowning event since the event displaces the continuity of space. Originary thinking tries to grasp this disruptive instant, this moment of transition, between the end of the first beginning and the eruption of another beginning.[3] Heidegger writes aphoristically and, at times, frenetically in this text so that his writing will allow for an opening up, both textually and in the thinking, of previously unheard-of spaces and discontinuous connections.[4] This is because the movement that is being traced from one beginning to another is not one that can be traversed by providing a link or bridge. The movement in this work is not a way or a path, for there is no pathway that can carry us along. That is why Heidegger says:

"All specific 'contents' and 'opinions' and 'pathways' of the first attempt in *Being and Time* are incidental and can disappear" (GA 65, 242; CP, 171).

The movement of thought from metaphysics and from phenomenology to the thinking of be-ing (*Seyn*)[5] is radically transitional. A μεταβολή, a transformative shift, a *Kehre*, according to Heidegger, is required if one is to enter into the time/space of this movement. Heidegger's *Contributions* is a meditation on the work of thinking in the age of transition (GA 65, 83; CP, 57). What is required of thinking in this time is to think transition in itself, apart from its usual rendering in terms of the poles from which and toward which something is moving. Thus the work of thinking can only be "a *passage* [*Gang*] in both senses of the word: a going and a way at the same time—thus a way that itself goes" (ibid.). Thinking becomes a path that is itself underway; what is called for is transitional thinking, thinking in transition.

To think in transition is to be attuned to the decisive moment of the enowning event. But this moment is, while remaining an instant, a join-ture, a transitional "between." Heidegger acknowledges the difficulty of thinking of such a passageway that is underway by stating that one can only enter into this underway movement through a leap. "What counts *in the other beginning* is the leap into the encleaving middle [*in die erklüf-tende Mitte*] of the turn of the event of being" (GA 65, 231; CP, 163–64). So the *Kehre* is not, first of all, a human activity per se, but rather the turning of *Ereignis*. This turning is to be understood as a middle (*Mitte*), which, like the Aristotelian mean, is not an expanse but a moment, the between of both the first and the other beginning. And despite the fact that this event is utterly singular, it nevertheless is, as essentially be-tween, bifurcated and cleaved. And the aesthetic listener[6] who hears the resonance of this divisive moment between two beginnings cannot traverse along a prepared path but is required to leap.

In each chapter of this text, Heidegger tries to relate what is being discussed to the question of being. In the chapter on the leap, Heidegger situates the altogether radical and difficult thought of *Ereignis* in *Contributions* in relationship both to the meaning of being in the history of metaphysics and the meaning of being in *Being and Time*. Heidegger claims that there is both a continuity and a disruption in the passage from the meaning of being in *Being and Time* to the sense of be-ing and the truth of being as *Ereignis* in his *Contributions*. He suggests that *Being and Time*, in terms of its relationship to *Ereignis*, is itself the preparation of a crossing. By transitional crossing (*Übergang*), Heidegger does not mean to claim that a link between metaphysics and *Ereignis* has been established by his major work. "Going from the guiding-question to the grounding-question, there is never an immediate, equi-directional and continual process that once again applies the guiding question (to being)" (GA 65, 77; CP, 53). *Being and Time* prepares a movement out of metaphysics and an opening of the space/time for a new beginning, without being able to initiate or occupy the beginning. The sense of being in *Being and Time* is between the being of metaphysics and the be-ing (*Seyn*) of *Contributions*. Although there is a sense in which an over-coming and crossing over is in fact accomplished already in *Being and Time,* any attempt to understand the character of this transition requires that one read Heidegger's early work retrospectively by first entering into the heart of Heidegger's concern in his later work. For there is no bridge to *Ereignis* as the truth of *Seyn.* A leap is required. *Being and Time* is a preparation, a clearing of the space for such a leap; but it does not attempt to articulate this *Sprung.*

Part IV of *Contributions* begins with the following statement, which says opaquely and compactly what is unfolded in the rest of the chapter:

> The leap, the most daring move in the advance of inceptual thinking, aban-dons and throws aside everything familiar, expecting nothing from beings immediately. Rather, above all else it releases [*erspringt*] belongingness to be-ing in its full essence as enowning event. Thus the leap gives the impression of being most restless—and yet it is precisely attuned by that *deep awe* . . . in which the will of reservedness exceeds itself into inabiding and sustaining the most distant nearness of the hesitating refusal. (GA 65, 227; CP, 161)

We learn from this initial statement that the leap is caught up in a double movement of a peculiar sort. On the one hand, it is a movement away from absorption in the affairs of beings. *Being and Time* has shown how this involvement in the particularity of things forsakes being as a whole and being as such.[7] In the sudden turning from beings, the originary thinking of the leap enters into the movement of the end; it undergoes the nullity of beings. On the other hand, at the same time and all at once, the leap opens out toward the movement of the essential unfold-ing of be-ing in its fullness. It is also the site (and of course a leap is essentially without location and not a place at all) of both extreme reti-cence that holds back in the face of beings (*Verhaltenheit*), and an insis-tent and unrelenting insertion into the space of the refusal and withdrawal of being. Finally, this refusal and default of being is both the most near to and the farthest from the leap—and both at once. The leap is not an extension—in either direction, either in the direction of *Ereig-nis* and the abandonment of being, or in the direction of the vanishing of beings in distress (*Not*). The space of transition from one to the other cannot be traversed; the springing is always fractured and rifted. The possibility of the leap is thus at the same time its impossibility. But it is not that something is impeding the leap from occurring. Rather the leap itself, the very character of leaping, *is* to be fissured and split. The leap has at its heart a divisiveness and twofoldness that belongs to its essence. The leap is an original juncture that both joins *and* parts. The leap is so close that there is nothing between its occurrence and that from which it departs. And yet the departure is so radical that everything is set aside and everything is too remote to be accessed. The leap occurs in the juxtaposition of these opposites, in the sameness of opposition that Heidegger calls an originary strife, "*strife* as the essence of the 'between,' not as letting the contrary also count" (GA 65, 264; CP, 186).

Heidegger argues in part V, on abysmal grounding, that the trembling (*Erzitterung*) of the strife in the cleft (*Erklüftung*), which is attained and sustained on the basis of the event of appropriation (*Ereignung*), constitutes the (non-subjective) selfhood of Da-sein, of being-there (GA 65, 321; CP, 226). Da-sein is essentially there in its fullness in the moment of *Ereignis* in a way more original than every I and you and we. "No 'we' and 'you' and no 'I' and 'thou,' no *community* setting itself up by itself, ever reaches the self; rather it only misses the self and continues to be excluded from the self, unless it grounds itself first of all on Da-sein" (GA 65, 321; CP, 226). But this moment is not only the ground of an originary self; it is the abysmal grounding that is undergone by the leap into the unsurpassable fissure, the tear in being. The grounding and primordial source of selfhood is abysmal and fundamentally an experience of being torn apart, an experience of departure from self.

One aspect of the leap of originary, inceptual thinking is the recognition that there is no pathway to the recovery of a self. Through the leap, Da-sein stands in relationship to this unsurpassable fissure and tear in being that makes being underway to the leap an impossibility. Heidegger hyphenates the word "Da-sein" throughout this text, and it becomes evident that the meaning of Da-sein has dramatically shifted in comparison to *Being and Time*. One indication of this is that thrownness, projecting-open, and other such modes of Dasein are now shown as belonging co-primordially to be-ing and the truth of be-ing and as occurring not solely on the basis of Dasein's being but in the inter-play, the between (GA 65, 239; CP, 169). Thus Heidegger says: "In opening up the essential unfolding of be-ing, it becomes manifest that Da-sein does not accomplish anything, unless it be to get hold of the counter-resonance of the en-owning occurrence (*Er-eignung*), i.e., to shift into this counter-resonance and thus first of all to become itself" (GA 65, 239; CP, 167).[8] Thus, the essence of Da-sein is the leap. Da-sein is the advent of the impossible occurrence of this leap.

I would like now to mark out more briefly and comment on four other important aspects of what Heidegger calls the leap: (1) its excessive concreteness that *posits* being-there and precludes any ordinary sense of transcendence; (2) its momentariness that abandons horizonal thinking in favor of the eternal lightning-flash that posits the event of being; (3) its unicity and singularity, a solitary singularity that distances itself from the earlier emphasis on belongingness; (4) its silence that respects the refusal and reticence of being.

In light of Heidegger's remarks on the difference between being and beings, and the central role of the notion of anxiety (entering into a detachment from beings) in *Sein und Zeit*, it is important to notice the concreticity that Heidegger nevertheless ascribes to the inceptual thinking of the event of be-ing. The concreteness of the leap is such that all references to the universal and transcendent in distinction from the particular need to be abandoned (GA 65, 239; CP, 169). It is not a matter of a radical immanence that forsakes essences in favor of the sheer facticity of beings. The leap is, from this point of view, a leap away from the world of appearances. But it is not for this reason a leap that aims toward universals that transcend particularity. "The task is not to surpass beings (transcendence) but rather to leap over the distinction and thus over transcendence and to inquire inceptually into be-ing and truth" (GA 65, 270; CP, 177). The leap enters even more profoundly into the specificity and concreteness of what is. This is, more than anything else, what Heidegger means by the inabiding character of being-there (*Dasein*) in this text. "One must think so far ahead—or better: so far into—the there (the *Da*) that the truth of be-ing lights up originarily" (GA 65, 175; CP, 249).

The leap is there in the space/time where the difference of beings emerges, where the irruption of the manifold of beings in their multiplicity unfolds; it occurs in the space where be-ing withdraws and thus initiates the discussion of beings. The originary thinking of the leap does not gather beings back into their essence and interpret them as representations of transcendental ideas; originary thinking is not representation at all. Rather it is a thinking that stays with and gives witness to the unrepresentable yet double moment of emergence/withdrawal. In this sense, its immediacy and concreteness surpass any other kind of thinking of immanence that takes the originary play of this space/time for granted.

Here Heidegger radically dis-places the vantage point of subjectivity, as well as the Nietzschean inversion that orients itself around life, and finally even the authenticity of humans in *Being and Time* (GA 65, 325; CP, 229). Thus, not even horizonal thinking and the thinking that turns from the in-timeness of beings to world is at issue in the thinking of the leap. The leap is not away from beings to world. These two senses of time—the sequential time of beings in the world, and the horizonal span of worldly time—are both left behind in the leap which opens up the play of originary time-space. "Time-space has nothing of what is commonly known as 'time' and 'space' in themselves" (GA 65, 386; CP, 270). Heidegger characterizes this time-space as eternal (GA 65, 259; CP, 371). But eternal here means something even more finite and more

utterly temporal than any previous sense of time. The leap belongs to
the divisive time of the instant, which Heidegger says flashes up sud-
denly and unexpectedly. It is called a divisive time because it is the time
of the between, an abysmal juncture, more original than what opens
out of this intersection: "Strife as the essence (*Wesung*) of the 'between,'
not as letting the opposite also count" (GA 65, 265; CP, 186).

The peculiar character of this moment of jointure is such that no
connection with other moments is possible. As the origin of all connections, it itself is radically disconnected. Originary, inceptual thinking therefore occurs in loneliness and cannot be shared; Heidegger
declares that *Contributions* is written to prepare for "the rare who bring
along the utmost courage for solitude, in order to think the nobility of
be-ing and to speak of its uniqueness" (GA 65, 11; CP, 9). This
unshareability of the thinking of the moment of leaping places peculiar demands on this work, which would pretend in some way to
speak about and communicate something of this event. Heidegger emphasizes repeatedly the unicity and singularity of this occurrence which
is inherently non-relational and yet the grounding of the very possibility of all relationality and belongingness.

Finally, the poetic saying of this leap is silent before and reverent
toward the refusal and default of being. It does not try to make up for
the loss of being. The absence of being is no longer an error rooted in
the metaphysical turn. The thinking of the essential unfolding of the
truth of being *is* the thinking of the moment of the withdrawing of
being. Originary thinking is attuned to the halcyon tones echoed in the
great stillness of this event.

The originary thinking of the leap occurs in relationship both to the
end of the first beginning and in anticipation of the second beginning
that is yet to come. It is a thinking that occurs in the space of the
between. It attempts to think a movement that is fundamentally finite,
momentary, unshareable, non-relational, unsayable, utterly singular,
torn apart from all else, and estranged from everything familiar. These
characteristics of the leap make it inevitable that Heidegger would turn
in this chapter on the leap to a discussion of being unto death. The connection between *Being and Time* and *Contributions* that is established in
this discussion of the transitional leap is especially evident in these passages that have to do with being-toward-death. Heidegger insists, in
confrontation with certain "misreadings" of *Being and Time,* that the
central importance of being-toward-death is not in the turn from being
to nothingness; rather, the turn is from beingness to the event of being
(GA 65, 283; CP, 199). Heidegger argues that being-toward-death is not
so much the basis of a nullity as the site of the sudden opening of time-
space; a play of time-space that advents in a decisive, non-epochal
instant of irruption and eruption. "Here the utmost appraisal of *tempo-*

rality is enacted, and thus along with it the occupying of the *space* of the truth of be-ing, *the announcing of time-space"* (GA 65, 284; CP, 200). Heidegger calls death the supreme and utmost witness of being, the witnessing of the utter estrangement and abandonment of being. Para- doxically, Da-sein's being-toward-death opens up its nearness to being in that Da-sein is singularized and de-parted from being. In other words, being and Da-sein are related as the event of a passing away, of a turning back. When this is connected to Heidegger's discussion of the passing away of the last god at the end of *Contributions,* one can better recognize the extent to which Heidegger has put aside any remaining sense of the subjectivity of Da-sein that entangled *Being and Time* with metaphysics. For the truth of being is not granted out of any subjective relationship to being on the part of Da-sein. Rather be-ing-toward- death encounters the refusal of being. It is no longer the call of conscience but the refusal of being that summons Da-sein to *Sorge.* Be-ing- toward-death radically singularizes Da-sein and thus unfolds being- there, not as the ground of beings but as the decisive site of an abysmal grounding of the truth of being that is independent of all beings. More- over, in his discussion of being-toward-death, Heidegger makes clear that the death of Da-sein is radically futural in a sense that was only hinted at in *Being and Time. Contributions* is haunted by an eschatological voice that addresses the coming, the advent of what is to come. In *Con- tributions,* Da-sein itself is yet to come.

The discussion of being-toward-death in part IV is situated between a treatment of *Zerklüftung,* the fissure and cleft of being, and a discus- sion of *Wesung,* the essential unfolding of being. The enowning event of be-ing is the strife between an unfolding opening into what is and a holding back, an untraversable rift that prevents any communication with what is. Be-ing-toward-death is the site of the play of this double character of *Ereignis.* Da-sein is thereby both the site of the origin of the belonging together that characterizes being-in-the-world, and the abys- mal attunement to the abandonment of be-ing that attends to a differ- ence that is beyond being. It is the latter part of Dasein's double character that *Being and Time* failed to adequately address. But this fail- ure is significant. For it is only in attending to this double character of Da-sein that the leap becomes possible. *Contributions* is Heidegger's attempt to prepare for such a possibility.

Notes

1. For bibliographical information on the texts referred to here, see the introduction to this volume, note 1.

2. Part II is entitled *Anklang.* Heidegger addresses in this chapter the way in which the other beginning "echoes" in the destitution that occurs through the

forgetting of being. Here he already finds a resonance of the abandonment of being toward which originary thinking and hearing is drawn.

3. In this moment is contained the hidden history of a great stillness in which "there can still *be* a people" (GA 65, 34; CP, 24). This time-space of the moment is other than what occurs in the presencing of horizonal temporality. In a future essay I hope to trace Heidegger's references to community in *Contributions*. On the basis of *Contributions,* it seems to me, an entirely different sense of being a people emerges, one which bears little resemblance to National Socialism. The primary characteristic of this coming community is that it is a community of singular beings wherein the way of being a people is governed by this singularity. "In its origin and destiny this people is singular, corresponding to the singularity of be-ing itself" (GA 65, 97; CP, 67). Reiner Schürmann must have been guided by a manuscript of this lecture course in his work *Heidegger on Being and Acting: From Principles to Anarchy* (Bloomington: Indiana University Press, 1986). In any case, *Contributions* appears to me to support his conclusions.

4. This juxtaposition of contradictory terms and notions is common throughout the text and requires us to think together what are, in a certain way, unable to be together, except in a certain peculiar space such as that opened up by the leap. Heidegger's project in *Contributions* is to think of another beginning "outside" the dualisms of metaphysics.

5. Heidegger changes the spelling of *Sein* in German to *Seyn* to indicate the question of the new beginning in distinction from previous questioning about being. The fact that *Seyn* is an older way to spell the verb indicates the complicated circling of inceptual thinking that tries to reach a new beginning and at the same time tries to recover the most ancient and forsaken question of all. In the Emad/Maly translation, *Seyn* is translated as "be-ing."

6. I borrow this term from Nietzsche's *The Birth of Tragedy,* where he says that the rebirth of tragedy after the end of Socratism requires the rebirth of the ability to hear. See Friedrich Nietzsche, *The Birth of Tragedy,* trans. W. Kaufmann (New York: Vintage Books, 1966), p. 133. Nietzsche too identifies what needs to be heard after the death of Socratism and metaphysics in terms of listening to the moment of juncture.

7. Later in this essay it will become clear that the turn from particularity is toward an even greater sense of concreteness, and that the thereness and finitude of Da-sein is even more thoroughgoing in this text.

8. This is a good example of the philosophical dimension of Heidegger's references to the "fugue" of thinking. Originary thinking of the leap is the counterpoint to *Ereignis.*

10. Grounders of the Abyss
John Sallis

How is one even to read, much less to write about, a work that at the very outset disclaims being a work, at least of the style heretofore, and declares that all fundamental words have been used up and that the genuine relation to the word has been destroyed? What is to be said of a book the very title of which is deliberately made to exemplify this destitution of words, even if with the utmost irony, as if the blandest of covers had been mockingly wrapped around this text, which, in starkest contrast, does not shy away from the most unheard-of—and, indeed, courageous[1]—ventures, letting words slide toward the most extreme limit, toward the unsayable to which saying would always already have submitted? As in what is, though parenthesized and set as if it were merely a subtitle, nonetheless called the proper, suitable, appropriate title: *Vom Ereignis.* How is one to read and to write (translating even into another language) of and from what would be said in this word that Heidegger himself later declared untranslatable?[2] What is one to make— or not make—of a text that says—and says that it says—"always the same of the same" (GA 65/CP, §39), weaving its tautological threads always around the same pole or at least around the single axis secured by that pole? What of a text that, at the other extreme, yokes together words that to all appearances speak against one another, issuing in such apparent contradictions as "grounders of the abyss"? To say nothing of the way in which the text crosses back over itself, crossing out what, in the crossing toward the other beginning, it could not but have put forth.

How is one to read this strange text otherwise than as Nietzsche once demanded of his readers: "slowly, deeply, looking cautiously back and forth, with reservations, with doors left open, with delicate fingers and eyes"?[3] How is one to write of *Contributions to Philosophy* otherwise than by trying to keep one's bearings alongside some short stretches of the "pathway which is first traced out by the crossing to the other beginning, into which Western thinking is now entering" (GA 65/CP, §23)?

It is remarkable that grounding weighs so heavily in the thinking that would cross to the other beginning. For, in this crossing, grounding would be exceeded, as would be indeed the entire orbit within which grounding was heretofore possible and was determined as such in the first beginning. Yet it is precisely through—as a result of—this transgression that the need for another grounding is exposed and the necessity of rehabilitating grounding, even if exorbitantly, is put into play. Grounding comes to figure so prominently that the word, even if used up in the history of metaphysics, can entitle one of the major fugal moments of

Heidegger's text. And, from its beginning, *Contributions* celebrates those who are called "grounders of the abyss."

The thinking inscribed in *Contributions* begins at the end of metaphysics, begins within that indefinitely extending end in order to break with it, out of it, for the sake of another beginning. *Metaphysics* designates "the whole history of philosophy up to now" (GA 65/CP, §258), that which began in the first beginning and which came to its end (in the double sense of completion and termination) in Nietzsche's reversal of what he called Platonism. With the Nietzschean inversion of the defining opposition between supersensible and sensible—that is, when the "true world" finally becomes a fable—the final possibility of Platonism is realized and the entire store of such possibilities, played out in the history of metaphysics, is exhausted (GA 65/CP, §91).[4]

What Nietzsche calls Platonism corresponds to what Heidegger calls the first beginning, though Heidegger's analysis goes well beyond any that Nietzsche ventured—except, in a very different register, in *The Birth of Tragedy*. According to Heidegger's analysis, the first beginning is marked by the eruption, among the Greeks, of the question regarding beings as a whole, regarding beings as such—the question as to what beings as such are, the question "What are beings?"[5]

In the arising of this question and thus in the first beginning as such, necessity is operative. Yet, as pertaining to the first beginning, necessity does not have the sense determined for it in and by the first beginning; Heidegger's thoughtful saying of the first beginning is itself already engaged in passing (*Zuspiel*) between this and another beginning. As thought in this passage, the necessity ascribed to the first beginning is not delimitable merely as one modal category alongside the other two, possibility and actuality. Rather, in the passing between beginnings, the necessary (*notwendig*) comes to be redetermined as a turning (*Wende*) out of a compelling need or distress (*nötigende Not*), a turning from need/distress and a turning compelled by need/distress. As that which is compelling in necessity, *Not* (perhaps best translated with the hendiadys need/distress) does not refer merely to misery and lack. Heidegger stresses that, though apparently just negative, it is something more originary, something that escapes the mere opposition between positive and negative. In the lecture course *Basic Questions of Philosophy*, which is contemporaneous with the composition of *Contributions*, Heidegger even says, of the need/distress that compels the first beginning, that "it is not a lack and not a deprivation but is the surplus of a gift, which, however, is more difficult to bear than any loss."[6] One would presume that it is difficult to bear precisely because of that to which, if one were to bear it, one would be compelled by it.

But what is the need/distress operative in the first beginning? The lecture course describes it as: "not knowing the way out or the way in:

out of and into that which such knowing first opens up as an unentered
and ungrounded 'space.'" He calls this space first opened up by such
knowing/not knowing the "between," where, as he says, "it has not yet
been determined what being [*seiend*] is or what non-being is, though
where also there is not such total confusion and undifferentiation of
beings and non-beings [*des Seienden und Unseienden*] as would sweep
everything away and into everything else."[7] Set forth needfully/dis-
tressfully into this "between," man for the first time has the experience
of finding himself in the midst of beings (*das Inmitten des Seienden*). Yet
the very knowing that opens up the "between" and sets man forth in
the midst of beings is haunted by not-knowing,[8] and it is precisely this
not-knowing that constitutes the need/distress that holds sway in this
opening. The need/distress breaks up beings so as to ground a possible
standpoint for man within this space; that is, it compels a casting asun-
der of what will be determined as beings in their being over against
non-beings. Thus this need/distress provides to thinking in the first
beginning its essential space, a space in which beings can come forth in
their being and can thus be apprehended and named in their being for
the first time. It is, then, this need/distress that attunes man to beings in
their being. This attunement is what the Greeks called Θαυμάζειν (wonder) and identified as the origin of philosophy.

Thus compelled and attuned, the first beginning issues in a determination of the being of beings. In the passing (*Zuspiel*) between beginnings, an understanding of being as constant presence (*beständige
Anwesenheit*) can be shown to have thoroughly guided this determination; indeed, this insight, that the Greek determination of being was
secretly guided by reference to a mode of time, was—as we know—
decisive for Heidegger in opening the way to *Being and Time* and
beyond. But in the first beginning as such, it was a matter of determining that which constitutes an answer to the question "What are beings
as such?" It was a matter of determining their beingness (*Seiendheit*—
Heidegger's translation of οὐσία), their whatness. The determination
proceeded as follows: the beingness or whatness of a being consists in
the look that is always presented by such a being, the look that indeed
is sighted in advance and that thus enables the very recognition of any
being as the being it is, the look that precedes the generation of any and
every being that looks thus and survives the destruction of every such
being. But the look, that is, what is seen when one sets out to see
(ἰδεῖν) something, is the ἰδέα. Thus is being determined in the first
beginning as the beingness of beings, and beingness, in turn, as ἰδέα.[9]

As the first beginning is carried through—and ever thereafter in the
history of metaphysics—philosophy thinks the circulation between beingness and beings, reenacting the circling that is continually under way
in the circuit linking beings to their beingness and beingness to those

beings whose beingness it constitutes. This circulation is generated, on the one side, by the requirement that the ἰδέα be sighted in advance of beings and, on the other side, by the capacity of beings to present their ἰδέα. This is the circulation that is itself presented in the Platonic images of line and cave. It is the circulation that Heidegger finds meant in the very name *metaphysics:* "The name is meant to say that thinking of being takes beings in the sense of what is present and extant as its starting point and goal for ascending to being, an ascending which immediately and at once turns again into a descending into beings" (GA 65/CP, §258). Thus metaphysics circles; thus it circles through all possible configurations of its circle until, with Nietzsche, it comes to its end. To the extent that ground and grounding are determined purely in reference to the circling between beings and beingness—as indeed they have been heretofore—the end of metaphysics is also the exhaustion of ground and grounding. The slightest move beyond, the merest gesture toward twisting free of the final—and thus of every—possibility of so-called Platonism, cannot but expose one to an abyss.

Crossing to another beginning would bring, then, an overcoming of metaphysics, a leap beyond the first beginning and everything possible within its orbit. And yet, it is only in the crossing to another beginning that an originary appropriation of metaphysics and of its history becomes possible; that is, it is precisely at the point of its overcoming that metaphysics "first becomes recognizable in its essence" (GA 65/CP, §85).[10] Recognizing it in its essence means, in a provisional formulation:[11] thinking and saying that which, in play in the first beginning as the very condition of its possibility, nonetheless went unthought and unsaid both in the first beginning and also, consequently, in the history of metaphysics. The unthought of the first beginning could, then, be said—provisionally—in a discourse on that by which the opening and sustaining of the difference between beings and their beingness becomes possible. In the same mode, one could say of this unthought that it is the condition that makes possible the circulation between beings and beingness, that enables the circling played out in the history of metaphysics. In the first beginning, philosophy would have passed over this condition—that is, the condition would have remained concealed precisely as it, at once, made possible everything that philosophy ventured in the first beginning. It is this unthought, unsaid condition, this "domain . . . completely hidden up to now" (GA 65/CP, unnumbered opening section) that would be thought and said in the crossing to another beginning ventured in *Contributions.*

One of the names for this unthought of the first beginning—provisionally characterized as condition of possibility—is *beyng,* the archaic spelling of which serves not only to distinguish it from being as beingness but also to suggest a certain anteriority with respect to the metaphysical concept of being.[12] As condition of possibility, as that by which the very space of the circulation between beings and beingness is first opened, beyng can itself be identified neither as a being nor as the beingness (whatness, ἰδέα) of beings.

Contributions ventures to say thoughtfully this unthought and unsaid condition of the very space of the first beginning, saying it, first of all, as beyng. Such saying will have to strategize between two impossibilities: on the one side, the impossibility of saying beyng "with the ordinary language that today is ever more widely misused and destroyed by incessant talking" and, on the other side, the impossibility of inventing "a new language for beyng." Whereas in the first beginning the language of beings had an appropriateness, as philosophy addressed beings in their beingness, now, in crossing to another beginning, now, with the turn from the exhausted circuit of beings and beingness back to beyng, now, with this leap to beyng, which is neither a being nor the beingness of a being, one will, as Heidegger says, have "to say the language of beings as the language of beyng" (GA 65/CP, §36). The impossibility even of the question "What is beyng?" — as if one could assume that beyng *is* and could ask about its whatness, its beingness — is indicative of the disruptive force of the turn. The only possibility will be some such strategy as the following: to grant within certain limits the everyday understanding of language as referring to beings and to "go a certain stretch of the way with it — in order then at the right moment to exact a turning in thinking" (GA 65/CP, §41). Whatever the strategy, the saying will remain precarious.

Yet *Contributions* ventures to think and say the unthought of the first beginning in at least four ways. The first way is simply as *beyng*, the archaic spelling signaling the turn back to what can be called — provisionally — an anterior condition. The second way says the same but says it as the *essence of beyng*. Heidegger is explicit that, in this phrase, *essence* (as essency [*Wesung*]) "does not name something that yet again lies *beyond* beyng" (GA 65/CP, §164). Again: it "is never a way of beyng that is added on to beyng or even one which persists in itself above beyng" (GA 65/CP, §166). Displaced from such senses as κοινόν and γένος, essence adds nothing to beyng, and *the essence of beyng* says the same as *beyng* itself. What the tautological inscription is to mark is only that beyng holds sway (*west*) as happening (*Geschehnis*).[13] Beyng is — to say it improperly — nothing other than its happening, and the essence of beyng is, as Heidegger expands the saying, the "happening of the truth of beyng" (GA 65/CP, §166). It goes without saying that everything will depend on properly determining the sense of happening; this determination, differentiating the happening of beyng from mere ontic occurrences, will lead directly into a renewal of the question of grounding, a renewal that, putting into play the old, used-up word, will attempt at the right moment to exact a turning in thinking.

The third way says the unthought of the first beginning as the truth of beyng. Heidegger observes that this expression does not mean the truth about beyng, as if it referred to one or several correct assertions about beyng that could be so entitled and taken to constitute a doctrine or theory about beyng. Heidegger observes also that the expression does not mean true beyng in the sense of beyng that is actual, as if beyng were not anterior to beings and to such modes as actuality. He says, rather: "This truth of beyng is nothing at all different from beyng, but rather its ownmost essence [Diese Wahrheit des Seyns ist gar nichts vom Seyn Verschiedenes, sondern sein eigenstes Wesen]" (GA 65/CP, §44). The tautology is explicit: the truth of beyng is beyng (which) is the essence of beyng. But what the expression *the truth of beyng* accentuates is the character of beyng as ἀλήΘεια, as the clearing/concealment in and through which beings come to show themselves in their being. In this expression the character of beyng as condition of possibility is—if still provisional—most prominent. As indicated by the following: "For truth is the between [*das Zwischen*] for the essency [*Wesung*] of being and the beingness of beings. This between grounds the beingness of beings" (GA 65/CP, §5). The point is not that the truth of beyng, because it is between the essence of beyng and the beingness of beings, is therefore something other than, something apart from, the essence of beyng. The point is, rather, that it is as truth, as clearing/concealment, that beyng happens, in such a way that beings can come to present themselves in their beingness. Around precisely this point Heidegger broaches the concept of another ground, assuming that, within the orbit of this other ground, one could continue to speak of concept. No longer identified with the beingness of beings, this other ground—the between, the truth of beyng—would ground the beingness of beings. One could call it a kind of ground of ground, a ground before ground—though only as long as one kept intact the metaphysical circuit and held back from the leap beyond its end. Outside and beyond, the very determination of the being (of beings) as beingness would erode in such a way as to prepare a transmutation of being itself.

In the fourth way of saying the unthought of the first beginning, the requirement of ground and grounding is decisive. Yet in this connection what is required is not just the grounding of beingness on the truth of beyng as its ground; rather, what must be grounded is the truth of beyng itself. Heidegger writes "that the essency of beyng requires the grounding of the *truth* of beyng and that this grounding must be enacted as *Da-sein*" (GA 65/CP, §88). Under the requirement that it be grounded, the truth of beyng—beyng in its very happening—makes its own those who are capable of such grounding; it appropriates those who, precisely by enacting Da-sein, can ground the truth of beyng. As appropriating those needed, beyng happens—and this is the fourth way of saying it—as *Ereignis*.[14] But how is it that grounding is enacted as Da-sein? How is it that, in Heidegger's stark formulation, "Da-sein is the grounding of the truth of beyng" (GA 65/CP, §83)? What kind of grounding can Da-sein provide? What kind of ground can Da-sein be? What is Da-sein?—to risk a question that crosses back over itself, putting in question the very appropriateness of the *what* (that is, of *whatness*) to that which is called Da-sein. These questions touch on the heart of the thinking and discourse of grounding.

"Beyng holds sway [*west*] as Ereignis" (GA 65/CP, §10): this is what is said—from a distinctive essential domain—in each of the fugal moments of *Contributions;* this is what is said in saying always the same of the same. Always it is said of beyng that it happens as *Ereignis*. Always it is said of beyng and of the essence of beyng and of the truth of beyng—for these are the same—that they happen as *Ereignis*.

In thus saying always the same of the same, *Contributions* would say the unthought of the first beginning. Yet Heidegger repeatedly underlines the difference between the question of beings, that is, the guiding-question belonging to the first beginning, and the question of beyng, that is, the grounding-question that was passed over in the first beginning but is now to become the question proper to the other beginning. In the first beginning, being is thought as the beingness of beings and hence within the purview of beings.[15] But in the other beginning, being is not to be thought within this purview, not to be thought from beings: "Thus beyng can no longer be thought from beings; it must be thought from out of itself" (GA 65/CP, §2). On the other hand, the truth of beyng requires a grounding, and the thoughtful saying that is under way to another beginning and that has crossed over to the grounding-question (*Grundfrage*) cannot but be indicative of this grounding: "This thoughtful saying is a directive. It indicates the open sheltering of the truth of beyng in beings as a necessity, without being a command" (GA 65/CP, §2). It is a necessity as turning out of need/distress: grounding the truth of beyng must involve sheltering the truth of beyng in beings, sheltering it in beings that are, on the other hand, themselves in the open, hence, in precisely this sense—conjoining apparent opposites—an open sheltering (*Freie der Bergung*). Yet, in turn, the determination of grounding through this conjunction belongs to a larger configuration in which is expressed one of the major tensions running through *Contributions:* on the one hand, the truth of beyng must be thought from itself and not (as in the first beginning) from beings; but, on the other hand, the truth of beyng must be sheltered in beings and to this extent still thought—if differently—within a certain purview of beings. Yet the difference is all-decisive: the truth of beyng is to be brought to an *open* sheltering in beings, to a sheltering in beings that not only are in the open but that, precisely by sheltering the truth of beyng, open up that very expanse.

Crossing to the other beginning would be, then, at the same time, going back into the first beginning, going back through the first beginning to the originary essence that remained concealed in the first beginning and throughout its entire course as metaphysics. This double movement, this passing (*Zuspiel*) between beginnings, is what is carried out in pursuing the question "What is metaphysics?" the *what* designating here not the whatness of a finally defined concept of metaphysics, but rather the concealed ground of metaphysics, the ground concealed so essentially that the concealment belonged to the very constitution of metaphysics. Thus it is that going back into the ground of metaphysics "is already no longer metaphysics but rather its overcoming" (GA 65/CP, §85).

But what about this concealed ground, which, provisionally, has been characterized as a condition of possibility, as that which makes possible the differentiation of beingness and beings and the circulation within the circuit of that difference? Did that which first made it possible for beings to be apprehended and named in their beingness remain utterly concealed in the first beginning? Was this making-possible, this enabling, simply, unknowingly assumed? Heidegger's own account in the contemporaneous lecture course would suggest otherwise: it is a knowing that first opens up the between, the *in the midst* of beings, where their determination in their beingness becomes possible. And what unfolds that possibility is the not-knowing, the need/distress, that haunts that knowing and that, in enabling the determination of beings, attunes man to beings in their being, gives him that attunement that the Greeks call Θαυμάζειν. That such enabling did not remain concealed is evident not only in Heidegger's account of it but also from the Platonic texts themselves, which recognize and celebrate the way in which philosophy originates from wonder and from a certain not-knowing, that is, ignorance, that haunts knowing.

In what sense, then, is the happening of beyng the concealed ground operative in the first beginning? How is it the concealed ground if not as that which enables, if not as condition of possibility, if not as that which is prior to the determination of beings in their being, that is, as what came to be called the a priori? For Heidegger leaves no doubt but that the happening of beyng is not, in this sense, prior: "But beyng is not something 'earlier'—subsisting for and in itself. Rather, Ereignis is the temporal-spatial simultaneity of beyng and beings" (GA 65/CP, §5). Not that Heidegger denies that the regress to prior conditions has, within limits, its legitimacy: "Within beings and the interpretation of beings on the basis of their beingness in the sense of representedness (and already of ἰδέα), the regress to 'presuppositions' and 'conditions' makes sense and is right" (GA 65/CP, §44). Not that Heidegger denies even that such a way of thinking remains inevitable in the crossing to the other beginning: "Such a return, therefore, has become the basic form of 'metaphysical' thinking in manifold modifications, to such a degree that even the overcoming of 'metaphysics' toward an inceptual understanding cannot do without this way of thinking" (GA 65/CP, §44). And yet, if one cannot but go a stretch of this way—as indeed we have—one must also break with it, recognizing that "the *a priori* is really only there where ἰδέα is—and that is to say that beingness (κοινόν) as ὄντως ὄν is more-being [*seiender*] and thus, *first of all*, a being" (GA 65/CP, §112). In other words, to think being as a priori is ultimately to place it in the purview of beings and would be simply to repeat the obliteration of the difference. In the crossing to the other beginning, there must come a point at which one breaks decisively with thinking beyng as the a priori.

Beyond this point one will no longer, on the way to beyng, engage a regress that merely redoubles the metaphysical regress from beings to a priori beingness. If there should eventually prove to be a way in which beyng grounds beings so as to let them come forth in their being, that way will depend on—will be itself grounded by—the grounding of beyng itself. If, in this grounding, as Heidegger writes, "the ground grounds as a-byss" (GA 65/CP, §9),[16] then everything will hinge on the grounding—or grounders—of the abyss.

Heidegger writes of them almost at the very outset of *Contributions*, sketching in broad strokes what comes about with them: "At times those grounders of the abyss must be consumed in the fire of that which is safeguarded [*das Verwahrten*], so that Da-sein becomes possible for man [*Menschen*] and thus constancy [*Beständigkeit*] in the midst of beings is rescued, so that in the open of the strife between earth and world beings themselves undergo a restoration" (GA 65/CP, §2).

Who are the grounders of the abyss? Among them are those who question: "Those who question have set aside all curiosity; their seeking loves the abyss, in which they know the oldest ground" (GA 65/CP, §5).[17] For those who question, being grounders of the abyss does not mean installing a ground that would cancel the abyss as such but rather apprehending the abyss as archaic ground, as an abysmal ground older than beingness as ground. Yet, before all else, what these grounders ground is beyng in its truth; their accomplishment—indeed the accomplishment of all grounders of the abyss—is to ground the truth of beyng in this abysmal ground.

Those who question are not the only grounders of the abyss. Indeed in what he says of them—that at times they must be consumed in the fire of that which is safeguarded—Heidegger's reference is primarily to the poet, to the poet of poets. For Hölderlin, poetizing the essence of poetry, depicts the poet as exposed to the danger of being consumed by the fire of that which otherwise would go unbequeathed but which the poet can receive and hand down to the people. Cited and discussed in

Heidegger's 1934/35 lecture course on Hölderlin,[18] the lines come from "Wie wenn am Feiertage . . ." ("As on a Holiday . . ."). In Michael Hamburger's translation:

> And hence it is that without danger now
> The sons of Earth drink heavenly fire.
> Yet, fellow poets, us it behoves to stand
> Bare-headed beneath God's thunderstorms,
> To grasp the Father's ray, no less, with our own two hands
> And, wrapping in song the heavenly gift,
> To offer it to the people.[19]

It is to the grounders of the abyss that Heidegger refers when he writes of the *"few individuals* . . . on the essential paths of grounding Da-sein [*des gründenden Da-seins*]," distinguishing them from "the random and resistless many who come later but who have nothing more before them and nothing more behind them" (GA 65/CP, §45). The allusions to Nietzsche, to *Thus Spoke Zarathustra*, could hardly be more transparent: set apart from the last men, those called grounders of the abyss and grounders of the truth of beyng are to *go under*. Somewhat as Zarathustra went under so as to expose what underlies Platonism (and "Platonism for the people") and to bring about the going-under of man himself.[20] Those who go under are given over to what is to come (GA 65/CP, §250). These grounders of the abyss are the ones who come to something, to something beyond man as heretofore extant; they are the ones to whom something thus comes. They are the ones to come, those of the future (*die Zukünftigen*).

Whether exposing themselves to the consuming fire of heaven or erotically seeking in the abyss the oldest ground or going under so as to remain true to the earth, the grounders of the abyss do so in order that Da-sein becomes possible for man. It is a matter of enabling man not just to be a being but to let there open a clearing in which beings can come to presence — perhaps even at the cost of man's becoming less a being (*unseiender*) (see GA 65/CP, §83). Thus would it become possible for man "to be the Da as the ground needed by the essence of beyng" (GA 65/CP, §5). And thus would "constancy in the midst of beings" be rescued amidst the collapse of beingness, that is, of the constancy (constant presence) that was established through the yoke of the ἰδέα in the first beginning. And thus "in the open of the strife between earth and world beings themselves [are to] undergo a restoration." The task is "to restore beings from out of the truth of beyng" (GA 65/CP, §4): to restore to them, to be sure, something of what they have lost through the onslaught of machination, but in what in the other beginning is the only way possible, by letting them *be* within such happening of the truth of beyng as happens in the strife between earth and world.

And yet, a restoration of beings can come to pass only from out of a grounding of the truth of beyng. And, in turn, a grounding of the truth of beyng can come about only from out of a leap—a daring, venturesome, dangerous leap by which everything familiar is abandoned. Indeed it is not just a matter of abandoning everything on which everyday life depends but of leaping away from all this; it is not just a matter of abstaining, as in adopting an ascetic stance, but of leaving everything behind in the most decisive and essential way: "The leap, the most daring move in the proceeding of inceptual thinking, abandons and casts behind itself [*wirft . . . hinter sich*] everything familiar, expecting nothing from beings immediately" (GA 65/CP, §115). It is a matter of a leap away from beings as providing any immediate support, guidance, direction; more fundamentally, it is a leap away from beings as capable of providing any understanding of being, of supplying the sense either of their own being or of the being of that being that we ourselves are. The leap thus constitutes a break with, a decisive turn from, the determination of being within the purview of beings, the determination that determined the first beginning. Once one lets go entirely of beings, even the possibility of grounding being on beings dissolves, and one loses—even for oneself as being—all possibility of ground. Through the leap all grounds fall away, and one exposes oneself utterly to the abyss. The grounders *of the abyss* are such, first of all, in the sense that they are utterly exposed to the abyss and must endure being *in and of it*. To be sure, Heidegger declares that the leap releases also a certain belongingness to beyng: the grounders of the abyss are claimed, appropriated, for grounding the truth of beyng and are attuned (in awe) to this claim (see GA 65/CP, §115). Nonetheless, neither the claim nor the attunement gives them anything, as it were, to hold onto. Even as claimed and attuned, the grounders remain in the abyss, of the abyss; for it is only through their grounding the truth of beyng that a ground—though ever so precarious—is gained. The grounders are of the abyss in that, from within the abyss, they bring forth (through grounding) a ground within the abyss. From out of the abyss, their grounding is a "grounding of the abysmal ground" (GA 65/CP, §226).

With the grounding question it is man's engagement that gets put to the question. In *Contributions* Heidegger continues to stress, as he had in the Marburg lectures, that, from the Greeks on, the development of the question of being had always followed the guiding thread provided by reference to such things as soul, reason, spirit, thinking, that is, by essential reference to man. But in these lectures what Heidegger brings out is the continuity with this recurrent reference to man: "the ontology of Dasein represents the latent goal and constant and more or less evident demand of the whole development of Western philosophy."[21] In

Contributions, on the other hand, what emerges is "that somehow man and yet again not man, namely, in an extension and a displacement, is in play in the grounding of the truth of beyng." Heidegger adds: "And it is precisely this question-worthy [matter] that I call Da-sein" (GA 65/ CP, §193).

Beyng comes to truth only on the ground of Da-sein, only through the grounding brought by Da-sein (see GA 65/CP, §168). Da-sein is the ground of the truth of beyng, the ground through whose grounding beyng happens. Da-sein is not to be identified with man; its name is not to be taken as just an updated name for the being previously called man. Da-sein is not something to be found in extant man, neither an inherent structure nor an emergent form nor an intrinsic capability; on the contrary, through the grounding brought by Da-sein, the grounding of the truth of beyng, "man is transformed from the ground up [*vom Grund aus*]" (GA 65/CP, §170) — from out of this very ground and its grounding. Or, in another idiom, man as he was heretofore — "a rope over an abyss" — goes under.

Needed in order that beyng be brought to its truth, Da-sein is appropriated by beyng. Only in and through this appropriation does beyng happen at all. Its essential happening can, then, be called *Ereignis;* and, in English, this word will then need to be woven into a discourse charged by the significations of *ownness* (*making its own* — in the double sense), *appropriation,* and *happening.* Man, too, while going under as he was heretofore, is, on the other side, also appropriated: "The Da is appropriated [*ereignet*] by beyng itself, and consequently man, as guardian of the truth of beyng, is appropriated and thus belongs to Da-sein in a distinctive and unique way" (GA 65/CP, §175). But how is it that man is the guardian of the truth of beyng? And how is man related to Da-sein such that he can come to belong to Da-sein in a distinctive, indeed unique way?

These questions can be addressed only if the question of Da-sein itself is first taken up. One would like to ask: What is Da-sein, if not simply man or some aspect of extant man? — yet one can do so only to the extent that one frees the *what,* letting it metamorphize in the direction indicated by the displacement of essence in play in Heidegger's work from 1930 on.[22] Here is one answer to the question: Da-sein "is itself the being of the Da [*das Sein des Da*]." Heidegger continues: "The Da, however, is the openness of beings as such as a whole, the ground of more originarily thought ἀλήθεια." What Da-sein says is *that there is a Da* — not just a determinable here and there (*hier und dort*) but, as Heidegger says, a "clearing [*Lichtung*] of beyng itself whose openness first spaces the space for every here and there." What Da-sein says is *that a clearing opens.* Even further: Da-sein is "the essency of that opening which first opens up the self-concealing (the essence of beyng) and which is thus the truth of beyng" (GA 65/CP, §173).[23] The grounding that Da-sein brings to the truth of beyng by the opening of a clearing for—within—the self-concealing of beyng itself is so essential to the happening of the truth of beyng that Heidegger lets *grounding* slide virtually into identity.

But what, then, of Da-sein and man? On the one hand, the grounding is such as to require that man come to it (GA 65/CP, §130). This connection is also borne by the expression *menschliches Dasein*, in which, says Heidegger, the reference to man indicates "the uniqueness of that being, man, to whom alone Da-*sein* is proper" (GA 65/CP, §176). This connection—though not only it—leads Heidegger to say: "Beyng needs man in order that it hold sway [*wese*], and man belongs to beyng that he might accomplish his utmost vocation [*Bestimmung*] as Da-sein" (GA 65/CP, §133).

In another regard, the relation between Da-sein and man is said to lie in Da-sein's being the ground of the possibility of man's future (*des künftigen Menschseins*), that is, "man *is* futural insofar as he undertakes to be the Da" (GA 65/CP, §173). Otherwise he remains among the many who come along later but have nothing more before them and nothing more behind them—that is, he remains apart from the grounders of the abyss, apart even from those allied with them (see GA 65/CP, §45).

Da-sein is what both under-grounds man and raises him to excess (*zugleich unter-gründet und überhöht*) (GA 65/CP, §176). Da-sein grounds man but in a grounding in which man, as he was hitherto, goes under. This under-grounding is precisely what is at issue in the declaration that Da-sein is both ground and abyss for historical man (see GA 65/CP, §194). Da-sein grounds future man and buries man as he has been. At the same time, man is raised, elevated: belonging to beyng, man (grounded by Da-sein) contributes to opening and preserving a clearing in the midst of concealment, a clearing within a concealment (the self-concealing withdrawal of beyng) that utterly exceeds all clearing. It seems that man can come to be so engaged by this excess that he broaches an exceeding of himself as (a) being—in the sense thus outlined by Heidegger: "The less a being [*unseiender*] man is and the less he insists upon the being [*das Seiende*] that he finds himself to be, so much nearer does he come to being [*Sein*]" (GA 65/CP, §83). Presumably it is thus that man is *überhöht* by Da-sein—not just raised or elevated but raised to excess, elevated excessively.

But *how* is it that man comes to be grounded in Da-sein (and thus under-grounded and raised in excess)? How, in particular, is it that the grounders of the abyss come to be grounded by Da-sein, by that abysmal ground itself? Heidegger's answer is unequivocal: they come to be grounded in Da-sein precisely by becoming grounders of Da-sein; and this they do in and by creating (GA 65/CP, §195). But creating means: sheltering (*Bergen*) the truth of beyng in beings (GA 65/CP, §7). It is because man is the one by whom the truth of beyng comes to be sheltered in a being that man can be the guardian of the truth of being.

Heidegger says: "The grounding of Da-sein happens as the sheltering of truth," its sheltering, through creating, in a being (GA 65/CP, §219). In a sense, everything pertinent to grounding is gathered in the phrase *the grounding of Da-sein*. At least three distinct senses are in play and in interplay. The phrase signifies (1) the grounding of the truth of beyng by Da-sein, that is, through the opening of a clearing for beyng; (2) the grounding (as under-grounding) of man by Da-sein (through which man comes to the opening and preserving of clearing); and (3) the grounding of Da-sein by man through the creating in which the truth of beyng comes to be sheltered in a being. The point is that these three groundings happen at once (ἅμα), and this *at once* is said in the word *Ereignis*. This is why in the passage (cited above) in which Heidegger sets beyng apart from the concept of the a priori, he says that "Ereignis is the temporal-spatial simultaneity of beyng and beings" (GA 65/CP, §5).

Man becomes a grounder of the abyss—that is, of the abysmal ground Da-sein—by creating, by sheltering the truth of beyng in a being. For instance, in an artwork, which, in instigating the strife of earth and world, lets the truth of beyng happen. As with the temple at Paestum, which once opened and sustained a Greek world borne by the self-secluding earth. But it is of utmost significance that such sheltering is not something *nachträglich:* "Sheltering is not a subsequent housing [*das nachträgliche Unterbringen*] of an extant, subsistent truth within a being" (GA 65/CP, §243). Or, as Heidegger declares decisively in *The Origin of the Work of Art:* "But truth does not exist in itself beforehand, somewhere among the stars, only subsequently to descend elsewhere among beings. . . . Clearing of openness [i.e., the truth of beyng] and establishment in the open [i.e., being sheltered in a being such as an artwork] belong together. They are the same single essence of the happening of truth."[24] The opening of a clearing (grounding the truth of beyng) happens as the grounders of the abyss come, within the clearing, to shelter the truth of beyng in a being. Yet it is not as though there is first the truth of beyng, which then, subsequently, gets sheltered. From the point of view of man, who has leaped into the abyss, it is not as though he somehow already—perhaps even always already—had the truth in view and then (keeping his gaze fixed on it, holding to it) could eventually shelter it, that is, express it or translate it. But if—letting the *is* slide toward *Ereignis*—one can say that there is no truth before it is sheltered, this does not mean, on the other hand, that the sheltering brings the truth of beyng about as a result; it is not as though there is creative sheltering and only then, subsequently, the truth of beyng. Rather, the truth of beyng and its sheltering happen *at once*. What is perhaps most demanding is to think this *at once*.

The truth of beyng can be sheltered in many ways: "in thinking, poetizing, building, leading, sacrificing, suffering, celebrating" (GA 65/CP, §177).[25]

Aside from—but also including—the distinctive beings in which truth is sheltered, beings are grounded in the truth of beyng; it is only from out of this grounding—and not through mere explanatory derivation from other beings—that beings can be known (GA 65/CP, §118). Yet this grounding of beings as such occurs only within the opening and sheltering accomplished in the grounding of Da-sein. Thus Heidegger says that beyng "holds sway [*west*] *before* all beings that stand within it, something that of course can never be grasped according to the hitherto '*a priori*'" (GA 65/CP, §180).

Neither can Da-sein as ground (of the truth of beyng and, mediately, of beings as such) be grasped according to the concept of ground that identifies ground with the constant presence constituted as beingness in the first beginning. Heidegger marks this differentiation by saying with regard to the grounding of Da-sein that "the ground grounds as a-byss" (GA 65/CP, §9); he calls this grounding a "grounding of the abysmal ground" (GA 65/CP, §226). Heidegger links the abysmality of Da-sein to being-toward-death (see GA 65/CP, §163) but also—and in the end there is perhaps no difference—to the character of Da-sein as time-space. The utter differentiation from the concept of ground as nonspatial, eternal beingness goes without saying as Heidegger displaces ground (as Da-sein) into a displaced time-space: "Da-sein is to be taken as time-space, not in the sense of the usual concepts of time and space but as the momentary site [*Augenblicks-stätte*] for the grounding of the truth of beyng" (GA 65/CP, §200). At such a momentary site ground will always be also abyss, the retreat of ground.

Thus will the few who take up the grounding of Da-sein be grounders of the abyss. Precisely as they ground and shelter the unspeakable excess of the utterly strange truth of beyng. In going under, while standing, aloof, courageously reaching for the heavenly fire.

Notes

1. Referring to the beginning as the always withdrawing origin, Heidegger writes: "This unused-up power of the closure of the richest possibilities of courage (of the attuned-knowing will to *Ereignis*) is the only rescue and attestation" (GA 65/CP, §23). For bibliographical information on the texts referred to here, see the introduction to this volume, note 1.

2. Heidegger, *Identität und Differenz* (Pfullingen: Günther Neske, 1957), p. 29.

3. Friedrich Nietzsche, *Morgenröthe*, in vol. 5/1 of *Werke: Kritische Gesamtausgabe*, ed. Giorgio Colli and Mazzino Montinari (Berlin: Walter de Gruyter, 1971), p. 9.

4. See also Heidegger, *Nietzsche* (Pfullingen: Günther Neske, 1961), vol. l, pp. 231–42.

5. See Heidegger, *Vom Wesen der Wahrheit* in *Wegmarken*, vol. 9 of the Gesamtausgabe (Frankfurt am Main: Vittorio Klostermann, 1976), §4.

6. Heidegger, *Grundfragen der Philosophie: Ausgewählte "Probleme" der "Logik,"* vol. 45 of the Gesamtausgabe (Frankfurt am Main: Vittorio Klostermann, 1984), p. 153.

7. Ibid., p. 152.

8. Heidegger elaborates the not-knowing that constitutes the need/distress. He refers to "the open 'between' in which beings and non-beings stand forth as a whole, though still in their undifferentiatedness" and then continues: "Since the between is the *whole* of these undifferentiated beings, there is nothing outside to which an exit would be possible. And because it is a whole that is undifferentiated, there is nothing inside to which a way might lead as to a standpoint" (ibid., p. 160).

9. See ibid., pp. 60–71.

10. Here and throughout I have retained the traditional translation of *Wesen* as "essence." While the two words do not have identical significations, both have served in the history of modern philosophy to translate the Latin *essentia*. While no one will dispute the fact that in *Contributions* the word *Wesen* comes to have a sense that diverges radically from that of *essentia*, it is, on the other hand, a major accomplishment of Heidegger's text to inscribe this common (and philosophically traditional) German word in a discourse so originary as to transform the sense of the word. To try to build that transformation into the very translation cannot but obscure it. For *Wesung*, which is not a common German word, I use the uncommon form *essency*, which was still current in seventeenth-century English.

11. This formulation, though for other reasons provisional, already engages the successively more originary redeterminations to which Heidegger submits essence in *On the Essence of Truth*. A marginal note by Heidegger makes explicit the succession of senses already virtually manifest in the text itself: "Essence: (1) *quidditas* — the 'what' — κοινόν; (2) enabling — condition of possibility; (3) ground of enabling" (*Vom Wesen der Wahrheit*, p. 177). Not only is essence thus linked to ground at an entirely new level (that of freedom as the essence/ground of truth) but also even essence as ground is referred to a still "more originary essence" at a level at which the determinations of essence and of truth converge.

12. Since the archaic character of the spelling is significant, it is preferable to translate *Seyn* as *beyng*, a form that was extant in English at least as late as the fourteenth century, rather than with the hyphenized *be-ing*.

13. Thus, near the end of *On the Essence of Truth*, at a point where the full displacement of the sense of *essence* has been accomplished, Heidegger says that *essence* is to be understood verbally (*verbal*), even though, still remaining at this point within metaphysical representation, thinking identifies essence "as the difference holding sway between being and beings [als den waltenden Unterschied von Sein und Seiendem]" (*Vom Wesen der Wahrheit*, p. 201).

14. Taking Heidegger at his word that *Ereignis* can no more be translated than can the Greek λόγος and the Chinese Tao (*Identität und Differenz*, 29), I have left it untranslated throughout, while, on the other hand, developing in the discourse around it its affinity with happening and with appropriation.

15. ". . . from the very beginning being as beingness is experienced and

thought *only* in terms of 'beings'—from beings, so to speak, from *and* back to the manifold" (GA 65/CP, §110).

16. Instead of the neologism *abground* (and in view of Heidegger's own remark against inventing new language [*B*, §36], *abyss* has been retained to translate *Abgrund*. Since *abyss* transliterates ἄβυσσος (α-privative + βύσσος [bottom]), it corresponds closely to *Abgrund* and allows etymologically the same hyphenization (*a-byss*) that Heidegger employs.

17. *Curiosity* (Neugier) designates in *Being and Time* the form that understanding takes in everydayness: "When curiosity has become free, its concern is to see, not in order to understand what it sees, that is, to come into a being toward it, but *only* in order to see. It seeks novelty only to leap from it again to another novelty" (*Sein und Zeit* [Tübingen: Max Niemeyer, 1960], p. 172).

18. Heidegger, *Hölderlins Hymnen "Germanien" und "Der Rhein,"* vol. 39 of the Gesamtausgabe (Frankfurt am Main: Vittorio Klostermann, 1980), pp. 30–31. See also the 1939/40 lecture devoted to this hymn, published as "Wie wenn am Feiertage . . ." in *Erläuterungen zu Hölderlins Dichtung*, vol. 4 of the Gesamtausgabe (Frankfurt am Main: Vittorio Klostermann, 1981).

19. Friedrich Hölderlin, *Poems and Fragments*, trans. Michael Hamburger (Ann Arbor: University of Michigan Press, 1966), pp. 375, 377.

20. See Heidegger's discussion of Zarathustra's *Untergang* in the 1937 lecture course *Nietzsches metaphysische Grundstellung im abendländischen Denken*, vol. 44 of the Gesamtausgabe (Frankfurt am Main: Vittorio Klostermann, 1986), §5.

21. Heidegger, *Die Grundprobleme der Phänomenologie*, vol. 24 of the Gesamtausgabe (Frankfurt am Main: Vittorio Klostermann, 1975), p. 106.

22. That is, from the time of the initial version of "On the Essence of Truth." In this regard, one should note also Heidegger's insistence that *Da-sein* cannot be translated: "In *that* meaning which is for the first time and essentially introduced in *Being and Time* this word [*Da-sein*] cannot be translated, i.e., it resists the perspectives of previous ways of thinking and saying in Western history: *Da sein*" (GA 65/CP, §176).

23. ". . . grounding itself *clears* [lichtet] the self-concealing . . ." (GA 65/CP, §130). "The formulation 'Truth is, first of all, clearing concealment [*lichtende Verbergung*]' means: that a clearing is grounded for the self-concealing [*das Sichverbergende*]. The self-concealing of beyng in the clearing of the Da" (GA 65/CP, §217).

24. Heidegger, *Der Ursprung des Kunstwerkes*, in *Holzwege*, vol. 5 of the Gesamtausgabe (Frankfurt am Main: Vittorio Klostermann, 1977), p. 49. This work was first presented as lectures in 1935/36.

25. Another enumeration suggests an even broader range: "tool-preparation [*Zeuganfertigung*], machination-arrangement (technicity), creating works, deeds that establish states, thoughtful sacrifice" (GA 65/CP, §32). See also the enumeration in *The Origin of the Work of Art* (*Ursprung des Kunstwerkes*, p. 49).

11. Forgetfulness of God: Concerning the Center of Heidegger's *Contributions to Philosophy*

Günter Figal

I

Heidegger's *Contributions to Philosophy* seems strange and difficult to read in our times. This is attributable not only to its extremely concise, monumental, and lapidary style but to the difficulty of the thoughts articulated in it and often only sketched in. Nor is the difficulty attributable to the open, often only sketchy and elliptical form that Heidegger has given to his text. Much remains unfinished and appears to have been written more for self-understanding than for communication. Above all, the claim of the whole work is foreign, untimely, even if contemporary philosophy is marked by convictions that come to language — decisively — in *Contributions*. For instance, it has now become a general conviction that "the time of 'systems' is over" (GA 65, 5; CP, 4)[1] and that one can no longer do philosophy in a metaphysical way. The different varieties of "post-metaphysical thought" attributed to names like Habermas, Derrida, Foucault, Vattimo, or Rorty[2] — those varieties for which the philosophy of science is not philosophical enough — go back to Heidegger in one way or another. Nevertheless, the difference between them and Heidegger could not be greater. Whereas the former aim at a withdrawal or weakening of the philosophical claim, Heidegger wants to maintain it undiminished; on Heidegger's terms, philosophical thinking is not a late Alexandrian epilogue or a retreat to socially mediated, literary, genealogical, ironic, or pragmatic positions but a "crossing to another beginning," "the grounding opening of the free-play of the time-space of the truth of be-ing" (GA 65, 5; CP, 4, translation modified). But it must be even stranger that the attempt at such a preparatory, crossing, and opening thought is linked to the possibility of a theophany, the "passing" (GA 65, 412; CP, 290) of the "last god." It seems that rather than following out a departure from the myths and mystifications of the tradition, Heidegger puts to work new mystifications. Thus it seems, at best, possible to read this book, published from the "Nachlass" a considerable time after it was written, in a historical (*historisch*) way. Whether or not *Contributions* is Heidegger's second major work is open to question. Whereas *Being and Time* has belonged for a long time to the classic works of philosophy, the later book — granted all its relevance — seems nothing more than the document of a phase in the path of Heidegger's thinking.

Yet, assuming this would imply that one ought to view the whole of Heidegger's later philosophy historically (*historisch*). *Contributions* is not only a summary and concentration of what Heidegger philosophically worked out in the thirties but also the anticipation of his later philosophy. Indeed, viewed this way, *Contributions* is the center of Heidegger's thinking after *Being and Time*.[3] Also, the importance of the thought of the "last god" for Heidegger's late thought is documented in an interview in the *Spiegel* that was recorded in 1966 but published only in 1976. The often quoted sentence that astonished people in its time, "Only a god can save us" (GA 16, 671), points directly to *Contributions*, and this is made clear by Heidegger's explanatory comments in the interview. If one wanted to erase the theology of Heidegger's later thought, one would deprive it of its center.

But it could be that the skepticism with respect to this theology and thus with respect to *Contributions* does not touch Heidegger at all, that instead, with it, a certain narrowness of contemporary thinking becomes apparent. Indeed, anything religious and theological has become foreign to this thinking. The religious has been marginalized or diluted and reduced to no more than a helpful possibility for life and social ethics. As a consequence, it does not play any major role as a philosophical problem. One could again argue against this with a composed attitude and relativize current guidelines and orientations and stress that these too have already lost their unquestionability. As Ernst Jünger once stressed, the two hundred years that have been governed by Enlightenment thinking represent only "a very tiny section, and maybe only an interruption, compared with times in which one worshipped gods and demons." Therefore, one who "speaks (now or once again) about gods" does not make him or herself "as indisputable as in the first half of our [twentieth] century or among the elite even since Voltaire." Even when Nietzsche balances Apollo and Dionysus against each other, it is "more than mythological symbolism"; what is meant is "mythical substance."[4]

But Heidegger's theology of the "last god"—and with it the great thinking-attempt of *Contributions* as a whole—is not a defense of taking lightly the marginalization of the religious that has become characteristic for modernity and of placing oneself back into the religious normality of the history of human kind. In this theology the peculiar conditions of modernity are not only considered but are also explicitly acknowledged and taken up when Heidegger determines the "greatest nearness of the last god" as "refusal" (GA 65, 411; CP, 289). The last god does not manifest, does not reveal itself; it withdraws itself—and this means also that it withdraws from its mythical conception into a figure and from determination in philosophical concepts, insofar as this determination is obtained through an interpretation of beings as a whole, through an ontology. Thus one could call Heidegger's theology "negativistic" in the sense that it composes a procedure of thought that begins with a negative determination in order to—and only in order to—do

justice to the phenomenon in question.⁵ This does not mean that one
has to outline something in contrast to something else so that one says,
for example, what it is not in order to give at least an idea of what it
could be. The theology of the "last god" is not negativistic because it
withdraws from the human power to grasp it or because it is concealed
in its essence. Even if the negative concepts could suggest this, what
they do not mean to do is to name the essence of the "last god." This
god is thought out of a negative experience, but the experience of it is
itself such that the negative concepts ought to yield something positive
for understanding.

These are preliminary considerations that must now be developed
more fully; and this means clearing up a complex whole of intertwined
motives and thoughts in which Heidegger's theology can become understandable as the center of *Contributions*. At the same time, it is preferable
not to interpret the theology of the "last god" only through *Contributions*
but to consider other works as well for clarification of this issue. What
needs to come forth in this way is indicated by Heidegger's statement,
noted above, that the "nearness of the last god" means the same as
"refusal." One ought to understand this refusal and therefore ought first
to consider more closely and determine in this connection what leads to
the theology of the last god: the flight of the old gods. Heidegger develops this motive first in the Hölderlin lecture of winter semester 1934/35
and then takes it up as a guiding theme in *Contributions*.

II

Even at the beginning of *Contributions*, Heidegger writes that what matters is to belong "to those who are most remote," to belong "to those for
whom the flight of the gods in their farthest withdrawal remains most
near" (GA 65, 18; CP, 14). Most remote in this sense means "far away
and outside," and this means "outside the familiarity of 'beings' and
their interpretations." Even if the theme of the flight of the gods has
become important for Heidegger through Hölderlin, the figure of
thought wherein it is inscribed is not new in Heidegger's philosophy. In
the treatise *On the Essence of Ground* (1929), humans are determined as
"beings of farness [*Wesen der Ferne*]" (GA 9, 175) — as beings that,
"swaying over into possibilities," "project" the world as the leeway
(*Spielraum*) of their own being and possibility of being. As a connection
in which one can be or live, "world" is not just pre-given but is first
"formed" in a definite way in a more originary interpretation. As
"beings of farness" humans are "world-forming [*weltbildend*]" (GA 9,
158); their world exists only in an originary interpretation that first sets
free behavior and action, their dealings with beings, and also their
self-understanding. Thus scientific research as well as one's self-

understanding as a researcher depend upon the formation (*Bildung*) of a scientific world—they depend on the fact that world is understood as a connection in which beings are disclosed as being discoverable. This understanding is the condition of all research. Since this understanding exceeds research and its discoveries in the realm of beings that are immediately given, of the *phusei onta*, it can be determined as "metaphysics." Metaphysics is the occurrence of "the question of beings as such" (GA 65, 175; CP, 123); it determines in each case the leeway in which beings can be discovered in a determinate way, and in such a way that human being in the world also gains its determination from the response made possible with the question of beings as such.

If Heidegger could understand in such a way the farness in the being of humans, it is all the more remarkable that he links it to the experience of the flight of the gods—only this experience leads beyond the "familiarity of 'beings' and their interpretations." This experience now guarantees freedom from entanglement in a world that has become known and self-evident, a world that in *On the Essence of Ground* Heidegger had attributed to the new beginning of a "world-projection." Even in the earlier treatise he finds that this freedom is not possible without "withdrawal"; as Heidegger develops it, the "projection of possibility" gets its "binding force" by standing in opposition to people's involvement in a factual world. The simple fact that not all possibilities are open first gives weight to "the ones that are 'truly' graspable" (GA 9, 167). But the "withdrawal," understood as "flight of the gods," is not a counterweight to freedom; it is its springing forth. Heidegger believes that only this withdrawal is able to provide a solution to the constraint of a factical world.

We can explain to a certain extent why Heidegger thinks this by referring to his understanding of this factical world. The technically and scientifically determined world of modernity no longer allows world-projections because the world is already projected technically and scientifically. This projection sets free only already determined possibilities of comportment. In their turn, these possibilities are such that they deny themselves insofar as they are intrinsically directed to restless realization, to the marginalization of the open and the undecided, which were at one time characteristic of the projection of the world itself. "Calculation," "organization," and "acceleration" are fundamental traits of this world (GA 65, 120–24; CP, 84–86), with the projection of which humanity has entered an "epoch of total lack of questioning of all things and of all machination" (GA 65, 123; CP, 86). From the perspective of makeability and efficiency, there are tendentiously only problems that can be viewed as technical in the broadest sense and as resolvable technically. But this means that nothing truly problematic remains, nothing that could be accepted as a limit of human action. As

Heidegger says in *Contributions,* "the lack of distress is the greatest where self-certainty has become unsurpassable, where everything is held to be calculable and, above all, where it is decided, without a preceding question, who we are and what we are to do" (GA 65, 125; CP, 87). Even if this is only the tendency of the technically and scientifically impressed world, this world can no longer express itself from itself — since nothing in it points beyond the proceedings of control, possession, and processing of information. In order for this world to be experienced as such, an experience is needed that stands against the ways of thinking and comportment that are characteristic for it, an experience that stands against itself. This should be the experience of the flight of the gods.

But why this experience? Pointing to Hölderlin and to the fact that Heidegger reads him as the poet of the fled gods[6] does not give any answer but only indicates the place and importance of Hölderlin in Heidegger's thinking; even if Heidegger gets the theme of the flight of the gods through Hölderlin, it is still the importance of the matter that brings Heidegger to understand Hölderlin as a key figure of modernity. In terms of its matter, the experience of the flight of the gods is relevant for the modern world in two respects: on the one hand it belongs to modernity, and on the other hand it cannot be understood within the framework of modernity; with this experience something comes into play that does not fit into a world characterized by "self-certainty" and the gesture of makeability. This world can be called "profane," "of this world," "disenchanted"[7] only insofar as it is related to another, past world in whose place it stands. In this respect, the sacred in the forms of myth and revelation is a presupposition for understanding the modern world. The modern world is articulated as modern with respect to what is past in it.

But this does not yet mean that we would necessarily understand what is past in a way that is different from that of modernity — we might understand it, for instance, as the ensemble of representations in which we are caught so that we are prevented from using our own freedom and reason. Thus, seen from the perspective of enlightenment, the fled gods could also appear as the idols that have finally been recognized as such, and after the decline of which human self-consciousness finally can develop itself undisturbed. But if the flight of the gods is to be different and is not to mean the disappearance of "godliness," if this flight indicates their sway, then we can see that godliness does determine human life "as a power that is not fulfilled anymore, as a fading and dark, but still powerful power" (GA 39, 95). We can further see that with the flight of the gods a fundamental experience must be set free in human existence — an experience that touches human existence in such a way that one can escape it only at the cost of a total self-darkening.

I have already indicated that Heidegger thinks this way by pointing to the fact that the experience of the flight of the gods takes the place of the world-projection and that it thus becomes the experience of the origin of freedom. As in the case of the "formation of the world," freedom also speaks from the flight of the gods because this flight lets the character of possibility of Dasein become manifest. In *Contributions* we read that "refusal is the highest actuality of the highest possible *as* possible and is thus what is primary necessity" (GA 65, 294; CP, 207). In it a possibility shows itself to be actual that is simply inevitable and thus "necessary," and this can only mean that it concerns human existence as such immediately. We can see that possibility can be identified with the possibility of Dasein itself when we consider the central sentence of *Being and Time* according to which possibility is "the most primordial and ultimate positive ontological determination of Da-sein" (GA 2, 191; BT, 135).[8] Possibility constitutes that originary openness in which alone determinate possibilities can be experienced and anything encountered can show itself as such.

In *Being and Time* as well, Heidegger had bound the experience of this openness to negative phenomena: The uselessness, the lack or disturbance of something in connection with utensils, with things at hand (*Zeug*), first makes explicit the everyday and obvious environment (GA 2, 97–102; BT, 67–71); anxiety, as the experience of "complete insignificance" (GA 2, 247; BT, 174), first reveals the world as a relation of meaning in which one can comport oneself (GA 2, 244–53; BT, 172–78). The flight of the gods is an experience of possibility comparable to this, even though it is constituted in a quite different way. Like the experience of uselessness and like anxiety, the experience of the flight of the gods is involuntary. It must be involuntary so that Dasein's character of possibility, its openness, in which alone there is comportment and activity, *can* become manifest: Only where something happens, where something breaks into the connection of comportment, can this connection become explicit. Something must be different from normal behavior in order to lead to the ground of behavior, to the openness that surrounds it and sets it free. The enlightening myth of the fall of the gods obscures this involuntariness and is meant to intercept it, to repress it as an experience: The cult receives a rift, all of a sudden faith loses its force; nature is "deprived of godliness," and, as estimable as the representations of "godfather, Christ, and Maria" in art may be, "it does not help; our knees do not bend anymore."[9] A loss has occurred, and now it can be "rationalized," for instance, in such a way that one ascribes it to oneself as something one had always desired and maybe also always already enacted. Only when the gods have already gone away may one want to renounce them and persuade oneself that without them one lives freer and better. But if one does not want to get entangled in such rationalizations, one ought to allow again that to which they were a soothing response: the lack that occurred nonvoluntarily—

as when the behavior in the "environment" is interrupted unwillingly and, all of a sudden, without somebody wanting this, the world has "the character of complete insignificance" (GA 2, 247; BT, 174).

But the flight of the gods is also different in an essential way from the negative phenomena of the disturbance of the surroundings and of anxiety. What becomes explicit with the flight of the gods is not the possibility of being that is understood as belonging to each Dasein or in reference to the world as a whole that articulates itself as "resoluteness" or "world-formation" (GA 2, 391–99; BT, 272–77). What becomes explicit is rather a being open for what is occurring, a being possible for the possibility that is not at one's disposal, that is coming toward oneself and addresses oneself. It is not the case that something ungraspable or anonymous occurs, as when anxiety arises and no reason can be found for it. Instead, in the occurrence of the flight of the gods one is related toward something, something previously addressed in itself that now withdraws into silence. In the absence of address and response, the flight of the gods is an experience of Dasein in its alterity: Dasein as openness is always already beyond the immanence of a being that discloses itself in one's own view and always only as one's own.[10] When we experience being possible in the flight of the gods, it—being-possible—shows that it need not be understood in the sense of a "proper" becoming free for one's own possibilities or for the "world-formation."

This is significant because indeed Heidegger understands the flight of the gods as the fundamental experience of a world that has already been formed and that is in danger of remaining caught in its own formation in the essential possibilities provided by control and makeability. Because the flight of the gods composes the experience of a withdrawal, it lets appear Dasein's character of possibility and also makes manifest that this character of possibility is not fulfilled by forming a world. The fact is that, simultaneously with a determinate worldformation, something disappears that remains unavailable for the formed world. This disappearance can lead to the unavailability of precisely that Dasein in the openness of which this disappearing occurs. Then we can see that Hölderlin's poetry is more than an opposing word to the modernity that is about to establish itself; it would be especially different from a restoring nostalgia for the sense of a lost world and the problematic nature of all romanticism. Rather, Hölderlin's poetry would be a ground-word—a poetic word that leads to the ground of Dasein, to its openness before any specific comportment toward it.

Insofar as world-formation is a behavior that responds to the openness of Dasein, the experience of the flight of the gods also leads to the ground of the modern world, to the fundamental relation in Dasein that is carried out with world-formation. For Heidegger this can be grasped within the tradition of Western thought as the question of the "truth of beings" (GA 65, 179; CP, 125); and the modern world also shows itself to be a truth, an "unconcealedness" or a certain approachability of beings in this sense. With the flight of the gods, taken as an explicit experience of self-withdrawal and self-refusal, what withdraws becomes manifest with each answer to the unspoken question—how beings as such may be understood. What withdraws is precisely what questions and is in question and precedes not only Dasein but also other beings in their determinateness—in Heidegger's word "being," or, in distinction to the particular being of beings, also "be-ing" (*Seyn*). The flight of gods is an experience of being insofar as in it being itself—or be-ing—appears in its fundamental trait of withdrawal.

Thus, the withdrawal of the gods corresponds to an "abandonment of being" or "forgetfulness of being" that in *Contributions* Heidegger could call "the first dawning of be-ing" (GA 65, 293; CP, 207), and of which he could later say, in "Zur Seinsfrage" (1955), that it is "nothing negative, but as concealment probably a sheltering" (GA 9, 415). When forgetfulness is grasped this way, it is "nothing negative" in the sense that it does not exhaust itself in negativity. It is the negatively apprehended positive. Indeed forgetting is not just missing something, nor is it the erasure of something from memory—at least not if the experience of forgetting is really undergone. What one experiences is rather a knowing of the not-knowing-anymore; something that could be described but not determined anymore—a name, the precise course of an occurrence—intrudes in its own indeterminacy with an unmistakable, sometimes even painful intensity. Forgetfulness in this sense lays claim to someone, it is a possibility of guarding that which is unavailable in it, guarding its very unavailability. Therefore forgetfulness "shelters" what has withdrawn itself; it guards it because one is not able to be sure about it.

Because in *Contributions* this sheltering is entrusted to the experience of the flight of the gods, this flight cannot turn into an expectation of the gods' return. A Dasein which takes seriously its unavailable freedom "does not count gods and does not count on them and does not even reckon with an individual god" (GA 65, 293; CP, 207). A binding of this kind, a reawakened faith, a newly established cult, would immediately cover up the experience of being-possible; and under the presumption that in the flight of the gods "precisely dwells" godliness (GA 39, 95), they would lead to the vanishing of godliness. The last god is needed to preserve this experience of godliness.

III

Heidegger's thoughts regarding the "last god" are short and condensed, darker than many other things in *Contributions*. However, there are criteria for their comprehension: These thoughts belong together with what has previously been developed in the book, as a key, so to speak, through an allusion or correspondence, to the previously developed thought. The last god, Heidegger says, has its "essential swaying"—its peculiar way to occur that does not manifest itself as a reality that may be identified—"within the hint, the onset and staying-away of the arrival as well as the flight of the gods who have been, and within their sheltered and hidden transformation" (GA 65, 409; CP, 288). "Hinting" may be read here as "to give to understand." In the lecture course of winter semester 1931/32, Heidegger says that a hint "leads into something that is to be understood, i.e., in the domain of understandability," or, as Heidegger goes on to say in an elucidating way, into the "dimension within which one understands," "into a *sense*" (GA 34, 18). To give to understand thus does not mean "to allude," or "to communicate indirectly," but is meant in a literal sense and thus means the same as the introduction into the leeway of understanding—"into a sense." Something makes sense in a specific connection, for example, a move in a game played on a board, a gesture or a word in a conversation. But the game, the conversation, could be called "meaningful" if, as the connection that it is, it would again be in a connection. "What is understood," Heidegger says, is "never *itself* sense, but always only something 'in the sense of'. . . . Sense is never the *topic* of understanding" (GA 34, 18) but, as one could add, its horizon, i.e., that—the connection that is as open as it is limited—in which one understands something as being "meaningful."

What gives to understand, then, what opens the horizon or open field of understanding, stands all the more beyond understanding; it cannot be understood itself, and, on the other hand, it only gives to understand that which withdraws itself from understanding. What gives to understand is self-withdrawing, and it can be interpreted as the "godly" (*das Göttliche*). In the Hölderlin lecture course of 1934/35, Heidegger already conceived the "hinting" as the "originary saying" of the gods. He conceived it with Hölderlin as their "language" (GA 39, 128). As evidence for this he takes the saying of Heraclitus, fragment 9: "The master, whose place of saying is Delphi [god Apollo] neither says nor hides but *hints*" (GA 39, 127).[11] The last god is not Apollo, but it is *like* him, so that what is said about Apollo may also be said about it.

What the last god gives to understand is easily recognizable in the quoted first characterization that Heidegger gives of it, namely, as a space of understanding or horizon of meaning. The "hint" of the last god has been elucidated as "the onset and staying-away of the arrival as well as the flight of the gods who have been, and within their sheltered and hidden transformation." The hint of the last god is an openness that is marked only by possibilities. "Onset" and "staying-away"—between these two no decision is made, just as no decision is made between "arrival" and "flight." Rather, both are suspended through intertwinement: The arrival impacts and stays away, the flight impacts and stays away, and thus neither of the two can be established as occurring. And "onset" and "staying-away" occur in such a way that each turns into the opposite as soon as it is attributed differently: The onset of the flight is withdrawnness, the onset of arrival is presence (*Gegenwärtigkeit*), like the staying away of flight is presence, and the staying away of arrival is withdrawnness. Thus, what is given to understand in an *open time,* in an arrival that remains open and a withdrawal that remains open — a future and having been (*Gewesenheit*) without anything happening that could be established.

In this time that is opened through the "hint" of the last god one might see the "hidden transformation" of "the gods who have been." That which is given to understand, the timely openness of Dasein and being, has become a "time-space" through the forms that "sway," that are present by "having been" and having fled and that therefore may be called "those who have been" (GA 65, 412; CP, 290). In this time-space occurs a farness of the having been and the coming to be that is held together in itself. And what ought to be experienced now as the godly is what gives to understand, the last god.

We can now say directly what the last god itself is, namely, what gives to understand the open time, the time-space of Dasein and being. Through it one can experience the unity of this time, what unites its openness, as well as see that the unity can always only be in the disposition of the time-dimensions. The god holds together unity and disposition in its giving to understand. Said with the phrasing from the Hölderlin lecture it allows to become transparent "what conflicts in its accordance" and "the accord in its conflict" (GA 39, 128). But this unity of unity and strife could not be thought or followed through in thinking, and thus it unfolds dialectically when the god itself is not taken up into this enactment of thinking, when thus it is deprived of its godliness. Indeed, the fact is that god as such stands for the ungraspability of the belonging together of uniting openness and timely disposition. It must withdraw itself as it gives to understand the "time-space" of Dasein for understanding. The time-space is "the stillness of its [the god's] passing" (GA 65, 412; CP, 290), the god itself is "the highest form of withdrawal" (GA 65, 416; CP, 293).

In the light of these claims, the last god seems to come close to the others, to the gods that have been, and thus to lose its uniqueness. As the gods that have been had their time and then withdrew themselves, the last god too, so to speak, flashes up and goes away.[12] But Heidegger wants to understand this "passing" (*Vorbeigang*) in a different way than that of the appearing and disappearing of the other gods. The last god does not manifest itself in any individual form; it does not become the

center of a cult or belief in order then to withdraw, after more or less
time, and to pass into the circle of the gods that have been. Its refusal
does not follow an epiphany but is to be conceived "negatively" and has
the same meaning as epiphany. This is why it can be called the "highest" form of refusal. The last god is not a last one like the others but the
"last" one insofar as it "makes what is ownmost to the uniqueness of
the divine being [*Gottwesen*] most prominent" (GA 65, 406; CP, 286).
This is why—as Heidegger thinks—true experience of godliness forms
itself around the last god, an experience of godliness that is without rite
and statute, without theology in the traditional sense of the word and
thus also without a tradition that may be identified. What is experienced is exclusively the "grounding" of Dasein as timely openness that,
so to speak, holds the middle between the enhancement of a life that
only trusts its own force, and the turning toward a transcending power
beyond. Grounded in this way, Dasein is neither self-contained nor
bound to something; it is thus the perception of freedom—of a freedom
that institutes itself only without self-loss and without fear of self-loss.
Free Dasein is given only through the last god, and this last god can be
experienced only in the freedom of Dasein. Therefore this freedom "is"
not but occurs in that "enowning" that gives to *Contributions to Philosophy* its proper title;[13] it occurs in the encounter of god and humans,
which—with reference to Heraclitus—may also be called "strife,"
because with it both god and humans first come to their essence (GA
65, 413; CP, 291).

IV

In Heidegger's self-understanding, the path of thinking in *Contributions*
is a preparation of enowning as the strife between god and humans.
The enactment of this path of thinking is a "leap-off [*Ab-sprung*]" (GA
65, 178; CP, 125): It is a renunciation of the traditional forms of philosophy and a caesura in the questionlessness of the modern world—
this way of thinking happens as a question about what withdraws itself
that, according to its essence, cannot be determined but only reached
by questioning. Thus, from the "restlessness" of questioning a stillness
ought to arise "which, as gathering into the most question-worthy
(enowning), awaits the simple intimacy of the call and withstands the
utmost fury of the abandonment of being" (GA 65, 397; CP, 278, translation modified). Even though Heidegger's language has changed, with
a closer look one recognizes the gesture of thinking as it manifests itself
here. It concerns what Heidegger in *Being and Time*, and even earlier,
has called "deconstruction" (*Destruktion*) and what he has elucidated as
a "return to the originary sources of motivation."[14] But now decon-

struction no longer means a leading back to the philosophical tradition that has been marked by the Greeks, back to its origin in Aristotle; nor does it lead back, as in *Being and Time,* to the self-understanding in Dasein that gains back its beginning by repeating it. What now ought to be gained is the "other beginning" of Dasein, and this means the beginning in the situation of the godly "call" (*Zuruf*) that remains unavailable to humans. What Heidegger attempts to explore in thinking is the possibility of a "dialogue" in which god and humans can "hear from each other" (GA 39, 68–72).

Here, indeed, only the *possibility* of dialogue is meant, not its philosophical pursuit. Understood in the sense of a response to the openness of Dasein that is related to the godly, the latter would mean the same as what Heidegger calls "deification" (*Vergötterung*) in the text that immediately follows *Contributions* in the collected works, *Besinnung* (see GA 66, 239–43). Deification means the declaration of something—of a phenomenon, a category—as the determination of the god. This is complementary to "dis-godding" (*Entgötterung*), i.e., to treat gods themselves as an explanation of what one conceives to be "in the end not explainable" and what one consequently wants to interpret as "willed by god" (GA 66, 239). As "miscalculating determination" of the godly, both lead to different versions of "theism" that for Heidegger belong to the history of metaphysics insofar as they are bound to the pattern of the elucidation of something from the perspective of its origin and are bound methodically to the research of principles (GA 65, 411; CA, 289). In contrast to such "metaphysical" answers, one needs to gain back the *questionableness* of the godly, i.e., precisely that open domain that questioning itself opens and according to which one comports oneself not in an explanatory way but in "reticent accord" (GA 65, 414; CP, 291). And this comportment is not yet that of a thinking that is preparatory and fundamentally precedes the open domain. When philosophical examination determines the "dialogue" as the place and determines "enowning" as the moment of encounter of god and humans, this encounter fundamentally stands out.

But several things indicate that with this claim, Heidegger does not exhaust and probably underdetermines his philosophical theology. By exploring in thinking the possibility of the "dialogue" that we are and by delineating its structure in concepts, he not only explores an impending possibility but discovers something. He allows the place of all religious experience to become manifest in a fundamentally new way. By designating, at the same time, this place as the origin of philosophical experience—Dasein as open site of "be-ing"—he makes conceivable the common root of philosophy and religious experience. Thus he shows that religious experience needs philosophical thought in order not to get caught in inappropriate objectifying representations and in order not to misinterpret the "dialogue" between god and humans in relation to a figure beyond this world that manifests itself in this world.

The preceding discussion says something about the philosophical interpretability of these figures. Can they appear only as those "that have been" or "that fled," so that now the religious experience cannot be anything more than the experience of a god that withdraws in its "passing," a god to which no cult, no faith, no tradition belongs anymore? Or is it not the case that what Heidegger attempts to grasp in thinking as the last god is precisely that godliness into which one ought to bring back the figures of myth and revelation — the first and originary that first gives sense to myth and revelation as the free space in which they originate?

One can easily understand why considerations of this kind are not developed in *Contributions to Philosophy* but are at most only indicated; the book is far too much marked by schemes of historical thinking, as a meditation on what is transitory, where the experience of presence can always only be retrospective and a preparation for what is to come. Here Heidegger follows the conviction articulated by Nietzsche's Zarathustra that humans are "a bridge and no aim," "a transition and a going under,"[15] and at the same time gives it a different turn by not seeing the possibility for humans to overcome themselves through the "overman" (*Übermensch*) but through the "dialogue" between humans and god.[16] But because he remains oriented by the thought of transition and going under, this dialogue still is waiting for "enowning," instead of being able to become understandable as a structure that has always already been fulfilled, and one that has certainly also always already failed.

Viewed from this perspective, with his theology of the last god, Heidegger has not grasped a possibility that would have lent itself from an earlier work and that at the same time could be understood as a correction of the earlier conception. This correction would show the "understanding of being" (*Seinsverständnis*) that occurs in religious experience and theological conceptualization, and it would point to the religious dimension of the "understanding of being" (GA 9, 63) instead of claiming that with this theology of the last god a "purely rationally conceivable content" is brought to bear. But in principle there is no impediment to reading the philosophical theology in *Contributions* in this sense. When one orients oneself less according to the historical "situation" of the book than according to the structures revealed in it, Heidegger's investigation may be understood as a clarification of the "between" of god and humans, and this is a contribution to the hermeneutic task that, according to Plato's *Symposium*, philosophy has to accomplish according to the demon that enlivens it: to mediate between gods and humans.[17]

Notes

1. For bibliographical information on the texts referred to here, see the introduction to this volume, note 1. References to other volumes in the Gesamtausgabe (and, where they exist, to published translations), follow the same format as that used here for *Beiträge zur Philosophie*.

2. The formula of postmetaphysical thought goes back to Jürgen Habermas, *Nachmetaphysisches Denken* (Frankfurt am Main: Suhrkamp, 1988).

3. How far *Contributions* forms a unity with the other treatises that were written after 1937 can be judged only after they are all published. See the concluding remark of the editor of GA 66.

4. Ernst Jünger, *Gestaltwandel* (1993), in *Sämtliche Werke* (Stuttgart: Klett-Cotta, 1999), vol. 19, p. 609.

5. "Negativism" is the central concept of the philosophy of Michael Theunissen, who designates with it the attempt "to take away from the negative the positive." See Michael Theunissen, *Negative Theologie der Zeit* (Frankfurt am Main: Suhrkamp, 1991), p. 55. Theunissen has developed this concept in connection with his Kierkegaard interpretations. See "Kierkegaard's Negativistic Method," in Joseph H. Smith, ed., *Kierkegaard's Truth: The Disclosure of the Self* (New Haven: Yale University Press, 1981) (Psychiatry and the Humanities, vol. 5); translated into German as *Das Selbst auf dem Grunde der Verzweiflung. Kierkegaards negativistische Methode*, trans. Daniela Neu (Frankfurt am Main: Suhrkamp, 1991).

6. See the lecture *Hölderlins Hymnen "Germanien" und "Der Rhein,"* GA 39, esp. pp. 79–113.

7. Regarding the thought of dis-enchantment that goes back to Max Weber, see GA 65, 124; CP, 86–87.

8. Martin Heidegger, *Being and Time*, trans. Joan Stambaugh (Albany: State University of New York Press, 1996), p. 135 (GA 2, 191).

9. G. W. F. Hegel, *Vorlesungen über Ästhetik*, in *Werke in 20 Bänden*, "Auf der Grundlage der Werke von 1832–1845 neu edierte Ausgabe," ed. Eva Moldenhauer and Karl Markus Michel, vols. 13–15 (Frankfurt am Main: Suhrkamp, 1970). Here vol. 14, p. 137, and vol. 13, p. 142.

10. This thought could be a point of departure for rethinking fundamentally Emmanuel Levinas's critique of Heidegger. If Heidegger does not at all understand Dasein as immanence, the sharp opposition between him and the philosophy of the other developed by Levinas also becomes relative.

11. See also GA 16, 687.

12. At this point one ought to remember another fragment from Heraclitus, DK B 64, that Heidegger and Eugen Fink extensively interpreted in the seminar they held together: "but everything governs the lightening." Here Fink has interpreted, evidently with Heidegger's agreement, the lightening as "that which forms the universe," as "world-formation" (GA 15, 31).

13. In an earlier discussion of this connection I have identified the last god with enowning. See my *For a Philosophy of Freedom and Strife: Politics, Aesthetics, Metaphysics* (Albany: State University of New York Press, 1998), p. 168. I am now correcting that interpretation.

14. *Phänomenologische Interpretationen zu Aristoteles (Anzeige der hermeneutischen Situation)*, ed. Hans-Ulrich Lessing, in *Dilthey-Jahrbuch für Philosophie und*

Geisteswissenschaften, ed. Fritjof Rodi (Göttingen: Vandenhoeck & Ruprecht, 1989), vol. 6, pp. 237–69; this passage p. 249.

15. Friedrich Nietzsche, *Also sprach Zarathustra,* Zarathustra's Vorrede 4, *Sämtliche Werke. Kritische Studienausgabe,* ed. Giorgio Colli and Mazzino Montinari (Munich, Berlin, and New York: De Gruyter, 1980), vol. 4, pp. 16–17.

16. For a more detailed interpretation of the thought of the "overman," see my *Nietzsche* (Stuttgart: Reclam, 1999), pp. 200–16.

17. Plato, *Symposium* 202e.

12. The Last God

David Crownfield

The primary focus of this essay is the brief but dense and important section of *Contributions to Philosophy* entitled "The Last God" (GA 65, 403–17; CP, 285–93).[1] Throughout the work we encounter the question of the last god, an oscillation between the singular and the plural, the relation of god and be-ing, and the specific issue of "the passing of the last god."[2] This essay will focus on the specific section, but will draw substantially on these motifs in the work as a whole, as well as the notions of the event and the truth of be-ing, to indicate together the scope of the question of god in *Contributions*.

I begin with an overall interpretive preview, designed to give an orienting sketch of my understanding of the issue of the last god. In order to make more evident the textual basis of my reading of particular questions I will next identify a few key terms on which my reading would be made more evident by English expressions other than those chosen by the translators. These terms are *Ereignis, Wesen, Bergung,* and *berücken/entrücken.* (This also gives me a chance to show parenthetically my assumptions about some of Heidegger's central themes.) There follows a discussion of seven topics central to the theme of the last god: the passing of the last god, the wholly other, refusal, the turning, truth and the last god, the table of commandments, and ripeness. After a brief recapitulation, I identify in conclusion several unresolved problems that require future study and discussion.

Interpretive Preview

We need to be clear from the outset that Heidegger's discussion of the question of god(s) is not addressed either to the vindication of belief or to its repudiation. In his view, truth is a disclosiveness inherently inseparable from misdirection and occlusion; thus either affirmation or denial of god(s) must, to the extent it is true, mark also an essential untruth. Being is historical — is actual precisely in the sayings and practices and artworks, in the communities and institutions, where it occurs and is articulable. God is thus god in the texts, in the architecture and literature, the works and sacrifices, crusades and inquisitions, prayers and confessions, in which the name(s) of god(s) have their places and contexts. And actual also, in all of them, is the absence, default, negativity of god(s).

Heidegger's aim is not to vindicate or discredit faith in god/s, but formally to indicate the extremities in which the question of god/s arises and is contextualized. These extremities include the utter gratuity in which being-there occurs for the time being rather than nothing at all; the inescapable exigency, for each of us, of accepting the incomprehensible task of being-there; the constant hemorrhage of unachieved possibilities; the ever-renewed radicality of the turn away from the passing of what has already charmed us out of ourselves, and toward the ecstatic opening to the novelty of what comes; and the inseparability that binds together our moving toward anything whatever and the necessity of moving toward nothing at all.

Heidegger also makes clear that these extremities occur in determinate configurations and articulations for actual histories and communities. There is not a universal essence to be extracted from these particularities, but only the specific forms, practices, associations, and concepts in which a community already lives and comes to engagement with its gods and with their absences. We still face a long history before the extremity may come to some wholly new configuration. The passing away of the whole question of god is thus only a possibility for a remote future whose long preparation we can at most only await and seek to anticipate.

Throughout *Contributions,* Heidegger repeatedly speaks of the undecidability of whether the gods are, in their present remoteness, passing finally away or again coming toward us, and whether their remoteness is their assault or default (their wrath or their failure). He says that his frequent use of the plural "gods" indicates not a definite polytheism but the "inherent richness" and "immeasurable possibilities" of the question (GA 65, 411; CP, 289). And he often uses the singular, apparently also as a non-quantitative indicator, marking the singularity of the *question* of god/s. He speaks, without explanation, of "the gods' decision about their god" (GA 65, 239; CP, 169), which suggests the radical surpassability of every determinate figuring of the extremity, a "god beyond god" (cf. Tillich, *The Courage to Be,* pp. 182–90).

Gods, he says, do not have being, which they need. The whole treatment of be-ing in *Contributions* makes it difficult to see what it would be for *anything* to "have" being, but the notion that god "needs" being, or needs anything, is offensive to the theistic tradition. Heidegger's expression essentially repudiates ontotheological theism, which identifies god as first or highest being, cause or ground of being, or "being" itself taken absolutely. In Heidegger, "to be" means to occur, uniquely and surprisingly, lingeringly and departingly, and gods are not extant but figures of remembrance and expectation; only in moments of existential and historical eventuation can "god" be other than an empty intention. Insofar as god occurs in narratives of claim and promise, and in acts that venture to rely on the claim and promise, god needs being (enactment) in that god figures the exigency of the claim that calls out and calls home. In *Being and Time,* "conscience" (*Gewissen* [SZ, 272ff.; BT, 317ff.]) is the call of being-there to itself, calling it out of dispersion and reification back to resolute self-owning temporality. In *Contributions*, the call is at the same time the call of be-ing, claiming historical actualization in a shared withstanding of passing-on (GA 65, 413; CP, 290).

Contributions as a whole hinges on a turning from having been charmed by what is passing, toward an ek-static self-displacement and self-exceeding into the openness of the coming. This turning involves a salvaging of the passing by creating, naming, making and saying and doing. In such a turning, what-is acquires its names and configurations and uses, and so preserves what has passed as clues for anticipating what may be coming. (Churches, mosques, temples, rituals, divinities, and scriptures are thus implicitly among the things that, already having been, are now reconstrued and reappropriated—turning away from a closing down of the exposure to extremity and toward a beckoning summons out into the open, back into the homeland that has never been realized, by a short, steep path that is both open and mortal.)

Notes on Translation

Translation of this work is difficult, and no solution could satisfy all readers on every page. The present translation is strong and helpful on many points. There are inevitably a few issues on which the translators' choice of words may not make obvious to a reader why I interpret a passage the way I do, so I need to make clear the textual grounds for some of my interpretations. These issues center naturally around the most difficult and central terms. I will discuss briefly *Ereignis; Wesen* (noun and verb) and *Wesung; bergen* and *Verborgenheit;* and the pair *berücken* and *entrücken.* My purpose is to highlight themes central to the text as I read it, and I will not directly discuss the translators' choices. I do include after each of the terms that I discuss the translators' English expression, and a parenthetical page reference to the discussion of that term in the Translators' Foreword. In each instance, I will briefly note the specific bearing of the term on the question of god.

Ereignis ("enowning" [see CP, xix–xxii]). Heidegger's perennial theme is the meaning of *Sein* (being, to be). "Being" can mean something, anything, everything, or what "holds up" everything out of nothing; it can mean "is-ness"; it can be capitalized as Being, what is basic, first, highest, ultimate, God; it can indicate the problem Hamlet faces, "To be or not to be?" *Being and Time* and related work establishes that all these senses are involved with human temporality, but the work of that period does not succeed in founding all senses of "being" in that temporality. Retaining the results of the earlier work, *Contributions* shifts the focus from Dasein's ecstatic self-transcendence to the co-occurrence of being-there and what there is there, in its time-space specificity, and including its whole context in world, community, history, language, memory and anticipation, textures of practice, etc. Heidegger had ended "What Is Metaphysics?" with Leibniz's question, "Why is there anything at all rather than nothing?" Heidegger now replies, *das Ereignis*, meaning the singular occurrence together, in their full configurations and spatiotemporal, sociohistorical context, of a "my being in the world" *and* of what there is there and then, and before and after and round about. Be-ing happens. (Sometimes *Ereignis* is hyphenated to emphasize its occurring ["er-"] and its coordination ["-eignis"] of "being-there" and "what is"; sometimes it is used in a verb form [*er-eignen*].) To represent *Ereignis*, I use "event"; but it needs to be taken in this sense of the occurrence of a unique transitory configuration of not-nothing, not just as a local happening.

(What can the notion of God mean in such a radical ontology of spatiotemporal singularity?)

Wesen ("essential sway" [see CP, xxiv–xxvii]). While one use of this word in German philosophy is to translate the Latin *essentia*, it may often indicate instead a distinctive characterization of an individual rather than the common essence of a class. For Heidegger, anything whatever occurs in an already articulated context and with a distinctive relevance to a horizon of expectation. This point, made clear in *Being and Time* from the perspective of the anticipatory openness of being-there, is correlated in *Contributions* with both the already-giving historical and social articulation of the context and the distinctive givenness of the thing as granted *to* Dasein *in* that context. The occurring of this co-giving is *Wesung*, the whole focused configuration is *Wesen*, and thus one can say of the event that be-ing "*west*." (Though it would be awkward, I would say it "essences.") The translators' term "sway" works fairly well as a noun, for the *Wesen* of something, in the sense of what "holds sway." The verb "to sway" is more of a problem because the ordinary sense of the English verb "sway" is independent of the sense needed for Heidegger.

(To understand the question of God in this context will require a recognition that "God" too is a word in the language, already a historical and social component of the whole articulation in which the event of being-at-all "essences." Both theism and atheism, as traditionally conceived, assume that entire onto-theo-logical context and background without recognizing their own relativization by it.)

Bergen and its cognates ("shelter" [see CP, xxxii]). *Bergen* has a core sense of "salvage," to retrieve or rescue from shipwreck, storm, conflagration, or the like. In translations of Heidegger (including *Contributions*), it is often rendered "shelter." The problem with this is the connotation that someone doing the retrieving would be the source of shelter, security, and protection, which I do not find consistent with Heidegger. (Translating *bergen* as "to salvage" could result in a similar problem, if emphasis were put on the "salvager.") Heidegger's emphasis is on the turning of the matter from passing to ongoing, not on any act of saving or sheltering or protecting.[3] Most commonly I use "retrieve," and sometimes "salvage."

This leads us to the pair *berücken/entrücken* (see CP, xxxiii–xxxiv). Being-there is (always already) charmed (*berückt*) out of itself into what surrounds it and, bereft of the charming presence by its passing, is enraptured away (*entrückt*) into the coming, the possible. (I use "enraptured" here in something like the apocalyptic sense of being snatched out of the world that is about to pass away, rather than in an emotive sense. The translators' "removal unto" lacks the ecstatic discontinuity between passing and coming that is implicit in "rapture" and in the German.) When being charmed is bereft and the lingering traces hint of a possible coming, being-there is enraptured toward that unknown coming and acts to retrieve those passing traces by engraving them in artworks, words, deeds, sacrifices, and institutions—the configurings of "what there is." This is the *Bergung* (retrieval) which salvages the traces as beckonings (or even as promises) but at the same time, through projecting them forward and so in some sense continuing them, renders *verborgen* (concealed) the reality of passing.

(The works, words, deeds, sacrifices, and institutions in which having-been has been salvaged and concealed include the naming and worshipping of gods and all the works and the textures of practice and discourse of which gods are part or context. In a time when gods are remote and perhaps passing out of relevance, or perhaps repelled by our ungodliness, how may the turning creatively salvage these traces of having-been as beckonings forward toward what gods once promised and called us to?)

Specific Issues

1. The passing of the last god. Repeatedly throughout the work, Heidegger uses the phrase, "*der Vorbeigang des letzten Gottes.*" John Bailiff has translated this as "the departure of the final God." Jeff Prudhomme has translated it as "the passing by of the ultimate God." Both readings are fully in accord with the German; the ambiguity is essential to Heidegger's treatment. He several times indicates that it is *undecidable* whether gods are departing finally or whether they are coming back. They are absent, utterly remote, but whether in wrath or failure, and whether still receding or beginning the way back, is absolutely indeterminable. This, I think, must be read in Derrida's sense of "undecidable" as indicating precisely what requires a decision but provides no preferential guide that might mitigate the risk.

The "passing" is thus not to be merely equated with the death of god. In the slightly later essay, "Nietzsche's Word, 'God is Dead'" (1939), Heidegger understands Nietzsche's phrase to mean the disestablishment of the supersensory and of the highest values. Of this, he observes:

> [I]f God in the sense of the Christian God has disappeared from his authoritative position in the supersensory world, then this authoritative place itself is still always preserved, even though [preserved] as that which has become empty. . . . What is more, the empty place demands to be occupied anew [by other ideals and doctrines]. (*The Question Concerning Technology*, p. 69)

This disappearance/preservation, Heidegger is quite clear, has already occurred.[4] The passing (by or away) of the ultimate or final god is something else. Its ambiguity marks the indeterminability of whether the empty place will be itself superseded by an unforseeable gift of weal and transformation or by an utter relinquishment of the ontological residues of the god/s (or by the exhaustion of the human in the manipulative degradation of the earth). Indeed, when it is stated in these terms, the still-pending antithesis (exit or return) is seen to figure a turning between utter loss and utter gift. Such a turning itself enacts the central structural dynamics of *Ereignis*, the event of be-ing.

2. *The wholly other.* On the title page of the section "The Last God," Heidegger has the following note: "The wholly Other [*ganz Andere*] against those that have been, especially against the Christian." (The word "God" is not repeated after "Christian" in the German, as it is in the translation.) "Wholly Other" is a phrase common in Christian theology in the 1920s and 1930s, especially in characterizing the place of God in the early work of Karl Barth and the religious thought of Kierkegaard. God, for early Barth, is utterly alien to any perspective that is grounded in anything but the event of gratuitous givenness of God itself. The concrete appropriation of the event is always prone to lapse into idolatry; the god can in no way be properly contained in doctrines, texts, or any words or acts except, as Barth put it (quoting the Augsburg Confession), "where and when it pleaseth God."[5] Even the Christian doctrines of Trinity and of Christ, even the church at its best, even the sacramental bread and wine, do not for Barth "contain" God in some degree but merely confess the gift and indicate the sites and contexts of its remembered and expected occurrence. (Both this temporal structure of remembering expectation and the indicative, non-essentializing method, are explicit in Barth, as they are in Heidegger.)

The very affirmation of one transcendent and ultimate god can be, in its most thoroughgoing form, the radical negation of all determinate and determinable gods, in the name of God. Such a "wholly other" cannot be equated with a specific remembered deity, not even a biblical or Christian "god that has been." In an important twentieth-century reading of the revelation of God to Moses in Exodus 3:14, God answers Moses' question, "What is [god's] name?" with "I will be what I will be" (Revised Standard Version, note): futural, wholly other than any already-known gods — especially than the god of any established monotheism.

Clearly such a radical antithesis of God and god/s is irreducibly ambiguous, between highest actuality and utmost negativity, as the tradition of negative theology since Pseudo-Dionysius has always understood. A god that is wholly other than all gods borders on being identical with nothing at all. The extremes can thus be read either with Jean-Luc Marion as testimony to God or with Jacques Derrida as the recognition of the utter otherness of every other(ness). Heidegger, focusing as usual on a formal indication of the question, centers his treatment of the last god at the site of this equivocation rather than opting for either resolution of it.

3. Refusal. Early in the section, "The Last God," Heidegger says, "We move into the timespace of the decision over the flight and advent of gods" (GA 65, 405; CP, 285, translation slightly modified). But must that question not be determined factually by which alternative will occur? Or is it a matter of moving into a whole new timespace determined by truth/being/event (as a complex singularity)? After opening this question, he then asks,

> What if that whole domain of decision, flight or coming of gods, were itself precisely the end? What if, beyond that, be-ing for the first time would have to be grasped in its truth as the occurring as which That comes to pass which we call *refusal* [*Verweigerung*]?
>
> That is neither flight nor advent, nor equally flight and advent, but something originary, the fullness of the granting of being in refusal. (GA 65, 485, translation mine; cf. CP, 285)

The text goes on to say that refusal is the supreme nobility of granting and the fundamental movement of concealment (GA 65, 406; CP, 285).

Beyond this, *Contributions* offers no direct explication of refusal; yet the contexts in the work as a whole suggest a line of interpretation. What charms us out beyond ourselves and opens for us a place and space is a lingering happening, one that will not tarry long but will leave us abyssally exposed by its passing and to the coming, in their surprising singularity. The refusal to tarry abandons us to this exposure, to the claim of the coming. We stay the passing in enactments, sayings, works and sacrifices in which we aim to retain and repeat what has already been. Thus configuring a world, we find our figuration both sustained and refused in the resistant opacity of the earth. And we find in the retained trace of passing the hint of the inescapable passing of the open itself. Refusal is thus the "not" of both not yet and no longer (GA 65, 410;

CP, 288). It is this refusal that would be exposed if the question of god is "itself precisely the end" (GA 65, 485; CP, 285, translation modified).

So long as God can figure the extremity both of blessedness and of subjugation, and the absence of god can mark the extremity both of the abandonment and of the empowerment of the human, the question of god has not moved into the past. Historically we may at some time reach a point where the ambiguity of these extremes is directly posed as the openness of a decision. (Such a notion of decision comprises a full mutual concurrence between a radically Kierkegaardian self-commitment and a decisive historical and epochal coming-to-pass.) Such a decision is utterly exposed to the "no" of both the past and the future: the extremity of refusal. To live toward the return of the god, to keep the commandments and trust the promises, is exposed to nondelivery; to repudiate the god and strive toward mastery of our fate, or toward reconciliation with it, is equally vulnerable to nonattainment. And either way mortality is ineluctable. Both the essential exposure to refusal and its intractability are decisive for the sense of "to be."

When refusal is understood as the heart of be-ing, we find ourselves exposed to the silence of the passing of the last god. (The god's passing must be a silence, at least in part, because the language of our sayings is configured by the gods' having-been; we thus cannot *say* the passing without thereby repeating the implicit retention of the god/s.) "Flight and advent of gods now together move into having-been [*das Gewesene*], and come to be withdrawn from what is over with [*dem Vergangenen*]" (GA 65, 406, translation mine; cf. CP, 285). The over-with is that which we put behind us, turn away from, and so are still oriented by. The having-been is that which we take up again in word and work, which we reinvent and aim to surpass, and out of which we thus construct our projection of possibilities and meanings. It is not that we repeat its past forms, preserving its residues, but that we find in its traces hints of the coming, intimations of the excess of surprise. In this turning forward we respond to the summons to invent the future of the works of the god and so expose ourselves anew to the utmost refusal.[6] The god's move from over-with to having-been is thus a move within and beyond both the extremity of faith and the Nietzschean self-overcoming.

4. *The turning.* "The event has its inmost occurring and its broadest scope in the turning" (GA 65, 407, translation mine; cf. CP, 286). Heidegger had known since before *Being and Time* that the fundamental ontology of Dasein's temporality was preparatory to a projected turning, toward a thinking of the essential temporality of *to be* in its core sense. The turning, indeed, turns out to be itself intrinsic to that core sense of "to be." What *Being and Time* read as the resolute projecting of the horizon of being-there must become at the same time a silent and reserved expectation, hovering between awe and alarm, opening the

"there" for the surprising coming-to-pass of the unique event that concretely grants and articulates "am" and "is" and "are."

What brings being *there* to itself, he says (GA 65, 407; CP, 286), is the onset of the event. In its resoluteness being-there appropriates and enacts traces of what is passing, thus both construing and participating in the historical constitution of what-is. "And *in the turning*" what grounds *being* there is its openness, its being charmed out beyond itself and snatched away ahead of itself toward the hints of disclosiveness in what is coming to pass. Being-there thus is a turning between resolute appropriation of the lingering and bondage to the yet-unknowable that is befalling (GA 65, 407; CP, 286).

Through the event, being-there is thrown to itself and becomes a self. It *needs* this possibility opened in the event. And in the turning, the event needs the human (as the site of its being an event, the locus of its meaning and relevance, the place of its "taking place" at all). The summons of this need to be, together with refusal, marks the passing of the last god. The turning between self-becoming and being granted and claimed is already the turning between the god's abandonment and the god's onset, and so it is also the turning from the last god toward the truth of refusal.

The extreme claim of the event is at the same time the silent call of most-hidden self-knowledge (GA 65, 408; CP, 287). This formulation openly entwines the extreme claim of the god with the notion in *Being and Time* of conscience as the call of care. Each (inmost self-knowledge and outermost claim) overreaches and displaces the other in a turn and turn about. The depth of silent self-knowledge opens a further extremity of the claim of the event. The extreme displacement of self effected in the claim brings home a more silent, more intrinsic self-knowledge. The claim again exceeds and displaces this self-knowing and so brings it home even more. Neither is Dasein's self-resolution the foundation of the world it opens up and by which it is charmed beyond itself, nor is the world of what-already-is an ultimate foundation that grants us to ourselves and claims us back in bondage to its limits. Rather, there is a turning and turning back between the two so that whichever we start from is exceeded by the other, which is exceeded again in its turn.

To speak of gods is to speak of the utmost precedence of the granting, the claiming, the overriding that exceeds our self-resolution. To say that gods need being is on the other hand to speak of the originative and inventive character of Dasein's self-resolving world-projecting, where alone all senses of being, of relevance, of priority, can occur. This self-resolving projecting is needed precisely as the turning toward the overriding excess that displaces and summons us, turns us, beyond ourselves. The extremity of the alternation Heidegger's figure of turning maintains—between existential being-there and the historicality of being, between the charming lingering of the passing-away and the enrapturing surprise of the coming, between summons and homecoming—is sustained by the focal figure of the passing of the last god. This passing may leave momentous traces, such as a table of commandments. But at the same time it is a passing away, an abandonment, a death of god, an exposure to ineluctable refusal.

5. *Truth and the Last God.* The work of truth, as an earlier section of *Contributions* developed it (GA 65, 326–92; CP, 229–74), is one of retrieving the lingering traces of what is passing as hints of the coming. This truth-work preserves these traces/hints through concrete enactments—articulated and stabilized in specific linguistic utterances and artistic creations, actualized in material and public acts that mark and shape and reorder the world, shared in historical and communal interactions and institutions, paid for in specific sacrifices and accommodations. All these acts of salvaging and preserving truth conceal in repetition the novelty of the coming and conceal in their preservation the utterly transitory character of each word and act and sacrifice. Heidegger gives only condensed, poetic indications on this theme; I will enlarge on its specific bearing on the question of truth and god.

We can see that among the acts and works that are a transitory preservation of traces and hints as truth are those that recall and anticipate the god/s. These traces are inscribed in scriptures and sanctuaries, liturgies and ministries, prayers and hymns, acts of charity and of crusade. The equivocal character of these traces hints at the equivocal character of the god and of truth itself. The disclosive moments marked with the name of the god are preserved in these enactments and residues, and at the same time concealed in them. The remembered/expected occurrence that is named as the god claims and empowers these acts of salvage and preservation but does not preserve them from the equivocation. Nor could it. Essential to the event of god is the call to decision and enactment. Such enactment, if it is to bear traces of the god, must pose that claim again. To relieve us of it, to erase the undecidability that founds decision, would erase the claim and thus negate the "godding" (*Götterung* [GA 65, 245; CP, 172]) of the god.

In turning from the god's having been, we may be open to what the memory of divinity traces as a beckoning toward what is to come. One aspect of what is involved here may be illuminated by looking at other contexts. In the lectures on Hölderlin's "Germanien" in 1934, Heidegger attends to Hölderlin's evocation of the gods whose day is past and speaks of the appropriate mood for dealing with them as "grieving relinquishment" (GA 39, 93ff.). "Grieving is not hanging on to what is gone, but a standing firm and enduring of the 'there' (da) and 'here'" (GA 39, 94). Hanging on would not be love for the god, because it is not a will that the beloved *be* (as itself, as gone). "It is because the poet loves these gods to excess that he consents to their being dead, for their flight does not destroy their having been, but creates and maintains it" (ibid.). To try to bring them back to life doesn't give them new life but death. A creative renunciation, in surrendering the gods, preserves their divinity untouched.

We can see that such grieving renunciation "preserves" the god as gone yet also remembered as still tracing a past weal and summons. Thus, in moving us, the past god hints toward a yet-inconceivable future (promising both surprise and refusal, i.e., be-ing). For Hölderlin, the gods don't come back, but what they marked in the height of their giving and claiming can still beckon to a future excess both of blessing and of summons.[7] We must in-vent the sayings and hearings of this future, the creations and actions, the forms of community and the costs, that beckon toward what is coming. This invention is not anything we please but is a project of saying and enacting that futural weal and summons. It may be for some a transformation of the forms of thinking and engaging with divinity; it may be for others a self-exceeding abandonment of gods. By means of both, the overall configuration of truth may come to be refocused.

It is also appropriate to recall Hölderlin's image in "Wie, wenn am Feiertage . . . ," where he calls on his fellow poets

. . . to stand
Bareheaded beneath God's thunderstorms,
To grasp the Father's ray, no less, with our own two hands
And, wrapping in song the heavenly gift,
To offer it to the people.[8]

The *Bergung*—in my version, "retrieval"—of the passing of the god is a turning from the god's once-overwhelming but passing presence toward the human inscription that preserves the going in a singing onward for the people. It is this singing/inscribing that is the ambiguous and transitory locus of truth.

6. *The Table of Commandments.* In an important passage (GA 65, 413; CP, 290), Heidegger ties the question of the passing of the god specifically to the figure of a table of commandments, and thus implicitly to Exodus 33, where Moses asks to see Yahweh's glory. He is told that he may not see God's face but that after God has passed by he may see God going away. After this theophany (this "passing by of the ultimate god"), Moses returns to the people with his transcription of the renewed commandments. The turning toward the future that recalls the god that has passed by is traced in the table of commmandments, as it is for Hölderlin both in the song of the poet after the storm and in Germania's grieving renunciation of the ancient gods. All these turning retrievals hint of the surprising extremity of an unforeseeable summons and homecoming yet to come to pass.

To show more clearly the grounds for my treatment of this topic, I offer my own textual reading of this key paragraph:

> We must prepare the grounding of truth, and it might seem that that would already predetermine the honoring and thus the preservation of the last god. [But] we must at the same time know, and hold to it, that the retrieval [*Bergung*] of truth into what-is [*das Seiende*] (including the history of the preservation of the god, and the manner in which it needs us as grounding its existence) is called for first of all through [the god] itself: called for not merely as a table of commandments but more originarily, in such a way that its passing demands a continuity of what-is, and with it of the human in its midst: a continuity in which what-is, in the simplicity of its recovered essence (in artwork, tool, thing, deed, look, and word) first withstands the passing, not by stopping it but by letting it hold sway as a going. (GA 65, 413, translation mine; cf. CP, 290)

The configuration and articulation of what occurs, in its lingering passing, must be retrieved in the turning toward what is to come. This retrieval gathers the materials for our anticipatory sketch of the coming, by enacting (real-izing) that anticipation in word and work. The gods that are passing are only preserved in that retrieval, in that turning, in that sketch and enactment. The god is not metaphysically postulated but is traced in the text and observance of the commandments and in other words and works. If Nietzsche is right that the funeral of a god requires a higher humanity than any hitherto (see *The Gay Science*, #125), the claim and promise in relation to which the god is relinquished into what has-been must exceed that of the table of commandments (and the promised land). In this exceeding, Heidegger indicates, we must not erase the passing god but let it go and, in its going, claim us to a coming summons and promise, beyond any that has been.

This is a call neither to preserve the god nor to abandon the god but rather to turn to the greater openness of a future beyond the god's passing—a future which is beyond specification either by the expectation of a greater or newer god or by a richer godlessness, a future hinted at both by the god's passing away and by the god's divinity as the excess of claim and promise. In the turning we inscribe the memory of the passing god in saying and doing, as Moses inscribed it on the tablets of the Law, and we let the god's refusal to stay mark out the utter novelty of the coming and evoke from us the utter inventiveness of our way forward.

7. Ripeness. Heidegger's discussion of ripeness (*Reife* [GA 65, 410; CP, 288]) emerges from his treatment of the beckoning hint (*Wink*). Here, he says, we encounter the elemental strife of earth and world, of purest closedness (opacity, inertia, durability) and highest radiance (light, meaning, possibility), playing out between the most charming enchantment and the most fearful enrapturing (GA 65, 410; CP, 288). Ripeness is the readiness of the fruit both for its goodness and for its falling from the tree. Heidegger would have us turn from its preservation on the tree to letting it fall and taking up its fruitfulness.

What is the fruitfulness, the richness, the ripeness, hinted at in the falling/passing of the last god? What is the gift of the god which, in its very passing away, calls and moves us outward to a higher homecoming than anything hitherto?

(This question summons us to ultimate exposure and inventive response and in summoning calls us home [to the unprecedented extremity of the question itself].)

Conclusion

The question of the last god is integral to the path of Heidegger's turning from *Being and Time* to his later work for several reasons. To move beyond the traditional onto-theo-logical foundation of being requires moving beyond the notion of a first, highest, absolute, originative being. To understand being historically and temporally is to understand passing as integral to being; the god is thus passing in an ironic ambiguity between passing as ceasing to hold absolute sway and passing in the sense of "coming to pass." The traces of the god—commandments, song, grieving renunciation—are marks of passing that hint of an excess of summons and of homecoming: alternately coming home to selfhood beyond the god and to god beyond self (and beyond any god hitherto). The fruitfulness of the memory of the god is the same ripeness in which it falls from the tree: passing and bearing fruit are inseparable. The realization of the god is history, enactment in words and works, lives and institutions, thus in coming to pass.

The key question of truth with respect to the last god is the question of a turning enactment, marked by the traces of the god that has passed, following beckoning hints that are inventively construed and enacted. Such enactment both remembers and relinquishes the god, moves both toward exceeding the work of the god and toward acknowledging a claim and summons of futurity—toward what is wholly other not only than ourselves and our inventions but than all gods hitherto (and all previous conceptions of god).

In this turning enactment, the truth of Schleiermacher's emphasis on existence as absolute dependence (see *The Christian Faith*, pp. 12–18) is exceeded by the truth, yet to be performed, of Nietzsche's superhuman, and the truth of the superhuman is exceeded by the coming anew of the utter givenness on which we are dependent as we turn again from the passing toward the coming.

Questions for Further Discussion and Study

The following questions are all to some degree interrelated and over-lapping.

1. How has Heidegger's move from *Being and Time* to the approach of *Contributions* affected the question of god? Specifically, is his general subsumption and retention of the approach of *Being and Time* under a broader perspective reflected in a subsumption and retention of the overtly theological thinking of the 1920s under the broader scope of the passing of the last god?

2. Is *Contributions* the basic document for the thinking that underlies the specific studies of the postwar years, or is there a further substantial move involved in those works? If so how does that move further modify the question of god?

3. How are we to understand the change of tone from the extremity of *Contributions* to the greater tranquility of dwelling in the fourfold in the later years? Given Heidegger's strong emphasis on the fundamental disclosive significance of *Stimmung* (mood), we obviously must not dismiss it as a "mere" change of mood. Is the utter extremity a function of Heidegger's struggle with the dominance of absolute monotheism in Western thought, later fading as that theism is more effectively disestablished? Or is the whole question relocated and decentered after *Contributions,* and if so specifically how and in what texts?

4. Are there fundamental shifts in the sense of be-ing that accompany the shift from *Contributions'* mood of anticipation, ambivalently suspended between awe and alarm, to the postwar quiet sense of releasement to what gives itself? Or is the change simply a calming coming-to-dwell in the waiting for the passing of the god and for the coming of the surprising?

5. Is the mutual exceeding in which the god overwhelms (*übermächtigt*) the human and the human surpasses (*übertrifft*) the god (GA 65, 415; CP, 292) compatible with, or displaced by, the later notion of mortals dwelling in the fourfold before the (absence of) divinities?

Notes

1. For bibliographical information on the texts referred to here, see the introduction to this volume, note 1.

2. The capitalization of "God" creates an ambiguity between the formal indication of the matter of the question of god and the affirmation of a specific god by personal name. I prefer to use the capital only when referring to a specific god affirmed in the tradition, or in titles.

3. The same problem arises when *Wächter* is translated as "guardian." Heidegger's *Wächter* does not "watch over" and give security to something but "watches out for" what may come or what may pass.

4. Heidegger's repeated criticisms of "onto-theo-logy," most focused in _Identity and Difference,_ are not merely aimed at the attribution of being to God but equally to the whole notion of being that remains in modern thought even after god is subtracted. This is the preserving of that (empty) authoritative place.

5. Schaff, _The Creeds of Christendom,_ vol. 3, p. 10. See also Barth, _The Doctrine of the Word of God,_ part 1, pp. 24–25.

6. "Invent" here translates _erdenken,_ which in ordinary German means to invent or concoct. Heidegger makes quite clear that he does not mean making up anything we please but an exposure of thinking to the claim of the event of be-ing in its articulated coming to be. It is thus entirely and concurrently imagination and apprehension of what gives. "In-vent" thus retains the colloquial sense of _erdenken_ and at the same time also says at once "imagine" and "come upon" "in-venire."

7. In his 1939 discussion of Hölderlin's "Wie wenn am Feiertage . . ." (_Erläuterungen zu Hölderlins Dichtung,_ pp. 49–77), Heidegger gives particular attention to _das Heilige,_ the holy. Here the emphasis is not on the god's summons (as in _Contributions_) but on the _Heil,_ the whole, healing, weal, blessing. My juxtaposition of "blessing and summons" here and "summons and promise" elsewhere relies on the indication in _Contributions_ that the summons is not only a calling out but a calling home, with summons and blessing treated as coordinate modes of extremity. Whether this combination is appropriate in _Contributions_ or whether _Heil_ reflects a significant later development is a question involved with the issues proposed for further discussion at the end of this essay.

8. Hölderlin, _Poems and Fragments,_ pp. 397–98.

Bibliography

Barth, Karl. _The Doctrine of the Word of God (Church Dogmatics_ I/1 and I/2). Edinburgh: T. & T. Clark, 1936, 1948.

Bible. _The Oxford Annotated Bible with the Apocrypha,_ ed. Herbert G. May and Bruce M. Metzger. New York: Oxford University Press, 1965.

Derrida, Jacques. "How to Avoid Speaking: Denials." In _Derrida and Negative Theology,_ ed. Harold Coward and Toby Forshay. Albany: State University of New York Press, 1992.

Heidegger, Martin. _Being and Time,_ trans. John Macquarrie and Edward Robinson. New York: Harper & Row, 1962.

——— . _Beiträge zur Philosophie (Vom Ereignis),_ ed. Friedrich-Wilhelm von Herrmann. Gesamtausgabe, vol. 65. Frankfurt am Main: Vittorio Klostermann, 1989. Translated by Parvis Emad and Kenneth Maly as _Contributions to Philosophy (From Enowning)._ Bloomington: Indiana University Press, 1999.

——— . _Erläuterungen zu Hölderlins Dichtung._ Frankfurt am Main: Vittorio Klostermann, 1963 [1951].

——— . _Hölderlins Hymnen "Germanien" und "Der Rhein."_ Gesamtausgabe, vol. 39. Frankfurt am Main: Vittorio Klostermann, 1980.

——— . _Identity and Difference,_ trans. Joan Stambaugh. New York: Harper & Row, 1969.

——— . _The Question Concerning Technology and Other Essays,_ ed. and trans. William Lovitt. New York: Harper & Row, 1977.

Hölderlin, Friedrich. *Poems and Fragments,* trans. Michael Hamburger. London: Anvil Press Poetry, 1994.

Marion, Jean-Luc. *God without Being,* trans. Thomas A. Carlson. Chicago: University of Chicago Press, 1991.

Nietzsche, Friedrich. *The Gay Science,* trans. Walter Kaufmann. New York: Random House, 1974.

Otto, Rudolf. *The Idea of the Holy,* trans. John W. Harvey. London: Oxford University Press, 1958.

Pöggeler, Otto. *The Paths of Heidegger's Life and Thought,* trans. John Bailiff. Atlantic Highlands, N.J.: Humanities Press, 1997.

Prudhomme, Jeff Owen. "The Passing-By of the Ultimate God: The Theological Assessment of Modernity in Heidegger's *Beiträge zur Philosophie.*" *Journal of the American Academy of Religion* 61 (fall 1993): 443–54.

Schaff, Philip. *The Creeds of Christendom.* 3 vols. New York, 1878.

Schleiermacher, Friedrich. *The Christian Faith,* trans. H. R. Mackintosh and J. S. Stewart. Edinburgh: T. & T. Clark, 1976.

13. On "Be-ing": The Last Part of
Contributions to Philosophy (From Enowning)
Parvis Emad

> And any effort at wanting to force what is said in this
> beginning into a familiar intelligibility is futile and
> above all against the nature of such thinking.
> — *Contributions to Philosophy*, part VIII, "Be-ing," §259

In order to enter the last part of *Contributions to Philosophy (From Enowning)*,[1] entitled "Be-ing," we must be clear about the following questions. Considering the structure of this work, which precisely reflects its hermeneutic-phenomenological thrust, in what sense can "Be-ing" be said to be the last part of *Contributions*? Do words such as "last" and "part" apply to "Be-ing" without reservation? And more importantly, how does Heidegger's characterization of "Be-ing" as "an attempt to grasp the whole once again" (GA 65, 514; CP, 365) contribute to our understanding of the relation between "Be-ing" and the "parts" preceding it?

If what being-historical thinking achieves in the six "joinings" (*Fügungen* or *Fugen*) of *Contributions* (in "Echo," "Playing-Forth," "Leap," "Grounding," "The Ones to Come," and "The Last God") is indispensable for entering into "Be-ing," but "Be-ing" is not a "summary" and "conclusion" of the six preceding "joinings," then how are we to understand the relation between these "joinings" and "Being" and how are we to enter into this concluding part? If — considering their "contents" — neither the "Preview" nor the six "joinings" progressively develop an argument the way introductions and chapters usually do, then the relation between "Be-ing" and the six "joinings" cannot be grasped according to the assumption that in *Contributions* Heidegger steadily and gradually develops a central "thesis." If this is the case, then we should seek the guiding clue for grasping the relation between the six "joinings" and "Be-ing" *not* in such an assumption but in the so-called "turning" (*die Kehre*) as the "happening" that reverberates throughout *Contributions* and enables us to enter the last part of this work. Thus enabled, we shall understand what Heidegger means when he intends with "Be-ing" to grasp "the whole once again."

Beginning with a general characterization of the "turning" as the "happening" that reverberates in "Be-ing" as well as in the six "joinings" of *Contributions*, we shall see that Heidegger's attempt to grasp — with "Be-ing" — "the whole once again" should not be misconstrued as the attempt of a willful thinking that, at the end of the road, deems itself to be in control of be-ing and wants to do the impossible, namely to grasp be-ing as a whole. Rather, by trying to achieve a basic understanding of the "turning" we shall see that the last part of *Contributions*, "Be-ing," represents the attempt of a thinking that is claimed by be-ing in such a way as to respond in this part to that claim by *returning, once again*, to the full range of the "turning." Why once again? Because "turning" is not only the "happening" that reverberates in the six "joinings" of *Contributions* and its last part "Be-ing" but also a "happening" that reverberates throughout the transcendental-horizonal pathway of fundamental ontology. Given this proviso, we must set out from a basic understanding of the so-called "turning."[2]

I

When several decades after *Contributions* Heidegger had the opportunity to express himself on the matter of "turning," he precisely and concisely characterized the "turning" in three interconnected respects. First, he pointed out that "turning" marks "a turning point" (*eine Wendung*) in his own enactment in thinking of the "turning"; second, he indicated that "turning" is what occurs within the dynamic (*Sachverhalt*) named "being and time," "time and being"; and finally, he characterized the "turning" by stressing that this "happening" points directly to be-ing insofar as "the 'happening' of 'turning' . . . 'is' be-ing as such" (Das "Geschehen" der Kehre . . . "ist" das Seyn als solches).[3] Thus, if we want to enter "Be-ing" in a manner that behooves the matter called be-ing, we must first achieve a basic understanding of these characterizations of "turning."

We shall take our bearing from the last characterization of the "turning," because this characterization brings invaluable light to the entire matter of "turning." By characterizing the "turning" as the "happening which *is* be-ing as such," Heidegger tells us that this "happening" is nothing other than be-ing's way of holding sway, and that this "happening" should not be confused with a "move" that thinking might make. Heidegger makes this point by suggesting that "turning" should be differentiated from what might be instigated by thinking alone. He says:

> Turning is above all not a process in thinking-questioning [*das fragende Denken*]. . . . It is neither invented by me nor does it concern my thinking alone.[4]

Since "turning" is to be grasped as "the happening which is be-ing as such," it should be differentiated from what might be instigated by thinking-questioning and from what would appear to be "invented" by Heidegger and would concern his thinking alone. Once we realize this, we understand the first characterization of the "turning." Precisely because "turning" is be-ing's way of holding sway, "turning" must be distinguished from what is instigated by thinking-questioning. Precisely because "turning" is be-ing's way of holding sway, it needs to be enacted and projected open by thinking-questioning. When we take this projecting into account, then we understand why Heidegger refers to "turning" as a "turning point" in his thinking. It is a "turning point" because Heidegger enacts thinking as projecting-opening. Thus Heidegger's first characterization of "turning" reads:

> The thinking of the turning *is* a turning point in my thinking [Das Denken der Kehre ist eine Wendung in meinem Denken].[5]

With the first characterization Heidegger drives the point home that "turning" marks a "turning point" in his thinking insofar as thinking is taken in the specific sense of "projecting-opening,"[6] i.e., in the sense of what he calls *Entwurf* and *entwerfen*.

Understood as projecting-opening, this thinking is neither totally autonomous—designs and pursues its own "projects"—nor completely heteronomous—submitting, as it were, to "projects" that are handed down to it. If we insist on taking *Entwurf* to mean "projection" without any effort to show that this "projection" is actually a "projecting-opening," then we fail to preserve the distinction between what thinking does totally on its own and what Heidegger's thinking, as enactment of "the happening of the turning," does when *this* thinking responds to the sway of be-ing which is this "happening." Thus when Heidegger refers to the thinking of the "turning" as a "turning point" in his thinking, he refers to a thinking that is held fast within the "turning."

In order to grasp the second characterization of the "turning," namely the occurrence that pertains to the dynamic of "being and time" and "time and being," we must once again hold in our regard the distinction between "the happening of the turning which *is* be-ing as such," and the enactment in Heidegger's thinking of this "happening." The matter that belongs to the dynamic called "being and time" and "time and being" is the same "happening of the turning which is be-ing as such"—a matter which transcendental-horizonal thinking of fundamental ontology initially projects open as the horizon of presence for the presencing of beings. What in the course of transcendental-horizonal thinking Heidegger calls "metontological turning" presupposes that "the happening of the turning which is be-ing as such" is projected-open. This is another way of saying that metontological turning toward beings is possible only when "the happening of the turning which is be-ing as such" is projected-open as the horizon of presence.[7] (But this is not to suggest that the latter projecting accomplishes the same thing as projecting-open, which occurs within being-historical thinking. For, as we shall see projecting-open that determines transcendental-horizonal thinking undergoes a profound transformation in being-historical thinking.)

What do we learn from these three characterizations of the "turning" that might serve as a foothold for our entry into the concluding part of *Contributions* entitled "Be-ing"? First, that a proper understanding of the "turning" is the prerequisite for placing both the title of the concluding part and this part itself into a proper perspective. This means that a mere orientation toward "Be-ing" as a title—a noun—does not measure up to the task of entry into "Be-ing." Secondly, we become mindful of the intimate connection between thinking and language, because "turning" and its projecting by Heidegger's thinking determine the language of this part in its entirety. And this means, thirdly that we cannot divorce the language of this part, "Be-ing," from the thinking that projects open the "turning"; i.e., be-ing's swaying cannot propose to translate the language of this part into the language of familiar intelligibility. This is so because virtually every basic word of this concluding part becomes understandable against the background that Heidegger sets up when he projects-open the swaying of be-ing which is called "turning." Finally, we learn that central to entering "Be-ing" is the enactment of such a projecting-opening, which presents itself as something utterly inseparable from the "turning": There is no "turning" without a concomitant projecting-open. Which means that "turning as the happening which *is* be-ing as such" is also projecting-opening. And this means that Heidegger's projecting-opening of the "turning" is indispensable for getting into and coming to terms with the last part of *Contributions*, "Be-ing." Given the intimate relationship between "Be-ing" and the preceding six "joinings," we can also say that those "joinings" and "Be-ing" referentially depend on the "turning" and its concomitant projecting-opening.

II

The reader who stands at the threshold of "Be-ing" must be prepared to enter this part of *Contributions* by taking his bearings from the entire matter of "turning." This is to say that such a reader should understand that "turning" is not an event that happens without affecting thinking. On the contrary: standing at the threshold of "Be-ing," the reader should realize that what being-historical thinking achieves in the six "joinings" of *Contributions* as well as in its last part, "Be-ing," is enactable if thinking becomes aware of "the happening of the turning which is be-ing as such."

At this point the crucial question concerns this awareness. What is it that thinking receives from be-ing's swaying, "turning"? Can we determine in specific terms what *comes to* thinking *from* be-ing's swaying, i.e., "turning"? What is it that thinking receives from the "turning" when thinking projects-open *what it receives as* the echo of be-ing in abandonment of be-ing ("Echo"); *as* the playing of the first beginning forth unto the other beginning ("Playing-Forth"); *as* leaping into the full swaying of being ("Leap")—a leap that is ground*ing and* ground*ed* ("Grounding") by the ones to come ("The Ones to Come"), i.e., those who receive the hint of the last god ("The Last God")? Given that what being as such yields of its own accord is opened up and disclosed by the enactment of thinking, can this yield be determined in specific terms? As what does be-ing as such and of its own accord turn toward and enter the domains of thinking and language, thus shaping the text that is entitled "Be-ing"?

To respond to these questions, we must first hold in our regard what occurs as projecting-opening, since be-ing's swaying, the "turning," and thinking or projecting-opening are inseparable. The first time that we come upon this inseparability is in the course of transcendental-horizonal thinking when Heidegger puts forth projecting-opening as a *thrown* projecting-opening (*geworfener Entwurf*). However, at this point Heidegger does not work out the specific manner in which thrown projecting-opening is held fast and embedded within the "turning" that is be-ing. By addressing the being of Dasein as what this being *has to be,* Heidegger puts forth facticity as that beyond which transcendental-horizonal thinking cannot go in order for this thinking to hold in its regard the origin of thrown projecting-opening.

The evidence for this is to be found in the manner in which transcendental-horizonal thinking puts forth thrownness (*Geworfen-heit*). In the purview of this thinking, thrownness is constituted by facticity and is intimately, ultimately, and unsurpassably bound to projecting-opening. Observed from within transcendental-horizonal thinking, this thinking cannot go beyond thrownness of thrown projecting-opening and determine the origin of thrownness. By contrast, being-historical thinking is aware of the origin of thrownness and facticity, taking its clue from a movement within the matter of be-ing, which announces its "immanent transformation"[8] as enowning (*Ereignis*). Heidegger now realizes that thrownness as well as projecting-opening are enowned by be-ing as enowning.

If we ask as what be-ing's swaying enters the domain of thinking and is brought to language in the shape of "Be-ing," then we would have to respond by saying that be-ing's swaying enters the domain of thinking as an "enowning-throw" (*ereignender Zuwurf*)? No other word than "enowning-throw" describes more accurately the phenomenological dynamic which *is* the entry of be-ing's swaying into the domain of thinking.[10] For, the component "throw" (*Wurf*) blocks misunderstanding of that entry in terms of something extant; while the component "enowning" is fit precisely to reflect thinking's being enowned by the "throw" of be-ing, i.e., by its swaying into the domain of thinking. As an "enowning-throw," be-ing enters the domain of thinking, thus enowning and enabling thinking to become the thinking of be-ing.

What does "enowning-throw" bring to thinking when it enters the domain of thinking? We cannot respond to this question without first attending to the transformation of thinking by be-ing's "enowning-throw." The "enowning-throw" transforms thinking by enowning and enabling it to make a leap into and to become being-historical thinking. This can happen because be-ing's swaying, the "turning," resonates in the "enowning-throw." Heidegger has this resonance in mind when he speaks of "turning in enowning" (*die Kehre im Ereignis*). What does he mean by this? We respond to this question by holding in our regard both the "leap" and "turning in enowning" as addressed by Heidegger in the "joinings" that precede "Be-ing."

The primary and deciding consequence of the enabling of thinking by the "enowning-throw" is the realization that "the thrower" of projecting-opening experiences itself as thrown, i.e., as "en-owned by be-ing" (GA 65, 304; CP, 214). The transforming of thinking by the "enowning-throw" into being-historical thinking and the ensuing realization that the one who leaps—the thrower—is enowned by be-ing require Heidegger for the first time in his philosophical career to determine as "turning in enowning"[11] be-ing's swaying, or the "turning." Determining and opening up the "turning" as "turning in enowning" is possible because be-ing's "enowning-throw" is a historically *transforming* and historically *enabling* movement, which Heidegger calls enowning or *Ereignis*.[12]

The primary yield of holding in our regard the enabling power of be-ing consists in re-grasping the "turnings" that occur in transcendental-horizonal thinking. "Turning in enowning" now paves the way for reinterpreting the fundamental-ontological, metontological "turnings" and "circles." Heidegger says:

> Enowning has its innermost occurrence and its widest reach in the turning. The turning that holds sway in enowning is the sheltered ground of the entire series of turnings, circles, and spheres, which are of unclear origin, remain unquestioned, and are easily taken in themselves as the "last." (GA 65, 407; CP, 286)

This means that the "turning" to which transcendental-horizonal thinking is a response is in truth the "turning" that resonates in be-ing's "enowning-throw," which now reveals itself as "turning in enowning." Central to this "turning" is the "belonging" character of be-ing's "enowning-throw."

Unlike the turnings that are familiar to us from the domain of the extant (turning a page, turning in a road, etc.)—turnings that *do not intrinsically belong to* what is turning—"turning in enowning" is a turning that belongs intrinsically to *the one who belongs* to this turning *as* the *one who is destined* to belong to and be enowned by the "enowning-throw." We put "belonging" in the foreground when we suggest that it should be differentiated from the ordinary manners of belonging because of the intimacy of this "belonging" to be-ing's "call" (*Zuruf/ Zuwurf*),[13] i.e., to be-ing's "enowning-throw."[14]

Here "belonging" refers to the manner in which the being-historical thinker *belongs* to the "enowning-throw" *as the one who is destined to belong* to and be enowned by the "enowning-throw." This is to say that the being-historical thinker is not the one who decides but is the one who is called upon and in this vein is decided to *belong* to the "enowning-throw." Here we must carefully heed the nuance of difference between simply "belonging" to the "enowning-throw" and "belonging" as being called upon and being destined to belong to the "enowning-throw." Heidegger maintains this nuance of difference by drawing upon the following words: *Zuruf, Zugehörige, Zugehör,* and *Angerufene,* the English rendition of all of which had to draw in the word "belonging." The word "belonging" in "the call (to the one belonging)" (*der Zuruf, dem Zugehörigen*) (GA 65, 407; CP, 287) simply refers to the being-historical thinker as the one belonging. However, the word "belonging" in "belonging (of the one who is called)" (*der Zugehör [des Angerufenen]*) (ibid.) indicates being called upon, being destined to belong, and being enowned by be-ing's "enowning-throw."

Heeding this nuance, we realize that be-ing's "enowning-throw" evokes this particular manner of belonging and thus brings about a movement which has no terminus a quo and no terminus ad quem because as "turning in enowning" this movement happens as a movement that runs from the "enowning-throw" to "belonging" and back from "belonging" to the "enowning-throw." The being-historical thinker is the one who belongs to the "enowning-throw" insofar as this "throw" comes from the movement called "turning in enowning." But the being-historical thinker is also the one who is called upon and destined to belong to the "enowning-throw" insofar as this "throw" is destined for the thinker, who, by dint of being *so* called upon and destined, *turns toward* the "enowning-throw." Thus "enowning-throw" and being-historical thinking find themselves in a counter-turning movement which reveals that, strictly speaking, "turning in enowning" is a "counter-turning." Heidegger puts all of this succinctly when he says:

> Turning holds sway between the call [*Zuruf/Zuwurf* ("enowning-throw"); interpolation mine] (to the one belonging) and the belonging (of the one who is called). Turning is counter-turning [*Widerkehre*]. (GA 65, 407; CP, 287)

Unlike the manners of "belonging" familiar to us from the domain of the extant (belonging that indicates appropriation and possession), the notion of "belonging" that functions here is thoroughly void of any connection with the extant. Heidegger points in this direction when he indicates that "belonging" and "enowning-throw" are *mirrored* in Da-sein. He says: "Da-sein is . . . the mirroring of call ["enowning-throw"] and belongingness" (GA 65, 311; CP, 219; interpolation mine). The orienting power of this word "mirroring" shows being-historical thinking as what is *inseparable* but *distinguishable* from be-ing's "enowning-throw": being-historical thinking mirrors that "throw" as be-ing's "throw" — thus remaining inseparable from the "throw" — while that "throw" mirrors being-historical thinking by enowning and enabling it to project open the "throw" — thus remaining distinguishable from that thinking.

Thus it becomes clear that "turning" reverberates as a counter-turning between "enowning-throw" and "belonging." Holding this counter-turning in our regard, we realize that the entry into the last part of *Contributions*, "Be-ing," is not mainly a matter of reading. More originary and, therefore, more decisive than reading this part of *Contributions* is being drawn into, and thus being guided by, the "enowning-throw" and "belonging" in their counter-turning, which, as we shall see, is temporal-temporalizing and spatial-spatializing. This is to say that the entry into "Be-ing" is to be made through a reading that is aware of its own placement in that counter-turning as a temporal-temporalizing, spatial-spatializing counter-turning. Thus, in order to enter this part of *Contributions* in a manner that is commensurate with that counter-turning, we will have to find out in what way it is a temporal-temporalizing spatial-spatializing counter-turning.

First, we must note that the "enowning-throw" not only reveals thinking as what belongs to the "enowning-throw" but also brings to thinking a ground that is simultaneously *ur-ground, ab-ground*, and *un-ground*. As the onefold of an ur-ground, ab-ground, and un-ground, the "enowning-throw" brings to thinking a ground that is held unto an ab-ground, i.e., a ground that "grounds . . . and yet does not actually ground" because "it is hesitating" (GA 65, 380; CP, 265). A ground that grounds and yet does not actually ground is a ground that grounds as an ab-ground, i.e., as "the staying away of ground" (ibid.). In *Contributions* Heidegger captures the process of a hesitating grounding with striking brevity when he says: "*Ab*-ground is ab-*ground*" (ibid.). Depending on whether we observe the "ab-" or the "-ground," we might hold in our regard a ground that *remains* while it stays *away* — a ground whose grounding brings to thinking a "hesitating refusal" (*zögernde Versagung*) (ibid.). This shows that "enowning-throw" brings to thinking a ground that *stays* in hesitatingly being *away*.

Since hesitating, staying, and being away indicate temporality, we can say that the ground which "enowning-throw" brings to thinking is a ground that is temporal and temporalizing. But "enowning-throw" also brings to thinking a ground that is spatial and spatializing. This is a ground that *stays* and by staying makes room *as* (not for) what is *coming*. Since staying points to spatiality, the ground that stays is a ground brought to thinking by the "enowning-throw" as a ground that charms into making room, i.e., it is spatial and spatializing.

To sum up, we can say that "enowning-throw" brings to thinking a ground that is temporal-temporalizing and spatial-spatializing; and as such it is held in a temporalizing- spatializing-encircling hold, or "time-space."[15] All of this is brought to thinking insofar as *all of this* is held in reserve for thinking in the grounding-attunement of reservedness—an attunement which is also brought to thinking by be-ing's "enowning-throw."

Considering the task of entry into "Be-ing," we have to say that we cannot enter this part of *Contributions* without first becoming aware of how *we* stand with respect to the grounding of a ground that is held in a temporalizing-spatializing-encircling hold, or "time-space," and is thus reserved in the grounding attunement of reservedness. Following such an awareness we can hold in our regard the counter-turning between an "enowning-throw" and a "belonging" as a counter-turning which shapes each "joining" of *Contributions* as well as "Be-ing."

III

Holding in our regard the entire matter of "turning" as it marks a turning point (*eine Wendung*) in Heidegger's thinking of the "turning," and as it unfolds in *Contributions* as "turning in enowning," which is grasped as the "counter-turning" between an "enowning-throw" and "belonging," we ask: How does thinking *belong to* the "enowning-throw" insofar as "enowning-throw" attunes thinking by bringing to it the grounding-attunement of reservedness and concomitantly a ground that is held in a temporalizing-spatializing encircling hold? Thinking belongs to the "enowning-throw" to the extent that "enowning-throw" brings to and attunes thinking by the grounding-attunement of reservedness. Thus attuned, thinking is actually enacted as an "enowned projecting-opening" (*ereigneter Entwurf*).[16]

It should be pointed out that (a) the component "enowned" in the expression "enowned projecting-opening" would be misconstrued if "enowning-throw" were mistaken for something extant, an *addendum,* and that (b) thinking as attuned and enowned by be-ing's "enowning-throw" is enowned by a ground which is held unto an ab-ground and which manifests the temporalizing-spatializing-encircling hold or "time-space." The component "projecting-opening" indicates that, as attuned and enowned, thinking is enabled to project open and disclose a being as enowned while thinking continues to inhere in the "enowning-throw." And that means that the component "projecting-opening" points to the capability inherent in thinking to open up and disclose a being, while thinking continues to inhere in and be aware of be-ing's "enowning-throw" as that which attunes, enowns, and enables thinking, and brings to it a ground that is held unto an ab-ground and manifests the temporalizing-spatializing-encircling hold or "time-space."

Virtually *everything* Heidegger says in the entirety of "Be-ing," especially in §§262 to 269, should be grasped against the background of these two coalescing components. The "enowning-throw" attunes and enowns thinking by bringing to it a ground that manifests the encircling hold or "time-space." Both the "enowning-throw" and the ground are always already projected-open when a being is disclosed. Whether such a disclosure brings a being to the fore that is dis-enowned by be-ing (a being that belongs to the epoch of machination and unfolds from within the first beginning),[17] or whether this disclosure puts forth a being that shelters be-ing[18] (a being that belongs to the other beginning), in either case experiencing a being amounts to enacting an "attuned enowned projecting-opening." However, when we hold such an enactment in our regard, we find that projecting-opening might nevertheless move away from be-ing's "enowning-throw" — without severing itself from the "enowning-throw" — while at the same time disclosing an erectable and preservable "something" which, insofar as it *is*, receives the mark of be-ing and is thus called *a being*. Holding in our regard such an enactment of thinking amounts to experiencing the disclosure of a being through a projecting opening which Heidegger calls a preparatory projecting:

> For experiencing a being and for sheltering its truth, "projecting-open" is only what is preparatory, which then passes over in proceeding to that which is erectable and preservable in the domain of projecting-opening — and as *preserving* receives the seal of be-ing. (GA 65, 447; CP, 314)

Continuing to hold in our regard such an enactment of thinking, we find further that, as it is enacted, projecting-opening displays a movement which is a *move away from* and a simultaneous *returning to* be-ing's "enowning-throw." This simultaneous returning reveals a hitherto unheeded aspect of the "attuned enowned projecting-opening" which Heidegger describes when he says

> In thinking's knowing awareness, projecting-opening is not something preparatory *for* something else, but rather the most unique and the last and thus the most rare, which holds sway unto itself as the grounded truth of be-ing. (ibid.)

Continuing to hold in our regard such an enactment of thinking, we ask: From where does projecting-opening receive the impetus to move away from be-ing's "enowning-throw," without severing itself from it, and to simultaneously return to be-ing's "enowning-throw"? Undoubtedly from be-ing's "enowning-throw," since projecting-opening *is attuned* by the "enowning-throw" and is thus an *"attuned* enowned projecting-opening." Holding in our regard that moving away from "enowning-throw" and this simultaneous returning to it, we realize that while *moving away* and *returning* to be-ing's "enowning-throw," the initiator of projecting-opening, the thrower, might relinquish a being and, as Heidegger puts it in §263, experience himself as the one who

> throws himself free of a being unto be-ing without a being's having already been enopened as such. (GA 65, 452; CP, 318)

In §263 Heidegger calls this experience "free-throw" (*Loswurf*) or "throwing-oneself free" (*Sichloswerfen*). In order to understand what this "free-throw" or "throwing-oneself free" of a being is all about, we must continue to hold in our regard the aforementioned "moving away from" and "simultaneous returning" at the same time as we steer clear of the traditional conception of man as *animal rationale*.

As long as we abide by *animal rationale,* we have no way of grasping the "free-throw," or "throwing-oneself free," of a being. We cannot depart from familiar properties of man (e.g., reason) in the expectation of locating the "free-throw" in those properties. The truth is that as an originary phenomenon, "free-throw" or "throwing-oneself free" of a being, is not a property of *animal rationale.* Rather, as originary, "free-throw" grounds man's being anew from the ground up. Heidegger says:

> We must not take man as pre-given in the heretofore familiar properties and now seek the free-throw in him, but rather: throwing-oneself-free must itself first ground for us what is ownmost to man. (GA 65, 454; CP, 319)

We cannot proceed from the properties of *animal rationale* not only because "free-throw" is not a property of *animal rationale* but also because "free-throw" presupposes the "moves" that are blocked by the conception of man as *animal rationale.*

Continuing further to hold in our regard the move away from be-ing's "enowning-throw," which in moving away does not sever itself from the "enowning-throw" and simultaneously returns to the "enowning-throw," we realize that what up to now we called "free-throw," or "throwing-oneself free" of a being, is the same as a specific direction taken by the "attuned enowned projecting-opening," which Heidegger calls venturing the open (*das Offene wagen*). This is a projecting which belongs neither to oneself nor to what is over against and yet to both—not as object and subject but knowing oneself as countering in the open—intimating that *what* throws itself free and that from which it throws itself free holds sway in the same way as the over against. (GA 65, 454; CP, 319–20)

Thinking (attuned enowned projecting-opening) might occur as such a venturing, might throw itself free of a being unto be-ing, when thinking realizes that it does not come from a subject vis-à-vis be-ing as an object—when it knows itself as "countering in the open" (*Ent-gegnend im Offenen*). What counts here is this countering. Heidegger talks about *venturing* (*wagen*), because the "attuned enowned projecting-opening," which moves away from be-ing's "enowning-throw" and returns to it, is a venture, i.e., it does not enjoy the security and certainty of a principle of epistemology. Since that from which thinking throws-itself-free is an as yet unenopened (not yet disclosed) being (which is nonetheless a being), and since that which throws itself free is a thinking that simultaneously returns to a disclosed being, we can say that in "venturing the open," in "knowing oneself as countering in the open," in "free-throw," and in "throwing-oneself-free," thinking enacts a returning to a disclosed being. And thus returning, thinking experiences a returnership (*Rückkehrerschaft*), which means that moving away from and simultaneously returning to be-ing's "enowning-throw" is not a one-time occurrence but ongoing.

Thus "enowning-throw" not only attunes, enowns, and enables thinking to disclose a being as belonging to a ground that is held unto the temporalizing-spatializing ab-ground but also enables thinking to experience a returnership that goes on as moving away from and simultaneous returning to be-ing's "enowning-throw." This experience entails the "free-throw," "throwing-oneself-free," "venturing the open," and "knowing oneself as countering in the open." It thus shows that "enowning-throw" and all that it brings to thinking—attunement, enownment, the onefold of a temporalizing-spatializing unground, abground, and urground—is impregnated with an ongoing returnership. And this means that it is the "enowning-throw" that actually places man's being squarely within the ongoing experience of that returnership. Since the returnership entails man's throwing himself free of "a being" unto be-ing, this returnership holds the possibility open for man to gain access to what is "most-ownmost most-remote" (*das Eigenst-Fernste*)[19] to him, thus becoming man:

> By throwing himself free of "a being," man first becomes man. For only in this way does he return to a being and *is* he the one who has returned. (GA 65, 452; CP, 318)

Insofar as experiencing the returnership amounts to man's throwing himself free of a being unto be-ing, such an experience also entails a manner of dwelling that takes place in the light of what the "enowning-throw" brings to thinking. This is a dwelling that is attuned to the truth of be-ing, i.e., to a ground that is held unto an ab-ground and manifests "time-space." Depending on how man realizes the dwelling, and depending on how man is destined to and gifted for that realization, returnership holds a view of be-ing:

> One must first know the manner of dwelling and the concomitant gift, as well as the manner in which in the re-turn what was before and fettering is initially met with as what a being is found or what is found as a being—which view of being man as the returner (*Zurückkehrer*) retains. (GA 65, 453; CP, 319)

An almost total blindness to the experience of throwing himself free of a being, and an exposure to the full range of the ongoing experience of returnership, is what actually shapes man's dwelling as well as the view of be-ing that he as the returner retains. What view of be-ing he holds depends on how his dwelling is shaped.

However, the possibilities that are adumbrated in the dwelling, namely throwing-oneself-free of a being and returnership, are forgotten. This forgottenness is an indication that

> man was *not* capable of mastering the returnership (*Rückkehrerschaft*). This "not" [is] the ground of his hitherto Western history. (ibid.)

This means that man was not capable of holding on to what the "enowning-throw" brings, was not able to hold unto the truth of be-ing as what is held unto the ab-ground. But since man's relationship to be-ing cannot be severed or eliminated, following this "not mastering" he continues to be exposed to be-ing's "enowning-throw"—to the truth that is held unto the ab-ground—but with one important difference. The "enowning-throw" that comes to thinking after that "not mastering" is a "dis-enowned enowning-throw" and belongs to the "time-space" of machination. The "dis-enowned enowning-throw" that is held unto the *unground* called machination brings to the fore the forgottenness of the returnership and the forgottenness of be-ing's "enowning-throw." Accordingly, this forgottenness serves as a measure for understanding

> how a colossal disturbance runs through all human progress; how be-ing itself as machination sets itself into what is precisely not its ownmost. (ibid.)

This means that, as it is presently shaped, human progress is interpenetrated by a colossal disturbance. This progress is thus capable neither of providing an access to what is "most-ownmost most-remote" to humans nor of rendering superfluous what is "most-ownmost most-remote" to humans by replacing it.

IV

With the attempt to determine more closely the "free-throw," or "throwing-oneself free of a being unto be-ing," we come upon the experience of a returnership that occurs as moving away from and returning to be-ing's "enowning-throw." We now suggest that the experience of this returnership constitutes the backbone of the entirety of the last part of *Contributions*, "Be-ing," that it holds the key for grasping what Heidegger means when he says that with "Be-ing" he intends to grasp the whole once again, and that it is this experience that allows thinking to enter this last part of *Contributions*.

The experience of returnership sustains Heidegger's accomplishments in each section of "Be-ing" because what he says in each section is understandable and co-enactable on the basis of what he calls "throwing-oneself free of a being unto be-ing." But we must caution against confusing this "throwing-oneself free of a being" with a "freedom from" or detachment à la Buddhism, or with any other doctrine of liberation. Strictly speaking, thinking can never free itself from beings; it can only move away from disclosing a being toward be-ing's "enowning-throw" — in short, it can only undergo the experience of returnership. This is the experience that sustains the entirety of "Be-ing" when Heidegger addresses "the essential swaying of be-ing" (§§265, 266, 269, 270), "history" (§273), "calculation as the ground of the gigantic" (§§260, 274), "the ontological difference" (§§266, 268), "gods' needfulness of be-ing" (§§259, 279), "transformation of man's being by an originary thinking of be-ing" (§§259, 270, 271, 272) — a transformation that leads to what is ownmost to language and what is ownmost to the work of art, and to history (§§273, 276, 277) — and in particular when he lays out the "manifoldness of enownings" (§§267, 268, 269).

The experience of returnership also holds the key for understanding Heidegger's intention to grasp the whole once again with "Be-ing." In its entirety "Be-ing" is referentially dependent upon the experience of returnership — *not* because here Heidegger returns to the preceding six "joinings" and gathers together the "results" as a whole. As a quick look at "Be-ing" might show, he never enacts such a returning. Besides, were such a returning to occur, it would be reminiscent of the familiar surveys at the end of a work that are consummated in a summary and conclusion — it would be a far cry from the experience of returnership which shapes the last part of *Contributions*. Heidegger makes it quite clear that with "Be-ing" he does not intend to sum up the "results" of the preceding six "joinings" and conclude the work, since he indicates explicitly that this is an attempt which happens *once again*. He says explicitly "once again" because he also grasps the whole throughout each of the preceding six "joinings." This whole is not the whole *of* what lies "between" disclosing a being and be-ing's "enowning-throw" but is the whole *as* what occurs or transpires when thinking moves away from and returns to be-ing's "enowning-throw." (The "whole *of* " would imply summing up and concluding, the "whole *as*" indicates a manner of self-showing and manifesting.) Grasping this whole happens once again, because with "Be-ing" Heidegger *returns* to the whole *as* what occurs when thinking moves away from and returns to be-ing's "enowning-throw." That is why he has to characterize "Be-ing" as an attempt to grasp the whole once again.

Finally, the experience of returnership provides the actual entry into "Be-ing" since this experience, as we saw, is irrevocably bound to be-ing's "enowning-throw" as it enters the domain of thinking via "the happening of the turning." The experience of returnership and the "happening of turning" thus prove to be so profoundly intertwined that we can say that, by unearthing the experience of returnership, Heidegger in *Contributions* brings to *a preliminary* completion his thinking of the "turning."

But "turning" is not an "event" which occurs outside language and which may or may not leave language alone. Be-ing's swaying, i.e., "turning" is at the same time a turning *of* and *in* language. This being the case, it should be understandable why this present attempt deliberately stays with Heidegger's basic words instead of abandoning them in favor of the language of the tradition which is "more familiar" and "more intelligible." Precisely because "turning" marks a "turning point" in Heidegger's thinking of be-ing, and precisely because no one else in our time attempts to articulate the "turning," it is incumbent upon us to stay with Heidegger's language. And this is to say that whether we take the "turning" as that to which transcendental-horizonal thinking is a response, or whether we take the "turning" as that to which being-historical thinking is a response, we should stay with Heidegger's words because they emerge from within the turning as the onefold of being and language. Only insofar as these words emerge from within that onefold are they words "of" thinking and not ours to manipulate as we please. The notion of a more familiar, more intelligible, more traditional language is a notion with which metaphysics attempts to obfuscate *Ereignis* by interpreting it according to metaphysical criteria of "comprehensibility and incomprehensibility of things." Such a notion is based on the total lack of grasping what is ownmost to Heidegger's language and its unfolding within the swaying that is called be-ing. Since "turning" marks a "turning point" in Heidegger's thinking, then it should be clear why we who come after Heidegger should stay with his words as words that come from and shelter the swaying of be-ing called "turning."

Notes

1. For bibliographical information on the text referred to here, see the introduction to this volume, note 1. All references in the text are to the Emad/ Maly translation of the *Beiträge zur Philosophie (Vom Ereignis)*. For the English renditions of the key words of *Contributions* as used in this essay, see "Translators' Foreword," CP, xv–xliv.

2. In addition to Heidegger's own account of the "turning" dealt with below, see Friedrich-Wilhelm von Herrmann, *Wege ins Ereignis: Zu Heideggers "Beiträgen zur Philosophie"* (Frankfurt am Main: Vittorio Klostermann, 1994), pp. 5–26, 64–84; idem, "Wahrheit-Zeit-Raum," in *Die Frage nach der Wahrheit*, vol. 4, *Schriftenreihe Martin-Heidegger-Gesellschaft*, ed. Ewald Richter (Frankfurt am Main: Vittorio Klostermann, 1997), pp. 243–56; and Paola-Ludovica Coriando, *Der letzte Gott als Anfang: Zur ab-gründigen Zeit-Räumlichkeit des Übergangs in Heideggers "Beiträge zur Philosophie"* (Munich: Wilhelm Fink Verlag, 1998), pp. 33–34.

3. Cf. the "Preface" to W. J. Richardson, *Heidegger: Through Phenomenology to Thought* (The Hague: Martinus Nijhoff, 1967), pp. xvii, xix, xxi. It should be pointed out that my renditions of these crucial terms differ significantly from Richardson's in his translation of Heidegger's letter to him. This letter appears in Richardson's work as a *Vorwort*. On this point see, "Vorwort: Brief an P. William J. Richardson von Martin Heidegger," *Philosophisches Jahrbuch* 72 (1964–65): 385, 397. Regarding the matter of "turning" it should be pointed out that by interpreting Heidegger's "it worlds" (*es weltet*) from his 1919 war emergency course (GA 56, 57) as a "turning before the turning," Hans-Georg Gadamer totally obfuscates the threefold characterizations of the "turning" and unleashes an avalanche of misunderstandings. See his *Gesammelte Werke*, vol. 3 (Tübingen: J. C. B. Mohr, 1987), p. 418. This obfuscation determines Theodore Kiesel's understanding of the "war emergency course of 1919" (see his *Genesis of Heidegger's Being and Time* [Berkeley: University of California Press, 1993], pp. 3, 16 and passim); Manfred Riedel's interpretation of the "turning" (see his "Die Urstiftung der phänomenologischen Hermeneutik: Heideggers frühe Ausein-andersetzung mit Husserl," in *Phänomenologie im Widerstreit: Zum 50. Todestag Husserls*, ed. Christoph Jamme and Otto Pöggeler [Frankfurt am Main: Suhrkamp, 1989], pp. 215–33); and John van Buren's understanding of Hei-degger's early Freiburg lecture courses (see his *The Young Heidegger: Rumor of the Hidden King* [Bloomington: Indiana University Press, 1994], pp. 136–37). For a thoroughgoing criticism of these misunderstandings, see Tomy S. Kalariparam-bil, *Das befindliche Verstehen und die Seinsfrage* (Berlin: Duncker und Humblot, 1999), pp. 72ff.

4. Richardson, *Heidegger*, p. xix, translation modified.

5. Ibid., p. xvii.

6. For more on "projecting-opening" and the inadequacies of "project" and "projection" as possible renditions of *entwerfen* and *Entwurf*, see "Translators' Foreword," CP, xxvii–xxx.

7. For metontological turning, see *Metaphysische Anfangsgründe der Logik im Ausgang von Leibniz* (Frankfurt am Main: Vittorio Klostermann, 1978), GA 26, 199–201; *The Metaphysical Foundations of Logic*, trans. Michael Heim (Blooming-ton: Indiana University Press, 1984), pp. 156–57. For a precise understanding of

this "turning," see Friedrich-Wilhelm von Herrmann, *Heideggers "Grundprobleme der Phänomenologie": Zur "Zweiten Hälfte" von "Sein und Zeit"* (Frankfurt am Main: Vittorio Klostermann, 1991), pp. 53ff.

8. Von Herrmann, *Wege ins Ereignis*, pp. 55ff.

9. Regarding this expression, see von Herrmann, *Wege ins Ereignis*, pp. 92 and passim.

10. What Richardson calls "mittence" (*Heidegger*, p. 435) should not be confused with "enowning-throw." First, "mittence" is Richardson's rendition of Heidegger's *Geschick*, and secondly, the words "mittence" and *Geschick* do not reflect be-ing's enowning character. But this is not to say that "mittence" or *Geschick* and "enowning-throw" are unrelated.

11. See CP, 255. The phrase "for the first time" is meant to remind us of what Heidegger alludes to when he characterizes the "turning" as a "turning point in his thinking."

12. Here attention should be paid to the prefix "en" in enowning for capturing the enabling power which is indicated by the prefix "Er," in *Er-eignis*. See ibid., "Translators' Foreword," pp. xix–xxii.

13. See von Herrmann, *Wege ins Ereignis*, p. 92: "den Zuruf, den wir auch als Zuwurf fassen können."

14. From this point on we will use the expression "enowning-throw" as synonymous with "call."

15. This means that thinking or projecting-opening *belongs* to this temporalizing-spatializing-encircling hold, or "time-space." This refutes the assumption that in *Contributions* thinking *becomes* a dimension of time and space. Understood in the context of the counter-turning, we cannot talk about "time" and "space" and dimension without obfuscating "time-space."

16. For this expression, see von Herrmann, *Wege ins Ereignis*, p. 92 and passim.

17. See part II, "Echo" (CP, 84), in which Heidegger characterizes the epoch of machination as one in which "beings . . . are dis-enowned by be-ing."

18. See part V, "Grounding" (CP, 271-73), in which Heidegger addresses the possibility of a being that shelters be-ing.

19. The expression *das Eigenst-Fernste* is Paola-Ludovica Coriando's. See her "Die 'Formale Anzeige' und das Ereignis: Vorbereitende Überlegungen zum Eigencharakter seinsgeschichtlicher Begrifflichkeit mit einem Ausblick auf den Unterschied von Denken und Dichten," *Heidegger Studies* 14 (1998): 32.

Contributors

Walter A. Brogan is Professor of Philosophy at Villanova University. He is coeditor of *American Continental Philosophy: A Reader;* cotranslator of *Metaphysics Theta 1–3: On the Essence and Actuality of Force* by Martin Heidegger; and author of many articles on Greek philosophy in relation to contemporary authors.

David Crownfield is Professor Emeritus of Religion and Philosophy at the University of Northern Iowa. He is editor of *Body/Text in Julia Kristeva: Women, Religion, and Psychoanalysis;* coeditor of *Lacan and Theological Discourse;* and author of many articles in religion and philosophy, including articles on Martin Heidegger's *Contributions to Philosophy.* He is past president of the American Theological Society, Midwest Division.

Parvis Emad is Emeritus Professor of Philosophy at DePaul University and founding coeditor of *Heidegger Studies.* He is cotranslator of Martin Heidegger's *Hegel's Phenomenology of Spirit, Phenomenological Interpretation of Kant's* Critique of Pure Reason, and *Contributions to Philosophy (From Enowning).*

Günter Figal is Professor of Philosophy at the University of Tübingen. His books include *For a Philosophy of Freedom and Strife: Martin Heidegger; Phänomenologie der Freiheit; Das Untier und die Liebe: Sieben platonische Essays; Der Sinn des Verstehens;* and *Heidegger zur Einführung.*

Friedrich-Wilhelm von Herrmann is Emeritus Professor of Philosophy at the University of Freiburg. His most recent book is *Die helle aber zarte Differenz: Heidegger und Stefan George.* His previous books include *Wege ins Ereignis: Zu Heideggers "Beiträgen zur Philosophie," Heideggers Philosophie der Kunst,* and *Hermeneutische Phänomenologie des Daseins.* He is the German editor of *Heidegger Studies* and executive director of the Heidegger Gesamtausgabe.

Kenneth Maly is Professor of Philosophy at the University of Wisconsin–La Crosse and founding coeditor of *Heidegger Studies.* He is cotranslator of Martin Heidegger's *Hegel's Phenomenology of Spirit, Phenomenological Interpretation of Kant's* Critique of Pure Reason, and *Contributions to Philosophy (From Enowning).* He is also editor of the journal *Call to Earth.*

William McNeill is Associate Professor of Philosophy at DePaul University, Chicago. He is author of *The Glance of the Eye: Heidegger, Aristotle, and the Ends of Theory* and of various articles on Heidegger. He has translated or edited a number of Heidegger's texts, including *The Concept of Time; The Fundamental Concepts of Metaphysics: World, Finitude, Solitude; Hölderlin's Hymn "The Ister"*; and *Pathmarks*.

Richard Polt is Associate Professor of Philosophy at Xavier University in Cincinnati. He is author of *Heidegger: An Introduction;* cotranslator of *Heidegger's Introduction to Metaphysics;* and coeditor of *A Companion to Heidegger's Introduction to Metaphysics*.

John Sallis is Edwin Erle Sparks Professor of Philosophy at The Pennsylvania State University. He is author of *Force of Imagination: The Sense of the Elemental; Chorology: On Beginning in Plato's* Timaeus; *Shades — Of Painting at the Limit; Double Truth; Stone; Crossings: Nietzsche and the Space of Tragedy; Echoes: After Heidegger; Spacings — Of Reason and Imagination; Delimitations: Phenomenology and the End of Metaphysics; The Gathering of Reason; Being and Logos: Reading the Platonic Dialogues;* and *Phenomenology and the Return to Beginnings*. He has also edited numerous volumes, including three collections of essays on Heidegger. He is general editor of the Indiana University Press book series Studies in Continental Thought.

Dennis J. Schmidt is Professor of Philosophy at Villanova University. He is author of *The Ubiquity of the Finite* and *On Germans and Other Greeks*. He is translator of Ernst Bloch's *Natural Law and Human Dignity* and editor of the State University of New York Press Series in Continental Philosophy.

Susan M. Schoenbohm has taught philosophy at Vanderbilt University, The University of the South, and The Pennsylvania State University. She has published articles on Heidegger, contemporary Continental thought, ancient Greek philosophy, and ancient Asian thought.

Charles E. Scott is Edwin Erle Sparks Professor of Philosophy at The Pennsylvania State University. His previous books include *Boundaries in Mind: A Study of Immediate Awareness in Psychotherapy; The Language of Difference; The Question of Ethics: Nietzsche, Heidegger, Foucault; On the Advantages and Disadvantages of Ethics and Politics;* and *The Time of Memory*. He is coeditor of the Pennsylvania State University Press series American and European Thought. Among his edited and coedited books are *Martin Heidegger: In Europe and America,* and *Ethics and Danger: Essays on Heidegger and Continental Thought*.

Alejandro Vallega was born in Chile and educated in Latin America, the United States, and Europe. He teaches philosophy at California State University, Stanislaus. His work focuses on issues of identity and alterity in Continental thought and ancient philosophy. He is also a Latinamericanist.

Daniela Vallega-Neu was educated in Germany, France, and Italy. She previously taught in Germany and now teaches philosophy at California State University, Stanislaus. In addition to articles on Continental and ancient Greek thought, she is author of *Die Notwendigkeit der Gründung im Zeitalter der Dekonstruktion: Zur Gründung in Heideggers Beiträge zur Philosophie unter Hinzuziehung der Derridaschen Dekonstruktion.*

Index

Abandonment of/by be-ing: as distress, 39, 142, 145; and machination, 40, 151–153; and echo, 70, 114, 232–233; and startled dismay, 74; and language, 74, 76

Ab-ground, 3; in questioning, 18; as the truth of be-ing, 57; and echo, 72; and silence, 73; in da-sein, 70n25, 161; and enowning, 236, 240. *See also* Abyssal ground

Abyss, 181–195

Abyssal ground: in questioning, 20; and be-ing's "not character," 20; and transition, 20; as a determination of da-sein, 26; and sheltering, 26, 189. *See also* Ab-ground

Aletheia, 63n30; as unconcealment, 83–85, 186, 192. *See also* Truth of be-ing

Alterity, 56

Anticipatory Resoluteness: in insistence, 75; and decision, 133

Anxiety, 133, 176, 203–204

Apprehension, 83

Aristotle, 37, 83, 86, 100n21, 174, 209; and metaphysics, 19; and *Augenblick*, 129–149

Assistance, 171, 172. *See also* Passing; Play-encounter; Playing-forth

Attempt: as temptation, 2; as the thinking of *Contributions*, 48, 106; in the transition, 49; in enowning, 60

Attunement: in stillness, 21; as grounding 73, 183; and enowning, 239–240

Augenblick, 79, 130–149, 173, 195

Auseinandersetzung, 107, 152

Authenticity, 6, 141

Awe: as "guarding," 23; and the other beginning, 23; as guiding attunement, 74, 114, 191, 225

Basic Problems of Phenomenology, 87, 132, 136

Basic Questions of Philosophy, 150, 182

Beginning: in be-ing-historical thinking, 54–57; in inceptual thinking, 54; as essential sway, 54; the first and the other, 54–55; in temporality, 57; as be-ing, 57; and enowning, 94, 103n41; and history, 153

Be-holding, 83–104

Be-ing, 1, 110, 139–142, 184–195, 230–245; as breakage from the tradition, 6; and questioning, 18; and transition, 19; as da-sein, 20; and the First Beginning, 24; as outside of presence, 51; as *phusis*, 54; as beginning, 57; and echo, 70; and turning, 152, 154, 157–162; as historical, 214

Being and Time, 1, 66, 106, 109, 132, 137, 141, 150, 154, 157, 171, 174–175, 178, 183, 198–199, 203, 208–209, 214–215, 220–221, 225–226; and the tradition, 5; failed interpretations of, 6, 8–9; and the meaning of being, 15; and temporality, 16; and da-sein, 38; as revolutionary, 39; its failure, 45n14; and the ontological difference, 52; and history, 53; and "ecstasis," 73, 87; and language, 78n22; and enowning, 90

Be-ing-historical thinking: and metaphysics, 17; in transition, 19, 48, 53–54; in *Contributions*, 48–65, 105, 229; in the closure of metaphysics, 51–52; different from historiography, 52; as returning, 57; as underway, 57; as overcoming, 57; as resounding, 58; from enowning, 58, 105–126; as enacting an ungrounding moment, 59; and turning, 153, 162–167; and thrownness, 233–234, 236

Belonging: to be-ing, 71, 158, 171, 235–236; to da-sein, 72

Bergen, 216–217, 223. *See also* Sheltering

Berücken/entrücken, 217. *See also* Charming-moving-unto; Removal-unto

Besinnung, 172, 209. *See also* Meditative awareness

Beyng. *See* Be-ing

Boredom, 142–144

Call: and enowning, 18, 158; and language, 69; in echo, 71–72; and refusal, 74–76, 111, 114–115; and joining, 123; and the last god, 209, 224

Care: and transition, 20; in *Contributions*, 20; as *Inständigkeit*, 20; in *Being and Time*, 134

Charming-moving-unto, 3, 23, 58. See also *Berücken/entrücken*; Removal-unto

Clearing, 3, 114, 119, 190, 192
Cleavage, 117–118
Cogito, 86
Coming to pass, 5, 225; and temporality, 16; and sonority, 18; and gift, 23; in time/space, 23; of da-sein, 26. *See also* Essence; Essency; Essential sway
Conscience, 214
Correspondence, 5
Crossing, 106, 112, 122, 155, 156, 181, 184, 188
Counter-resonance, 111, 118, 121, 158, 160, 161

Da-sein: and transition, 19; and the other beginning, 20; and silence, 22; and withdrawal, 24; and sheltering, 26; in *Being and Time*, 38; and temporality, 67, 88; disclosing the truth of be-ing, 73–74; and insistence, 75; as abysmal, 79n25; and questioning, 82; and enowning, 89–90, 110–111; and *Augenblick*, 134, 137–138, 142; and turning, 151–168; and the leap, 171–180; and grounding, 181–195; and the last god, 204–210
Death: and machination, 40; being-towards, 78n18, 178
Decision, 91; and displacement, 25; determines da-sein, 25; in space/time, 60; and *Augenblick*, 133, 135
Deconstruction, 208
Derrida, Jacques, 76, 217, 219
Disenowning, 115, 152. *See also* Enowning
Displaced: from familiarity, 25; in startled dismay, 74
Distress, 91, 114, 142, 175, 182; of the author, 6; of absence of distress, 39

Earth, 1, 75, 189, 190, 224
Echo, 4, 70, 106, 151, 232; and the call, 71
Eidos, 84, 100n21, 130
Enactment, 1, 4, 6, 9–10, 17–18, 214; of thinking, 21, 159; as the occurrence of be-ing, 55; in *The History of Be-ing*, 56; as be-ing-historical thinking, 59; *Contributions* as enactment, 60, 106. *See also* Enowning; *Ereignis;* Event
Enchantment, 24
Encleaving, 3, 151, 153, 164
Engrounding, 119
En-grounding-projecting-opening, 119
Enopening, 3, 108, 124, 160

Enowned projecting-open, 111–113, 121, 158, 167, 237–238
Enowning, 1, 3, 4, 9, 18–20, 23, 76, 87–94, 102n41, 106–126, 151–168, 233–235, 238, 240; and transition, 26–27; and beginning, 58; and be-ing-historical thinking, 58; as leap, 59, 72; as the truth of be-ing, 70–71; and language, 71–76; and the turn, 71; and da-sein, 73; and enthinking, 82; different from presence, 89–90; and enthinking, 91–92
Enowning-historical-thinking, 105–125
Enowning-throw, 166, 233–241
Enthinking, 81–104, 161
Entscheidung. See Decision
Entwurf, 231. *See also* Opening projection; Projecting-open
Ereignis, 108, 130, 135, 137, 140, 171, 174, 187–188, 215–216, 218, 233–234, 243. *See also* Enactment; Enowning; Event
Erfahrung, 1–2
Essence, 10, 19, 52, 185, 196n10; as coming to pass, 29n13. *See also* Coming to pass; Essency; Essential sway
Essency, 186. *See also* Coming to pass; Essence; Essential sway
Essential sway, 3; and essence, 10, 29n13, 106; and occurrence, 51; as *phusis*, 54, 57, 61n4; and beginning, 54; as language, 67; saying of, 70; and presencing, 99n15; and enowning, 110; and turning, 150–170
Event, 34, 40, 44n1, 66, 81–104. See also Enactment; Enowning; *Ereignis*
Eventuation, 2, 18; of thought, 2; as temporal, 5–6; as non-representational, 7; in the event of be-ing, 9; and reticence, 23; in language, 66–67

Facets, 41, 46n23. *See also* Joinings; Jointure
Facticity, 17
First Beginning, 19–24, 106, 152–156, 173, 181–188, 233, 238; and wonder, 22; in Nietzsche, 49; and the other beginning, 54, 55, 116; in the play-encounter, 54–56; and presence, 81
Fore-grasping, 3
Freedom, 43, 203, 208
Fugal structure, 10, 60, 70, 172, 181; as the structure of *Contributions*, 17. *See also* Joinings; Jointure
Fundamental Concepts of Metaphysics, 138
Futural ones, 41, 120, 193, 233

Gift, as refusal 23, 182
Ground, 17, 21, 106, 118–120, 181–197, 233; in enowning, 87
Grounding question, 187
Guiding question, 187

Heraclitus, 83
Hermeneutics, 105, 123–125, 152, 157, 210, 229
Hesitating refusal, 175, 236. *See also* Refusal
Hint, 4–5, 6–7, 9–10, 18, 123, 206, 224–225; and withdrawal, 21
Historiography: as different from be-ing-historical thinking, 52–54, 162; as different from history, 52, 153; and occurrence, 60n3
History: historical context of *Contributions*, 36; historical crisis, 39; and race, 41; at the end of metaphysics, 50; and occurrence, 52; different from historiography, 52; in *Being and Time*, 53; and da-sein, 111; of the first beginning, 116–117; and turning, 153, 162–167
History of Being, 56, 60, 109, 153, 162
Hölderlin, 36, 189, 202, 222–223; and language, 37, 75, 97, 206; as exemplary poet, 42; and Mnemosyne, 56

Inceptual thinking: as be-ing-historical thinking, 54, 106, 108; and beginning, 57; and turning, 161; and the leap, 176
Ingrasping, 81, 104n51, 124
Insistence, 79n26; in the truth of be-ing, 73; and ecstasis, 73; in da-sein, 75; and ingrasping, 104n51
Intimation, 141, 148n44. *See also* Echo
Introduction to Metaphysics, 83, 89, 90

Joinings, 8, 108, 112–113, 121–124, 150–155, 162, 173, 229, 232, 237. *See also* Fugal structure; Jointure
Jointure, 106, 108–109, 112, 121–124; its rigor, 122. *See also* Fugal structure; Joinings
Jünger, Ernst: and machination, 37; and the last god, 199

Kierkegaard, 132, 218, 220

Language, 1, 2, 32–34, 66–80, 185, 232, 242–243; in turning, 5; in metaphysics, 34, 35, 38, 66–67; as performative, 35;

76; exhaustion of, 35; use of commonplace words, 35–36; and poetry, 36; and reticence, 36; and Hölderlin, 37; as transformative, 38, 69; as the eventuation of be-ing, 66–69; fails in *Being and Time*, 67–70; and presentation, 67; as temporality, 67; and leap, 69; as poietic, 69; in *Being and Time*, 78n22; and naming, 97
Last god, 41–42, 108, 120–121, 213–228, 233; and Schelling, 46n25; and reticence, 79n28; the passing of, 198–212
Lastness, 39–41
Leading or guiding question, in Nietzsche, 50
Leap, 6, 51–52, 91, 98, 108–110, 117–118, 150–170, 208, 233–234; as ungrounding, 59, 191; over transcendence, 68; overcoming horizons, 68; as turning, 69; and withdrawal, 71; and language, 77; and da-sein, 171–180
Letter on Humanism, 67, 77n2, 78n15, 111, 136, 139
Logos, 83

Machination, 8, 10, 39, 88, 115, 151, 190, 201–202, 241; and Jünger, 37; and metaphysics, 40; and Nietzsche, 40, 46n19; as the obliteration of da-sein, 40
Meditative awareness, 22. *See also* Besinnung
Memory, 56, 225
Metaphysical Foundations of Logic, 143
Metaphysics, 5–6, 15–16, 138–142, 152, 171, 175, 181–184, 188; and the familiarity of beings, 22–24; and presence, 25; untenability of, 27; and language, 34–38; and the event, 35; and time, 38; and nature, 38; and truth, 38; and machination, 40; and race, 40; and politics, 42; and transcendence, 48; as presence, 48–49; and the ontological difference, 52
Mnemosyne, 56, 145
Myth, 198–199, 210

National Socialism, 39; and race, 40
Nature, 1, 203; as substance, 38
Need: of original thinking, 21; and startled dismay, 22; in enowning, 23; of needlessness, 142
Nicomachean Ethics, 130–135
Nietzsche, Friedrich: use of *Versuch*, 2; and

nihilism, 30n23, 49; and the overcoming of metaphysics, 37, 49, 182, 184, 190; and machination, 40; and the failure of ethics, 43; as the end of the First Beginning, 49; as metaphysical, 50; and presence, 51; Heidegger's reading of, 61n15; his style, 172; and life, 177; and myth, 199; and transition, 210; and the last god, 218, 220, 224, 225

Nihilism: at the end of metaphysics, 30n23, 49–52, 148n64; and language, 77

Occurrence, 49, 50; as appearance, 50; outside the ontological difference, 52; and history, 52–53; and historiography, 52–53; and memory, 56; as ungrounding, 58; and language, 74

On The Essence of Ground, 110, 200–201

The ones to come, 108, 112, 113, 120, 233

The Origin of the work of Art, 75, 146n16, 194, 196n11

Ontological difference: and metaphysics, 52, 68, 138, 140; in *Being and Time,* 52; its limitations, 68; and turning, 154–157, 167

Opening projection, 3; in the leap, 71, 117–118, 176, 153; in *Being and Time,* 71; and thrownness, 72, 87; in enowning, 111–112; and the last god, 121; and the hint, 123; and be-ing, 231–233, 237, 239, 244n6. *See also* Projecting-open

Other beginning, 20, 23, 106, 139, 152–156, 173, 181–189, 233–238; and transition, 54; and the first beginning, 54–55; and Hölderlin, 75; and Nietzsche, 75

Parmenides, 83

Passing, 182. *See also* Assistance; Play-encounter; Playing-forth

Performative thinking, 1, 66

Perspective, 105, 112

Phronesis, 130–135

Phusis, 54, 57, 63n29, 83, 84

Plato, 1, 37, 83, 99–100, 210; the *Seventh Letter,* 45n8, 10

Platonism, 182, 184, 190

Play-encounter, of the first and other beginning, 55

Playing-forth, 108, 115–117, 152–153. *See also* Assistance; Passing; Play-encounter

Poiesis: and machination, 40; erasing the passage of be-ing, 55; poietic language, 69

Politics, 33–42

Praxis, 131, 136

Presence, 10, 16, 25, 48–49, 88, 132, 134, 138, 146n13, 207, 210, 231; in Nietzsche, 51; and appearing, 61; and enthinking, 81; in the first beginning, 81; and *phusis,* 83–84; as different from enowning, 89

Pre-Socratics, 83–84

Preview, 17, 112

Proairesis, 135

Projecting-open, 231–233, 237–239. *See also* Enowned projecting-open; Opening projection

Race: and National Socialism, 40; and metaphysics, 40; and the obliteration of history 40–41

Refusal, 21, 74, 114, 141, 143, 151–152, 175, 178, 199–200, 205, 219–220; and reticence, 23; in the occurrence of be-ing, 70; and the origin of language, 76. *See also* Hesitating refusal

Removal-unto: and time/space, 23, 58; and charming-moving-unto, 23; and ab-ground, 58. *See also Berücken/ entrücken*

Representational Thinking, 6, 83–86, 94–96, 138, 161, 202; and Hegel, 88, 122

Reservedness, 74–75, 114, 141, 147n37, 151, 173, 175

Resounding, 58

Reticence: in writing *Contributions,* 5, 171; and the abyss, 22; and refusal, 23, 175; and language, 36; and awe, 74; and silence, 74; and the last god, 79n28, 209

Retrieval, 133, 217, 222, 224

Returnership, 240–245

Revolution: in *Being and Time,* 39; and the closure of metaphysics, 42–43

Ripeness, 224–225

Schelling, 37, 46n25

Sheltering, 24, 26, 30n24, 114, 119, 161, 187, 193–194, 205; and language, 75–76; and insistence, 75; and thrownness, 111

Silence, 22, 34, 51, 72, 74, 76, 98

Sonority, 18

Space, 183, 185

Space/time, 60, 173, 177. *See also* Time/space

Startled dismay, 22, 30n24, 114; as guiding attunement, 74

Stillness, 21, 171

Strife, 75, 176, 178

Techne: and machination, 40; erases the passage of be-ing, 55; in Aristotle, 130

Temporality, 5, 8, 16, 52, 88, 94, 137, 236, 240; and history, 53; and production, 55; and beginning, 57

Thrown projecting-open, 110–112, 115, 159, 233

Thrownness: in the leap, 71, 159–160, 176; and the turn, 71; responding to the call, 71; and opening projection, 72, 87; and enthinking, 92; and enowning, 109–112, 233–242; and ground, 133

Time/space: and *Entrückung,* 23; and the occurrence of be-ing, 58; as historical site, 76; as horizon, 88; and sheltering, 119; and *Augenblick,* 140; and da-sein, 207; and be-ing, 237–238, 241. *See also* Space/time

Tonality, 21, 173

Tragedy, 36

Transcendence, 5, 6, 9, 18, 68, 109–112, 118, 144, 176, 233; in metaphysics, 48–49; and the ontological difference, 52

Transition, 15, 18–19, 171, 174–175; as a change in human being, 19; into be-ing-

historical thinking, 19, 27n3, 48, 53, 54, 70; and abyssal ground, 20; and coming to pass, 26; and the truth of be-ing, 48

Truth of be-ing, 15, 17, 150, 160, 193–195; and sheltering, 26; and metaphysics, 35; and transition, 48; as ab-ground, 57; and strife, 75; and poetry, 76; restoration from, 119, 140

Turn, 5, 62, 67, 69, 111, 150–170, 174, 182, 185, 187, 191, 220–223; in enowning, 71, 89–90; in Heidegger's thinking, 130, 137; in be-ing, 229–245

Underway, 53–54, 57, 174

Ungrounding, 2, 236, 240; in enactment, 6; of da-sein, 25; and sheltering, 26; and metaphysics, 58; and occurrence, 58

Ur-ground, 236, 240

Versuch. See Attempt

Verweigerung. See Refusal

Wesen, 215–216

Withdrawal, 16, 20, 24, 70, 72–75, 175; in enowning, 9; and questioning, 18; and startled dismay, 22; of familiarity, 25, 26; in the leap, 71; and turning, 71; and the last god, 201, 205, 207

Wonder, 22, 64n52, 183, 188

World, 75, 189, 224; world-forming, 200–202